PANAMA

COUNTRY STUDY GUIDE

International Business Publications, USA
Washington, DC, USA - Panama

PANAMA

COUNTRY STUDY GUIDE

Editorial content: International Business Publications, USA

Editor-in-Chief: **Dr. Igor S. Oleynik**
Editor: **Natasha Alexander**
Assistant Editor: **Karl Cherepanya**

Published by
International Business Publications, USA
P.O.Box 15343, Washington, DC 20003
Phone: (202) 546-2103, Fax: (202) 546-3275.
E-mail: rusric@erols.com

UPDATED ANNUALLY

We express our sincere gratitude to all government agencies and international organizations which provided information and other materials for this guide

Databases & Information: International Business Publications, USA
Cover Design: International Business Publications, USA

ISBN 0-7397-5823-3

For customer service and information, please contact:
in the USA: **International Business Publications, USA**
P.O.Box 15343, Washington, DC 20003
Phone: (202) 546-2103, Fax: (202) 546-3275.
E-mail: rusric@erols.com

Printed in the USA

PANAMA

COUNTRY STUDY GUIDE

TABLE OF CONTENTS

BUSINESS AND DEVELOPMENT PROFILES

PANAMA: STRATEGIC PROFILE

COUNTRY OVERVIEW

President: Mireya Elisa Moscoso
Independence: 1903 (from Colombia)
Population (1999E): 2.8 million
Location/Size: Middle America, bordering both the Caribbean Sea and the North Pacific Ocean, between Colombia and Costa Rica/30,200 square miles
Capital City: Panama City
Languages: Spanish (official), English (14%; many Panamanians are bilingual)
Ethnic Groups: Mestizo (mixed Amerindian and white) 70%, Amerindian and mixed (West Indian) 14%, White 10%, Amerindian 6%
Religions: Roman Catholic 85%, Protestant 15%

ECONOMIC OVERVIEW

Currency: Balboa
Market Exchange Rate: US $1=1 Balboa (fixed)
Nominal Gross Domestic Product (GDP, 1999E): $9.6 billion
Real GDP Growth Rate (1999E): 3.4% **(2000E):** 2.6%
Inflation Rate (1999E): 1.3% **(2000E):** 1.5%
Colon Free Zone Imports (3/99-3/00): $330 million
Colon Free Zone Re-exports (3/99-3/00): $410 million
Number of ships through Panama Canal per month (average, 3/99-3/00): 1,154
Foreign Debt: $7.9 billion

ENERGY OVERVIEW

Oil Production (1999E): 1,000 barrels per day (bbl/d)
Oil Consumption (1999E): 52,000 bbl/d
Net Oil Imports (1999E): 51,000 bbl/d
Crude Refining Capacity (1/1/00): 60,000 bbl/d
Coal Consumption (1998E): 60,000 Short tons
Electric Generation Capacity (1/1/98): 1.05 million kilowatts
Electricity Generation (1998E): 4.5 billion kilowatthours
Electricity Consumption (1998E): 4.3 billion kilowatthours

ENVIRONMENTAL OVERVIEW

Total Energy Consumption (1999E): 0.16 quadrillion Btu* (<0.1% of world total energy consumption)
Energy-Related Carbon Emissions (1999E): 2.5 million metric tons of carbon (<0.1% of world total carbon emissions)
Per Capita Energy Consumption (1999E): 56.2 million Btu (vs U.S. value of 355.8 million Btu)
Per Capita Carbon Emissions (1999E): 0.88 metric tons of carbon (vs U.S. value of 5.5 metric tons of carbon)
Energy Intensity (1999E): 19,685 Btu/$1990 (vs U.S. value of 12,638 Btu/$1990)**
Carbon Intensity (1999E): 0.31 metric tons of carbon/thousand $1990 (vs U.S. value of 0.19 metric tons/thousand $1990)**
Sectoral Share of Energy Consumption (1998E): Industrial (16.2%), Transportation (46.5%), Residential (36.3%), Commercial (1.0%)
Sectoral Share of Carbon Emissions (1998E): Industrial (24.7%), Transportation (41.0%), Residential (32.2%), Commercial (2.1%)
Fuel Share of Energy Consumption (1999E): Coal (1.0%), Oil (78.4%), Natural Gas (0.0%)
Fuel Share of Carbon Emissions (1998E): Coal (1.5%), Oil (98.5%), Natural Gas (0.0%)
Renewable Energy Consumption (1998E): 41 trillion Btu*
Number of People per Motor Vehicle (1998): 9.8 (vs U.S. value of 1.3)
Status in Climate Change Negotiations: Non-Annex I country under the United Nations Framework Convention on Climate Change (ratified on May 23rd, 1995). Ratified the Kyoto Protocol on March 5th, 1999.
Major Environmental Issues: water pollution from agricultural runoff threatens fishery resources; deforestation of tropical rain forest; land degradation.
Major International Environmental Agreements: Biodiversity, Climate Change, Climate Change-Kyoto Protocol, Desertification, Endangered Species, Hazardous Wastes, Law of the Sea, Marine Dumping, Nuclear Test Ban, Ozone Layer Protection, Ship Pollution, Tropical Timber 83, Tropical Timber 94, Wetlands, Whaling.

GEOGRAPHY

Location: Middle America, bordering both the Caribbean Sea and the North Pacific Ocean, between Colombia and Costa Rica

Geographic coordinates: 9 00 N, 80 00 W

Map references: Central America and the Caribbean

Area:
total: 78,200 sq km

land: 75,990 sq km
water: 2,210 sq km

Area—comparative: slightly smaller than South Carolina

Land boundaries:
total: 555 km
border countries: Colombia 225 km, Costa Rica 330 km

Coastline: 2,490 km

Maritime claims:
territorial sea: 200 nm

Climate: tropical; hot, humid, cloudy; prolonged rainy season (May to January), short dry season (January to May)

Terrain: interior mostly steep, rugged mountains and dissected, upland plains; coastal areas largely plains and rolling hills

Elevation extremes:
lowest point: Pacific Ocean 0 m
highest point: Volcan de Chiriqui 3,475 m

Natural resources: copper, mahogany forests, shrimp

Land use:
arable land: 7%
permanent crops: 2%
permanent pastures: 20%
forests and woodland: 44%
other: 27% (1993 est.)

Irrigated land: 320 sq km (1993 est.)

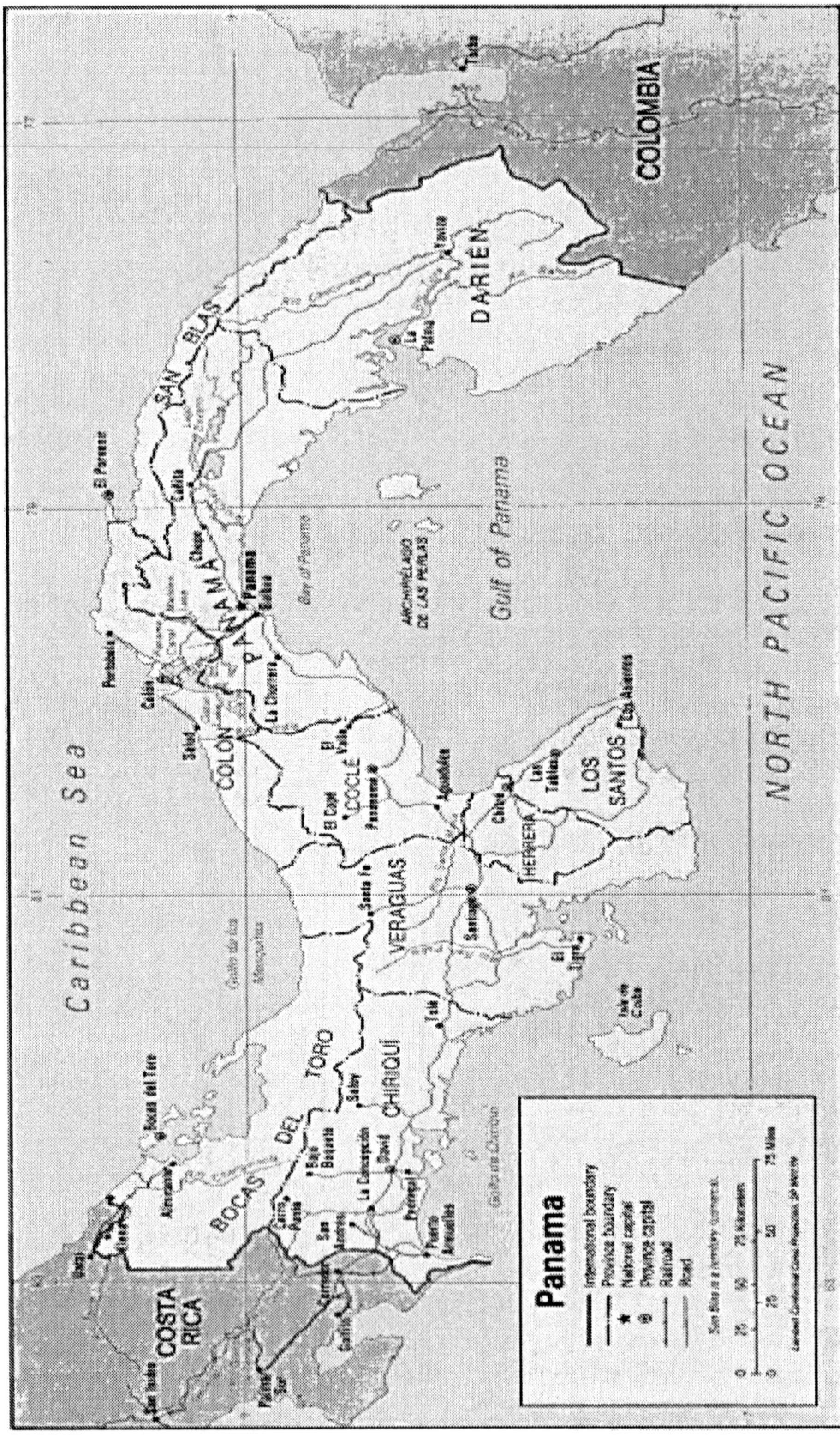
Panama
Caribbean Sea
Gulf of Panama
NORTH PACIFIC OCEAN
COLOMBIA
COSTA RICA
BOCAS DEL TORO
CHIRIQUI
VERAGUAS
HERRERA
LOS SANTOS
COCLE
COLON
PANAMA
SAN BLAS
DARIEN
ARCHIPIELAGO DE LAS PERLAS

Natural hazards: NA

Environment—current issues: water pollution from agricultural runoff threatens fishery resources; deforestation of tropical rain forest; land degradation

Environment—international agreements:
party to: Biodiversity, Climate Change, Desertification, Endangered Species, Hazardous Wastes, Law of the Sea, Marine Dumping, Nuclear Test Ban, Ozone Layer Protection, Ship Pollution, Tropical Timber 83, Tropical Timber 94, Wetlands
signed, but not ratified: Marine Life Conservation

Geography—note: strategic location on eastern end of isthmus forming land bridge connecting North and South America; controls Panama Canal that links North Atlantic Ocean via Caribbean Sea with North Pacific Ocean

PEOPLE

Population: 2,735,943 (July 1998 est.)

Age structure:
0-14 years: 32% (male 446,001; female 428,532)
15-64 years: 62% (male 864,382; female 841,870)
65 years and over: 6% (male 74,529; female 80,629) (July 1998 est.)

Population growth rate: 1.56% (1998 est.)

Birth rate: 21.99 births/1,000 population (1998 est.)

Death rate: 5.14 deaths/1,000 population (1998 est.)

Net migration rate: -1.28 migrant(s)/1,000 population (1998 est.)

Sex ratio:
at birth: 1.04 male(s)/female
under 15 years: 1.04 male(s)/female
15-64 years: 1.03 male(s)/female
65 years and over: 0.92 male(s)/female (1998 est.)

Infant mortality rate: 24 deaths/1,000 live births (1998 est.)

Life expectancy at birth:
total population: 74.47 years
male: 71.73 years
female: 77.31 years (1998 est.)

Total fertility rate: 2.57 children born/woman (1998 est.)

Nationality:
noun: Panamanian(s)
adjective: Panamanian

Ethnic groups: mestizo (mixed Amerindian and white) 70%, Amerindian and mixed (West Indian) 14%, white 10%, Amerindian 6%

Religions: Roman Catholic 85%, Protestant 15%

Languages: Spanish (official), English 14%
note: many Panamanians bilingual

Literacy:
definition: age 15 and over can read and write
total population: 90.8%
male: 91.4%
female: 90.2% (1995 est.)

GOVERNMENT

Country name:
conventional long form: Republic of Panama
conventional short form: Panama
local long form: Republica de Panama
local short form: Panama

Data code: PM

Government type: constitutional republic

National capital: Panama

Administrative divisions: 9 provinces (provincias, singular—provincia) and 2 territories* (comarca); Bocas del Toro, Chiriqui, Cocle, Colon, Darien, Herrera, Los Santos, Panama, San Blas*, Veraguas, and a new, as yet unnamed territory* or 'comarca' created 7 March 1997 when President PEREZ BALLADARES signed a bill designating a reserve stretched across three provinces

Independence: 3 November 1903 (from Colombia; became independent from Spain 28 November 1821)

National holiday: Independence Day, 3 November (1903)

Constitution: 11 October 1972; major reforms adopted April 1983

Legal system: based on civil law system; judicial review of legislative acts in the Supreme Court of Justice; accepts compulsory ICJ jurisdiction, with reservations

Suffrage: 18 years of age; universal and compulsory

Executive branch:
chief of state: President Ernesto PEREZ BALLADARES Gonzalez Revilla (since 1 September 1994); First Vice President Tomas Gabriel ALTAMIRANO DUQUE (since 1 September 1994); Second Vice President Felipe Alejandro VIRZI Lopez (since 1 September 1994); note—the president is both the chief of state and head of government
head of government: President Ernesto PEREZ BALLADARES Gonzalez Revilla (since 1 September 1994); First Vice President Tomas Gabriel ALTAMIRANO DUQUE (since 1 September 1994); Second Vice President Felipe Alejandro VIRZI Lopez (since 1 September 1994); note—the president is both the chief of state and head of government
cabinet: Cabinet appointed by the president
elections: president and vice presidents elected on the same ticket by popular vote for five-year terms; election last held 8 May 1994 (next to be held 2 May 1999)
election results: Ernesto PEREZ BALLADARES elected president; percent of vote—Ernesto PEREZ BALLADARES (PRD) 33%, Mireya MOSCOSO DE GRUBER (PA) 29%, Ruben BLADES (MPE) 17%, Ruben Dario CARLES (MOLIRENA) 16%

Legislative branch: unicameral Legislative Assembly or Asamblea Legislativa (72 seats; members are elected by popular vote to serve five-year terms)
elections: last held 8 May 1994 (next to be held 2 May 1999)
election results: percent of vote by party—NA; seats by party—PRD 32, PS 4, PALA 1, PA 14, MPE 6, MOLIRENA 4, PLA 3, PRC 3, PLN 2, PDC 1, UDI 1, MORENA 1
note: legislators from outlying rural districts are chosen on a plurality basis while districts located in more populous towns and cities elect multiple legislators by means of a proportion-based formula

Judicial branch: Supreme Court of Justice (Corte Suprema de Justicia), nine judges appointed for 10-year terms; five superior courts; three courts of appeal

Political parties and leaders:
governing coalition: Democratic Revolutionary Party (PRD), Gerardo GONZALEZ; National Liberal Party (PLN), Raul ARANGO, founder; Popular Nationalist Party, Jorge FLORES
other parties: Solidarity Party (PS), Samuel LEWIS GALINDO; Nationalist

Republican Liberal Movement (MOLIRENA), Guillermo FORD; Arnulfista Party (PA), Mireya MOSCOSO DE GRUBER; Christian Democratic Party (PDC), Ruben AROSEMENA; Papa Egoro Movement (MPE), Ruben BLADES; Civic Renewal Party (PRC), Carlos ABADIA; National Renovation Movement (MORENA), Pedro VALLARINO; Authentic Liberal Party (PLA); Labor Party (PALA); Independent Democratic Union (UDI)

Political pressure groups and leaders: National Council of Organized Workers (CONATO); National Council of Private Enterprise (CONEP); Panamanian Association of Business Executives (APEDE); National Civic Crusade; Chamber of Commerce; Panamanian Industrialists Society (SIP); Workers Confederation of the Republic of Panama (CTRP)

International organization participation: AG (associate), CACM, CCC, ECLAC, FAO, G-77, IADB, IAEA, IBRD, ICAO, ICFTU, ICRM, IDA, IFAD, IFC, IFRCS, ILO, IMF, IMO, Inmarsat, Intelsat, Interpol, IOC, IOM, ISO, ITU, LAES, LAIA (observer), NAM, OAS, OPANAL, PCA, RG, UN, UNCTAD, UNESCO, UNIDO, UPU, WCL, WFTU, WHO, WIPO, WMO, WToO, WTrO

Diplomatic representation in the US:
chief of mission: Ambassador Eloy ALFARO de Alba
chancery: 2862 McGill Terrace NW, Washington, DC 20008
telephone: [1] (202) 483-1407
consulate(s) general: Atlanta, Houston, Miami, New Orleans, New York, Philadelphia, San Francisco, San Juan (Puerto Rico), Tampa

Diplomatic representation from the US:
chief of mission: Ambassador William John HUGHES
embassy: Avenida Balboa and Calle 38, Apartado 6959, Panama City 5
mailing address: American Embassy Panama, Unit 0945, APO AA 34002
telephone: [507] 227-1777
FAX: [507] 227-1964

Flag description: divided into four, equal rectangles; the top quadrants are white (hoist side) with a blue five-pointed star in the center and plain red, the bottom quadrants are plain blue (hoist side) and white with a red five-pointed star in the center

ECONOMY

Economy—overview: Because of its key geographic location, Panama's economy is service-based, heavily weighted toward banking, commerce, and tourism. Since taking office in 1994, President PEREZ BALLADARES has advanced an economic reform program designed to liberalize the trade regime, attract foreign investment, privatize state-owned enterprises, institute fiscal reform, and encourage job creation through labor code reform. The government privatized its two remaining ports along the Panama Canal in 1997 and approved the sale of the railroad in early 1998. It also plans to sell other assets, including the electric company. Panama joined the World Trade Organization (WTrO) and approved a tariff reduction that will give the country the lowest average tariff rates in Latin America. A banking reform law was approved by the legislature in early 1998 and will take effect in June. After two years of near stagnation, the reforms are beginning to take root; GDP grew by 3.6% in 1997 and is expected to grow by more than 5% in 1998. The most important sectors driving growth have been the Panama Canal and the shipping and port activities. The Colon Free Zone also rebounded from a slow year in 1996.

GDP: purchasing power parity—$18 billion (1997 est.)

GDP—real growth rate: 3.6% (1997 est.)

GDP—per capita: purchasing power parity—$6,700 (1997 est.)

GDP—composition by sector:
agriculture: 8%
industry: 18%
services: 74% (1997 est.)

Inflation rate—consumer price index: 1.2% (1997)

Labor force:
total: 1.044 million (1997 est.)
by occupation: government and community services 31.8%, agriculture, hunting, and fishing 26.8%, commerce, restaurants, and hotels 16.4%, manufacturing and mining 9.4%, construction 3.2%, transportation and communications 6.2%, finance, insurance, and real estate 4.3%
note: shortage of skilled labor, but an oversupply of unskilled labor

Unemployment rate: 13.1% (1997 est.)

Budget:
revenues: $2.4 billion
expenditures: $2.4 billion, including capital expenditures of $341 million (1997 est.)

Industries: construction, petroleum refining, brewing, cement and other construction materials, sugar milling

Industrial production growth rate: 0.4% (1995 est.)

Electricity—capacity: 957 million kW (1995)

Electricity—production: 3.6 billion kWh (1995)

Electricity—consumption per capita: 1,355 kWh (1995)

Agriculture—products: bananas, rice, corn, coffee, sugarcane, vegetables; livestock; fishing (shrimp)

Exports:
total value: $592 million (f.o.b., 1997 est.)
commodities: bananas 43%, shrimp 11%, sugar 4%, clothing 5%, coffee 2%
partners: US 37%, EU, Central America and Caribbean

Imports:
total value: $2.95 billion (c.i.f., 1997 est.)
commodities: capital goods 21%, crude oil 11%, foodstuffs 9%, consumer goods, chemicals
partners: US 48%, EU, Central America and Caribbean, Japan

Debt—external: $7.26 billion (1996 est.)

Economic aid:
recipient: NA

Currency: 1 balboa (B) = 100 centesimos

Exchange rates: balboas (B) per US$1—1.000 (fixed rate)

Fiscal year: calendar year

COMMUNICATIONS

Telephones: 273,000 (1991 est.)

Telephone system: domestic and international facilities well developed
domestic: NA
international: 1 coaxial submarine cable; satellite earth stations—2 Intelsat (Atlantic Ocean); connected to the Central American Microwave System

Radio broadcast stations: AM 91, FM 0, shortwave 0

Radios: 564,000 (1992 est.)

Television broadcast stations: 23

Televisions: 420,000 (1992 est.)

TRANSPORTATION

Railways:
total: 355 km
broad gauge: 76 km 1.524-m gauge
narrow gauge: 279 km 0.914-m gauge

Highways:
total: 11,100 km
paved: 3,730 km (including 30 km of expressways)
unpaved: 7,370 km (1996 est.)

Waterways: 800 km navigable by shallow draft vessels; 82 km Panama Canal

Pipelines: crude oil 130 km

Ports and harbors: Balboa, Cristobal, Coco Solo, Vacamonte, Manzanillo

Merchant marine:
total: 4,350 ships (1,000 GRT or over) totaling 89,622,112 GRT/137,529,188 DWT
ships by type: bulk 1,240, cargo 1,033, chemical tanker 195, combination bulk 67, combination ore/oil 19, container 426, liquefied gas tanker 175, livestock carrier 9, multifunction large-load carrier 5, oil tanker 524, passenger 40, passenger-cargo 6, railcar carrier 1, refrigerated cargo 296, roll-on/roll-off cargo 101, short-sea passenger 40, specialized tanker 15, vehicle carrier 158
note: a flag of convenience registry; includes ships from 76 countries among which are Japan 1,236, Greece 418, Hong Kong 273, South Korea 247, Taiwan 227, China 185, Singapore 119, US 112, Switzerland 85, and Indonesia 60 (1997 est.)

Airports: 109 (1997 est.)

Airports—with paved runways:
total: 40
over 3,047 m: 1
2,438 to 3,047 m: 1
1,524 to 2,437 m: 5
914 to 1,523 m: 14
under 914 m: 19 (1997 est.)

Airports—with unpaved runways:
total: 69
914 to 1,523 m: 17
under 914 m: 52 (1997 est.)

MILITARY

Military branches: an amendment to the Constitution abolished the armed forces, but there are security forces (Panamanian Public Forces or PPF includes the National Police, National Maritime Service, and National Air Service)

Military manpower—availability:
males age 15-49: 733,019 (1998 est.)

Military manpower—fit for military service:
males: 502,731 (1998 est.)

Military expenditures—dollar figure: $78 million (1995); note—for police and security forces

Military expenditures—percent of GDP: NA%

TRANSNATIONAL ISSUES

Disputes—international: none

Illicit drugs: major cocaine transshipment point and major drug money-laundering center; no recent signs of coca cultivation; monitoring of financial transactions is improving

NARCOTICS IN PANAMA

The government of Panama (GOP) continues to demonstrate its willingness to combat transnational drug trafficking. The GOP seized significant amounts of illicit drugs in 1999, despite apparent changes in trafficking routes. The new Mireya Moscoso Administration has demonstrated its commitment to combat money laundering, corruption, drug trafficking, and other transnational crimes. Immediately after taking office, the new Administration set up an anti-corruption unit in the Ministry of Economy and Finance. Talks on a full maritime agreement moved forward. A draft agreement is under review by the Ministry of Foreign Affairs. Panama's law enforcement agencies continue to maintain excellent relations with their U.S. counterparts. Panama is a party to the 1988 UN Drug Convention.

Panama is a major transshipment point for illicit drugs smuggled from Colombia. Cocaine is stockpiled in Panama prior to being repackaged for passage to the U.S. and Europe. Panama's location, largely unpatrolled coastlines, advanced infrastructure, underdeveloped judicial system, and well-developed financial services sector make it a crossroads for transnational crime, such as drug trafficking, money laundering, illicit arms sales and alien smuggling. Panama's Canal, containerized seaports, the Pan-American Highway, an active international airport, and numerous uncontrolled airfields provide organized crime groups almost unlimited transportation options through the country.

Panama's international banking center, a long established tax haven, combined with the Colon Free Zone (CFZ) and a U.S. dollar-based economy render Panama vulnerable to money laundering. Panama hosted the "Third Hemispheric Congress on the Prevention of Money Laundering" in August 1999. The new Administration has expressed its interest in improving money-laundering controls and cooperating in these efforts with the U.S. and other countries in the region.

STATUS OF COUNTRY

Panama continued to be a major drug transit country because of its proximity to the world's largest cocaine producer and because of its inadequate border, airport, and maritime controls. Domestic drug abuse continues to increase. Panama is not a significant producer of drugs or precursor chemicals. Panama's large and sophisticated banking and trading center, its dollar-based economy, and proximity to Colombia, make it an attractive site for money laundering, especially through the Colombian Black Market Peso Exchange (BMPE). The BMPE is a complex network dedicated to changing U.S. dollars into Colombian pesos and is used by drug traffickers and smugglers, as well as by legitimate industry attempting to avoid trade tariffs. The new Moscoso Administration has expressed interest in bolstering Panama's anti-money laundering measures (See Money Laundering Section). Panama is a member of the Caribbean Financial Action Task Force (CFATF).

COUNTRY ACTIONS AGAINST DRUGS

Policy Initiatives. CONAPRED, Panama's national drug policy office, took a major step forward in 1999 through active efforts to establish a national chemical control policy. The initiative seeks to integrate government entities regulating chemical control with private sector businesses involved in the chemical industry and transportation of precursor chemicals.

Accomplishments. Panama continued to implement its own national counternarcotics plan, the "National Drug Strategy -1996-2001," through CONAPRED. This program, under the authority of the Attorney General, coordinates GOP and non-governmental organization (NGO) work and stresses prevention, treatment, rehabilitation, control of supply, and interdiction. Panama also made significant progress in implementing its comprehensive chemical control program. In August, Panama hosted the "Third Hemispheric Congress on the Prevention of Money Laundering," organized by the GOP's Financial Analysis Unit (UAF) and the Panama Banking Association. Officials and experts from Latin America, the U.S. and Europe gathered to focus on money laundering issues.

Law Enforcement Efforts. GOP agencies seized 2,576 kilograms (kgs) of cocaine, 1,558 kilos of marijuana, 46 kilos of heroin, 600 liters of acetic anhydride, and made 131 arrests for international drug-related offenses in 1999. Although 1999 cocaine seizures declined from record 1997-98 seizures, decreased seizures were due to changes in drug trafficking patterns rather than change in flow. Heroin seizures continued to increase, further establishing Panama as a principal link in the chain that funnels Colombian heroin to the U.S.

In January 1999, the National Assembly passed a law changing authority to designate and dismiss Technical Judicial Police (PTJ) executives from the Attorney General to the Supreme Court. The transfer led to confrontation between the two organizations that resulted in a serious deterioration in law enforcement cooperation to the extent that meaningful investigations, police work, and ultimately, successful prosecutions have been negatively affected. Nevertheless, U.S.-Panama bilateral cooperation with the PTJ's counternarcotics squad, which is co-housed with the Public Ministry's drug prosecutor, continues to be excellent.

The National Maritime Service (SMN) has been Panama's interdiction success story. In 1999, the SMN conducted operations resulting in seizures of 453 kilos of cocaine and over 600 liters of acetic anhydride. The SMN seized several go-fast boats that were subsequently provided by the Attorney General to be utilized as SMN patrol craft. The SMN has a strong working relationship with the National Air Service (SAN), the Panamanian National Police (PNP), the PTJ, and the drug prosecutor's office and with their USG counterparts. The key to the SMN's strength is its leadership, both within the institution and as a lead agency in counternarcotics operations and seizures. SMN participation in high seas operations led to the seizure of 27 Mt. of cocaine from Panamanian flagged vessels outside of Panamanian territorial waters. The presence of U.S. Coast Guard (USCG) personnel to train and assist in joint mission planning and professional exchanges that are conducted during joint operations has been invaluable.

Despite limited air assets and internal structural problems, the SAN conducted two cannabis eradication operations in coordination with the Attorney General's drug prosecutor's office and provided excellent logistical support for USCG air assets.

The Direccion de Fiscalia Aduanal (DFA), the Customs branch responsible for interdiction efforts at seaports and international airports, seized multi-kilo shipments along the Costa Rican border and at Tocumen international airport. During 1999, DFA personnel assigned to Tocumen successfully seized in excess of two million dollars in U.S. currency concealed within airfreight. DFA was also responsible for a number of heroin seizures and for increasing coordination and cooperation with the PTJ, leading to all-around better drug enforcement.

Precursor Chemicals. Panama is not a major producer or significant consumer of chemicals used in processing illegal drugs. However, a large volume of chemicals transits the CFZ for other countries. This year, with the assistance of the Inter-American Drug Abuse Control Commission (CICAD), Panama took significant steps toward developing a regulatory/enforcement infrastructure to control the use and shipment of precursor chemicals.

Asset Forfeiture. The Panamanian legal system provides for asset forfeiture, including a system for identifying and forfeiting narcotics-related assets. Forfeiture actions have supplemented the PTJ, the PNP and other GOP law enforcement agencies with numerous vehicles. Although Panama has not enacted a specific law that provides for sharing seized narcotics assets with other governments, the GOP shares assets with other countries on a case-by-case basis. Current negotiations between the United States Attorney's office and the office of Panama's Attorney General to permit asset sharing in the multi-million dollar Gonzalo Rodriguez Gacha case exemplify this cooperation.

Money Laundering. Although cooperation between the U.S. and Panama on money laundering improved with the new Administration, the pursuit of money laundering cases remains constrained by laws requiring prosecutors to present an unusually high burden of proof and to meet extremely difficult evidentiary standards. (See money laundering section).

Corruption. The Moscoso Administration took office in September 1999 with a publicly-stated commitment to integrity and transparency. A presidential decree established a National Anti-Corruption Office in the Ministry of Economy and Finance. In 2000, the anti-corruption office is expected to propose legislation to define ethical conduct by government employees and specific sanctions for those breaking the law.

The GOP pursues those who produce, distribute, or traffic in narcotics and/or other controlled substances. However, outdated procedures and corruption undermine Panama's judicial system. Lack of prosecutions coupled with relatively low pay for law enforcement officers and insufficient resources negatively affects police morale. These factors inherently foster individual corruption and make it challenging to develop long-term, criminal investigations against top-echelon drug and money laundering violators. The new president of the Supreme Court is committed to making the judicial system more effective and transparent.

Agreements and Treaties. Panama is a party to the 1988 UN Drug Convention, the 1961 UN Single Convention and its 1972 Protocol, and the 1971 UN Convention on Psychotropic Substances. A mutual legal assistance treaty and an extradition treaty are in force between the U.S. and Panama. The Panamanian constitution, does not permit the extradition of Panamanian nationals. In 1991, the USG and the GOP signed a maritime operations agreement, which included provisions for shipriders and USCG support and assistance to the SMN. The USG concluded a Customs Mutual Assistance Agreement (CMAA) with the GOP in 1999. The GOP participates in CICAD, the Caribbean Financial Action Task Force (CFATF), and the Basle Committees' Offshore Group of Bank Supervisors (OGBS). In addition, Panama has bilateral agreements on drug trafficking with the United Kingdom, Colombia, Mexico, Cuba, and Peru and MLATs with the UK, Colombia, Costa Rica, El Salvador, Guatemala, Honduras, and Nicaragua. In 1997, Panama became the first Latin American country to join the Egmont group, an alliance of some 30 nations with centralized financial analysis units to combat money laundering.

The GOP has not signed a US-Panama bilateral comprehensive maritime counternarcotics treaty, although a draft agreement is currently under review by the Ministry of Foreign Affairs. Discussions with the new Administration on the text will continue in 2000.

Cultivation and Production. In 1996, the entire coca cultivation in the traditional growing areas of the eastern Darien region along the Colombian border was eradicated. Aerial reconnaissance confirms that the cultivators have not replanted any fields. The limited amounts of marijuana being cultivated supply the local market and are insufficient for export. The presence of significant quantities of Colombian heroin transiting Panama during 1999 indicates that South American drug organizations remain committed to increasing their share of the highly profitable heroin market.

Drug Flow and Transit. Panama is a key hub for the transit and distribution of South American cocaine and increasingly, precursor chemicals and heroin. Fishing vessels, cargo ships and "go-fast" boats transit Panamanian waters and either continue on to other Central American countries or drop off their cargo in Panama. Shipments dropped off in Panama are repackaged and moved northward on the Pan-American Highway or depart in sea freight containers. There were reports of small, low-flying planes entering Panamanian airspace and dropping drug loads in remote, sparsely populated areas. Cocaine and heroin are also moved to the U.S. and Europe by couriers transiting Panama by commercial air flights.

Domestic Programs (Demand Reduction). Drug abuse continues to plague Panama, with use of cocaine and its derivatives reaching ever-higher levels. About 20 percent of seizures in 1999 consisted of drugs destined for Panamanian consumption. Several years ago, Colombian trafficking organizations began giving their Panamanian associates cocaine as payment rather than cash. In order for the Panamanian middlemen to convert the cocaine to cash, it had to be distributed locally. This change was the genesis of Panama's current cocaine/crack epidemic. Crack or "bazuco" is sold to urban youth and Kuna Indians, whose home, the San Blas autonomous region, has emerged as a major drug airdrop center. Kuna leaders have expressed concern over the impact of the drug trade on their society. GOP officials fear that the increase of heroin trafficking will give rise to a serious heroin abuse problem.

Panama continued to vigorously implement CONAPRED's counternarcotics plan developed under the auspices of the Attorney General's National Drug Strategy. The demand reduction portion of the strategy stresses prevention, as well as treatment, rehabilitation and reinsertion of drug users into the labor force. The Ministry of Education and CONAPRED promote demand reduction through training for teachers, information programs, anti-drug abuse training for youth, school curriculum programs and support for the National Drug Information Center (CENAID). These efforts are integrated with the Ministry of Health's treatment and rehabilitation programs and those of the Catholic church, Panamanian NGO "Cruz Blanca (White Cross)," the University of Panama, the "Panama Coalition For A Drug- Free Community," and the "Pride Foundation." One weakness in GOP drug treatment programs is that there are no long-term rehabilitation programs outside of the major urban centers.

U.S.POLICY INITIATIVES AND PROGRAMS

Program agreements between the U.S. and Panama provide crucial equipment, training, and information to enhance the performance of GOP counternarcotics institutions. The key objectives of these programs are to improve Panama's prosecutorial and investigative capabilities, strengthen Panama's judicial system, encourage the enactment of more effective laws and regulations covering counternarcotics, money laundering and corruption, and ensure strict enforcement of existing Panamanian laws. The U.S., through USAID and ICITAP, is assisting the GOP to develop a comprehensive Administration of Justice (AOJ) program to strengthen law enforcement and judicial institutions and procedures.

During 1999, the U.S. Coast Guard continued to work closely with the SMN, enhancing its effectiveness as a maritime interdiction force. In 1999, the U.S. provided the SMN with two 82-foot Point class Coast Guard patrol boats and helped the GOP to establish an SMN station on the Caribbean mouth of the Panama Canal. The U.S. has traditionally had an excellent relationship with

Panamanian Customs and U.S. programs have provided Panamanian Customs with training and operational tools.

Other U.S. projects in 1999 supported the Ministry of Education's teacher training for demand reduction programs and joint counternarcotics operations between DEA, Customs and the Coast Guard and their Panamanian counterparts in PTJ, Customs, and the SMN. The USG provided training, equipment, and operational support to the PTJ, the PNP, CONAPRED, the Joint Intelligence Coordination Center (JICC), the office of the drug prosecutor, Customs and Immigration. The Embassy has also purchased an ion scanner machine for the use of Panama's law enforcement community and is working with the PTJ forensics laboratory to examine upgrading its equipment. The U.S. continued to fund and develop Panama's JICC, including upgrading software and training for the JICCs employees and providing precursor chemical control training.

Bilateral Cooperation. The new Administration has demonstrated its political will to increase joint counternarcotics efforts and strengthen national law enforcement institutions. The GOP cooperates with U.S. requests to board and search Panamanian-flagged vessels suspected of drug smuggling in international waters. In 1999, U.S. and Panama carried out four joint operations. The PTJ and the PNP, with support from the U.S. Immigration Service, U.S. Customs and DEA, executed three major joint interdiction operations along the Costa Rican border against alien smuggling and drug trafficking.

The Moscoso Administration requested U.S. assistance in developing Panama's law enforcement/national security strategy. The U.S. and Panama held the first bilateral meeting of the new Administration in November 1999 to address U.S. support for strategy development. The U.S. and Panama discussed an array of issues in the context of four working groups: society and the environment, law enforcement, trade, and security. The Law Enforcement Working Group exchanged information and presented recommendations on counternarcotics, extradition, asset forfeiture, justice reform, alien smuggling, and money laundering. These meetings demonstrated the new Administration's determination to build successful law enforcement and justice institutions and enhance Bilateral Cooperation.

The GOP pursued major drug kingpins. Pierre Janeiro Barbe was implicated as the principal transporter/owner of over 5 mt of cocaine seized from two ships. Concluding a thirteen-month investigation in October 1999 by the Panama drug prosecutor's office, PTJ and DEA, the GOP executed arrest, search, and seizure warrants. While Barbe remains at large, he has been declared a fugitive from Panamanian justice and his assets have been seized.

The Panamanian drug prosecutor's office participated in a bilateral investigation to target a Panamanian export company involved in the seizure of 432 kgs of cocaine in June 1999 in New York and obtained evidence in the U.S. case for prosecution in Panama. The drug prosecutor authorized the initial arrest of individuals in Panama believed to be integral members of the cocaine distribution network.

Road Ahead. The Moscoso Administration has demonstrated willingness to build strong law enforcement institutions, combat money laundering, and ensure security of the canal. The GOP has repeatedly noted its interest in maintaining the security of the Darien region from infiltration by Colombian "narco-guerillas." The U.S. and Panama will continue to cooperate in these areas and strengthen joint counternarcotics efforts. Conclusion of a bilateral maritime agreement will greatly facilitate joint cooperation.

Panama's law enforcement efforts would be enhanced through closer coordination between its law enforcement agencies and with U.S. counterparts. The U.S. will work with the GOP to help strengthen Panama's law enforcement institutional capacity, particularly in training, interdiction, investigation and prosecution. The U.S. will support anti-corruption efforts and criminal justice reform. Panama's anti-money laundering efforts would be strengthened through implementation of banking reforms. A major goal will be to seek enactment of legislation to widen the existing law against drug money laundering to include the proceeds from all serious crimes, and to permit the UAF to share information with domestic and international counterparts.

The USG will continue to work with the Ministries of Health and Education and NGOs to expand Panama's demand reduction program. While realizing that the GOP has budgetary limits, the USG will encourage the GOP to seek new sources of funds, such as those available through effective money laundering prosecutions and asset forfeiture, to provide sufficient resources to law enforcement agencies.

PANAMA STATISTICS

(1991-1999)

	1999	**1998**	**1997**	**1996**	**1995**	**1994**	**1993**	**1992**
Coca								
Net Cultivation (ha)		-	0	0	0	10	10	-
Eradication (ha)	-	-	0	125	110	90	60	-

Cultivation (ha)			0	125	110	100	70	-
Seizures								
Cocaine (mt)	2.58	1.00	9.96	8.60	5.89	8.60	5.68	9.80
Cannabis (mt)	1.56	10.47	13.82	18.12	0.06	0.01	32.5	7.33
Heroin (mt)	0.046	0.022	0.033	0.010	0.030	0.007	0.013	0.001
Arrests/Detentions								
Nationals	-	1,393	1,143	1,113	737	879	696	412
Foreigners	131	139	217	139	137	284	104	105
Total Arrests	*131*	*1,532*	*1,360*	*1,252*	*874*	*1,163*	*800*	*517*

IMPORTANT INFORMATION FOR UNDERSTANDING PANAMA

Official Name: Republic of Panama

GEOGRAPHY

Area: 77,381 sq. km. (29,762 sq. mi.); slightly smaller than South Carolina. Panama occupies the southeastern end of the isthmus forming the land bridge between North and South America.
Cities: *Capital*--Panama City (827,828). *Other cities*--Colon (140,908), David (102,678).
Terrain: Mountainous (highest elevation Cerro Volcan, 3,475 m.--11,468 ft.); coastline 2,857 km. (1,786 mi.).
Climate: Tropical, with average daily rainfall 28 mm. (1 in.) in winter.

PANAMA CANAL HISTORICAL OVERVIEW

Among the great peaceful endeavors of mankind that have contributed significantly to progress in the world, the construction of the Canal stands as an awe-inspiring achievement. The unparalleled engineering triumph was made possible by an international work force under the leadership of American visionaries, who made the centuries-old dream of uniting the two great oceans a reality.

In 1534, Charles V of Spain ordered the first survey of a proposed canal route through the Isthmus of Panama. More than three centuries passed before the first construction was started. The French labored 20 years, beginning in 1880, but disease and financial problems defeated them.

In 1903, Panama and the United States signed a treaty by which the United States undertook the construction of an interoceanic ship canal across the Isthmus of Panama. The following year, the United States purchased from the French Canal Company its rights and properties for $40 million and began construction. The monumental project was completed in ten years at a cost of about $387 million. Since 1903 the United States has invested about $3 billion in the Canal enterprise, approximately two-thirds of which has been recovered.

The building of the Panama Canal involved three main problems - engineering, sanitation, and organization. Its successful completion was due principally to the engineering and administrative skills of such men as John F. Stevens and Col. George W. Goethals, and to the solution of extensive health problems by Col. William C. Gorgas.

The engineering problems involved digging through the Continental Divide; constructing the largest earth dam ever built up to that time; designing and building the most massive canal locks ever envisioned; constructing the largest gates ever swung; and solving environmental problems of enormous proportions.

In 1977, the United States and Panama embarked on a partnership for the management, operation and maintenance of the Panama Canal. Under two new treaties signed in a ceremony at OAS headquarters in Washington, D.C., on September 7, 1977, the Canal was to be operated until the turn of the century under arrangements designed to strengthen the bonds of friendship and cooperation between the two countries. The treaties were approved by Panama in a plebiscite on October 23, 1977, and the U.S. Senate gave its advice and consent to their ratificaton in March and April 1978. The new treaties went into effect October 1, 1979.

The Panama Canal Commission, a U.S. government agency, operated the Canal during the 20-year transition period that began with the Panama Canal Treaty implementation on October 1, 1979. The Commission was supervised by a nine-member binational board. For the first 10 years, a U.S. citizen served as the Canal Chief Executive Officer, under the title of Administrator, and a Panamanian was the Deputy. Effective January 1, 1990, as mandated by the treaty, a Panamanian served as Administrator and a U.S. citizen was the Deputy.

The Panama Canal Commission replaced the former Panama Canal Company, which, together with the Canal Zone and its government, was disestablished on October 1, 1979. On December 31, 1999, as required by treaty, the United States transferred the Canal to Panama.

The Republic of Panama assumed full responsibility for the administration, operation, and maintenance of the Panama Canal at noon, Eastern Time, December 31, 1999. Panama complies with its responsibilities through a governmental entity, designated as Panama Canal Authority, created by the Political Constitution of the Republic of Panama, and organized by Law 19 of June 11, 1997.

The Panama Canal Authority is the autonomous agency of the Government of Panama in charge of managing, operating, and maintaining the Panama Canal. The operation of the Panama Canal Authority is based on its organic law and the regulations approved by its Board of Directors.

The Canal administration remains committed to serving world trade with the standards of excellence that have been the tradition of the waterway throughout its history. With prudent investment in maintenance, modernization and training programs, the Canal will remain a viable, economic transportation artery for world trade well into the future.

The opening of the waterway to world commerce on August 15, 1914, represented the realization of a heroic dream of over 400 years. The 50 miles across the isthmus were among the hardest ever won by human ingenuity. Some interesting facts: A ship traveling from New York to San Francisco can save 7'872 miles using the Panama Canal instead of going around South America. In the fiscal year 1994 there where 14'029 transits, which carried 170.8 million long tons of cargo and paid US $ 419.2 million in tolls. The highest Canal toll was US $ 141,344.91 paid by the Crown Princess and the lowest toll ever paid was 36 cents by Richard Halliburton for swimming the Canal in 1928. The average time spent in transit from port to port is approx. 8 - 10 hours. Until Lake Mead was formed by the building of the Hoover Dam, Gatun Lake was the largest artificial body of water in the world.

FLORA & FAUNA

No other country in Central America has highly developed urban areas and dense tropical jungles at such close distance as Panama. You can literally go wildlife watching "over lunch," and return to the office in the afternoon, having added new and astonishing sights to your memory archives. A slow walk for a few hours along Pipeline Road, near Gamboa will on many occasions allow the visitor to see a higher diversity of wildlife than he could see spending a day at any park in Central America. But the possibility of easy access is only the wrapping paper of this special gift.

Panama is the Central American land bridge with South America and its wildlife shows the strong southern influence. Algae-covered sloths, tiny marmosets and night monkeys make their home in the canopy. The strange bushdog and the giant anteater hunt and forage in the undergrowth, and the capybara, largest rodent in the world, moves in groups along the edge of rivers and lakes. Most of these mammals do not occur farther north into Central America, and Panama provides a unique opportunity to observe these fascinating creatures in their habitat.

Birdwatchers have enjoyed Panama's natural wealth for over a century and bird collectors operated in this rich environment as far back as the mid-nineteenth century. This is no wonder since Panama is home to many of the most-sought jewels on any birders list. The majestic harpy eagle, largest of the neotropical raptors, is still seen occasionally by birders in the Darien and along Pipeline road, as well as its close relatives, the solitary and the crested eagle. Five species of macaws and a dozen and a half species of parrots, parakeets and parrotlets add more than just a visual treat, a lot of decibels to the jungle's dawn symphony. Toucans, bell birds, umbrellabirds and motmots, and even the resplendent quetzal, mostly restricted to the cloud forest of Chiriqui, are other beautiful elements to enrich the country's avifauna, exceeding 900 species.

But natural wealth is not restricted only to terrestrial environments. Panama is fish heaven, whether for the aquarium enthusiast, dip-netting jungle pools and streams, or the deep-sea fisherman trolling offshore. From the small multicolored Killifish and dwarf armored catfish, inhabiting the fresh-water streams and lakes, to the monstrous black marlin off Hannibal Bank and Pinas Bay, Panama has it all. Before the Central American land bridge was formed, Panama was an island which developed many typical freshwater species. As it joined South America and the bridge connected with North America, it started to receive species moving in from adjoining areas, on both versants.

Plant enthusiasts will be equally astonished by the incredible biodiversity found in a country smaller than South Carolina, barely 30,000 square miles. Scientists estimate that over 10,000 species of vascular plants exist in Panama, and many first-time visitors to the lowland rainforests will get the impression that they are all growing right in front of them. But there is more than rainforest in Panama. Dense mangrove thickets fringe large portions of both coastlines, slowly changing into riparian forests, bordering the bodies of water land inwards. The foothills of the central highlands hold tall, broadleaf forests which with increasing altitude, fade into the deep blue-green cloud forests of the upper ranges. The country's highest areas receive frost regularly during the dry season and there is even a report of snow on the summit of Volcan Chiriqui The vast flora covering Panama arose from this broad range of altitude and climatic conditions, combined with a very rich hydrography.

Among the showpiece groups of Panamanian flora are the orchids, with over 1,000 species, ranging from sea-level to the highest mountain peaks. The highest diversity can be found at mid-elevations, where one large tree can have over twenty species growing on trunk and branches, amidst dozens of other epiphytes. Heliconias, a group plants closely related to bananas and birds-of-paradise, display their brightly colored, crab-claw shaped inflorescences in dense thickets along streams and freshwater lakes. These plants evolved together with the hummingbird species that pollinate them, creating an interaction that displays such intense beauty and complexity, that it inspired wildlife artists since the Victorian days.

But Panama's natural world has inspired more than artists and amateur naturalists. Inquisitive visitors will find that this wealthy environment has been studied and documented for well over century. One of the world's most famous centers for the study of tropical ecology and a pioneer project in the field of island biogeography is the island of Barro Colorado, in Lake Gatun. Formed in 1914, when Lake Gatun was flooded it became a permanent study station of the Smithsonian Institute in 1923. Since then, a multidisciplinary team of resident and visiting researchers have kept a highly detailed account of the island's population dynamics of fauna and flora. This living laboratory has allowed scientist to gain a better understanding of the gradual changes that affect small, isolated areas of tropical forests. But the research programs at Barro Colorado are only one of the many ongoing studies, trying to get a better understanding of the country's vast natural wealth.

Whether you are only marginally interested in natural history, or enjoying nature is a main goal in your travel plans, Panama will provide you with an experience that can only be surpassed if you come back. And you will.

PEOPLE

Nationality: *Noun and adjective*--Panamanian(s).
Population (1997 est.): 2.82 million.
Annual growth rate: 2%.
Ethnic groups: Mestizo (mixed Indian and European ancestry) 70%, West Indian 14%, Caucasian 10%, Indian 6%.
Religions: Roman Catholic 85%, Protestant (Evangelical) 15%.
Languages: Spanish (official); 14% speak English as their native tongue; various Indian languages.
Education: *Years compulsory*--6. *Attendance*--95% for primary school-age children, 96% for secondary. *Literacy*--about 90% overall: urban 94%, rural 62%.
Health: *Infant mortality rate*--17/1,000. *Life expectancy*--74 yrs.
Work force (910,000): *Government and community services*--32%; *agriculture*--27%; *commerce, restaurants, and hotels*--16%; *manufacturing and mining*--9%; *transportation and communication*--6%; *construction*--3%; *finance, insurance, and real estate*--4%.

The culture, customs, and language of the Panamanians are predominantly Caribbean Spanish. Ethnically, the majority of the population is mestizo (mixed Spanish and Indian) or mixed Spanish, Indian, Chinese, and West Indian. Spanish is the official and dominant language; English is a common second language spoken by the West Indians and by many in business and the professions. More than half the population lives in the Panama City-Colon metropolitan corridor.

Panama is rich in folklore and popular traditions. Brightly colored national dress is worn during local festivals and the pre-Lenten carnival season, especially for traditional folk dances like the tanborito. Lively salsa--a mixture of Latin American popular music, rhythm and blues, jazz, and rock--is a Panamanian specialty. Indian influences dominate handicrafts such as the famous Kuna textile molas. Artist Roberto Lewis' Presidential Palace murals and his restoration work and ceiling in the National Theater are well known and admired.

More than 65,000 Panamanian students attend the University of Panama, the Technological University, and the University of Santa Maria La Antigua, a private Catholic institution. Including smaller colleges, there are 14 institutions of higher education in Panama.

The first 6 years of primary education are compulsory, and there are about 357,000 students currently enrolled in grades one through six. The total enrollment in the six secondary grades is about 207,000. Nearly 90% of Panamanians are literate.

HISTORY

Panama's history has been shaped by the evolution of the world economy and the ambitions of great powers. Rodrigo de Bastidas, sailing westward from Venezuela in 1501 in search of gold, was the first European to explore the isthmus of Panama. A year later, Christopher Columbus visited the isthmus and established a short-lived settlement in the Darien. Vasco Nunez de Balboa's tortuous trek from the Atlantic to the Pacific in 1513 demonstrated that the isthmus was indeed the path between the seas, and Panama quickly became the crossroads and marketplace of Spain's empire in the New World. Gold and silver were brought by ship from South America, hauled across the isthmus, and loaded aboard ships for Spain. The route became known as the Camino Real, or Royal Road.

Panama was part of the Spanish empire for 300 years (1538-1821). From the outset, Panamanian identity was based on a sense of "geographic destiny," and Panamanian fortunes fluctuated with the geopolitical importance of the isthmus. The colonial experience also spawned Panamanian nationalism as well as a racially complex and highly stratified society, the source of internal conflicts that ran counter to the unifying force of nationalism.

BUILDING THE CANAL

Modern Panamanian history has been shaped by its trans-isthmian canal, which had been a dream since the beginning of Spanish colonization. From 1880 to 1900, a French company under Ferdinand de Lesseps attempted unsuccessfully to construct a sea-level canal on the site of the present Panama Canal. In November 1903, with U.S. encouragement and French financial support, Panama proclaimed its independence and concluded the Hay/Bunau-Varilla Treaty with the United States.

The treaty granted rights to the United States "as if it were sovereign" in a zone roughly 10 miles wide and 50 miles long. In that zone, the U.S. would build a canal, then administer, fortify, and defend it "in perpetuity." In 1914, the United

States completed the existing 83-kilometer (50-mi.) lock canal, which today is one of the world's greatest engineering triumphs. The early 1960s saw the beginning of sustained pressure in Panama for the renegotiation of this treaty. (See discussion of United States-Panama relations and the 1977 Panama Canal Treaties below.)

MILITARY COUPS AND COALITIONS

From 1903 until 1968, Panama was a constitutional democracy dominated by a commercially oriented oligarchy. During the 1950s, the Panamanian military began to challenge the oligarchy's political hegemony. In October 1968, Dr. Arnulfo Arias Madrid, twice elected president and twice ousted by the Panamanian military, was again ousted as president by the National Guard after only 10 days in office. A military junta government was established, and the commander of the National Guard, Brig. Gen. Omar Torrijos, emerged as the principal power in Panamanian political life. Torrijos' regime was harsh and corrupt, but he was a charismatic leader whose populist domestic programs and nationalist foreign policy appealed to the rural and urban constituencies largely ignored by the oligarchy.

Torrijos' death in 1981 altered the tone but not the direction of Panama's political evolution. Despite 1983 constitutional amendments which appeared to proscribe a political role for the military, the Panama Defense Force (PDF), as they were then known, continued to dominate Panamanian political life behind a facade of civilian government. The PDF's hand-picked candidate won the presidential election in 1984. Pro-government parties also won a majority of Legislative Assembly seats, in races tainted by charges of corruption. By this time, Gen. Manuel Noriega was firmly in control of both the PDF and the civilian government.

The rivalry between civilian elites and the Panamanian military, a recurring theme in Panamanian political life since the 1950s, developed into a grave crisis in the 1980s. Prompted by government restrictions on media and civil liberties, in the summer of 1987 more than 100 business, civic, and religious groups formed a loose coalition that organized widespread anti-government demonstrations.

Panama's developing domestic crisis was paralleled by rising tensions between the Panamanian Government and the United States. The United States froze economic and military assistance to Panama in the summer of 1987 in response to the political crisis and an attack on the U.S. embassy. The Government of Panama countered by ousting the U.S. Agency for International Development in December 1987; before the end of the year, the U.S. Congress cut off all assistance to Panama. General Noriega's February 1988 indictment in U.S. courts on drug-trafficking charges sharpened tensions. In April 1988, President Reagan invoked the International Emergency Economic Powers Act, freezing

Panamanian Government assets in U.S. banks and prohibiting payments by American agencies, firms, and individuals to the Noriega regime.

When national elections were held in May 1989, Panamanians voted for the anti-Noriega candidates by a margin of over three-to-one. Although the size of the opposition victory and the presence of international observers thwarted regime efforts to control the outcome of the vote, the Norieiga regime promptly annulled the election and embarked on a new round of repression.

By the fall of 1989, the regime was barely clinging to power. An unsuccessful PDF coup attempt in October produced bloody reprisals. Deserted by all but a small number of cronies, and distrustful of a shaken and demoralized PDF, Noriega began increasingly to rely on irregular paramilitary units called Dignity Battalions. In December 1989, the regime's paranoia made daily existence unsafe for U.S. forces and other U.S. citizens.

On December 20, President Bush ordered the U.S. military into Panama to protect U.S. lives and property, to fulfill U.S. treaty responsibilities to operate and defend the Canal, to assist the Panamanian people in restoring democracy, and to bring Noriega to justice. The U.S. troops involved in Operation Just Cause achieved their primary objectives quickly, and troop withdrawal began on December 27. Norieiga eventually surrendered to U.S. authorities voluntarily. He is now serving a 40-year sentence in Florida for drug trafficking.

REBUILDING DEMOCRACY

Panamanians moved quickly to rebuild their civilian constitutional government. On December 27, 1989, Panama's Electoral Tribunal invalidated the Norieiga regime's annulment of the May 1989 election and confirmed the victory of opposition candidates under the leadership of President Guillermo Endara, and Vice Presidents Guillermo Ford and Ricardo Arias Calderon.

President Endara took office as the head of a four-party minority government, pledging to foster Panama's economic recovery, transform the Panamanian military into a political force under civilian control, and strengthen democratic institutions. During its 5-year term, the Endara government struggled to meet the public's high expectations. Its new police force proved to be a major improvement in outlook and behavior over its thuggish predecessor but was not fully able to deter crime. Its overall record was not enough to convince a skeptical public that it deserved re-election in 1994.

Ernesto Perez Balladares was sworn in as President on September 1, 1994, after an internationally monitored election campaign. The campaign was Panama's largest, with seven candidates for the presidency; over 2,500 for the legislature;

2,000 for mayoral posts; and more than 10,000 at the local level and was peaceful, orderly, and efficient.

Ernesto Perez Balladares ran as the candidate for a three-party coalition dominated by the Democratic Revolutionary Party (PRD), the erstwhile political arm of the military dictatorship during the Torrijos and Norieiga years. A long-time member of the PRD, Perez Balladares worked skillfully during the campaign to rehabilitate the PRD's image, emphasizing the party's populist Torrijos roots rather than its association with Noriega. He won the election with only 33% of the vote when the major non-PRD forces, unable to agree on a joint candidate, splintered into competing factions.

Perez Balladares governed with a multi-party cabinet that included prominent experts in their fields as well as several members who publicly opposed Noriega. His administration carried out economic reforms and often worked closely with the U.S. on implementation on the Canal treaties. In August 1998 a Perez Balladares-blocked referendum to allow presidential reelection failed by a large margin. Soon after, the Government of Panama asked that the 2-year-long negotiations to establish a multilateral counter-narcotics center be ended.

On May 2, 1999, Mireya Moscoso, the widow of former President Arnulfo Arias Madrid who had lost narrowly to Perez Balladares in 1994, defeated PRD candidate Martin Torrijos, son of the late dictator. The elections were considered free and fair. Moscoso took office on September 1, 1999. Though the PRD won a plurality of seats in the Legislative Assembly, Moscoso was able to create a razor-thin majority of PA deputies and members of other, smaller parties.

GOVERNMENT AND POLITICAL CONDITIONS

Type: Constitutional democracy.
Independence: November 3, 1903.
Constitution: October 11, 1972; amended 1983 and 1994.
Branches: *Executive*--president (chief of state), two vice presidents. *Legislative*--Legislative Assembly (unicameral, 72 members). *Judicial*--Supreme Court.
Subdivisions: Nine provinces and two (Indian) territories.
Political parties: President Mireya Moscoso belongs to the Arnulfista Party (PA). The PA, in coalition with smaller parties, holds a slim majority in the Legislative Assembly. Principal opposition parties include the Democratic Revolutionary Party (PRD) of former President Ernesto Perez Balladares.
Suffrage: Universal and compulsory at 18.

Panama is a representative democracy with three branches of government: executive and legislative branches elected by direct, secret vote for 5-year terms, and an independent appointed judiciary. The executive branch includes a president and two vice presidents. The legislative branch consists of a 72-member unicameral Legislative Assembly. The judicial branch is organized under a nine-member Supreme Court and includes all tribunals and municipal courts. An autonomous Electoral Tribunal supervises voter registration, the election process, and the activities of political parties. Everyone over the age of 18 is required to vote, although those who fail to do so are not penalized.

NATIONAL SECURITY

The Panamanian Government has converted the former Panama Defense Forces (PDF) into a civilian "public force," subordinate to civilian officials and composed of four independent units: the Panamanian National Police, the National Maritime Service (Coast Guard), the National Air Service, and the Institutional Protective Service (VIP Security). A constitutional amendment, passed in 1994, abolished the military permanently.

Law enforcement units that have been separated from the public force, such as the Technical Judicial Police, also are directly subordinate to civilian authorities. The public force budget--in contrast to the former PDF--is on public record and under control of the executive.

The United States, with congressional approval, is delivering assistance to help train and establish truly professional law enforcement agencies. In fiscal year 1997, the United States provided police skills training and technical assistance in civilian law enforcement development through a program managed by the International Criminal Investigative and Training Assistance Program (ICITAP).

PRINCIPAL GOVERNMENT OFFICIALS

President--Mireya E. MOSCOSO Rodriguez
First Vice President--Arturo VALLARINO Bartuano
Second Vice President--Dominador "Kaiser" BAZAN
Ministry of Foreign Affairs--Jose Miguel ALEMAN Healy
Ambassador to the United States--Guillermo FORD

Ambassador to the United Nations--Aquilino BOYD
Ambassador to the Organization of American States--Lawrence CHEWNING Fabrega

Panama maintains an embassy in the United States at 2862 McGill Terrace, N.W., Washington, D.C. 20008 (tel: 202-483-1407).

FOREIGN RELATIONS

Panama is a member of the UN General Assembly, most major UN agencies, and has served three terms as a member of the UN Security Council. It maintains membership in several international financial institutions, including the World Bank, the Inter-American Development Bank, and the International Monetary Fund.

Panama is a member of the Organization of American States, and was a founding member of the Rio Group. Although it was suspended from the Latin American Economic System (known informally both as the Group of Eight and the Rio Group) in 1988 due to its internal political system under Noriega, Panama was readmitted in September 1994 as an acknowledgment of its present democratic credentials.

Panama also is one of the founding members of the Union of Banana Exporting Countries and belongs to the Inter-American Tropical Tuna Commission. Panama is an active participant in Central American regional meetings, although it is not a formal participant in integration activities. Panama is a member of the Central American Parliament (PARLACEN) as well as the Central American Integration System (SICA). Panama joined its six Central American neighbors at the 1994 Summit of the Americas in signing the Alliance for Sustainable Development known as the Conjunta Centroamerica-USA or CONCAUSA to promote sustainable economic development in the region and participates in some Miami summit follow-on meetings.

Panama strongly backed efforts by the United States to implement UN Security Council Resolution 940, which was designed to facilitate the departure of Haiti's de facto authorities from power. Panama offered to contribute personnel to the Multinational Force, which restored the democratically elected government to Haiti in October 1994, and granted asylum to some former Haitian military leaders. Also in 1994, Panama agreed to accept 9,000 Cuban "rafters," who were housed temporarily on U.S. military range areas until 1995.

U.S.-PANAMANIAN RELATIONS

The Panama Canal Treaties provided the foundation for an enduring partnership. The U.S. and Panama implemented the treaties by preparing for the transfer to Panama of the Canal and the U.S. base properties. Headquarters of the U.S. Southern Command transferred to Miami in 1997. U.S. development assistance through USAID in FY 1997 was $3 million. Panama does not have a military; therefore, the United States provides no bilateral military assistance to the country. However, civic action projects, direct, and indirect military spending pump several $100 million annually into the Panamanian economy.

The United States cooperates with the Panamanian Government in promoting economic, political, and social development through U.S. and international agencies. Cultural ties between the two countries are strong, and many Panamanians come to the United States for higher education and advanced training. About 6,000 Americans reside in Panama, most of whom are retirees from the Panama Canal Commission and individuals who hold dual nationality. The number of U.S. visitors to Panama from July 1995 to June 1996 averaged around 3,600.

Panama continues to fight against illegal narcotics. The country's proximity to major cocaine-producing nations and its role as a commercial and financial crossroads make it a country of special importance in this regard. Although money laundering remains a problem, a new banking law of 1998 [should help--**helps**?] combat this crime. Panama has worked closely with the U.S. Treasury Department's Financial Crimes Enforcement Network.

THE PANAMA CANAL TREATIES

The 1977 Panama Canal Treaties entered into force on October 1, 1979. They replaced the 1903 Hay/Bunau-Varilla Treaty between the United States and Panama, and all other U.S.-Panama agreements concerning the Panama Canal which were in force on that date. The treaties comprise:

- A basic treaty governing the operation and defense of the Canal from October 1, 1979, to December 31, 1999 (Panama Canal Treaty); and
- A treaty guaranteeing the permanent neutrality of the Canal (Neutrality Treaty). The details of the arrangements for U.S. operation and defense of the Canal under the Panama Canal Treaty are spelled out in separate implementing agreements.

PURPOSE OF THE TREATIES

In negotiating the Panama Canal Treaties, four successive U.S. administrations acted to protect a fundamental national interest in long-term access to a secure and efficient Canal. Panama's cooperation is fundamental to this objective. By meeting Panamanian aspirations for eventual control of the Canal, the United States sought a new relationship with Panama based on friendship and mutual respect. The treaties make Panama a partner in the continued safe and efficient operation of the Canal. In serving the best interests of both nations, the treaties serve the interests of all users of the Canal.

HISTORY OF THE NEGOTIATIONS

Our bilateral relationship with Panama has centered on the Panama Canal since the beginning of the century. Under the 1903 treaty, the United States acquired unilateral rights to build and operate a canal in perpetuity. It also acquired the Canal Zone--a 553-square mile area in which the United States exercised the rights, power, and authority of a sovereign state. In January 1964, Panamanian dissatisfaction with this relationship boiled over into riots that resulted in the deaths of four U.S. Marines and more than 20 Panamanians. A 3-month suspension of diplomatic relations followed.

The growing bilateral tension in the 1960s gave weight to the views of those who believed that a new Canal Treaty was needed to replace the 1903 treaty and to establish a new relationship with Panama. In June 1967, United States and Panamanian negotiators completed draft treaties dealing with the existing Canal, a possible sea-level Canal through Panama, and defense matters. Neither country ratified the treaties, however, and they were publicly rejected by the new Torrijos government in 1970.

A resumption of treaty negotiations led to a declaration of principles signed in 1973 by Secretary of State Henry Kissinger and his Panamanian counterpart, Juan Antonio Tack. On September 7, 1977, President Carter and General Torrijos signed the Panama Canal Treaties at the headquarters of the Organization of American States in Washington, DC. The Panamanian people approved the new treaties in a plebiscite held on October 23, 1977. The U.S. Senate ratified the Neutrality Treaty on March 16, 1978, and the Panama Canal Treaty on April 18, 1978. The treaties entered into force on October 1, 1979. The protocol to the Neutrality Treaty is open to accession by all nations, and more than 35 have subscribed.

BASIC PROVISIONS OF THE TREATIES

The United States had primary responsibility for the operation and defense of the Canal until December 31, 1999. After that date, the United States and Panama will maintain a regime of neutrality for the Canal, including nondiscriminatory access and tolls for merchant and naval vessels of all nations. A U.S. Senate condition attached to the instruments of ratification allows the U.S. and Panama to negotiate a post-1999 defense-sites treaty, if both countries find such a treaty in their mutual interest. Negotiations for a possible post-1999 U.S. presence in Panama in a proposed multinational counter-narcotics center (MCC) ended in September 1998, and no further negotiations are planned.

In order to meet its treaty responsibilities, the United States has the right to use specified land and water areas and facilities in Panama necessary for the operation, maintenance, and defense of the Canal until December 31, 1999. After that date, U.S. warships will be entitled to expeditious passage through the Canal at all times, and the United States will continue to have the obligation to ensure that the Canal remains open and secure.

The United States operated the Canal through the Panama Canal Commission (PCC), which was a U.S. Government agency supervised by a Board of Directors consisting of five American and four Panamanian members, appointed by the President (the Panamanian members are initially nominated by their government). Until 1990, the Canal Administrator was an American, and the Deputy Administrator was Panamanian; these nationalities reversed for the final decade of the treaty on September 20, 1990, when Gilberto Guardia was installed as the first Panamanian Administrator.

He was succeeded in 1996 by another Panamanian, Alberto Aleman Zubieta. Pursuant to treaty obligations, the PCC trained Panamanians in all areas of Canal operations prior to the transfer of the Canal in 1999. In 1997 President Perez Balladares named the members of the Panama Canal Authority (PCA), the successor agency to the PCC.

During the life of the treaty, Panama received the following payments from Canal revenues:

- A fixed annual payment of $10 million;
- An annual payment of $10 million, adjustable for inflation, for public services provided to Canal operating areas by the Government of Panama (the Canal Zone and its government ceased to exist when the treaties entered into force, and Panama assumed jurisdiction over Canal Zone territories and functions);
- An annual percentage of toll revenues assessed at $0.39 (since October 1, 1996) per Panama Canal net ton transiting the Canal, worth $84.6 million in 1996; and
- A payment of up to $10 million in the event that revenues exceed PCC expenditures in a given year.

Under U.S. implementing legislation (the Panama Canal Act), the PCC was required to be self-sustaining; its costs could not exceed its revenues, nor could U.S. taxpayer funds be used for Canal operations or payments to Panama.

PRINCIPAL U.S. OFFICIALS

U.S. Embassy
Ambassador--Vacant
Deputy Chief of Mission--Fredrick Becker
Counselor for Political and Economic Affairs--Lewis Amselem
Counselor for Public Affairs--Joao Ecsodi
Counselor for Administrative Affairs--Trevor Snellgrove
Consul General--Robert Blohm

Smithsonian Tropical Research Institute
Director--Dr. Ira Rubinoff

The U.S. embassy in Panama is located at Avenida Balboa y Calle 38, Panama City (tel: 507-207-7000). Personal and official mail for the embassy and members of the mission may be sent to: U.S. Embassy Panama, Unit 0945, APO AA 34002.

E-mail: U.S. Information Service (USIS): usispan@pty.com Political/Economic Section--embpol@sinfo.net

OTHER CONTACT INFORMATION

American Chamber of Commerce & Industry in Panama
Estafeta Balboa
Apartado 168
Panama, Republica de Panama
Tel: (507) 269-3881
Fax: (507) 223-3508
E-mail: amcham@pan.gbm.net

U.S. Department of Commerce
International Trade Administration
Office of Latin American and the Caribbean
14th and Constitution, NW
Washington, D.C. 20230
Tel: (202) 482-0057
800-USA-TRADE
Fax: (202) 482-0464
Home Page: http://www.ita.doc.gov

ECONOMY

Real GDP (1982 baseline): $6.8 billion.
Annual growth rate: 3.1%.
Real per capita GDP: $2,502.
Natural resources: Timber, seafood, copper.
Services (72% of GDP): Finance, insurance, canal-related services, Colon Free Zone.
Agriculture (11% of GDP): *Products*--bananas and other fruit, corn, sugar, rice, coffee, shrimp, timber, vegetables, cattle. *Land*--agricultural 24%, exploitable forest 20%, other 56%.
Industry (19% of GDP): *Types*--food and drink processing, metalworking, petroleum products, chemicals, paper and paper products, printing, mining,

refined sugar, clothing, furniture, construction.
Trade: *Exports*--$640 million: bananas 33%, shrimp 11%, sugar 4%, coffee 2%, clothing 5%. *Major markets*--U.S. 40%. *Imports*--$3.15 million: capital goods 21%, crude oil 11%, foodstuffs 9 %, other consumer and intermediate goods 57%. *Major suppliers*--U.S. 40%.
Exchange rate: Fixed at unity with the U.S. dollar.

Panama's economy is primarily based on a well-developed services sector that accounts for 72% of GDP. Services include the Panama Canal, banking, insurance, government, and the Colon Free Zone--the world's second-largest free trade zone after Hong Kong. Mining, tourism, and maritime services are projected sources of future growth.

A major challenge facing the Moscoso administration is turning to productive use the 70,000 acres of U.S. military land and more than 5,000 buildings that reverted to Panama at the end of 1999. With this departure, Panama will have to replace jobs and income earned from U.S. bases. Estimates of Department of Defense contribution to the Panamanian economy through employing Panamanians, local procurement, and expenditures by personnel range from $170-$350 million.

Although the economic recovery of the early 1990s returned the economy to 1987 pre-crisis levels, sustained growth depends on Panama's ability to resolve long-standing problems of inequitable distribution of wealth, external debt, and dependence on U.S. Government and Canal revenues. Under- and unemployment continue to weigh down the national economy. Panama's working-age population is expected to grow 2.5% per year during the 1990s. Panama acceded to the World Trade Organization (WTO) in October 1996. During the Perez Balladares administration, in order to bring its regime into compliance with the WTO, Panama reduced tariffs over a broad range of products and eliminated non-tariff barriers. However, the Moscoso administration has moved to raise many tariffs back to WTO maximums.

In 1998, U.S. merchandise exports to Panama were $1.3 billion; U.S. imports from Panama were $280 million, for an overall U.S. trade surplus of just over $1 billion. Trade with the U.S. comprises roughly 40% of Panama's total merchandise trade.

Under the Perez Balladares administration, the water and electricity companies were slated for privatization in 1998, but those plans were dropped in the face of public opportunities. Panama privatized the ports of Cristobal and Balboa, the cement and telecom companies, and the casinos. The Moscoso government has indicated it does not favor further privatizations that it argues tend to perpetuate unemployment.

U.S. companies play an important role in the Panamanian economy. They are particularly active in banking, bananas, ports, and other services. Some 100 U.S. companies operate in Panama.

ROLE OF BUSINESS

The Government of Panama actively promotes Panama's long-standing reputation as an international trading, banking, and services center--and as a site for foreign direct investment. Panama's economy is characterized by low inflation and zero foreign exchange risk. In early 1998, Panama enacted a new banking law intended to detect and deter money laundering. The country is taking steps to improve its infrastructure with private and international financial institution financing.

OVERALL ECONOMIC SITUATION

Preliminary figures from Panama's General Comptroller indicate that Panama's GDP (the country's production of goods and services) grew 4.4% in 1997.

This is a significant increase compared to the 1996 2.5% growth rate. However, it is below the 5% growth average for the decade.

GDP grew faster than population growth in 1997, which is estimated at 1.8%. This implies that GDP per capita also grew in 1997. GDP per capita is higher by US$ 2 the 1987 figure. This means it has taken the country 10 years to overcome the 1987-1990 crisis.

The 1997 growth rate is also lower than the Latin American average. Economic Commission for Latin America (ECLA) of the United Nation estimated that the Latin American economy grew over 5% last year. Central America GDP grew 4%.

Panama's 1997 GDP growth was not enough to significantly reduce the country's high unemployment rate. According to ECLA this rate was 15.8% last year, among Latin America's highest. Latin America's average unemployment rate was 7.5% in 1997.

The trade and services sector (tertiary sector), which in Panama is highly export-oriented, is the one that grew most in 1997. Ports, Colon's Free Zone, tourism (including hotel and restaurant services), transportation and telecommunications grew the most.

Construction, mining and fishing also showed intermediate to high growth rates.

The primary sector was in worse shape. Agriculture suffered weather problems derived from El Niño phenomenon, and bananas are still affected by import restrictions imposed since 1992 by the European Community. The Panama Canal was also in bad shape. It was affected by the Asian crisis and ecological problems too.

Public finances worsened. Current income grew 4%, but current expenditures grew 8%. However, the government managed to reduce slightly its current foreign debt. ECLA estimated it was B/ 5,030 million by year end, compared to B/ 5,070 million by year end 1996. This means per capita debt is now B/ 2,500. In comparison, Latin America's debt grew to US$ 644,600 million, and per capita debt grew to US $ 2,000.

POLITICAL SITUATION

There were no great changes or extraordinary political events in 1997.

The Perez-Balladares Administration, with the support of the Revolutionary Democratic Party (PRD) and Solidaridad, continued implementing its liberalization program. The Telecommunications Institute was sold off to the private sector, and the government took steps towards the privatization of other state owned companies.

The implementation of the program and other events hurt the government's popularity. This was evidenced in several public opinion polls.

Political opposition parties coalesced around Arnulfista Party (PA), after that party's convention which elected Mireya Moscoso as president. Moscoso is the widow and former assistant to deceased populist leader Arnulfo Arias.

Another opposition sector, which includes the left, nationalist groups, and others, remained fragmented.

Political uncertainty continued with regards to an agreement extending the presence of U.S. military basis after the year 2000.

FORECAST

For 1998 slower growth is expected. Figures for the first few months of 1998 seem to confirm the forecast.

We expect weather problems will continue to hurt the economy, specially its primary sector, and that unfavorable external events (such as the Asian crisis and its impact on industrialized countries) will contribute to reduce exports and the tertiary sector's momentum.

Over half the population will adverse reelection of the President, but voter absenteeism at the referendum will probably favor the "Yes" vote.

The probability of Panama and the U.S. reaching an agreement with regards to the U.S. military presence in Panama beyond the year 2000 is less clear. Objections by Latin American nations and nationalist opposition both outside and within the ruling PRD could thwart the agreement.

It is also expected that two opposition alliances will be formed in 1998, which will give better winning probabilities to the government party in 1999.

GROSS DOMESTIC PRODUCT

(Million B/ of 1982

	'96	'97	Cr
TOTAL	6,348.2	6,628	4.4%
Sector I	521	516.3	-0.9%
Agriculture	288.2	266.3	-7.6%
Livestock	150.8	156.3	3.6%
Fishing	73.9	84.2	13.9%
Mining	8.1	9.5	17.3%
Sector II	1,179.4	1,224.8	3.8%
Electricity & water	620.3	642.6	3.6%
Industry	248.1	260.5	5%
Construction	311	321.7	3.4%
Sector III	4647.8	4886.9	5.1%
Whol. & Ret. Trade	676.7	703.4	3.9%
Free Zones	494.3	570.4	15.4%
Hotels & Rest.	100.7	106.1	5.4%
Panama Canal	429.9	422.2	-1.8%
Financia svces.	706.1	729.2	3.3%
Government	665.3	690.6	3.8%
Other svices.	1,574.8	1,665	5.7%

Data: Panama's General Comptroller.

TRAVEL AND BUSINESS INFORMATION

The U.S. Department of State's Consular Information Program provides Consular Information Sheets, Travel Warnings, and Public Announcements. **Consular Information Sheets** exist for all countries and include information on entry requirements, currency regulations, health conditions, areas of instability, crime and security, political disturbances, and the addresses of the U.S. posts in the country. **Travel Warnings** are issued when the State Department recommends that Americans avoid travel to a certain country. **Public Announcements** are issued as a means to disseminate information quickly about terrorist threats and other relatively short-term conditions overseas which pose significant risks to the security of American travelers. Free copies of this information are available by calling the Bureau of Consular Affairs at 202-647-5225 or via the fax-on-demand system: 202-647-3000. Consular Information Sheets and Travel Warnings also are available on the Consular Affairs Internet home page: http://travel.state.gov. Consular Affairs Tips for Travelers publication series, which contain information on obtaining passports and planning a safe trip abroad are on the internet and hard copies can be purchased from the Superintendent of Documents, U.S. Government Printing Office, telephone: 202-512-1800; fax 202-512-2250.

Emergency information concerning Americans traveling abroad may be obtained from the Office of Overseas Citizens Services at (202) 647-5225. For after-hours emergencies, Sundays and holidays, call 202-647-4000.

Passport information can be obtained by calling the National Passport Information Center's automated system ($.35 per minute) or live operators 8 a.m. to 8 p.m. (EST) Monday-Friday ($1.05 per minute). The number is 1-900-225-5674 (TDD: 1-900-225-7778). Major credit card users (for a flat rate of $4.95) may call 1-888-362-8668 (TDD: 1-888-498-3648). It also is available on the internet.

Travelers can check the latest health information with the U.S. Centers for Disease Control and Prevention in Atlanta, Georgia. A hotline at 877-FYI-TRIP (877-394-8747) and a web site at http://www.cdc.gov/travel/index.htm give the most recent health advisories, immunization recommendations or requirements, and advice on food and drinking water safety for regions and countries. A booklet entitled Health Information for International Travel (HHS publication number CDC-95-8280) is available from the U.S. Government Printing Office, Washington, DC 20402, tel. (202) 512-1800.

Information on travel conditions, visa requirements, currency and customs regulations, legal holidays, and other items of interest to travelers also may be obtained before your departure from a country's embassy and/or consulates in the U.S. (for this country, see "Principal Government Officials" listing in this publication).

U.S. citizens who are long-term visitors or traveling in dangerous areas are encouraged to register at the U.S. embassy upon arrival in a country (see "Principal U.S. Embassy Officials" listing in this publication). This may help family members contact you in case of an emergency.

GEOGRAPHY

Panama is located on the narrowest and lowest part of the Isthmus of Panama that links North America and South America. This S-shaped part of the isthmus is situated between 7° and 10° north latitude and 77° and 83° west longitude. Slightly smaller than South Carolina, Panama encompasses approximately 77,082 square kilometers, is 772 kilometers in length, and is between 60 and 177 kilometers in width.

Panama's two coastlines are referred to as the Caribbean (or Atlantic) and Pacific, rather than the north and south coasts. To the east is Colombia and to the west Costa Rica. Because of the location and contour of the country, directions expressed in terms of the compass are often surprising. For example, a transit of the Panama Canal from the Pacific to the Caribbean involves travel not to the east but to the northwest, and in Panama City the sunrise is to the east over the Pacific.

The country is divided into nine provinces, plus the Comarca de San Blas, which for statistical purposes is treated as part of Colón Province in most official documents. The provincial borders have not changed since they were determined at independence in 1903. The provinces are divided into districts, which in turn are subdivided into sections called *corregimientos*. Configurations of the *corregimientos* are changed periodically to accommodate population changes as revealed in the census reports.

The country's two international boundaries, with Colombia and Costa Rica, have been clearly demarcated, and in the late 1980s there were no outstanding disputes. The country claims the seabed of the continental shelf, which has been defined by Panama to extend to the 500-meter submarine contour. In addition, a 1958 law asserts jurisdiction over 12 nautical miles from the coastlines, and in 1968 the government announced a claim to a 200-nautical-mile Exclusive Economic Zone.

The Caribbean coastline is marked by several good natural harbors. However, Cristóbal, at the Caribbean terminus of the canal, had the only important port facilities in the late 1980s. The numerous islands of the Archipiélago de Bocas del Toro, near the Costa Rican border, provide an extensive natural roadstead and shield the banana port of Almirante. The over 350 San Blas Islands, near Colombia, are strung out for more than 160 kilometers along the sheltered Caribbean coastline.

The major port on the Pacific coastline is Balboa. The principal islands are those of the Archipiélago de las Perlas in the middle of the Gulf of Panama, the penal colony on the Isla de Coiba in the Golfo de Chiriquí, and the decorative island of

Taboga, a tourist attraction that can be seen from Panama City. In all, there are some 1,000 islands off the Pacific coast.

The Pacific coastal waters are extraordinarily shallow. Depths of 180 meters are reached only outside the perimeters of both the Gulf of Panama and the Golfo de Chiriquí, and wide mud flats extend up to 70 kilometers seaward from the coastlines. As a consequence, the tidal range is extreme. A variation of about 70 centimeters between high and low water on the Caribbean coast contrasts sharply with over 700 centimeters on the Pacific coast, and some 130 kilometers up the Río Tuira the range is still over 500 centimeters.

The dominant feature of the country's landform is the central spine of mountains and hills that forms the continental divide. The divide does not form part of the great mountain chains of North America, and only near the Colombian border are there highlands related to the Andean system of South America. The spine that forms the divide is the highly eroded arch of an uplift from the sea bottom, in which peaks were formed by volcanic intrusions.

The mountain range of the divide is called the Cordillera de Talamanca near the Costa Rican border. Farther east it becomes the Serranía de Tabasará, and the portion of it closer to the lower saddle of the isthmus, where the canal is located, is often called the Sierra de Veraguas. As a whole, the range between Costa Rica and the canal is generally referred to by Panamanian geographers as the Cordillera Central.

The highest point in the country is the Volcán Barú (formerly known as the Volcán de Chiriquí), which rises to almost 3,500 meters. The apex of a highland that includes the nation's richest soil, the Volcán Barú is still referred to as a volcano, although it has been inactive for millennia.

Nearly 500 rivers lace Panama's rugged landscape. Mostly unnavigable, many originate as swift highland streams, meander in valleys, and form coastal deltas. However, the Río Chepo and the Río Chagres are sources of hydroelectric power.

The Río Chagres is one of the longest and most vital of the approximately 150 rivers that flow into the Caribbean. Part of this river was dammed to create Gatun Lake, which forms a major part of the transit route between the locks near each end of the canal. Both Gatun Lake and Madden Lake (also filled with water from the Río Chagres) provide hydroelectricity for the area of the former Canal Zone.

The Río Chepo, another major source of hydroelectric power, is one of the more than 300 rivers emptying into the Pacific. These Pacific-oriented rivers are longer and slower running than those of the Caribbean side. Their basins are also more extensive. One of the longest is the Río Tuira, which flows into the Golfo de San Miguel and is the nation's only river navigable by larger vessels.

Panama has a tropical climate. Temperatures are uniformly high- -as is the relative humidity--and there is little seasonal variation. Diurnal ranges are low; on a typical dry-season day in the capital city, the early morning minimum may be 24°C and the afternoon maximum 29°C. The temperature seldom exceeds 32°C for more than a short time.

Temperatures on the Pacific side of the isthmus are somewhat lower than on the Caribbean, and breezes tend to rise after dusk in most parts of the country. Temperatures are markedly cooler in the higher parts of the mountain ranges, and frosts occur in the Cordillera de Talamanca in western Panama.

Climatic regions are determined less on the basis of temperature than on rainfall, which varies regionally from less than 1.3 to more than 3 meters per year. Almost all of the rain falls during the rainy season, which is usually from April to December, but varies in length from seven to nine months. The cycle of rainfall is determined primarily by two factors: moisture from the Caribbean, which is transported by north and northeast winds prevailing during most of the year, and the continental divide, which acts as a rainshield for the Pacific lowlands. A third influence that is present during the late autumn is the southwest wind off the Pacific. This wind brings some precipitation to the Pacific lowlands, modified by the highlands of the Península de Azuero, which form a partial rainshield for much of central Panama. In general, rainfall is much heavier on the Caribbean than on the Pacific side of the continental divide. The annual average in Panama City is little more than half of that in Colón. Although rainy-season thunderstorms are common, the country is outside the hurricane track.

Panama's tropical environment supports an abundance of plants. Forests dominate, interrupted in places by grasslands, scrub, and crops. Although nearly 40 percent of Panama is still wooded, deforestation is a continuing threat to the rain-drenched woodlands. Tree cover has been reduced by more than 50 percent since the 1940s. Subsistence farming, widely practiced from the northeastern jungles to the southwestern grasslands, consists largely of corn, bean, and tuber plots. Mangrove swamps occur along parts of both coasts, with banana plantations occupying deltas near Costa Rica. In many places, a multi-canopied rain forest abuts the swamp on one side of the country and extends to the lower reaches of slopes in the other.

HISTORY[1]

THE CONQUEST

Estimates vary greatly of the number of Indians who inhabited the isthmus when the Spanish explorers arrived. By some accounts, the population was considerably greater than that of contemporary Panama. Some Panamanian historians have suggested that there might have been a population of 500,000 Indians from some sixty "tribes," but other researchers have concluded that the Cuna alone numbered some 750,000.

Besides the Cuna, which constituted by far the largest group in the area, two other major groups, the Guaymí and the Chocó, have been identified by ethnologists. The Guaymí, of the highlands near the Costa Rican border, are believed to be related to Indians of the Nahuatlan and Mayan nations of Mexico and Central America. The Chocó on the Pacific side of Darién Province appear to be related to the Chibcha of Colombia.

Although the Cuna, now found mostly in the Comarca de San Blas, an indigenous territory or reserve considered part of Colón Province for some official purposes, have been categorized as belonging to the Caribbean culture, their origin continues to be a subject of speculation. Various ethnologists have indicated the possibility of a linguistic connection between the name *Cuna* and certain Arawak and Carib tribal names. The possibility of cultural links with the Andean Indians has been postulated, and some scholars have noted linguistic and other affinities with the Chibcha. The implication in terms of settlement patterns is that the great valleys of Colombia, which trend toward the isthmus, determined migration in that direction.

Lines of affiliation have also been traced to the Cueva and Coiba tribes, although some anthropologists suggest that the Cuna might belong to a largely extinct linguistic group. Some Cuna believe themselves to be of Carib stock, while others trace their origin to creation by the god Olokkuppilele at Mount Tacarcuna, west of the mouth of the Río Atrato in Colombia.

Among all three Indian groups-the Cuna, Guaymí, and Chocó- land was communally owned and farmed. In addition to hunting and fishing, the Indians raised corn, cotton, cacao, various root crops and other vegetables, and fruits. They lived then--as many still do-in circular thatched huts and slept in hammocks. Villages specialized in producing certain goods, and traders moved among them along the rivers and coastal waters in dugout canoes. The Indians were skillful potters, stonecutters, goldsmiths, and silversmiths. The ornaments

[1] This section based in part on the materials of the US Library of Commerce and other country related publications.

they wore, including breastplates and earrings of beaten gold, reinforced the Spanish myth of El Dorado, the city of gold.

Rodrigo de Bastidas, a wealthy notary public from Seville, was the first of many Spanish explorers to reach the isthmus. Sailing westward from Venezuela in 1501 in search of gold, he explored some 150 kilometers of the coastal area before heading for the West Indies. A year later, Christopher Columbus, on his fourth voyage to the New World, touched several points on the isthmus. One was a horseshoe-shaped harbor that he named Puerto Bello (beautiful port), later renamed Portobelo.

Vasco Núñez de Balboa, a member of Bastidas's crew, had settled in Hispaniola (present-day Dominican Republic and Haiti) but stowed away on a voyage to Panama in 1510 to escape his creditors. At that time, about 800 Spaniards lived on the isthmus, but soon the many jungle perils, doubtless including malaria and yellow fever, had killed all but 60 of them. Finally, the settlers at Antigua del Darién (Antigua), the first city to be duly constituted by the Spanish crown, deposed the crown's representative and elected Balboa and Martin Zamudio co-mayors.

Balboa proved to be a good administrator. He insisted that the settlers plant crops rather than depend solely on supply ships, and Antigua became a prosperous community. Like other conquistadors, Balboa led raids on Indian settlements, but unlike most, he proceeded to befriend the conquered tribes. He took the daughter of a chief as his lifelong mistress.

On September 1, 1513, Balboa set out with 190 Spaniards-among them Francisco Pizarro, who later conquered the Inca Empire in Peru-a pack of dogs, and 1,000 Indian slaves. After twenty-five days of hacking their way through the jungle, the party gazed on the vast expanse of the Pacific Ocean. Balboa, clad in full armor, waded into the water and claimed the sea and all the shores on which it washed for his God and his king.

Balboa returned to Antigua in January 1514 with all 190 soldiers and with cotton cloth, pearls, and 40,000 pesos in gold. Meanwhile, Balboa's enemies had denounced him in the Spanish court, and King Ferdinand appointed a new governor for the colony, then known as Castilla del Oro. The new governor, Pedro Arias de Avila, who became known as "Pedrarias the Cruel," charged Balboa with treason. In 1517 Balboa was arrested, brought to the court of Pedrarias, and executed.

In 1519 Pedrarias moved his capital away from the debilitating climate and unfriendly Indians of the Darién to a fishing village on the Pacific coast (about four kilometers east of the present-day capital). The Indians called the village Panama, meaning "plenty of fish." In the same year, Nombre de Dios, a deserted early settlement , was resettled and until the end of the sixteenth century served as the Caribbean port for trans-isthmian traffic. A trail known as the Camino Real, or royal road, linked Panama and Nombre de Dios. Along this trail, traces of which can still be followed, gold from Peru was carried by muleback to Spanish galleons waiting on the Atlantic coast.

The increasing importance of the isthmus for transporting treasure and the delay and difficulties posed by the Camino Real inspired surveys ordered by the Spanish crown in the 1520s and 1530s to ascertain the feasibility of constructing a canal. The idea was finally abandoned in mid-century by King Philip II (1556-98), who concluded that if God had wanted a canal there, He would have built one.

Pedrarias's governorship proved to be disastrous. Hundreds of Spaniards died of disease and starvation in their brocaded silk clothing; thousands of Indians were robbed, enslaved, and massacred. Thousands more of the Indians succumbed to European diseases to which they had no natural immunity. After the atrocities of Pedrarias, most of the Indians fled to remote areas to avoid the Spaniards.

The regulations for colonial administration set forth by the Spanish king's Council of the Indies decreed that the Indians were to be protected and converted to Christianity. The colonies, however, were far from the seat of ultimate responsibility, and few administrators were guided by the humane spirit of those regulations. The Roman Catholic Church, and particularly the Franciscan order, showed some concern for the welfare of the Indians, but on the whole, church efforts were inadequate to the situation.

The Indians, nevertheless, found one effective benefactor among their Spanish oppressors. Bartolomé de las Casas, the first priest ordained in the West Indies, was outraged by the persecution of the Indians. He freed his own slaves, returned to Spain, and persuaded the council to adopt stronger measures against enslaving the Indians. He made one suggestion that he later regretted--that Africans, whom the Spaniards considered less than human, be imported to replace the Indians as slaves.

In 1517 King Charles V (1516-56) granted a concession for exporting 4,000 African slaves to the Antilles. Thus the slave trade began and flourished for more than 200 years. Panama was a major distribution point for slaves headed elsewhere on the mainland. The supply of Indian labor had been depleted by the midsixteenth century, however, and Panama began to absorb many of the slaves. A large number of slaves on the isthmus escaped into the jungle. They became known as *cimarrones* (sing., *cimarrón*), meaning wild or unruly, because they attacked travelers along the Camino Real. An official census of Panama City in 1610 listed 548 citizens, 303 women, 156 children, 146 mulattoes, 148 Antillean blacks, and 3,500 African slaves.

THE SPANISH COLONY

The period of free, though licensed, exploration gave way to a period in which the king exercised royal control by appointing governors and their staffs. All were to be paid from crown revenues expected from the royal profits on the colony. The king's representative was responsible for ensuring such returns; he tracked all gold, pearls, and income from trade and conquest; he weighed out and safeguarded the king's share.

Governors had some summary powers of justice, but *audiencias* (courts) were also established. The first such *audiencia*, in Santo Domingo, Hispaniola, had jurisdiction over the whole area of conquest. As settlement spread, other *audiencias* were set up. By a decree of 1538, all Spanish territory from Nicaragua to Cape Horn was to be administered from an *audiencia* in Panama. This *audiencia* lasted only until 1543 because of the impossibility of exercising jurisdiction over so vast an area. A new Panamanian *audiencia*, with jurisdiction over an area more nearly coinciding with the territory of present-day Panama, was established in 1563. The viceroy's position was revived for the rich empires of Mexico and Peru. After 1567 Panama was attached to the Viceroyalty of Peru but retained its own *audiencia*.

Beginning early in the sixteenth century, Nombre de Dios in Panama, Vera Cruz in Mexico, and Cartagena in Colombia were the only three ports in Spanish America authorized by the crown to trade with the homeland. By the mid-1560s, the system became regularized, and two fleets sailed annually from Spain, one to Mexico, and the other to southern ports. These fleets would then rendezvous at Havana and return together to Cádiz, Spain. In principle, this rigid system remained in effect until the eighteenth century. From the middle of the seventeenth century, however, as the strength and prosperity of Spain declined, annual visits became the exception.

Shipments of bullion and goods were to be delivered to Panama on the Pacific side for transport over the isthmus and return to Spain. Panama's own contribution to the loading of the fleet was relatively small. Gold production was never great, and little exportable surplus of agricultural and forest products was available. Nothing was manufactured; in fact, Spain discouraged the production of finished goods. The colony's prosperity, therefore, fluctuated with the volume of trade, made up largely of Peruvian shipments. When the Inca gold was exhausted, great quantities of silver mined in Peru replaced gold in trade for 150 years, supplemented eventually by sugar, cotton, wine, indigo, cinchona, vanilla, and cacao.

Except for traffic in African slaves, foreign trade was forbidden unless the goods passed through Spain. Africans were brought to the colonies on contract (*asiento*) by Portuguese, English, Dutch, and French slavers, who were forbidden to trade in any other commodities. Spanish efforts to retain their monopoly on the rich profits from trade with their colonies provided a challenge to the rising maritime nations of Europe. Intermittent maritime warfare resulted in the Caribbean and later in the Pacific. The first serious interference with trade came from the English.

From 1572 to 1597, Francis Drake was associated with most of the assaults on Panama. Drake's activities demonstrated the indefensibility of the open roadstead of Nombre de Dios. In 1597 the Atlantic terminus of the trans-isthmian route was moved to Portobelo, one of the best natural harbors anywhere on the Spanish Main (the mainland of Spanish America).

Despite raids on shipments and ports, the registered legal import of precious metals increased threefold between 1550 and 1600. Panama's prosperity was at its peak during the first part of the seventeenth century. This was the time of the famous *ferias* (fairs, or exchange markets) of Portobelo, where European merchandise could be purchased to supply the commerce of the whole west coast south of Nicaragua. When a *feria* ended, Portobelo would revert to its quiet existence as a small seaport and garrison town.

Panama City also flourished on the profits of trade. Following reconstruction after a serious fire in 1644, contemporary accounts credit Panama City with 1,400 residences "of all types" (probably including slave huts); most business places, religious houses, and substantial residences were rebuilt of stone. Panama City was considered, after Mexico City and Lima, the most beautiful and opulent settlement in the West Indies.

Interest in a canal project was revived early in the seventeenth century by Philip III of Spain (1598-1621). The Council of the Indies dissuaded the king, arguing that a canal would draw attack from other European nations--an indication of the decline of Spanish sea power.

During the first quarter of the seventeenth century, trade between Spain and the isthmus remained undisturbed. At the same time, England, France, and the Netherlands, one or all almost constantly at war with Spain, began seizing colonies in the Caribbean. Such footholds in the West Indies encouraged the development of the buccaneers--English, French, Dutch, and Portuguese adventurers who preyed on Spanish shipping and ports with the tacit or open support of their governments. Because of their numbers and the closeness of their bases, the buccaneers were more effective against Spanish trade than the English had been during the previous century.

The volume of registered precious metal arriving in Spain fell from its peak in 1600; by 1660 volume was less than the amount registered a century before.

Depletion of Peruvian mines, an increase in smuggling, and the buccaneers were causes of the decline.

Henry Morgan, a buccaneer who had held Portobelo for ransom in 1668, returned to Panama with a stronger force at the end of 1670. On January 29, 1671, Morgan appeared at Panama City. With 1,400 men he defeated the garrison of 2,600 in pitched battle outside the city, which he then looted. The officials and citizens fled, some to the country and others to Peru, having loaded their ships with the most important church and government funds and treasure. Panama City was destroyed by fire, probably from blown up powder stores, although the looters were blamed. After 4 weeks, Morgan left with 175 mule loads of loot and 600 prisoners. Two years later, a new city was founded at the location of the present-day capital and was heavily fortified.

The buccaneer scourge rapidly declined after 1688 mainly because of changing European alliances. By this time Spain was chronically bankrupt; its population had fallen; and it suffered internal government mismanagement and corruption.

Influenced by buccaneer reports about the ease with which the isthmus could be crossed--which suggested the possibility of digging a canal--William Paterson, founder and ex-governor of the Bank of England, organized a Scottish company to establish a colony in the San Blas area. Paterson landed on the Caribbean coast of the Darién late in 1698 with about 1,200 persons. Although well received by the Indians (as was anyone not Spanish), the colonists were poorly prepared for life in the tropics with its attendant diseases. Their notion of trade goods--European clothing, wigs, and English Bibles--was of little interest to the Indians. These colonists gave up after six months, unknowingly passing at sea reinforcements totaling another 1,600 people. The Spanish reacted to these new arrivals by establishing a blockade from the sea. The English capitulated and left in April 1700, having lost many lives, mostly from malnutrition and disease.

In Spain Bourbon kings replaced the Hapsburgs in 1700, and some liberalization of trade was introduced. These measures were too late for Panama, however. Spain's desperate efforts to maintain its colonial trade monopoly had been self-defeating. Cheaper goods supplied by England, France, and the Netherlands were welcomed by colonial officials and private traders alike. Dealing in contraband increased to the detriment of official trade. Fewer merchants came to the Portobelo *feria* to pay Spain's inflated prices because the foreign suppliers furnished cheaper goods at any port at which they could slip by or bribe the coastal guards. The situation worsened; only five of the previously annual fleets were dispatched to Latin America between 1715 and 1736, a circumstance that increased contraband operations.

Panama's temporary loss of its independent *audiencia*, from 1718 to 1722, and the country's attachment to the Viceroyalty of Peru were probably engineered by powerful Peruvian merchants. They resented the venality of Panamanian officials and their ineffectiveness in suppressing the pirates (outlaws of no flag, as distinct from the buccaneers of the seventeenth century). Panama's weakness was further shown by its inability to protect itself against an invasion by the Miskito Indians of Nicaragua, who attacked from Laguna de Chiriquí. Another Indian uprising in the valley of the Río Tuira caused the whites to abandon the Darién.

The final blow to Panama's shrinking control of the transit trade between Latin America and Spain came before the mid- eighteenth century. As a provision of the Treaty of Utrecht at the end of the War of the Spanish Succession in 1713, Britain secured the right to supply African slaves to the Spanish colonies (4,800 a year for 30 years) and also to send 1 ship a year to Portobelo. The slave trade provision evidently satisfied both countries, but the trade in goods did not. Smuggling by British ships continued, and a highly organized contraband trade based in Jamaica--with the collusion of Panamanian merchants--nearly wiped out the legal trade. By 1739 the importance of the isthmus to Spain had seriously declined; Spain again suppressed Panama's autonomy by making the region part of the Viceroyalty of New Granada (encompassing present-day Colombia, Venezula, Ecuador, and Panama).

In the same year, war broke out between Britain and Spain. A British military force took Portobelo and destroyed it. Panamanian historians maintain that this attack diverted Spanish trade from the trans-isthmian route. The Seville-Cádiz monopoly of colonial trade had been breached by royal decrees earlier in the century, and precedent was thus furnished for the merchants of the Latin American colonies to agitate for direct trade with Spain and for intercolonial trade. After 1740 the Pacific coast ports were permitted to trade directly via ships rounding Cape Horn, and the Portobelo *feria* was never held again.

Relaxing the trading laws benefited both Spanish America and Spain, but Panama's economic decline was serious. Transit trade had for so long furnished the profits on which Panama had flourished that there had been no incentive to develop any other economic base. After the suppression of its *audiencia* in 1751, Panama became a quiet backwater, a geographically isolated appendage of New Granada, scarcely self-supporting even in food and producing little for export.

In 1793, near the close of the colonial period, the first recorded attempt at a comprehensive census of the area that had comprised the Panamanian *audiencia* was made. Incomplete and doubtless omitting most of the Indian and *cimarrón* populat- ion, specifically excluding soldiers and priests, the census recorded 71,888 inhabitants, 7,857 of whom lived in Panama City. Other principal towns had populations ranging from 2,000 to a little over 5,000.

Social hierarchy in the colony was rigid. The most prestigious and rewarding positions were reserved for the *peninsulares*, those actually born in Spain.

Criollos, those of Spanish ancestry but born in the colonies, occupied secondary posts in government and trade. Mestizos, usually offspring of Hispanic fathers and Indian mothers, engaged in farming, retail trade, and the provision of services. African and Indian slaves constituted an underclass. To the extent possible, Indians who escaped enslavement avoided Hispanic society altogether.

The church held a special place in society. Priests accompanied every expedition and were always counselors to the temporal leaders. The first bishop on the mainland came with Pedrarias. The bishop's authority, received from the king, made him in effect a vice governor. The bishopric was moved from Darién to Panama City in 1521. The relationship between church and government in the colony was closer than in Spain. Both the Roman Catholic Church and the monastic orders gained great wealth through tithes and land acquisition.

THE COLOMBIA DEPARTMENT

INDEPENDENCE FROM SPAIN

Lacking communication except by sea, which the Spanish generally controlled, Panama remained aloof from the early efforts of the Spanish colonies to separate from Spain. Revolutionaries of other colonies, however, did not hesitate to use Panama's strategic potential as a pawn in revolutionary maneuvers. General Francisco Miranda of Venezuela, who had been attracting support for revolutionary activities as early as 1797, offered a canal concession to Britain in return for aid. Thomas Jefferson, while minister to France, also showed interest in a canal, but the isolationist policies of the new United States and the absorption of energies and capital in continental expansion prevented serious consideration.

Patriots from Cartagena attempted to take Portobelo in 1814 and again in 1819, and a naval effort from liberated Chile succeeded in capturing the island of Taboga in the Bay of Panama. Panama's first act of separation from Spain came without violence. When Simón Bolívar's victory at Boyacá on August 7, 1819, clinched the liberation of New Granada, the Spanish viceroy fled Colombia for Panama, where he ruled harshly until his death in 1821. His replacement in Panama, a liberal constitutionalist, permitted a free press and the formation of patriotic associations. Raising troops locally, he soon sailed for Ecuador, leaving a native Panamanian, Colonel Edwin Fábrega, as acting governor.

Panama City immediately initiated plans to declare independence, but the city of Los Santos preempted the move by proclaiming freedom from Spain on November 10, 1821. This act precipitated a meeting in Panama City on November 28, which is celebrated as the official date of independence. Considerable discussion followed as to whether Panama should remain part of

Colombia (then comprising both the present-day country and Venezuela) or unite with Peru. The bishop of Panama, a native Peruvian who realized the commercial ties that could be developed with his country, argued for the latter solution but was voted down. A third possible course of action, a union with Mexico proposed by emissaries of that country, was rejected.

Panama thus became part of Colombia, then governed under the 1821 Constitution of Cúcuta, and was designated a department with two provinces, Panamá and Veraguas. With the addition of Ecuador to the liberated area, the whole country became known as Gran Colombia. Panama sent a force of 700 men to join Bolívar in Peru, where the war of liberation continued.

The termination of hostilities against the royalists in 1824 failed to bring tranquillity to Gran Colombia. The constitution that Bolívar had drafted for Bolivia was put forward by him to be adopted in Gran Colombia. The country was divided principally over the proposal that a president would serve for life. The president would not be responsible to the legislature and would have power to select his vice president. Other provisions, generally centralist in their tendencies, were repugnant to some, while a few desired a monarchy. Panama escaped armed violence over the constitutional question but joined other regions in petitioning Bolívar to assume dictatorial powers until a convention could meet. Panama announced its union with Gran Colombia as a "Hanseatic State," i.e., as an autonomous area with special trading privileges until the convention was held.

In 1826 Bolívar honored Panama when he chose it as the site for a congress of the recently liberated Spanish colonies. Many leaders of the revolutions in Latin America considered the establishment of a single government for the former Spanish colonies the natural follow-up to driving out the *peninsulares*. Both José de San Martin and Miranda proposed creating a single vast monarchy ruled by an emperor descended from the Incas. Bolívar, however, was the one who made the most serious attempt to unite the Spanish American republics.

Although the league or confederation envisioned by Bolívar was to foster the blessings of liberty and justice, a primary purpose was to secure the independence of the former colonies from renewed attacks by Spain and its allies. In this endeavor Bolívar sought Britain's protection. He was reluctant to invite representatives of the United States, even as observers, to the congress of plenipotentiaries lest their collaboration compromise the league's position with the British. Furthermore, Bolívar felt that the neutrality of the United States in the war between Spain and its former colonies would make its representation inappropriate. In addition, slavery in the United States would be an obstacle in discussing the abolition of the African slave trade. Bolívar nevertheless acquiesced when the governments of Colombia, Mexico, and Central America invited the United States to send observers.

Despite the sweeping implications of the Monroe Doctrine, President John Quincy Adams--in deciding to send delegates to the Panama conference-was not disposed to obligate the United States to defend its southern neighbors. Adams instructed his delegates to refrain from participating in deliberations concerning regional security and to emphasize discussions of maritime neutrality and commerce. Nevertheless, many members of the United States Congress opposed participation under any conditions. By the time participation was approved, the delegation had no time to reach the conference. The British and Dutch sent unofficial representatives.

The Congress of Panama, which convened in June and adjourned in July of 1826, was attended by four American states-Mexico, Central America, Colombia, and Peru. The "Treaty of Union, League, and Perpetual Confederation" drawn up at that congress would have bound all parties to mutual defense and to the peaceful settlement of disputes. Furthermore, because some feared that monarchical elements sympathetic to Spain and its allies might regain control of one of the new republics, the treaty included a provision that if a member state substantially changed its form of government, it would be excluded from the confederation and could be readmitted only with the unanimous consent of all other members.

The treaty was ratified only by Colombia and never became effective. Bolívar, having made several futile attempts to establish lesser federations, declared shortly before his death in 1830 that "America is ungovernable; those who served the revolution have plowed the sea." Despite his disillusion, however, he did not see United States protection as a substitute for collective security arrangements among the Spanish-speaking states. In fact, he is credited with having said, "The United States seems destined by Providence to plague America with misery in the name of Liberty."

Three abortive attempts to separate the isthmus from Colombia occurred between 1830 and 1840. The first was undertaken by an acting governor of Panama who opposed the policies of the president, but the Panamanian leader reincorporated the department of Panama at the urging of Bolívar, then on his deathbed. The second attempted separation was the scheme of an unpopular dictator, who was soon deposed and executed. The third secession, a response to civil war in Colombia, was declared by a popular assembly, but reintegration took place a year later.

THE CALIFORNIA GOLD RUSH AND THE RAILROAD

Even before the United States acquired California after the Mexican War (1846-48), many heading for California used the isthmus crossing in preference to the long and dangerous wagon route across the vast plains and rugged mountain ranges. Discovery of gold in 1848 increased traffic greatly. In 1847 a group of

New York financiers organized the Panama Railroad Company. This company secured an exclusive concession from Colombia allowing construction of a crossing, which might be by road, rail, river, or a combination. After surveys, a railroad was chosen, and a new contract so specifying was obtained in 1850. The railroad track followed generally the line of the present canal. The first through train from the Atlantic to the Pacific side ran on the completed track on January 28, 1855.

The gold rush traffic, even before the completion of the railroad, restored Panama's prosperity. Between 1848 and 1869, about 375,000 persons crossed the isthmus from the Atlantic to the Pacific, and 225,000 crossed in the opposite direction. Prices for food and services were greatly inflated, producing enormous profits from meals and lodging.

The railroad also created a new city and port at the Atlantic terminus of the line. The town that immediately sprang up to accommodate the railroad offices, warehouses, docks, and shops and to lodge both railroad workers and passengers soon became, and remains, the second largest in the country. United States citizens named it Aspinwall, after one of the founders of the Panama Railroad Company, but the Panamanians christened it Colón, in honor of Columbus. Both names were used for many years, but because the Panamanians insisted that no such place as Aspinwall existed and refused to deliver mail so addressed, the name Colón prevailed.

The gold rush and the railroad also brought the United States "Wild West" to the isthmus. The forty-niners tended to be an unruly lot, usually bored as they waited for a ship to California, frequently drunk, and often armed. Many also displayed prejudice verging on contempt for other races and cultures. The so-called Watermelon War of 1856, in which at least sixteen persons were killed, was the most serious clash of races and cultures of the period.

In 1869 the first transcontinental railroad was completed in the United States. This development reduced passenger and freight traffic across the isthmus and diminished the amount of gold and silver shipped east. During the height of the gold rush, however, from 1855 to 1858, only one-tenth of the ordinary commercial freight was destined for or originated in California. The balance concerned trade of the North Americans with Europe and Asia. The railroad company, because of its exceptionally high return on a capitalization that never exceeded US$7 million, paid a total of nearly US$38 million in dividends between 1853 and 1905. Panama received US$25,000 from Colombia's annuity and benefited from transient trade and some inflow of capital.

THE UNCOMPLETED FRENCH CANAL

Throughout the nineteenth century, governments and private investors in the United States, Britain, and France intermittently displayed interest in building a canal across the Western Hemisphere. Several sites were considered, but from the start the ones in Nicaragua and Panama received the most serious attention. President Andrew Jackson sent Charles A. Biddle as his emissary in the 1830s to investigate both routes, but the project was aborted when Biddle abandoned his government mission and negotiated instead with Colombian capitalists for a private concession.

Nevertheless, Colombia continued to express interest in negotiating with the United States on building a canal. A treaty was signed in 1846 between the two countries. The treaty removed the existing restrictive tariffs and gave the United States and its citizens the right of free transit of persons and goods over any road or canal that might be constructed in the isthmus. In addition, the United States guaranteed the neutrality of the isthmus and Colombia's sovereignty over it, with a view to ensuring uninterrupted transit for the duration of the treaty, which was to be twenty years or as long thereafter as the parties gave no notice to revise it. Called the Bidlack-Mallarino Treaty of 1846, it was actually ratified and became effective in 1848.

Because the canal interests of Britain and the United States had continued to clash, particularly in Nicaragua, Britain and the United States sought to ease tensions by entering into the ClaytonBulwer Treaty of 1850. The governments agreed specifically that neither would acquire rights to or construct a Nicaraguan canal without the participation of the other. This general principle was extended to any canal or railroad across Central America, to include the Isthmus of Tehuantepec in Mexico and Panama. In effect, since neither government was then willing or able to begin a canal, the treaty was for the time an instrument of neutrality.

Colombia's attempt to attract canal interest finally brought French attention to bear on Panama. After several surveys, a concession of exclusive rights was obtained from Colombia, and a company was formed in 1879 to construct a sea-level canal generally along the railroad route. Ferdinand de Lesseps, of Suez Canal fame, headed the company. The terms of the concession required completion in twelve years, with the possibility of a six-year extension at Colombia's discretion. The lease was for ninety years and was transferable, but not to any foreign government. The company also purchased most of the stock of the Panama Railroad Company, which, however, continued to be managed by Americans.

A ceremonious commencement of work was staged by de Lesseps on January 1, 1880, but serious earth moving did not start until the next year. As work progressed, engineers judged that a sea-level canal was impracticable. De Lesseps, a promoter but not an engineer, could not be convinced until work had gone on for six years. Actual labor on a lock canal did not start until late in 1888, by which time the company was in serious financial difficulty. At the peak of its operations the company employed about 10,000 workers.

De Lesseps had to contend not only with enemies who hampered financing by spreading rumors of failure and dumping stocks and bonds on the market but also with venal French politicians and bureaucrats who demanded large bribes for approving the issue of securities. His efforts to get the French government to guarantee his bonds were blocked by the United States, on the grounds that such action would lead to government control in violation of the Monroe Doctrine. The end result in January 1889 was the appointment of a receiver to liquidate the company, whereupon all work stopped.

Despite the French company's disastrous financial experience, an estimated two-fifths of the excavation necessary for the eventual canal had been completed. Many headquarters and hospital buildings were finished. Some of the machinery left on the site was usable later, and the railroad had been maintained. Another legacy of the French company's bankruptcy was a large labor force, now unemployed, mostly Antillean blacks. More than half were repatriated, but thousands remained, many of whom eventually worked on the United States canal.

THE SPILLOVER FROM COLOMBIA'S CIVIL STRIFE

During the last half of the nineteenth century, violent clashes between the supporters of the Liberal and Conservative parties in Colombia left the isthmus' affairs in constant turmoil. Local selfgovernment for the department of Panama was extended when the Liberals were in power and withdrawn when the Conservatives prevailed. The Catholic Church was disestablished under the Liberals and reestablished under the Conservatives. The fortunes of local partisans rose and fell abruptly and often violently.

According to one estimate, the period witnessed forty administrations of the Panamanian department, fifty riots and rebellions, five attempted secessions, and thirteen interventions by the United States, acting under the provisions of the BidlackMallarino Treaty. Partisan clashes and foreign intervention exacerbated racial antagonisms and economic problems and intensified grievances against the central government of Colombia.

Between 1863 and 1886, the isthmus had twenty-six presidents. Coups d'état, rebellions, and violence were almost continuous, staged by troops of the central government, by local citizens against centrally imposed edicts, and by factions out of power. The chaotic conditions that had prevailed under the federalist constitution of 1863 culminated in the 1884 election of Rafael Nuñez as president of Colombia, supported by a coalition of moderate Liberals and Conservatives.

Nuñez called all factions to participate in a new constituent assembly, but his request was met by an armed revolt of the radical Liberals.

Early in 1885, a revolt headed by a radical Liberal general and centered in Panama City developed into a three-way fight. Colón was virtually destroyed. United States forces landed at the request of the Colombian government but were too late to save the city. Millions of dollars in claims were submitted by companies and citizens of the United States, France, and Britain, but Colombia successfully pleaded its lack of responsibility.

Additional United States naval forces occupied both Colón and Panama City and guarded the railroad to ensure uninterrupted transit until Colombian forces landed to protect the railroad. The new constitution of 1886 established the Republic of Colombia as a unitary state; departments were distinctly subordinate to the central government, and Panama was singled out as subject to the direct authority of the government. The United States consul general reported that three-quarters of the Panamanians wanted independence from Colombia and would revolt if they could get arms and be sure of freedom from United States intervention.

Panama was drawn into Colombia's War of a Thousand Days (1899- 1902) by rebellious radical Liberals who had taken refuge in Nicaragua. Like the rest of Colombia, opinion in Panama was divided, and revolts in the southwest had hardly been suppressed when Liberals from Nicaragua invaded the Pacific coastal region and nearly succeeded in taking Panama City in mid-1900. The fortunes of war varied, and although a local armistice gave supporters of the Colombian government temporary security in the Panama-Colón region, the rebels were in control throughout the isthmus. Meanwhile, by early 1902 the rebels had been defeated in most of Colombia proper. At that point, the Colombian government asked the United States to intercede and bring about an armistice in Panama, which was arranged aboard the U.S.S. *Wisconsin* in the Bay of Panama in 1902.

Throughout the period of turmoil, the United States had retained its interest in building a canal through either Nicaragua or Panama. An obstacle to this goal was overcome in December 1901 when the United States and Britain signed the Hay-Pauncefote Treaty. This treaty nullified the provisions of the Clayton-Bulwer Treaty of 1850 and signified British acceptance of a canal constructed solely by or under the auspices of the United States with guarantees of neutrality.

THE UNITED STATES PROTECTORATE

THE 1903 TREATY AND QUALIFIED INDEPENDENCE

Naval operations during the Spanish-American War (1898-1901) served to convince President Theodore Roosevelt that the United States needed to control a canal somewhere in the Western Hemisphere. This interest culminated in the Spooner Bill of June 29, 1902, providing for a canal through the isthmus of Panama, and the Hay-Herrán Treaty of January 22, 1903, under which Colombia gave consent to such a project in the form of a 100-year lease on an area 10 kilometers wide. This treaty, however, was not ratified in Bogotá, and the United States, determined to construct a canal across the isthmus, intensively encouraged the Panamanian separatist movement.

By July 1903, when the course of internal Colombian opposition to the Hay-Herrán Treaty became obvious, a revolutionary junta had been created in Panama. José Augustin Arango, an attorney for the Panama Railroad Company, headed the junta. Manuel Amador Guerrero and Carlos C. Arosemena served on the junta from the start, and five other members, all from prominent Panamanian families, were added. Arango was considered the brains of the revolution, and Amador was the junta's active leader.

With financial assistance arranged by Philippe Bunau-Varilla, a French national representing the interests of de Lesseps's company, the native Panamanian leaders conspired to take advantage of United States interest in a new regime on the isthmus. In October and November 1903, the revolutionary junta, with the protection of United States naval forces, carried out a successful uprising against the Colombian government. Acting, paradoxically, under the Bidlack-Mallarino Treaty of 1846 between the United States and Colombia--which provided that United States forces could intervene in the event of disorder on the isthmus to guarantee Colombian sovereignty and open transit across the isthmus --the United States prevented a Colombian force from moving across the isthmus to Panama City to suppress the insurrection.

President Roosevelt recognized the new Panamanian junta as the de facto government on November 6, 1903; de jure recognition came on November 13. Five days later Bunau-Varilla, as the diplomatic representative of Panama (a role he had purchased through financial assistance to the rebels) concluded the Isthmian Canal Convention with Secretary of State John Hay in Washington. Bunau-Varilla had not lived in Panama for seventeen years before the incident, and he never returned. Nevertheless, while residing in the Waldorf-Astoria Hotel in New York City, he wrote the Panamanian declaration of independence and constitution and designed the Panamanian flag. Isthmian patriots particularly resented the haste with which BunauVarilla concluded the treaty, an effort partially designed to preclude any objections an arriving Panamanian delegation might raise. Nonetheless, the Panamanians, having no apparent alternative, ratified the treaty on December 2, and approval by the United States Senate came on February 23, 1904.

The rights granted to the United States in the so-called HayBunau -Varilla Treaty were extensive. They included a grant "in perpetuity of the use, occupation, and control" of a sixteenkilometer -wide strip of territory and extensions of three nautical miles into the sea from each terminal "for the construction, maintenance, operation, sanitation, and protection" of an isthmian canal.

Furthermore, the United States was entitled to acquire additional areas of land or water necessary for canal operations and held the option of exercising eminent domain in Panama City. Within this territory Washington gained "all the rights, power, and authority . . . which the United States would possess and exercise if it were the sovereign . . . to the entire exclusion" of Panama.

The Republic of Panama became a de facto protectorate of the larger country through two provisions whereby the United States guaranteed the independence of Panama and received in return the right to intervene in Panama's domestic affairs. For the rights it obtained, the United States was to pay the sum of US$10 million and an annuity, beginning 9 years after ratification, of US$250,000 in gold coin. The United States also purchased the rights and properties of the French canal company for US$40 million.

Colombia was the harshest critic of United States policy at the time. A reconciliatory treaty with the United States providing an indemnity of US$25 million was finally concluded between these two countries in 1921. Ironically, however, friction resulting from the events of 1903 was greatest between the United States and Panama. Major disagreements arose concerning the rights granted to the United States by the treaty of 1903 and the Panamanian constitution of 1904. The United States government subsequently interpreted these rights to mean that the United States could exercise complete sovereignty over all matters in the Canal Zone. Panama, although admitting that the clauses were vague and obscure, later held that the original concession of authority related only to the construction, operation, and defense of the canal and that rights and privileges not necessary to these functions had never been relinquished.

ORGANIZING THE NEW REPUBLIC

The provisional governing junta selected when independence was declared governed the new state until a constitution was adopted in 1904. Under its terms, Amador became Panama's first president.

The constitution was modeled, for the most part, after that of the United States, calling for separation of powers and direct elections for the presidency and the legislature, the National Assembly. The assembly, however, elected three persons to stand in the line of succession to the presidency. This provision remained in effect until 1946, when a new constitution provided for direct election of the vice president. The new republic was unitary; municipalities were to elect their own officials, but provincial authorities were to be appointed by the central government. The most controversial provision of the constitution was that which gave the United States the right to intervene to guarantee Panamanian sovereignty and to preserve order.

A two-party system of Liberals and Conservatives was inherited from Colombia, but the party labels had even less precise or ideological meaning in Panama than they had in the larger country. By the early 1920s, most of the Conservative leaders of the independence generation had died without leaving political heirs. Thus, cleavages in the Liberal Party led to a new system of personalistic parties in shifting coalitions, none of which enjoyed a mass base. Politics remained the exclusive preserve of the oligarchy, which tended to be composed of a few wealthy, white families.

Having successfully severed their ties with Colombia, the secessionists of Panama's central government were soon faced with a secessionist problem of their own. The Cuna of the San Blas Islands were unwilling to accept the authority of Panama, just as they had been unwilling to accept the authority of Colombia or Spain. The Panamanian government exercised no administrative control over the islands until 1915, when a departmental government was established; its main office was in El Porvenir. At that time, forces of the Colonial Police, composed of blacks, were stationed on several islands. Their presence, along with a number of other factors, led to a revolt in 1925.

In 1903 on the island of Narganá, Charlie Robinson was elected chief. Having spent many years on a West Indian ship, he began a "civilizing" program. His cause was later taken up by a number of young men who had been educated in the cities on the mainland. These Young Turks advocated forcibly removing nose rings, substituting dresses for molas, and establishing dance halls like those in the cities. They were actively supported by the police, who arrested men who did not send their daughters to the dance hall; the police also allegedly raped some of the Indian women. By 1925 hatred for these modernizers and for the police was intense throughout the San Blas Islands.

The situation was further complicated by the factionalism that resulted when Panama separated from Colombia. The leader of one of these factions, Simral Coleman, with the help of a sympathetic American explorer, Richard Marsh, drew up a "declaration of independence" for the Cuna, and on February 25, 1925, the rebellion was underway. During the course of the rebellion, about twenty members of the police were killed. A few days later a United States cruiser appeared; with United States diplomatic and naval officials serving as intermediaries, a peace treaty was concluded. The most important outcome of this rebellion against Panama was a treaty that in effect recognized San Blas as a semiautonomous territory.

BUILDING THE CANAL

When the United States canal builders arrived in 1904 to begin their momentous task, Panama City and Colón were both small, squalid towns. A single railroad stretched between the towns, running alongside the muddy scars of the abortive French effort. The new builders were haunted by the ghosts of de Lesseps's failure and of the workers, some 25,000 of whom had died on the project. These new builders were able, however, to learn from de Lesseps's mistakes and to build on the foundations of the previous engineering. The most formidable task that the North Americans faced was that of ridding the area of deadly mosquitoes.

After a couple of false starts under a civilian commission, President Roosevelt turned the project over to the United States Army Corps of Engineers, guided by Colonel George Washington Goethals. Colonel William Crawford Gorgas was placed in charge of sanitation. In addition to the major killers--malaria and yellow fever--smallpox, typhoid, dysentery, and intestinal parasites threatened the newcomers.

Because the mosquito carrying yellow fever was found in urban areas, Gorgas concentrated his main efforts on the terminal cities. "Gorgas gangs" dug ditches to drain standing water and sprayed puddles with a film of oil. They screened and fumigated buildings, even invading churches to clean out the fonts of holy water. They installed a pure water supply and a modern system of sewage disposal. Goethals reportedly told Gorgas that every mosquito killed was costing the United States US$10. "I know, Colonel," Gorgas reportedly replied, "but what if one of those ten-dollar mosquitoes were to bite you?"

Gorgas's work is credited with saving at least 71,000 lives and some 40 million days of sickness. The cleaner, safer conditions enabled the canal diggers to attract a labor force. By 1913 approximately 65,000 men were on the payroll. Most were West Indians, although some 12,000 workers were recruited from southern Europe. Five thousand United States citizens filled the administrative, professional, and supervisory jobs. To provide these men with the comforts and amenities to which they were accustomed, a paternalistic community was organized in the Canal Zone.

The most challenging tasks involved in the actual digging of the canal were cutting through the mountain ridge at Culebra; building a huge dam at Gatún to trap the Río Chagres and form an artificial lake; and building three double sets of locks-Gatun Locks, Pedro Miguel Locks, and Miraflores Locks-to raise the ships to the lake, almost twenty-six meters above sea level, and then lower them. On August 15, 1914, the first ship made a complete passage through the canal.

By the time the canal project was completed, its economic impact had created a new middle class. In addition, new forms of discrimination occurred. Panamanian society had become segregated not only by class but by race and national origin as well. Furthermore, United States commercial competition and political intervention had already begun to generate resentment among Panamanians.

UNITED STATES INTERVENTION AND STRAINED RELATIONS

In the very first year of the Hay-Bunau-Varilla Treaty, dissension had already arisen over the sovereignty issue. Acting on an understanding of its rights, the United States had applied special regulations to maritime traffic at the ports of entry to the canal and had established its own customs, tariffs, and postal services in the zone. These measures were opposed by the Panamanian government.

Mounting friction finally led Roosevelt to dispatch Secretary of War William Howard Taft to Panama in November 1904. His visit resulted in a compromise agreement, whereby the United States retained control of the ports of Ancón and Cristóbal, but their facilities might be used by any ships entering Panama City and Colón. The agreement also involved a reciprocal reduction of tariffs and the free passage of persons and goods from the Canal Zone into the republic. Compromises were reached in other areas, and both sides emerged with most of their grievances blunted if not wholly resolved.

Before the first year of independence had passed, the intervention issue also complicated relations. Threats to constitutional government in the republic by a Panamanian military leader, General Estéban Huertas, had resulted, at the suggestion of the United States diplomatic mission, in disbanding the Panamanian army in 1904. The army was replaced by the National Police, whose mission was to carry out ordinary police work. By 1920 the United States had intervened four times in the civil life of the republic. These interventions involved little military conflict and were, with one exception, at the request of one Panamanian faction or another.

The internal dynamics of Panamanian politics encouraged appeals to the United States by any currently disgruntled faction for intervention to secure its allegedly infringed rights. United States diplomatic personnel in Panama also served as advisers to Panamanian officials, a policy resented by nationalists. In 1921 the issue of intervention was formally raised by the republic's government. When asked for a definitive, written interpretation of the pertinent treaty clauses, Secretary of State Charles Evans Hughes pointed to inherent difficulties and explained that the main objectives of the United States were to act against any threat to the Canal Zone or the lives and holdings of non-Panamanians in the two major cities.

Actual intervention took several forms. United States officials supervised elections at the request of incumbent governments. To protect lives of United States citizens and property in Chiriquí Province, an occupation force was stationed there for two years over the protests of Panamanians who contended that the right of occupation could apply only to the two major cities. United States involvement in the 1925 rent riots in Panama City was also widely resented. After violent disturbances during October, and at the request of the Panamanian government, 600 troops with fixed bayonets dispersed mobs threatening to seize the city.

At the end of the 1920s, traditional United States policy toward intervention was revised. In 1928 Secretary of State Frank B. Kellogg reiterated his government's refusal to countenance illegal changes of government. In the same year, however, Washington declined to intervene during the national elections that placed Florencio H. Arosemena in office. The Arosemena government was noted for its corruption. But when a coup d'état was undertaken to unseat Arosemena, the United States once again declined to intervene. Though no official pronouncement of a shift in policy had been made, the 1931 coup d'état-the first successful one in the republic's history--marked a watershed in the history of United States intervention.

Meanwhile, popular sentiment on both sides calling for revisions to the treaty had resulted in the Kellogg-Alfaro Treaty of 1925. The United States in this instrument agreed to restrictions on private commercial operations in the Canal Zone and also agreed to a tightening of the regulations pertaining to the official commissaries. At the same time, however, the United States gained several concessions involving security. Panama agreed to automatic participation in any war involving the United States and to United States supervision and control of military operations within the republic. These and other clauses aroused strong opposition and, amid considerable tumult, the National Assembly on January 26, 1927, refused to consider the draft treaty.

The abortive Kellogg-Alfaro Treaty involved the two countries in a critical incident with the League of Nations. During the fall of 1927, the League Assembly insisted that Panama could not legally participate in the proposed arrangement with the United States. The assembly argued that an automatic declaration of war would violate Panama's obligations under the League Covenant to wait three months for an arbitral decision on any dispute before resorting to war. The discussion was largely academic inasmuch as the treaty had already been effectively rejected, but Panama proposed that the dispute over sovereignty in the Canal Zone be submitted to international arbitration. The United States denied that any issue needed arbitration.

A NEW ACCOMMODATION

In the late 1920s, United States policymakers noted that nationalist aspirations in Latin America were not producing desired results. United States occupation of the Dominican Republic, Haiti, and Nicaragua had not spawned exemplary political systems, nor had widespread intervention resulted in a receptive attitude toward United States trade and investments. As the subversive activities of Latin American Nazi and Fascist sympathizers gained momentum in the 1930s, the United States became concerned about the need for hemispheric solidarity.

The gradual reversal of United States policy was heralded in 1928 when the Clark Memorandum was issued, formally disavowing the Roosevelt Corollary to the Monroe Doctrine. In his inaugural address in 1933, President Franklin D. Roosevelt enunciated the Good Neighbor Policy. That same year, at the Seventh Inter-American Conference in Montevideo, the United States expressed a qualified acceptance of the principle of nonintervention; in 1936 the United States approved this principle without reservation.

In the 1930s, Panama, like most countries of the Western world, was suffering economic depression. Until that time, Panamanian politics had remained a competition among individuals and families within a gentleman's club--specifically, the Union Club of Panama City. The first exception to this succession was Harmodio Arias Madrid (unrelated to the aristocratic family of the same name) who was elected to the presidency in 1932. A mestizo from a poor family in the provinces, he had attended the London School of Economics and had gained prominence through writing a book that attacked the Monroe Doctrine.

Harmodio and his brother Arnulfo, a Harvard Medical School graduate, entered the political arena through a movement known as Community Action (Acción Communal). Its following was primarily mestizo middle class, and its mood was antioligarchy and anti- Yankee. Harmodio Arias was the first Panamanian president to institute relief efforts for the isolated and impoverished countryside. He later established the University of Panama, which became the focal point for the political articulation of middle-class interests and nationalistic zeal.

Thus, a certain asymmetry developed in the trends underway in the 1930s that worked in Panama's favor. While the United States was assuming a more conciliatory stance, Panamanians were losing patience, and a political base for virulent nationalism was emerging.

A dispute arose in 1932 over Panamanian opposition to the sale of 3.2-percent beer in the Canal Zone competing with Panamanian beers. Tension rose when the governor of the zone insisted on formally replying to the protests, despite the Panamanian government's well-known view that proper diplomatic relations should involve only the United States ambassador. In 1933 when unemployment in Panama reached a dangerous level and friction over the zone commissaries rekindled, President Harmodio Arias went to Washington.

The result was agreement on a number of issues. The United States pledged sympathetic consideration of future arbitration requests involving economic issues that did not affect the vital aspects of canal operation. Special efforts were to be made to protect Panamanian business interests from the smuggling of cheaply purchased commissary goods out of the zone. Washington also promised to seek appropriations from Congress to sponsor the repatriation of the numerous immigrant canal workers, who were aggravating the unemployment situation. Most important, however, was President Roosevelt's acceptance, in a joint statement with Harmodio Arias, that United States rights in the zone applied only for the purposes of "maintenance, operation, sanitation, and protection" of the canal. The resolution of this long-standing issue, along with a clear recognition of Panama as a sovereign nation, was a significant move in the direction of the Panamanian interpretation of the proper United States position in the isthmus.

This accord, though welcomed in Panama, came too early to deal with a major problem concerning the US$250,000 annuity. The devaluation of the United States dollar in 1934 reduced its gold content to 59.6 percent of its former value. This meant that the US$250,000 payment was nearly cut in half in the new devalued dollars. As a result, the Panamanian government refused to accept the annuity paid in the new dollars.

Roosevelt's visit to the republic in the summer of 1934 prepared the way for opening negotiations on this and other matters. A Panamanian mission arrived in Washington in November, and discussions on a replacement for the Hay-Bunau-Varilla Treaty continued through 1935. On March 2, 1936, Secretary of State Cordell Hull and Assistant Secretary of State Sumner Welles joined the Panamanian negotiators in signing a new treaty--the Hull-Alfaro Treaty-and three related conventions. The conventions regulated radio communications and provided for the United States to construct a new trans-isthmian highway connecting Panama City and Colón.

The treaty provided a new context for relations between the two countries. It ended the protectorate by abrogating the 1903 treaty guarantee of the republic's independence and the concomitant right of intervention. Thereafter, the United States would substitute negotiation and purchase of land outside the zone for its former rights of expropriation. The dispute over the annuity was resolved by agreeing to fix it at 430,000 balboas (the balboa being equivalent to the devalued dollar) which increased the gold value of the original annuity by US$7,500. This was to be paid retroactively to 1934 when the republic had begun refusing the payments.

Various business and commercial provisions dealt with longstanding Panamanian complaints. Private commercial operations unconnected with canal operations were forbidden in the zone. This policy and the closing of the zone to foreign commerce were to provide Panamanian merchants with relief from competition. Free entry into the zone was provided for Panamanian goods, and the republic's customhouses were to be established at entrances to the zone to regulate the entry of goods finally destined for Panama.

The Hull-Alfaro revisions, though hailed by both governments, radically altered the special rights of the United States in the isthmus, and the United States Senate was reluctant to accept the alterations. Article X of the new treaty provided that in the event of any threat to the security of either nation, joint measures could be taken after consultation between the two. Only after an exchange of interpretative diplomatic notes had permitted Senator Key Pittman, chairman of the Foreign Relations Committee, to advise his colleagues that Panama was willing under this provision to permit the United States to act unilaterally, did the Senate give its consent on July 25, 1939.

THE BISECTED REPUBLIC

THE WAR YEARS

After ratifying the Hull-Alfaro Treaty in 1939, Panama and the United States began preparation for and collaboration in the coming war effort. Cooperation in this area proceeded smoothly for more than a year, with the republic participating in the series of conferences, declarations, and protocols that solidified the support of the hemisphere behind Washington's efforts to meet the threat of Axis aggression. This cooperation halted with the inauguration of Arnulfo Arias.

Arnulfo Arias has been elected to the presidency at least three times since 1940 (perhaps four or five if, as many believe, the vote counts of 1964 and 1984 were fraudulent), but he has never been allowed to serve a full term. He was first elected when he headed a mass movement known as Panameñismo. Its essence was nationalism, which in Panama's situation meant opposition to United States hegemony. Arias aspired to rid the country of non-Hispanics, which meant not only North Americans, but also West Indians, Chinese, Hindus, and Jews. He also seemed susceptible to the influence of Nazi and Fascist agents on the eve of the United States declaration of war against the Axis.

North Americans were by no means the only ones in Panama who were anxious to be rid of Arias. Even his brother, Harmodio, urged the United States embassy to move against the leader. United States officials made no attempt to conceal their relief when the National Police, in October 1941, took advantage of Arias's temporary absence from the country to depose him.

Arnulfo Arias had promulgated a new constitution in 1941, which was designed to extend his term of office. In 1945 a clash between Arias's successor, Ricardo Adolfo de la Guardia, and the National Assembly, led to the calling of a constituent assembly that elected a new president, Enrique A. Jiménez, and drew up a new constitution. The constitution of 1946 erased the innovations introduced by Arias and restored traditional concepts and structures of government.

In preparation for war, the United States had requested 999- year leases on more than 100 bases and sites. Arias balked, but ultimately approved a lease on one site after the United States threatened to occupy the land it wanted. De la Guardia proved more accommodating; he agreed to lease the United States 134 sites in the republic but not for 999 years. He would extend the leases only for the duration of the war plus one year beyond the signing of the peace treaty.

The United States transferred Panama City's water and sewer systems to the city administration and granted new economic assistance, but it refused to deport the West Indians and other non-Hispanics or to pay high rents for the sites. Among the major facilities granted to the United States under the agreement of 1942 were the airfield at Río Hato, the naval base on Isla Taboga, and several radar stations.

The end of the war brought another misunderstanding between the two countries. Although the peace treaty had not entered into effect, Panama demanded that the bases be relinquished, resting its claim on a subsidiary provision of the agreement permitting renegotiation after the cessation of hostilities. Overriding the desire of the United States War Department to hold most of the bases for an indefinite period, the Department of State took cognizance of growing nationalist dissatisfaction and in December 1946 sent Ambassador Frank T. Hines to propose a twenty-year extension of the leases on thirteen facilities. President Jiménez authorized a draft treaty over the opposition of the foreign minister and exacerbated latent resentment. When the National Assembly met in 1947 to consider ratification, a mob of 10,000 Panamanians armed with stones, machetes, and guns expressed opposition. Under these circumstances the deputies voted unanimously to reject the treaty. By 1948 the United States had evacuated all occupied bases and sites outside the Canal Zone.

The upheaval of 1947 was instigated in large measure by university students. Their clash with the National Police on that occasion, in which both students and policemen were killed, marked the beginning of a period of intense animosity between the two groups. The incident was also the first in which United States intentions were thwarted by a massive expression of Panamanian rage.

THE NATIONAL GUARD IN ASCENDANCE

A temporary shift in power from the civilian aristocracy to the National Police occurred immediately after World War II. Between 1948 and 1952, National Police Commander José Antonio Remón installed and removed presidents with unencumbered ease. Among his behind-the-scenes manipulations were the denial to Arnulfo Arias of the presidency he apparently had won in 1948, the installation of Arias in the presidency in 1949, and the engineering of Arias's removal from office in 1951. Meanwhile, Remón increased salaries and fringe benefits for his forces and modernized training methods and equipment; in effect, he transformed the National Police from a police into a paramilitary force. In the spheres of security and public order, he achieved his long-sought goal by transforming the National Police into the National Guard in 1953 and introduced greater militarization into the country's only armed force. The missions and functions were little changed by the new title, but for Remón, this change was a step toward a national army.

From several preexisting parties and factions, Remón also organized the National Patriotic Coalition (Coalición Patriótico Nacional--CPN). He ran successfully as its candidate for the presidency in 1952. Remón followed national tradition by enriching himself through political office. He broke with tradition, however, by promoting social reform and economic development. His agricultural and industrial programs temporarily reduced the country's overwhelming economic dependence on the canal and the zone.

Remón's reformist regime was short-lived, however. In 1955 he was machine-gunned to death at the racetrack outside Panama City. The first vice president, José Ramón Guizado, was impeached for the crime and jailed, but he was never tried, and the motivation for his alleged act remained unclear. Some investigators believed that the impeachment of Guizado was a smokescreen to distract attention from others implicated in the assassination, including United States organized crime figure "Lucky" Luciano, dissident police officers, and both Arias families. The second vice president, Ricardo Arias (of the aristocratic Arias family), served out the remainder of the presidential term and dismantled many of Remón's reforms.

Remón did not live to see the culmination of the major treaty revision he initiated. In 1953 Remón had visited Washington to discuss basic revisions of the 1936 treaty. Among other things, Panamanian officials wanted a larger share of the canal tolls, and merchants continued to be unhappy with the competition from the nonprofit commissaries in the Canal Zone. Remón also demanded that the discriminatory wage differential in the zone, which favored United States citizens over Panamanians, be abolished.

After lengthy negotiations a Treaty of Mutual Understanding and Cooperation was signed on January 23, 1955. Under its provisions commercial activities not essential to the operation of the canal were to be cut back. The annuity was enlarged to US$1,930,000. The principle of "one basic wage scale for all . . . employees . . . in the Canal Zone" was accepted and implemented. Panama's request for the replacement of the "perpetuity" clause by a ninety-nine-year renewable lease was rejected, however, as was the proposal that its citizens accused of violations in the zone be tried by joint United States-Panamanian tribunals.

Panama's contribution to the 1955 treaty was its consent to the United States occupation of the bases outside of the Canal Zone that it had withheld a few years earlier. Approximately 8,000 hectares of the republic's territory were leased rent-free for 15 years for United States military maneuvers. The Río Hato base, a particularly important installation in defense planning, was thus regained for the United States Air Force. Because the revisions had the strong support of President Ricardo Arias, the National Assembly approved them with little hesitation.

THE POLITICS OF FRUSTRATED NATIONALISM

The CPN placed another candidate, Ernesto de la Guardia, in the presidency in 1956. The Remón government had required parties to enroll 45,000 members to receive official recognition. This membership requirement, subsequently relaxed to 5,000, had excluded all opposition parties from the 1956 elections except the National Liberal Party (Partido Liberal Nacional-PLN) which traced its lineage to the original Liberal Party.

De la Guardia was a conservative businessman and a member of the oligarchy. By Panamanian standards, he was by no means anti- Yankee, but his administration presided over a new low in United States-Panamanian relations. The Egyptian nationalization of the Suez Canal in 1956 raised new hopes in the republic, because the two canals were frequently compared in the world press. Despite Panama's large maritime fleet (the sixth greatest in the world), Britain and the United States did not invite Panama to a special conference of the major world maritime powers in London to discuss Suez. Expressing resentment, Panama joined the communist and neutral nations in a rival Suez proposal. United States secretary of state John Foster Dulles's unqualified statement on the Suez issue on September 28, 1956--that the United States did not fear similar nationalization of the Panama Canal because the United States possessed "rights of sovereignty" there-- worsened matters.

Panamanian public opinion was further inflamed by a United States Department of the Army statement in the summer of 1956 that implied that the 1955 treaty had not in fact envisaged a total equalization of wage rates. The United States attempted to clarify the issue by explaining that the only exception to the "equal pay for equal labor" principle would be a 25-percent differential that would apply to all citizens brought from the continental United States.

Tension mounted in the ensuing years. In May 1958 students demonstrating against the United States clashed with the National Guard. The violence of these riots, in which nine died, was a forecast of the far more serious difficulties that followed a year later. In November 1959 anti-United States demonstrations occurred during the two Panamanian independence holidays. Aroused by the media, particularly by articles in newspapers owned by Harmodio Arias, Panamanians began to threaten a "peaceful invasion" of the Canal Zone, to raise the flag of the republic there as tangible evidence of Panama's sovereignty. Fearful that Panamanian mobs might actually force entry into the Canal Zone, the United States called out its troops. Several hundred Panamanians crossed barbedwire restraints and clashed with Canal Zone police and troops. A second wave of Panamanian citizens was repulsed by the National Guard, supported by United States troops.

Extensive and violent disorder followed. A mob smashed the windows of the United States Information Agency library. The United States flag was torn from the ambassador's residence and trampled. Aware that public hostility was getting out of hand, political leaders attempted to regain control over their followers but were unsuccessful. Relations between the two governments were severely strained. United States authorities erected a fence on the border of the Canal Zone, and United States citizens residing in the Canal Zone observed a voluntary boycott of Panamanian merchants, who traditionally depended heavily on these patrons.

On March 1, 1960-Constitution Day-student and labor groups threatened another march into the Canal Zone. The widespread disorders of the previous fall had had a sobering effect on the political elite, who seriously feared that new rioting might be transformed into a revolutionary movement against the social system itself. Both major coalitions contesting the coming elections sought to avoid further difficulties, and influential merchants, who had been hard hit by the November 1959 riots, were apprehensive. Reports that the United States was willing to recommend flying the republic's flag in a special site in the Canal Zone served to ease tensions. Thus, serious disorders were averted.

De la Guardia's administration had been overwhelmed by the rioting and other problems, and the CPN, lacking effective opposition in the National Assembly, began to disintegrate. Most dissenting factions joined the PLN in the National Opposition Union, which in 1960 succeeded in electing its candidate, Roberto Chiari, to the presidency. De la Guardia became the first postwar president to finish a full four-year term in office, and Chiari had the distinction of being the first opposition candidate ever elected to the presidency.

Chiari attempted to convince his fellow oligarchs that change was inevitable. He cautioned that if they refused to accept moderate reform, they would be vulnerable to sweeping change imposed by uncontrollable radical forces. The tradition-oriented deputies who constituted a majority in the National Assembly did not heed his warning. His proposed reform program was simply ignored. In foreign affairs, Chiari's message to the Assembly on October 1, 1961, called for a new revision of the Canal Zone arrangement. When Chiari visited Washington on June 12 to 13, 1962, he and President John F. Kennedy agreed to appoint high-level representatives to discuss controversies between their countries regarding the Canal Zone. The results of the discussions were disclosed in a joint communique issued on July 23, 1963.

Agreement had been reached on the creation of the Bi-National Labor Advisory Committee to consider disputes arising between Panamanian employees and zone authorities. The United States had agreed to withhold taxes from its Panamanian employees to be remitted to the Panamanian government. Pending congressional approval, the United States agreed to extend to Panamanian employees the health and life insurance benefits available to United States citizens in the zone.

Several other controversial matters, however, remained unresolved. The United States agreed to increase the wages of Panamanian employees in the zone, but not as much as the Panamanian government requested. No agreement was reached in response to Panamanian requests for jurisdiction over a corridor through the zone linking the two halves of the country.

Meanwhile, the United States had initiated a new aid program for all of Latin America--the Alliance for Progress. Under this approach to hemisphere relations, President Kennedy envisioned a long-range program to raise living standards and advance social and economic development. No regular United States government development loans or grants had been available to Panama through the late 1950s. The Alliance for Progress, therefore, was the first major effort of the United States to improve basic living conditions. Panama was to share in the initial, large-scale loans to support self-help housing. Nevertheless, pressure for major revisions of the treaties and resentment of United States recalcitrance continued to move.

THE NEGOTIATION OF NEW TREATIES

THE 1964 RIOTS

Public demonstrations and riots arising from popular resentment over United States policies and the overwhelming presence of United States citizens and institutions had not been uncommon, but the rioting that occurred in January 1964 was uncommonly serious. The incident began with a symbolic dispute over the flying of the Panamanian flag in the Canal Zone.

For some time the dispute had been seriously complicated by differences of opinion on that issue between the Department of Defense and the Department of State. On the one hand, the military opposed accepting a Panamanian flag, emphasizing the strategic importance of unimpaired United States control in the Canal Zone and the dangerous precedent that appeasement of the rioters' demands would set for future United States-Panamanian relations. The Department of State, on the other hand, supported the flag proposal as a reasonable concession to Panamanian demands and a method of avoiding major international embarrassment. Diplomatic officials also feared that the stability of Panamanian political institutions themselves might be threatened by extensive violence and mob action over the flag issue.

The United States finally agreed to raise the Panamanian and United States flags side by side at one location. The special ceremony on September 21, 1960, at the Shaler Triangle was attended by the new governor of the zone, Major General William A. Carter, along with all high United States military and diplomatic officers and the entire Panamanian cabinet. Even this incident, however, which marked official recognition of Panama's "titular" sovereignty, was marred when the United States rejected de la Guardia's request to allow him to raise the flag personally. De la Guardia, as a retaliatory measure, refused to attend the ceremony and extended invitations to the presidential reception after the ceremony only to the United States ambassador and his senior diplomatic aides; United States Canal Zone and military officials were excluded.

Panamanians remained dissatisfied as their flag appeared at only one location in the Canal Zone, while the United States flag flew alone at numerous other sites. An agreement was finally reached that at several points in the Canal Zone the United States and Panamanian flags would be flown side by side. United States citizens residing in the Canal Zone were reluctant to abide by this agreement, however, and the students of an American high school, with adult encouragement, on two consecutive days hoisted the American flag alone in front of their school.

Word of the gesture soon spread across the border, and on the evening of the second day, January 9, 1964, nearly 200 Panamanian students marched into the Canal Zone with their flag. A struggle ensued, and the Panamanian flag was torn. After that provocation, thousands of Panamanians stormed the border fence. The rioting lasted 3 days, and resulted in more than 20 deaths, serious injuries to several hundred persons, and more than US$2 million of property damage.

At the outbreak of the fighting, Panama charged the United States with aggression. Panama severed relations with the United States and appealed to the Organization of American States (OAS) and the United Nations (UN). On January 10 the OAS referred the case to the Inter-American Peace Committee. When the UN Security Council met, United States ambassador Adlai E.

Stevenson noted that the Inter-American Peace Committee had already scheduled an on-the- spot investigation and urged that the problem be considered in the regional forum. A proposal by the Brazilian delegate that the president of the Security Council address an appeal to the two parties to exercise restraint was agreed on, and the UN took no further action.

The United States had hoped to confine the controversy to the Inter-American Peace Committee. But when negotiations broke down, Panama insisted that the Organ of Consultation under the 1947 Inter-American Treaty of Reciprocal Assistance (the so-called Rio Treaty) be convoked. The OAS Council, acting provisionally as the Organ of Consultation, appointed an investigating committee consisting of all the members of the Council except the two disputants. A joint declaration recommended by the Committee was signed by the two countries in April, and diplomatic relations were restored. The controversy smoldered for almost a year, however, until President Lyndon B. Johnson announced that plans for a new canal would be drawn up and that an entirely new treaty would be negotiated.

Negotiations were carried on throughout the first half of the presidency of Chiari's successor, Marcos Aurelio Robles. When the terms of three draft treaties--concerning the existing lock canal, a possible sea-level canal, and defense matters--were revealed in 1967, Panamanian public reaction was adverse. The new treaties would have abolished the resented "in perpetuity" clause in favor of an expiration date of December 13, 1999, or the date of the completion of a new sea-level canal if that were earlier. Furthermore, they would have compensated the Panamanian government on the basis of tonnage shipped through the canal, an arrangement that could have increased the annuity to more than US$20 million.

The intensity of Panamanian nationalism, however, was such that many contended that the United States should abandon involvement in Panama altogether. Proposals for the continued United States military bases in the Canal Zone, for the right of the United States to deploy troops and armaments anywhere in the republic, and for a joint board of nine governors for the zone, five of which were to be appointed by the United States, were particularly unpopular. Robles initially attempted to defend the terms of the drafts. When he failed to obtain treaty ratification and he learned that his own coalition would be at a disadvantage in the upcoming elections, he declared that further negotiations would be necessary.

THE OLIGARCHY UNDER FIRE

In the mid-1960s, the oligarchy was still tenuously in charge of Panama's political system. Members of the middle class, consisting largely of teachers and government workers, occasionally gained political prominence. Aspiring to upper-class stations, they failed to unite with the lower classes to displace the oligarchy. Students were the most vocal element of the middle class and the group most disposed to speak for the inarticulate poor; as graduates, however, they were generally coopted by the system.

A great chasm separated the rural section from the urban population of the two major cities. Only the rural wageworkers, concentrated in the provinces of Bocas del Toro and Chiriquí, appeared to follow events in the capital and to express themselves on issues of national policy. Among the urban lower classes, antagonism between the Spanish speakers and the English- and French-speaking blacks inhibited organization in pursuit of common interests.

Literacy was high-about 77 percent-despite the scarcity of secondary schools in the rural areas. Voter turnout also tended to be high, despite the unreliability of vote counts. (A popular saying is "He who counts the votes elects.") Concentration on the sins of the United States had served as a safety valve, diverting attention from the injustices of the domestic system.

The multi-party system that existed until the coup d'état of 1968 served to regulate competition for political power among the leading families. Individual parties characteristically served as the personal machines of leaders, whose clients (supporters or dependents) anticipated jobs or other advantages if their candidate were successful. Of the major parties competing in the 1960s, only the highly factionalized PLN had a history of more than two decades. The only parties that had developed clearly identifiable programs were the small Socialist Party and the Christian Democratic Party (Partido Demócrato Cristiano---PDC). The only party with a mass base was the Panameñista Party (Partido Panameñista-PP), the electoral vehicle of the erratic former president, Arnulfo Arias. The Panameñista Party appealed to the frustrated, but lacked a clearly recognizable ideology or program.

Seven candidates competed in the 1964 presidential elections, although only three were serious contenders. Robles, who had served as minister of the presidency in Chiari's cabinet, was the candidate of the National Opposition Union, comprising the PLN and seven smaller parties. After lengthy backstage maneuvers, Robles was endorsed by the outgoing president. Juan de Arco Galindo, a former member of the National Assembly and public works minister and brother-in-law of former President de la Guardia, was the candidate of the National Opposition Alliance (Alianza Nacional de Oposición) coalition, comprising seven parties headed by the CPN. Arnulfo Arias was supported by the PP, already the largest single party in the country.

As usual, the status of the canal was a principal issue in the campaign. Both the liberal and the CPN coalitions cultivated nationalist sentiment by denouncing the United States. Arias, abandoning his earlier nationalistic theme, assumed a cooperative and conciliatory stance toward the United States. Arias attracted lower-class support by denouncing the oligarchy. The Electoral Tribunal announced that Robles had defeated Arias by a margin of more than 10,000 votes of the 317,312 votes cast. The CPN coalition trailed far behind the top two contenders. Arias supporters, who had won a majority of the National Assembly seats, attributed Robles's victory to the "miracle of Los Santos"; they claimed that enough corpses voted for Robles in that province to enable him to carry the election.

The problems confronting Robles were not unlike those of his predecessors but were aggravated by the consequences of the 1964 riots. In addition to the hardships and resentments resulting from the losses of life and property, the riots had the effect of dramatically increasing the already serious unemployment in the metropolitan areas. Despite his nationalistic rhetoric during the campaign, the new president was dependent on United States economic and technical assistance to develop projects that Chiari's government, also with United States assistance, had initiated. Chiari emphasized building schools and low-cost housing. He endorsed a limited agrarian-reform program. Like his predecessor, Robles sought to increase the efficiency of tax collection rather than raise taxes.

By 1967 the coalitions were being reshuffled in preparation for the 1968 elections. By the time Arias announced his candidacy, he had split both the coalitions that had participated in the 1964 elections and had secured the support of several factions in a coalition headed by the Panameñista Party. Robles's endorsement went to David Samudio of the PLN. A civil engineer and architect of middle-class background, Samudio had served as an assemblyman and had held several cabinet posts, including that of finance minister under Robles. In addition to the PLN, he was supported by the Labor and Agrarian Party (Partido Laborista Agrario--PALA) and other splinter groups. (Party labels are deceptive; the PALA, for example, had neither an agrarian base nor organized labor support.) A PDC candidate, Antonio González Revilla, also entered the race.

Because many of Arias's supporters believed that the 1964 election had been rigged, the principal issue in the 1968 campaign became the prospective validity of the election itself. The credibility crisis became acute in February 1968 when the president of the Electoral Tribunal, a Samudio supporter, closed the central registration office in a dispute with the other two members of the tribunal, Arias supporters, over electoral procedures. The government brought suit before the Supreme Court for their dismissal, on the grounds that each man had a son who was a candidate for elective office. Thereupon González Revilla, with the backing of Arias, petitioned the National Assembly to begin impeachment proceedings against Robles for illegal interferences in electoral matters. Among other issues, Robles was accused of diverting public funds to Samudio's campaign.

The National Assembly met in special session and appointed a commission to gather evidence. Robles, in turn, obtained a judgment from a municipal court that the assembly was acting unconstitutionally. The National Assembly chose to ignore a stay order issued by the municipal court pending the reconvening of the Supreme Court on April 1, and on March 14 it voted for impeachment. On March 24, the National Assembly found Robles guilty and declared him deposed. Robles and the National Guard ignored the proceedings, maintaining that they would abide by the decision of the Supreme Court when it reconvened.

The Supreme Court, with only one dissenting vote, ruled the impeachment proceedings unconstitutional. The Electoral Tribunal subsequently ruled that thirty of the parliamentary deputies involved in the impeachment proceedings were ineligible for reelection. Robles, with the support of the National Guard, retained the presidency.

The election took place on May 12, 1968, as scheduled, and tension mounted over the succeeding eighteen days as the Election Board and the Electoral Tribunal delayed announcing the results. Finally the Election Board declared that Arias had carried the election by 175,432 votes to 133,887 for Samudio and 11,371 for González Revilla. The Electoral Tribunal, senior to the Board and still loyal to Robles, protested, but the commander of the National Guard, Brigadier General Bolívar Vallarino, despite past animosity toward Arias, supported the conclusion of the Board.

Arias took office on October 1, demanding the immediate return of the Canal Zone to Panamanian jurisdiction and announcing a change in the leadership of the National Guard. He attempted to remove the two most senior officers, Vallarino and Colonel José María Pinilla, and appoint Colonel Bolívar Urrutia to command the force. On October 11 the Guard, for the third time, removed Arias from the presidency. With seven of his eight ministers and twentyfour members of the National Assembly, Arias took refuge in the Canal Zone.

THE GOVERNMENT OF TORRIJOS AND THE NATIONAL GUARD

The overthrow of Arias provoked student demonstrations and rioting in some of the slum areas of Panama City. The peasants in Chiriquí Province battled guardsmen sporadically for several months, but the Guard retained control. Urrutia was initially arrested but was later persuaded to join in the two-man provisional junta headed by Pinilla. Vallarino remained in retirement. The original cabinet appointed by the junta was rather broad based and included several Samudio supporters and one Arias supporter. After the first three months, however, five civilian cabinet members resigned, accusing the new government of dictatorial practices.

The provisional junta moved swiftly to consolidate government control. Several hundred actual or potential political leaders were arrested on charges of corruption or subversion. Others went into voluntary or imposed exile, and property owners were threatened with expropriation. The National Assembly and all political parties were disbanded, and the University of Panama was closed for several months while its faculty and student body were purged. The communications media were brought under control through censorship, intervention in management, or expropriation.

Pinilla, who assumed the title of president, had declared that his government was provisional and that free elections were to be scheduled. In January 1969, however, power actually rested in the hands of Omar Torrijos and Boris Martínez, commander and chief of staff, respectively, of the Guard. In early March, a speech by Martinez promising agrarian reform and other measures radical enough to alarm landowners and entrepreneurs provoked a coup within the coup. Torrijos assumed full control, and Martinez and three of his supporters in the military government were exiled.

Torrijos stated that "there would be less impulsiveness" in government without Martinez. Torrijos did not denounce the proposed reforms, but he assured Panamanian and United States investors that their interests were not threatened.

Torrijos, now a brigadier general, became even more firmly entrenched in power after thwarting a coup attempted by Colonels Amado Sanjur, Luis Q. Nentzen Franco, and Ramiro Silvera in December 1969. While Torrijos was in Mexico, the three colonels declared him deposed. Torrijos rushed back to Panama, gathered supporters at the garrison in David, and marched triumphantly into the capital. The colonels followed earlier competitors of Torrijos into exile. Because the governing junta (Colonel Pinilla and his deputy, Colonel Urrutia) had not opposed the abortive coup, Torrijos replaced them with two civilians, Demetrio B. Lakas, an engineer well liked among businessmen, and Arturo Sucre, a lawyer and former director of the national lottery. Lakas was designated "provisional president," and Sucre was appointed his deputy.

In late 1969 a close associate of Torrijos announced the formation of the New Panama Movement. This movement was originally intended to organize peasants, workers, and other social groups and was patterned after that of Mexico's Institutional Revolutionary Party. No organizational structure was established, however, and by 1971 the idea had been abandoned. The government party was revived under a different name, the Democratic Revolutionary Party (Partido Revolucionario Democrático--PRD) in the late 1970s.

A sweeping cabinet reorganization and comments of high-ranking officials in 1971 portended a shift in domestic policy. Torrijos expressed admiration for the socialist trends in the military governments of Peru and Bolivia. He also established a mutually supportive relationship with Cuba's Fidel Castro. Torrijos carefully distanced himself from the Panamanian Marxist left. The political label he appeared to wear most comfortably was "populist." In 1970 he declared, "Having finished with the oligarchy, the Panamanian has his own worth with no importance to his origin, his cradle, or where he was born."

Torrijos worked on building a popular base for his government, forming an alliance among the National Guard and the various sectors of society that had been the objects of social injustice at the hands of the oligarchy, particularly the long-neglected campesinos. He regularly traveled by helicopter to villages throughout the interior to hear their problems and to explain his new programs.

In addition to the National Guard and the campesinos, the populist alliance that Torrijos formed as a power base included students, the People's Party (Partido del Pueblo-PdP), and portions of the working classes. Support for Torrijos varied among interest groups and over time. The alliance contained groups, most notably the Guard and students, that were traditionally antagonistic toward one another and groups that traditionally had little concern with national politics, e.g., the rural sector. Nationalism, in the form of support of the efforts of the Torrijos regime to obtain control over the canal through a new treaty with the United States, provided the glue for maintaining political consensus.

In the early 1970s, the strength of the alliance was impressive. Disloyal or potentially disloyal elements within the National Guard and student groups were purged; increased salaries, perquisites, and positions of political power were offered to the loyal majority. The adherence of the middle classes was procured partly through more jobs. In return for its support, the PdP was allowed to operate openly when all other political parties were outlawed.

The Torrijos effort to secure political support in the rural sector was an innovation in Panamanian politics. With the exception of militant banana workers in the western provinces of Chiriquí and Bocas del Toro, the campesinos traditionally have had little concern with national political issues. Unlike much of Latin America, in Panama the elite is almost totally urban based, rather than being a landed aristocracy.

No elections were held under the military government until April 1970, when the town of San Miguelito, incorporated as the country's sixty-fourth municipal district, was allowed to elect a mayor, treasurer, and municipal council. Candidates nominated by trade groups and other nonpartisan bodies were elected indirectly by a council that had been elected by neighborhood councils. Subsequently, the new system was extended throughout the country, and in 1972 the 505-member National Assembly of Municipal Representatives met in Panama City to confirm Torrijos's role as head of government and to approve a new constitution. The new document greatly expanded governmental powers at the expense of civil liberties. The state also was empowered to "oversee the rational distribution of land" and, in general, to regulate or initiate economic activities. In an obvious reference to the Canal Zone, the Constitution also declared the ceding of national territory to any foreign country to be illegal.

The governmental initiatives in the economy, legitimated by the new Constitution, were already underway. The government had announced in early 1969 its intention to implement 1962 legislation by distributing 700,000 hectares of land within 3 years to 61,300 families. Acquisition and distribution progressed much more slowly than anticipated, however.

Nevertheless, major programs were undertaken. Primary attention and government assistance went to farmers grouped in organizations that were initially described as cooperatives but were in fact commercial farming operations by state-owned firms. The government also established companies to operate banana plantations--partly because a substantial amount of the land obtained under the land- reform laws was most suited to banana cultivation and had belonged to international fruit companies.

Educational reforms instituted by Torrijos emphasized vocational and technical training at the expense of law, liberal arts, and the humanities. The programs introduced on an experimental basis in some elementary and secondary schools resembled the Cuban system of "basic schools in the countryside." New schools were established in rural areas in which half the student's time was devoted to instruction in farming. Agricultural methods and other practical skills were taught to urban students as well, and ultimately the new curriculum was to become obligatory even in private schools. Although the changes were being instituted gradually, they met strong resistance from the upper-middle classes and particularly from teachers.

Far-reaching reforms were also undertaken in health care. A program of integrated medical care became available to the extended family of anyone who had been employed for the minimal period required to qualify for social security. A wide range of services was available not only to the worker's spouse and children, but to parents, aunts, uncles, cousins--to any dependent relative. Whereas in the past medical facilities had been limited almost entirely to Panama City, under Torrijos hospitals were built in several provincial cities. Clinics were established throughout the countryside. Medical-school graduates were required to spend at least two years in a rural internship servicing the scattered clinics.

Torrijos also undertook an ambitious program of public works. The construction of new roads and bridges contributed particularly to greater prosperity in the rural areas. Although Torrijos showed greater interest in rural development than in urban problems, he also promoted urban housing and office construction in

Panama City. These projects were funded, in part, by both increased personal and corporate taxes and increased efficiency in tax collection. The 1972 enactment of a new labor code attempted to fuse the urban working class into the populist alliance. Among other things the code provided obligatory collective agreements, obligatory payroll deduction of union fees, the establishment of a superior labor tribunal, and the incorporation of some 15,000 additional workers, including street vendors and peddlers, into labor unions. At the same time, the government attempted unsuccessfully to unite the nation's three major labor confederations into a single, government-sponsored organization.

Meanwhile, Torrijos lured foreign investment by offering tax incentives and provisions for the unlimited repatriation of capital. In particular, international banking was encouraged to locate in Panama, to make the country a regional financial center. A law adopted in 1970 facilitated offshore banking. Numerous banks, largely foreign owned, were licensed to operate in Panama; some were authorized solely for external transactions. Funds borrowed abroad could be loaned to foreign borrowers without being taxed by Panama.

Most of the reforms benefiting workers and peasants were undertaken between 1971 and 1973. Economic problems beginning in 1973 led to some backtracking on social programs. A new labor law passed in 1976, for example, withdrew much of the protection provided by the 1972 labor code, including compulsory collective bargaining. The causes of these economic difficulties included such external factors as the decline in world trade, and thus canal traffic. Domestic problems included a decline in agricultural production that many analysts attributed to the failure of the economic measures of the Torrijos government. The combination of a steady decline in per capita gross national product (GNP), inflation, unemployment, and massive foreign debts adversely affected all sectors of society and contributed heavily to the gradual erosion of the populist alliance that had firmly supported Torrijos in the early 1970s.

Increasingly, corruption in governing circles and within the National Guard also had become an issue in both national and international arenas. Torrijos's opponents were quick to note that his relatives appeared in large numbers on the public payroll.

THE TREATY NEGOTIATIONS

During the first two years after the overthrow of Arias, while the Guard consolidated its control of the government and Torrijos rooted out his competitors within the Guard, the canal issue was downplayed and generally held in abeyance. By 1971, however, the negotiation of new treaties had reemerged as the primary goal of the Torrijos regime.

In the 1970s, about 5 percent of world trade, by volume, some 20 to 30 ships daily, were passing through the canal. Tolls had been kept artificially low, averaging a little more than US$10,000 for the 8- to 10-hour passage, and thus entailing a United States government subsidy. Nevertheless, canal use was declining in the 1970s, because of alternate routes, vessels being too large to transit the canal, and the decline in world trade.

The canal, nevertheless, was clearly vital to Panama's economy. Some 30 percent of Panama's foreign trade passed through the canal. About 25 percent of the country's foreign exchange earnings and 13 percent of its GNP were associated with canal activities. The level of traffic and the revenue thereby generated were key factors in the country's economic life.

Under the 1903 treaty, the governor of the Canal Zone was appointed by the president of the United States and reported to the secretary of war. The governor also served as president of the Canal Zone Company, and reported to a board of directors appointed by the secretary of war. United States jurisdiction in the zone was complete, and residence was restricted to United States government employees and their families. On the eve of the adoption of new treaties in 1977, residents of the Canal Zone included some 40,000 United States citizens, two-thirds of whom were military personnel and their dependents, and about 7,500 Panamanians. The Canal Zone was, in effect, a United States military outpost with its attendant prosperous economy, which stood in stark contrast to the poverty on the other side of its fences.

By the 1960s military activities in the zone were under the direction of the United States Southern Command (SOUTHCOM). The primary mission of SOUTHCOM was defending the canal. In addition, SOUTHCOM served as the nerve center for a wide range of military activities in Latin America, including communications, training Latin American military personnel, overseeing United States military assistance advisory groups, and conducting joint military exercises with Latin American armed forces.

Negotiations for a new set of treaties were resumed in June 1971, but little was accomplished until March 1973 when, at the urging of Panama, the UN Security Council called a special meeting in Panama City. A resolution calling on the United States to negotiate a "just and equitable" treaty was vetoed by the United States on the grounds that the disposition of the canal was a bilateral matter. Panama had succeeded, however, in dramatizing the issue and gaining international support.

The United States signaled renewed interest in the negotiations in late 1973, when Ambassador Ellsworth Bunker was dispatched to Panama as a special envoy. In early 1974, Secretary of State Henry Kissinger and Panamanian foreign minister Juan Antonio Tack announced their agreement on eight principles to serve as a guide in negotiating a "just and equitable treaty eliminating once and for all the causes of conflict between the two countries." The principles included recognition of Panamanian sovereignty in the Canal Zone; immediate enhancement of economic benefits to Panama; a fixed expiration date for United States control of the canal; increased Panamanian participation in the operation and defense of the canal; and continuation of United States participation in defending the canal.

American attention was distracted later in 1974 by the Watergate scandal, impeachment proceedings, and ultimately the resignation of President Richard M. Nixon. Negotiations with Panama were accelerated by President Gerald R. Ford in mid-1975 but became deadlocked on four central issues: the duration of the treaty; the amount of canal revenues to go to Panama; the amount of territory United States military bases would occupy during the life of the treaty; and the United States demand for a renewable forty- or fifty-year lease of bases to defend the canal. Panama was particularly concerned with the open-ended presence of United States military bases and held that the emerging United States position retained the bitterly opposed "perpetuity" provision of the 1903 treaty and thus violated the spirit of the 1974 KissingerTack principles. The sensitivity of the issue during negotiations was illustrated in September 1975 when Kissinger's public declaration that "the United States must maintain the right, unilaterally, to defend the Panama Canal for an indefinite future" provoked a furor in Panama. A group of some 600 angry students stoned the United States embassy.

Negotiations remained stalled during the United States election campaign of 1976 when the canal issue, particularly the question of how the United States could continue to guarantee its security under new treaty arrangements, became a major topic of debate. Torrijos replaced Foreign Minister Tack with Aquilino Boyd in April 1976, and early the next year Boyd was replaced by Nicolás González Revilla. Rómulo Escobar Bethancourt, meanwhile, became Panama's chief negotiator. Panama's growing economic difficulties made the conclusion of a new treaty, accompanied by increased economic benefits, increasingly vital.

The new Panamanian negotiating team was thus encouraged by the high priority that President Jimmy Carter placed on rapidly concluding a new treaty. Carter added Sol Linowitz, former ambassador to the OAS, to the United States negotiating team shortly after taking office in January 1977. Carter held that United States interests would be protected by possessing "an assured capacity or capability" to guarantee that the canal would remain open and neutral after Panama assumed control. This view contrasted with previous United States demands for an ongoing physical military presence and led to the negotiation of two separate treaties. This changed point of view, together with United States willingness to provide a considerable amount of bilateral development aid in addition to the revenues associated with Panama's participation in the operation of the canal, were central to the August 10, 1977 announcement that agreement had been reached on two new treaties.

THE 1977 TREATIES AND ASSOCIATED AGREEMENTS

On September 7, 1977, Carter and Torrijos met in Washington to sign the treaties in a ceremony that also was attended by representatives of twenty-six other nations of the Western Hemisphere. The Panama Canal Treaty, the major document signed on September 7, abrogated the 1903 treaty and all other previous bilateral agreements concerning the canal. The treaty was to enter into force six months after the exchange of instruments of ratification and to expire at noon on December 31, 1999.

The Panama Canal Company and the Canal Zone government would cease to operate and Panama would assume complete legal jurisdiction over the former Canal Zone immediately, although the United States would retain jurisdiction over its citizens during a thirty-month transition period. Panama would grant the United States rights to operate, maintain, and manage the canal through a new United States government agency, the Panama Canal Commission. The commission would be supervised by a board of five members from the United States and four from Panama; the ratio was fixed for the duration of the treaty. The commission would have a United States administrator and Panamanian deputy administrator until January 1, 1990, when the nationalities of these two positions would be reversed. Panamanian nationals would constitute a growing number of commission employees in preparation for their assumption of full responsibility in 2000. Another binational body, the Panama Canal Consultative Committee, was created to advise the respective governments on policy matters affecting the canal's operation.

Article IV of the treaty related to the protection and defense of the canal and mandated both nations to participate in that effort, though the United States was to hold the primary responsibility during the life of the treaty. The Combined Board, composed of an equal number of senior military representatives from each country, was established and its members charged with consulting their respective governments on matters relating to protection and defense of the canal. Guidelines for employment within the Panama Canal Commission were set forth in Article X, which stipulated that the United States would establish a training program to ensure that an increasing number of Panamanian nationals acquired the skills needed to operate and maintain the canal. By 1982 the number of United States employees of the commission was to be at least 20 percent lower than the number working for the Panama Canal Company in 1977. Both nations pledged to assist their own nationals who lost jobs because of the new arrangements in finding employment. The right to collective bargaining and affiliation with international labor organizations by commission employees was guaranteed.

Under the provisions of Article XII, the United States and Panama agreed to study jointly the feasibility of a sea-level canal and, if deemed necessary, to negotiate terms for its construction. Payments to Panama from the commission ("a just and equitable return on the national resources which it has dedicated to the . . . canal") were set forth in Article XIII. These included a fixed annuity of US$10 million, an annual contingency payment of up to US$10 million to be paid out of any commission profits, and US$0.30 per Panama Canal net ton of cargo that passed through the canal, paid out of canal tolls. The latter figure was to be periodically adjusted for inflation and was expected to net Panama between US$40 and US$70 million annually during the life of the treaty. In addition, Article III stipulated that Panama would receive a further US$10 million annually for services (police, fire protection, street cleaning, traffic management, and garbage collection) it would provide in the canal operating areas.

The second treaty, the Treaty Concerning the Permanent Neutrality and Operation of the Panama Canal, or simply the Neutrality Treaty, was a much shorter document. Because it had no fixed termination date, this treaty was the major source of controversy. Under its provisions, the United States and Panama agreed to guarantee the canal's neutrality "in order that both in time of peace and in time of war it shall remain secure and open to peaceful transit by the vessels of all nations on terms of entire equality." In times of war, however, United States and Panamanian warships were entitled to "expeditious" transit of the canal under the provisions of Article VI. A protocol was attached to the Neutrality Treaty, and all nations of the world were invited to subscribe to its provisions.

At the same ceremony in Washington, representatives of the United States and Panama signed a series of fourteen executive agreements associated with the treaties. These included two Agreements in Implementation of Articles III and IV of the Panama Canal Treaty that detailed provisions concerning operation, management, protection, and defense, outlined in the main treaty. Most importantly, these two agreements defined the areas to be held by the United States until 2000 to operate and defend the canal. These areas were distinguished from military areas to be used jointly by the United States and Panama until that time, military areas to be held initially by the United States but turned over to Panama before 2000, and areas that were turned over to Panama on October 1, 1979.

One foreign observer calculated that 64 percent of the former Canal Zone, or 106,700 hectares, came under Panamanian control in 1979; another 18 percent, or 29,460 hectares, would constitute the "canal operating area" and remain under control of the Panama Canal Commission until 2000; and the remaining 18 percent would constitute the various military installations controlled by the United States until 2000. The agreements also established the Coordinating Committee, consisting of one representative of each country, to coordinate the implementation of the agreement with respect to Article III of the Panama Canal

Treaty, and an analogous Joint Committee to perform the defense-related functions called for in the agreement with respect to Article IV of the treaty.

Ancillary agreements signed on September 7 allowed the United States to conduct certain activities in Panama until 2000, including the training of Latin American military personnel at four schools located within the former Canal Zone; provided for cooperation to protect wildlife within the area; and outlined future United States economic and military assistance. This latter agreement, subject to the availability of congressionally approved funds, provided for United States loan guarantees, up to US$75 million over a 5-year period, for housing; a US$20-million loan guarantee by the United States Overseas Private Investment Corporation for financing projects in the Panamanian private sector; loans, loan guarantees, and insurance, up to a limit of US$200 million between 1977 and 1982, provided by the United States Export-Import Bank for financing Panamanian purchases of United States exports; and up to US$50 million in foreign military sales credits over a 10-year period.

The speeches of Carter and Torrijos at the signing ceremony revealed the differing attitudes toward the new accords by the two leaders. Carter declared his unqualified support of the new treaties. The statement by Torrijos was more ambiguous, however. While he stated that the signing of the new treaties "attests to the end of many struggles by several generations of Panamanian patriots," he noted Panamanian criticism of several aspects of the new accords, particularly of the Neutrality Treaty: Mr. President, I want you to know that this treaty, which I shall sign and which repeals a treaty not signed by any Panamanian, does not enjoy the approval of all our people, because the twenty-three years agreed upon as a transition period are 8,395 days, because during this time there will still be military bases which make my country a strategic reprisal target, and because we are agreeing to a treaty of neutrality which places us under the protective umbrella of the Pentagon. This pact could, if it is not administered judiciously by future generations, become an instrument of permanent intervention.

Torrijos was so concerned with the ambiguity of the Neutrality Treaty, because of Panamanian sensitivity to the question of United States military intervention, that, at his urging, he and President Carter signed the Statement of Understanding on October 14, 1977, to clarify the meaning of the permanent United States rights. This statement, most of which was subsequently included as an amendment to the Neutrality Treaty and incorporated into its instrument of ratification, included a declaration that the United States "right to act against any aggression or threat directed against the Canal . . . does not mean, nor shall it be interpreted as the right of intervention of the United States in the internal affairs of Panama." Despite this clarification, the plebiscite that took place the next week and served as the legal means of ratification in Panama, saw only two-thirds of Panamanians registering their approval of the new treaties, a number considerably smaller than that hoped for by the government.

Ratification in the United States necessitated the approval of two-thirds of the Senate. The debates, the longest in Senate history, began on February 7, 1978. The Neutrality Treaty was approved on March 16, and the main treaty on April 18, when the debate finally ended. To win the necessary sixty-seven Senate votes, Carter agreed to the inclusion of a number of amendments, conditions, reservations, and understandings that were passed during the Senate debates and subsequently included in the instruments of ratification signed by Carter and Torrijos in June.

Notable among the Senate modifications of the Neutrality Treaty were two amendments incorporating the October 1977 Statement of Understanding, and interpreting the "expeditious" transit of United States and Panamanian warships in times of war as being preferential. Another modification, commonly known as the DeConcini Condition, stated that "if the Canal is closed, or its operations are interfered with [the United States and Panama shall each] have the right to take such steps as each deems necessary, ... including the use of military force in the Republic of Panama, to reopen the Canal or restore the operations of the Canal." Modifications of the Panama Canal Treaty included a reservation requiring statutory authorization for payments to Panama set forth in Article XIII and another stating that any action taken by the United States to secure accessibility to the Canal "shall not have as its purpose or be interpreted as a right of intervention in the internal affairs of the Republic of Panama or interference with its political independence or sovereign integrity." Reservations attached to both treaties made the United States provision of economic and military assistance, as detailed in the ancillary agreements attached to the treaties, nonobligatory.

The inclusion of these modifications, which were never ratified in Panama, was received there by a storm of protest. Torrijos expressed his concern in 2 letters, the first to Carter and another sent to 115 heads of state through their representatives at the UN. A series of student protests took place in front of the United States embassy. The DeConcini Condition was the major object of protest. Although the reservation to the Panama Canal Treaty was designed to mollify Panamanian fears that the DeConcini Condition marked a return to the United States gunboat diplomacy of the early twentieth century, this provision would expire in 2000, whereas the DeConcini Condition, because it was attached to the Neutrality Treaty, would remain in force permanently.

Despite his continuing concern with the ambiguity of the treaties with respect to the United States role in defense of the canal after 2000, the close Senate vote made Torrijos aware that he could not secure any further modification at that time. On June 16, 1978, he and Carter signed the instruments of ratification of each treaty in a ceremony in Panama City. Nevertheless, Torrijos added the following statement to both Panamanian instruments: "The Republic of Panama will reject, in unity and with decisiveness and firmness, any attempt by any country to intervene in its internal or external affairs." The instruments of ratification became effective on June 1, 1979, and the treaties entered into force on October 1, 1979.

TORRIJOS GOVERNMENT UNDERTAKES "DEMOCRATIZATION"

Ironically, the successful conclusion of negotiations with the United States and the signing of the Panama Canal treaties in August 1977 added to the growing political difficulties in Panama. Virtually all observers of Panamanian politics in the late 1970s agreed that the situation in the late 1970s could only be understood in terms of the central role traditionally played by nationalism in forming Panamanian political consensus. Before August 1977, opponents of Torrijos were reluctant to challenge his leadership because of his progress in gaining control over the Canal Zone. The signing of the treaties eliminated that restraint; in short, after August 1977, Panamanian resentment could no longer be focused exclusively on the United States.

The widespread feeling among Panamanians that the 1977 treaties were unacceptable, despite their being approved by a two-thirds majority in the October 1977 plebiscite, contributed to growing opposition to the government. Critics pointed especially to the amendments imposed by the United States Senate after the October 1977 plebiscite, which they felt substantially altered the spirit of the treaties. Furthermore, political opponents of Torrijos argued that the government purposely limited the information available on the treaties and then asked the people to vote "yes" or "no," in a plebiscite that the opposition maintained was conducted fraudulently.

Another factor contributing to the erosion of the populist alliance built by Torrijos during the early 1970s was the graduated and controlled process of "democratization" undertaken by the Torrijos government after signing the new canal treaties. In October 1978, a decade after the government declared political parties illegal in the aftermath of the 1968 military coup d'état, the 1972 Constitution was reformed to implement a new electoral law and legalize political parties. In the spirit of opening the political system that accompanied the ratification of the Panama Canal treaties, exiled political leaders, including former President Arnulfo Arias, were allowed to return to the country, and a flurry of political activity was evident during the subsequent eighteen months. Foremost among the activities were efforts to obtain the 30,000 signatures legally required to register a party for the October 1980 elections.

The 1978 amendments to the 1972 Constitution markedly decreased the powers of the executive branch of government and increased those of the legislature, but the executive remained the dominant branch. From October 1972 until October 1978, Torrijos had acted as the chief executive under the titles of head of government and "Maximum Leader of the Panamanian Revolution." After the 1978 amendments took effect, Torrijos gave up his position as head of government but retained control of the National Guard and continued to play an important role in the government's decision-making process. Before stepping down, Torrijos had agreed to democratize Panama's political system, in order to gain United States support for the canal treaties. In October 1978, the National Assembly elected a thirty-eight-year-old lawyer and former education minister, Aristides Royo, to the presidency and Ricardo de la Espriella to the vice presidency, each for a six-year term.

The PRD-a potpourri of middle-class elements, peasant and labor groups, and marginal segments of Panamanian society-was the first party to be officially recognized under the registration process that began in 1979. Wide speculation held that the PRD would nominate Torrijos as its candidate for the presidential race planned for 1984. Moreover, many assumed that with government backing, the PRD would have a substantial advantage in the electoral process.

In March 1979, a coalition of eight parties called the National Opposition Front (Frente Nacional de Oposición--FRENO) was formed to battle the PRD in the 1980 legislative elections, the first free elections to be held in a decade. FRENO was composed of parties on both the right and the left of center in the political spectrum, including the strongly nationalistic, anti-Yankee Authentic Panameñista Party (Partido Panameñista Auténtico--PPA), which was led by the aged but still popular former president, Arnulfo Arias; the PLN; the reform-oriented PDC; and the Social Democratic Party (Partido Social Democrático--PSD), which was left of center and reform-oriented. Three right-of-center parties--the Republican Party (Partido Republicano--PR), the Third Nationalist Party, and PALA--had also joined the FRENO coalition. The Independent Democratic Movement, a small, moderately left-of-center party, completed the coalition. Such diverse ideologies in the opposition party suggested a marriage of convenience. FRENO opposed the Panama Canal treaties and called for their revision on terms more favorable to Panama.

All qualified parties competed in the 1980 legislative elections, but these elections posed no threat to Torrijos's power base because political parties vied for only nineteen of the fifty seven seats in the legislature. The other two-thirds of the representatives were appointed, in essence by Torrijos's supporters. The PRD won twelve of the available nineteen seats; the PLN won five seats, and the PDC, one. The remaining seat was won by an independent candidate running with the support of a communist party, the Panamanian People's Party (Partido Panameño del Pueblo-- PPP). The PPP had failed to acquire the signatures required for a place on the ballot. Despite the lopsided victory of the progovernment party and the weakness of the National Legislative Council (budgeting and appropriations were controlled by President Royo, who had been handpicked by Torrijos), this election represented a small step toward restoring democratic political processes. The election also demonstrated that Panama's political party system was too fragmented to form a viable united front against the government.

THE POST-TORRIJOS ERA

TORRIJOS'S SUDDEN DEATH

Omar Torrijos was killed in an airplane crash in western Panama on July 31, 1981. His death deprived Central America of a potential moderating influence when that region was facing increased destabilization, including revolutions in Nicaragua and El Salvador. His death also created a power vacuum in his own country and ended a twelve-year "dictatorship with a heart," as Torrijos liked to call his rule. He was succeeded immediately as Guard commander by the chief of staff, Colonel Florencio Florez Aguilar, a Torrijos loyalist. Although Florez adopted a low profile and allowed President Royo to exercise more of his constitutional authority, Royo soon alienated the Torrijos clique, the private sector, and the Guard's general staff, all of whom rejected his leadership style and his strongly nationalistic, anti-United States rhetoric.

Royo had become the leader of leftist elements within the government, and he used his position to accuse the United States of hundreds of technical violations in the implementation of the canal treaties. The general staff considered the Guard to be the country's principal guarantor of national stability and began to challenge the president's political authority. Royo attempted to use the PRD as his power base, but the fighting between leftists and conservatives within the party became too intense to control. Meanwhile, the country's many and diverse political parties, although discontented with the regime, were unable to form a viable and solid opposition.

Torrijos had been the unifying influence in Panama's political system. He had kept Royo in the presidency, the PRD functioning, and the Guard united. The groups were loyal to him but distrustful of each other.

Florez completed twenty-six years of military service in March 1982 and was forced to retire. He was replaced by his own chief of staff, General Rubén Darío Paredes, who considered himself to be Torrijos's rightful successor and the embodiment of change and unity (Torrijos had been grooming Paredes for political office since 1975). In a press interview, Paredes stated that he had become "what some people sometimes call a strong man." Without delay the new Guard commander asserted himself in Panamanian politics and formulated plans to run for the presidency in 1984.

Many suspected that Paredes had struck a deal with Colonel Manuel Antonio Noriega Moreno, who had been the assistant chief of staff for intelligence since 1970, whereby Noriega would assume command of the Guard and Paredes would become president in 1984. Paredes publicly blamed Royo for the rapidly deteriorating economy and the pocketing of millions of dollars from the nation's social security system by government officials.

In July 1982, growing labor unrest led to an outbreak of strikes and public demonstrations against the Royo administration. Paredes, claiming that "the people wanted change," intervened to remove Royo from the presidency. With National Guard backing, Paredes forced Royo and most of his cabinet to resign on July 30, 1982, almost one year to the day after the death of Torrijos. Royo was succeeded by Vice President Ricardo de la Espriella, a United States-educated former banking official. De la Espriella wasted no time in referring to the National Guard as a "partner in power."

In August 1982, President de la Espriella formed a new cabinet that included independents and members of the Liberal Party and the PRD; Jorge Illueca Sibauste, Royo's foreign minister, became the new vice president. Meanwhile, Colonel Armando Contreras became chief of staff of the National Guard. Colonel Noriega continued to hold the powerful position of assistant chief of staff for intelligence-the Panamanian government's only intelligence arm. In December 1982, Noriega became chief of staff of the National Guard.

NORIEGA TAKES CONTROL

In November 1982, a commission was established to draft a series of proposed amendments to the 1972 Constitution. The PRD supported the amendments and claimed that they would limit the power of the Guard and help the country return to a fully democratic system of government. These amendments reduced the term of the president from six to five years, created a second vice presidency, banned participation in elections by active members of the Guard, and provided for the direct election of all members of the legislature (renamed the Legislative Assembly) after nomination by legitimate political parties. These amendments were approved in a national referendum held on April 24, 1983, when they were considered to be a positive step toward lessening the power of the National Guard. In reality, however, the National Guard leadership would surrender only the power it was willing to surrender.

General Paredes, in keeping with the new constitutional provision that no active Guard member could participate in an election, reluctantly retired from the Guard in August 1983. He was succeeded immediately by Noriega, who was promoted to brigadier general. During the same month, Paredes was nominated as the PRD candidate for president. National elections were only five months away, and Paredes appeared to be the leading presidential contender. Nevertheless, in early September, President de la Espriella purged his cabinet of Paredes loyalists, and Noriega declared that he would not publicly support any candidate for president. These events convinced Paredes that he had no official government or military backing for his candidacy. He withdrew from the presidential race on September 6, 1983, less than a month after retiring from the Guard. Although Paredes subsequently gained the support of the Popular Nationalist Party (Partido Nacionalista Popular--PNP) and was able to appear on the 1984 ballot, he was no longer a major presidential contender. Constitutional reforms notwithstanding, the reality of Panamanian politics dictated that no candidate could become president without the backing of the National Guard and, especially, its commander.

With Paredes out of the way, Noriega was free to consolidate power. One of his first acts was to have the Legislative Assembly approve a bill to restructure the National Guard, which thereafter would operate under the name of Panama Defense Forces (Fuerzas de Defensa de Panamá-FDP). Nominally, the president of the republic would head the FDP, but real power would be in the hands of Noriega, who assumed the new title of commander in chief of the FDP.

Meanwhile, the PRD--the military-supported party-was left without a candidate. To strengthen its base for the upcoming election, the PRD created a coalition of six political parties called the National Democratic Union (Unión Nacional Democrática-- UNADE), which included the PALA, PLN, and PR, as well as the smaller PP and the left-of-center Broad Popular Front (Frente Amplio Popular-FRAMPO). With the approval of the military, UNADE selected Nicolás Ardito Barletta Vallarino to be its presidential candidate. Ardito Barletta, a University of Chicago-trained economist and former minister of planning, had been a vice president of the World Bank for six years before his nomination in February 1984. Ardito Barletta was considered well qualified for the presidency, but he lacked his own power base.

Opposing Ardito Barletta and the UNADE coalition was the Democratic Opposition Alliance (Alianza Democrática de Oposición- ADO) and its candidate, the veteran politician, Arnulfo Arias. ADO, formed by the PPA, the PDC, the center-right National Liberal Republican Movement (Movimiento Liberal Republicano Nacional- MOLIRENA), and an assortment of leftist parties, was a diverse coalition made up of rural peasants (especially from Arias's home province of Chiriquí) and lower- and middle-class elements that opposed military rule and government corruption. During the campaign, Arias emphasized the need to reduce military influence in Panamanian politics. He called for the removal of the defense bill passed in September 1983, which had given the FDP control over all security forces and services.

The campaign proved to be bitterly contested, with both sides predicting victory by a large margin. Arias and his backers claimed that Ardito Barietta was conducting the campaign unfairly. Indeed, UNADE took advantage of being the pro-government coalition, and used government vehicles and funds to help conduct its campaign. In addition, most of the media--television, radio stations, and newspapers-favored the government coalition. For example, only one of the country's five daily newspapers supported the ADO.

Voting day, May 6, 1984, was peaceful. Violence broke out the next day between supporters of the two main candidates in front of the Legislative Palace, where votes were being counted. One person was killed, and forty others were injured. Irregularities and errors in the voter registration and in the vote count led to credible charges of electoral misconduct and fraud. Thousands of people, who believed that they had registered properly, showed up at the polling places only to discover that their names had been inexplicably left off the voting list. Large-scale vote-buying, especially in rural areas, was reported.

More serious problems developed during the next several days. Very few official vote tallies were being delivered from the precinct and district levels to the National Board of Vote Examiners, with no apparent reason for the delay. The vote count proceeded slowly amid a climate of suspicion and rumor. On May 9, the vote tabulation was suspended. On May 11, the members of the National Board of Vote Examiners declared that they could not fulfill their function because of 2,124 allegations of fraud, and they turned the process over to the Electoral Tribunal. The opposition coalition publicized evidence showing that many votes had been destroyed before they had been counted. These charges and all subsequent challenges by the opposition were rejected by the tribunal, even though the head of the three-man tribunal demanded a further investigation into the allegations. The election results were made public on May 16. Ardito Barletta won the election with 300,748 votes; Arias came in second with 299,035; retired General Paredes received 15,976. The military-supported candidate had won the election, and the threat to the political power of the FDP had been circumvented.

The United States government acknowledged that the election results were questionable but declared that Ardito Barletta's victory must be seen as an important forward step in Panama's transition to democracy. Relations between the United States and Panama worsened later in the year because of Panama's displeasure at the alleged slowness with which the United States-controlled Panama Canal Commission was replacing American workers with Panamanians.

The resignation of President Ricardo de la Espriella and his cabinet on February 13, 1984 was barely noticed during the intense election campaign. De la Espriella was forced out by Noriega. De la Espriella had opposed the military's manipulation of the election and strongly advocated free elections for 1984. During his brief tenure, de la Espriella had failed to institute any significant policy changes, and his presidency was lackluster. De la Espriella was succeeded immediately by Vice President Jorge Illueca, who formed a new cabinet.

Ardito Barletta, a straitlaced and soft-spoken technocrat, took office on October 11, 1984. He quickly launched an attack on the country's economic problems and sought help from the International Monetary Fund (IMF) to refinance part of the country's US$3.7-billion debt-the world's highest on a per-capita basis. He promised to modernize the government's bureaucracy and implement an economic program that would create a 5-percent annual growth rate. On November 13--to meet IMF requirements for a US$603-million loan renegotiation-he announced economic austerity measures, including a 7-percent tax on all services and reduced budgets for cabinet ministries and autonomous government agencies. He revoked some of the measures ten days later in response to massive protests and strikes by labor, student, and professional organizations.

Negative popular reaction to Ardito Barletta's efforts to revive the country's stagnant economy troubled opposition politicians, the military, and many of his own UNADE supporters. Ardito Barletta's headstrong administrative style also offended Panamanian politicians who had a customary backslapping and back-room style of politicking. Moreover, Arditto Barletta's economic program conflicted with the military's traditional use of high government spending to keep the poor and the political left placated.

On August 12, 1985, Noriega stated that the situation in the country was "totally anarchic and out of control;" he also criticized Ardito Barletta for running an incompetent government. Observers speculated that another reason-and probably the real one-for the ouster of Ardito Barletta was FDP opposition to the president's plan to investigate the murder of Dr. Hugo Spadafora, a prominent critic of the Panamanian military. Shortly before his death, Spadafora had announced that he had evidence linking Noriega to drug trafficking and illegal arms dealing. Relatives of Spadafora claimed that witnesses had seen him in the custody of Panamanian security forces in the Costa Rican border area immediately before his decapitated body was found on September 14, just a few miles north of the Panamanian border.

Because of uneasiness within the FDP over the Spadafora affair, Noriega, using Ardito Barletta's ineffectiveness as an excuse, pressured Ardito Barletta to resign, which he did on September 27, 1985, after only eleven months in office. Ardito Barletta was succeeded the next day by his first vice president, Eric Arturo Delvalle Henríquez, who announced a new cabinet on October 3, 1985. Noriega's policies, especially regarding future control of the Panama Canal, and his personal activities, produced very strained relations with the country's key ally, the USA. US development aid and military assistance were cut, but with little effect. US intervention became more likely after the presidential election of May

1989. This was a straight fight between the pro-government *Coalicion de Liberacion Nacional* (COLINA) and the principal opposition movement, the *Alianza Democratica de Oposicion Civilista* (ADOC). The ADOC candidate, Guillermo Endara Galimany, won with 62% of the vote. However, the election was almost immediately annulled. After an attempted coup in October 1989, believed to have had US backing, was quickly crushed by Noriega's forces, the only means of getting rid of the troublesome dictator was military intervention. In December 1989, US President Bush authorised an invasion of the country. After a few days of fierce fighting, US forces secured control of the country and the capture of noriega (who had taken refuge with the Papal Nuncio).

As Noriega was flown to the USA – where in April 1992 he was tried, convicted and sentenced to 40 years imprisonment – Guillermo Endara was installed at the head of a new administration drawn from the ADOC coalition which had won the May 1989 election. After a low start caused by chronic lack of finance, the Endara government gradually started to put the country back on its feet. Early discontent was reflected in a number of coup attempts during 1991 and 1992, although all were easily put down. Endara's term ended in 1994. At the presidential election held that May, the victor was Ernesto Perez Balladares, backed by a three-party centre-left coalition under the banner of Pueblo Unido. Five years later, Panamanians reverted to the conservative bloc now led by Mireya Elisa Rodriguez, who won the presidential race, and which took control of the national assembly where a four-party coalition is in government.

Rodriguez presided over the defining event in recent Panamanian politics: the return of the Panama canal Zone to Panama under the terms of the agreement negotiated by the Panamanians and the US Carter administration in 1980. (The prospect of Noriega enjoying unrestricted control of the canal had been an important reason behind the US invasion). Despite obvious American irritation at the unusual phenomenon of ceding territory to a foreign government, the Americans pulled out on schedule in a low-key ceremony in December 1999.

POPULATION AN SOCIETY

REGIONS OF SETTLEMENT

Panama has no generally recognized group of geographic regions, and no single set of names is in common use. One system often used by Panamanian geographers, however, portrays the country as divided into five regions that reflect population concentration and economic development as well as geography.

Darién, the largest and most sparsely populated of the regions, extends from the hinterlands of Panama City and Colón to the Colombian border, comprising more than one-third of the national territory. In addition to the province of Darién, it includes the Comarca de San Blas and the eastern part of Panamá Province. Darién-a name that was once applied to the entire isthmus-is a land of rain forest and swamp.

The Central Isthmus does not have precisely definable boundaries. Geographically, it is the low saddle of land that bisects the isthmus at the canal. It extends on the Pacific side from the Darién as far west as the town of La Chorrera. On the Atlantic, it includes small villages and clustered farms around Gatun Lake. East of the canal it terminates gradually as the population grows sparse, and the jungles and swamps of the Darién region begin. More a concept than a region, the Central Isthmus, with a width of about 100 kilometers, is the densely populated historical transportation route between the Atlantic and the Pacific and includes most of Colón Province.

Central Panama lies to the southwest of the canal and is made up of all or most of the provinces of Veraguas, Coclé, Herrera, and Los Santos. Located between the continental divide and the Pacific, the area is sometimes referred to as the Central Provinces. The sparsely populated Santa Fe District of Veraguas Province is located across the continental divide on the Atlantic side, however, and a frontier part of Coclé is also on the Atlantic side of the divide.

The hills and lowlands of Central Panama, dotted with farms and ranches, include most of the country's rural population. Its heartland is a heavily populated rural arc that frames the Bahía de Parita and includes most of the country's largest market towns, including the provincial capitals of Penonomé, Santiago, Chitré, and Las Tablas. This agriculturally productive area has a relatively long dry season and is known as the dry zone of Panama.

The remaining part of the Pacific side of the divide is taken up by Chiriquí Province. Some geographers regard it and Central Panama as a single region.

But, the lowlands of the two areas are separated by the hills of the Península de Las Palmas, and the big province of Chiriquí has sufficient individuality to warrant consideration as a separate region. The second largest and second most populous of the nine provinces, Chiriquí is to some extent a territory of pioneers as well as one of considerable economic importance. It is only in Chiriquí that the frontiers of settlement have pushed up well into the interior highlands, and the population has a particular sense of regional identity. A native of Chiriquí can be expected to identify himself, above all, as a Chiricano.

Atlantic Panama includes all of Bocas del Toro Province, the Caribbean coastal portions of Veraguas and Coclé, and the western districts of Colón. It is home to a scant 5 percent of the population, and its only important population concentrations are near the Costa Rican border where banana plantations are located.

SIZE AND GROWTH

In mid-1997, Panama's population was estimated at 2.6 million, when 40 percent of the population was under 15 years of age. This high proportion suggested continued pressure on the educational system to provide instruction and on the economy to create jobs in the next two decades. Population had increased more than 600 percent since the country's first census in 1911. The annual rate of increase ranged from less than 0.5 percent in the economically depressed 1920s to more than 3 percent in the decade from 1910 to 1920 and in the 1960s. Demographers projected an annual growth rate of 2.2 percent in the early 1990s, declining to 1.5 percent by 2000.

Provincial growth rates in the 1990s ranged from a low of 0.5 percent in Los Santos to a high of 3.5 percent in Panamá. The population in Bocas del Toro, both in remote and rural areas, grew at an average annual rate of approximately 3.1 percent. This high growth rate was due to a significant influx of migrants in response to the development of the Cerro Colorado copper project in the eastern part of that province. Population density was seventy-five persons per square kilometer. The highest densities and the region of the most concentrated urbanization were located in the corridor along the former Canal Zone from Colón to Panama City.

The crude death rate was 5 persons per 1,000 in the mid-1990s, a decline of nearly 50 percent from the mid-1960s. The crude birth rate was 21 per 1,000, a drop of one-third during the same period. Organized family planning began in 1966 with the establishment of the Panamanian Family Planning Organization, a private group. By 1969 the Ministry of Health was actively involved in family planning; clinics, information, and instruction were becoming more available to the population as a whole. By the late 1980s and early 1990s, more than 60 percent of women of childbearing age were using some form of contraception.

ETHNIC GROUPS

Because the isthmus holds a central position as a transit zone, Panama has long enjoyed a measure of ethnic diversity. This diversity, combined with a variety of regions and environments, has given rise to a number of distinct subcultures. But by the mid- 1990s, these subcultures were often diffuse in the sense that individuals were frequently difficult to classify as members of one group or the other, and statistics about the groups' respective sizes were rarely precise. Panamanians nonetheless recognized racial and ethnic distinctions, and considered them social realities of considerable importance.

Broadly speaking, Panamanians viewed their society as composed of three principal groups: the Spanish-speaking, Roman Catholic mestizo majority; the English-speaking, Protestant Antillean blacks; and tribal Indians. Small numbers of those of foreign extraction-Chinese, Jews, Arabs, Greeks, South Asians, Lebanese, West Europeans, and North Americans-were also present. They generally lived in the largest cities, and most were involved in the retail trade and commerce. There were a few retired United States citizens-mostly former Canal Zone officials-residing in Chiriquí. The Chinese were a major source of labor on the transisthmian railroad, completed in the mid-nineteenth century. Most went on to California in the gold rush beginning in 1848; of those who remained, most owned retail shops. They suffered considerable discrimination in the early 1940s under the nationalistic government of President Arnulfo Arias Madrid, who sought to rid Panama of non-Hispanics.

There were also small groups of Hispanic blacks, blacks (*playeros*), and Hispanic Indians (*cholos*) along the Atlantic coast lowlands and in the Darién. Their settlements, dating from the end of the colonial era, were concentrated along coasts and rivers. They had long relied on mixed farming and livestock raising, adapted to the particular exigencies of the tropical forest environment. In the mid-twentieth century, they began marketing small quantities of livestock, tropical fruits, rice, and coffee. In the 1980s, they were under pressure from the mestizo population, as farmers from the central provinces expanded into these previously isolated regions.

ANTILLEAN BLACKS

Black laborers from the British West Indies came to Panama by the tens of thousands in the first half of the twentieth century. Most were involved in the effort to improve the isthmus transportation system, but many came to work on the country's banana plantations as well. By 1910, the Panama Canal Company had employed more than 50,000 workers, three-quarters of whom were Antillean blacks. They formed the nucleus of a community separated from the larger society by race, language, religion, and culture.

Since World War II, immigration from the Caribbean islands has been negligible. Roughly 7 to 8 percent of the population were Antillean blacks in the 1980s. Their share in the total population was decreasing, as younger generations descended from the original immigrants became increasingly assimilated into the Hispanic national society.

The Antillean community continued to be marked by its immigrant, West Indian origins in the 1980s. Some observers noted that Antillean families and gender ideals reflected West Indian patterns and that Antillean women were less submissive than their mestizo counterparts. The Antilleans were originally united by their persistent loyalty to the British crown, to which they had owed allegiance in the home islands. Many migrated to Panama with the intention of returning home as soon as they had earned enough money to permit them to retire. This apparently transient status, coupled with cultural differences, further separated them from the local populace. Another alienating factor was the hostility of Hispanic Panamanians, which increased as the Antilleans prolonged their stay and became entrenched in the canal labor force. They faced racial discrimination from North Americans as well. Their precarious status was underscored by the fact that the 1941 constitution deprived them of their Panamanian citizenship (it was restored by the 1946 constitution). The hostility they faced welded them into a minority united by the cultural antagonisms they confronted.

The cleavage between older and younger generations was particularly marked. Younger Antilleans who opted for inclusion in the Hispanic society at large generally rejected their parents' religion and language in so doing. Newer generations educated in Panamanian schools and speaking Spanish well identified with the national society, enjoying a measure of acceptance there. Nevertheless, there remained substantial numbers of older Antilleans who were trained in schools in the former Canal Zone and spoke English as a first language. They were adrift without strong ties to either the West Indian or the Panamanian Hispanic culture. Isolated from mainstream Panamanian society and increasingly removed from their Antillean origins, they existed, in a sense, on the margins of three societies.

In common with most middle- and many lower-class Panamanians, Antillean blacks valued education as a means of advancement. Parents ardently hoped to give their children as good an education as possible because education and occupation underlay the social hierarchy of the Antillean community. At the top of that hierarchy were ministers of the mainline Protestant religions, professionals such as doctors and lawyers, and white-collar workers. Nonetheless, even a menial worker could hope for respect and some social standing if he or she adhered to middle-class West Indian forms of marriage and family life, membership in an established church, and sobriety. The National Guard, formerly known as the National Police and subsequently called the Panama Defense Forces (Fuerzas de Defensa de Panamá--FDP), served as a means of integration into the national society and upward mobility for poorer blacks (Antilleans and Hispanics), who were recruited in the 1930s and 1940s when few other avenues of advancement were open to them.

INDIANS

According to the 1990 census, Panama's indigenous population numbered slightly over 90,000, or 5 percent of the total population. Censuses showed Indians to be a declining proportion of the total population; they had accounted for nearly 6 percent of all Panamanians in 1960. The figures were only a rough estimate of the numbers of Indians in Panama, however. Precise numbers and even the exact status of several smaller tribes were uncertain, in part because many Indians were in the process of assimilation. Language, although the most certain means of identifying a person as an Indian, was by itself an unreliable guide. There were small groups of people who spoke only Spanish and yet preserved other indigenous practices and were considered Indians by their neighbors. The Guaymí, for example, showed little concern about linguistic purity and had adopted a wide variety of words of Spanish origin; nonetheless, they assiduously preserved indigenous religious belief and practice. By contrast, the far more acculturated Térraba would not use foreign words, even for nonindigenous items.

The Indian population was concentrated in the more remote regions of the country, and for most tribes, isolation was a critical element in their cultural survival. The Guaymí, numbering roughly 50,000 to 55,000, or slightly more than half of the Indian population, inhabited the remote regions of northwest Panama. The Cuna (also referred to as the Kuna) were concentrated mainly along the Caribbean coast east of Colón; their population was approximately 30,000, about one-third of all Indians.

In addition, there were a number of smaller groups scattered in the remote mountains of western Panama and the interior of Darién. The Chocó (or Embera) occupied the southeastern portion of Darién along the border with Colombia. Most were bilingual in Spanish and Chocó, and they reportedly had intermarried extensively with Colombian blacks. They appeared to be in a state of advanced acculturation.

The Bribri were a small section of the Talamanca tribe of Costa Rica. They had substantial contact with outsiders. Many were employed on banana plantations in Costa Rica, and Protestant missionaries were active among them, having made significant numbers of converts.

The Bókatá lived in eastern Bocas del Toro along the Río Calovébora. Linguistically, Bókatá speech was similar to Guaymí, but the two languages were not mutually intelligible. The tribe had not been as exposed to outsiders as had the Guaymí. In the mid- 1980s, there were virtually no roads through Bókatá territory; by the mid-1990s, there was a small dirt road passable only in dry weather.

The Térraba were another small tribe, living in the environs of the Río Teribe. In the twentieth century, the tribe suffered major population swings. It was decimated by recurrent tuberculosis epidemics between 1910 and 1930, but population expanded rapidly with the availability of better medical care after the 1950s. Contact with outsiders also increased. A Seventh Day Adventist mission was active in the tribe for years, and there was substantial acculturation with the dominant mestizo culture. By the mid- 1990s, the Térraba had abandoned most of their native crafts production, and their knowledge of the region's natural history was declining. They even looted their ancestral burial mounds for gold to sell. They refused employment on nearby banana plantations until the early 1970s, when a flood swept away most of the alluvial soil they had farmed. The Guaymí attempted to include the Térraba in Guaymí territory, but the Térraba stoutly resisted these efforts.

All of the tribes were under the jurisdiction of both the provincial and national governments. The Indigenous Policy Section of the Ministry of Government and Justice bore primary responsibility for coordinating programs that affected Indians, serving as a liaison between the tribes and the national government. There were a number of special administrative arrangements made for those districts in which Indians constituted the majority of the population. The 1972 Constitution required the government to establish reserves (*comarcas*) for indigenous tribes, but the extent to which this mandate had been implemented varied. By the mid-1980s, the Cuna were established in the Comarca de San Blas and the Chocó had government approval for official recognition of their own *comarca* in Darién. The Guaymí and the government continued negotiations about the extent of Guaymí territory. The Guaymí contended that government proposals would leave about half the tribe outside the boundaries of the reserve.

Indian education has frequently been under the de facto control of missionaries. The national government made a late entry into the field, but by the late 1970s there were nearly 200 Indian schools with nearly 15,000 students. Nevertheless, illiteracy among Indians over 10 years of age was almost 80 percent, in comparison with less than 20 percent in the population at large.

CUNA

The vast majority of Cuna Indians inhabited the San Blas Islands, with an estimated 3,000 additional Cuna living in small scattered settlements in Darién and in Colombia. The San Blas Islands are clusters of small coral islands, each only a few feet above sea level, along Panama's northeast coast. They contain some fifty densely settled Cuna villages. The density of settlement was one indication of a dramatic increase in population. Official census figures showed a population increase of nearly 60 percent between 1960 and 1990. The 1990 census revealed that village size ranged from 37 to nearly 1,500 inhabitants; half the total population was accounted for in 19 villages ranging in population from 300 to 1,000, with one-third in settlements of more than 1,000. The census seriously undercounted the total Cuna population, however, because it excluded absent workers, whose numbers were significant, given the prevalence of out-migration for wage labor.

Before settling on the San Blas Islands, the Cuna lived in inland settlements concentrated on rivers and streams throughout the Darién. Their contacts with outsiders were confined to trade with pirates and limited interaction with two abortive European colonies attempted in the region in the late seventeenth and early eighteenth centuries. Then, a 1787 treaty with Spain began roughly a century of profitable trade, and the Cuna specialized in coconut farming, which continues to produce their main cash crop. Pressure from mestizo and Chocó Indians migrating into the Darién from Colombia toward the end of the nineteenth century, gradually pushed the Cuna toward the coast and the villages they still occupied in the mid- 1990s.

The Cuna's contact with outsiders remained limited and circumscribed until around 1910. Panamanian settlement was focused along the isthmus, and the Colombian government was, in every significant sense, very distant. Although the Cuna themselves traded with passing ships, they did not permit the crews to debark. An individual Cuna might, however, serve a stint as a sailor, and groups would take a large canoe full of trading goods to Colón.

The Cuna were extensively dependent on outside sources for goods--indigenously produced items played little role in farming and fishing. In contrast to many rural mestizos and Indians elsewhere in Panama, the terms on which they bought outside manufactures were relatively favorable. The Cuna dealt only in cash; they bought from many suppliers; and Cuna themselves owned retail stores in San Blas.

By the early years of the twentieth century, the modern settlement pattern of the San Blas Cuna was well defined. Settlements varied in scale from temporary working camps of one to two families to permanent communities numbering in the hundreds. Social life then, as now, was organized around the twin foci of household and village. Descent was reckoned bilaterally, individuals tracing their ancestors and their progeny through both males and females. The household was the most significant grouping of kin. A 1976 survey found that households numbered on average 9.9 persons, with multiple family households the rule. Larger groupings of kin had no formal role in social relations. Adult siblings were rarely close, and contacts between more distant relatives, such as cousins, were even more diffuse.

Cuna households, in their ideal form, were composed of a senior couple, their unmarried children, and their married daughters and sons-in-law and their offspring. The head of the household directed the work of those residing there; a son-in-law's position was extremely subordinate, particularly during the early years of his marriage. After several years of marriage, husbands usually tried to establish their own households, but the shortage of suitable land made this difficult.

Women were a major force in household decisions. Their sewing and household activities were respected work. Men dominated the public-political sphere of Cuna life, however, and women were overwhelmingly subordinate to men outside their homes. Only a few women had been elected to public office, but daughters of leaders sometimes held government appointments.

Politics and kinship were separate aspects of Cuna life. Kin, even close relatives, did not necessarily support one another on specific issues. Although the children of past leaders enjoyed some advantage in pursuing a career in politics, kinship did not define succession to political office.

Villages had formal, ranked elective political offices, including the chiefs and the chiefs' spokespersons (also known as interpreters). Most communities also had a set of committees charged with specific tasks. Chiefs (except in the most acculturated communities where the chiefs did not sing) derived their authority from their knowledge of the sacred chants, and the spokespersons derived theirs from their ability to interpret the chants for the people. Elected officials conducted elaborate meetings dealing with both religious and secular affairs. The number of officials, the presence or absence of a specifically designated meeting place, and the number and complexity of the meetings themselves were all measures of a village's stature.

Meetings or gatherings fell into two categories: chanting or singing gatherings attended by all members of a village, and talking gatherings attended by adult men only. Singing gatherings were highly formalized, combining both indigenous and Spanish elements. The ritualized dialogue that chiefs chanted to their followers was common Indian practice throughout much of Latin America. Much of the actual vocabulary reflected Spanish influence. For example, the Cuna word for chief's spokesperson, *arkar*, is probably a corruption of the Spanish, *alcalde*.

Talking gatherings focused on exchanging information and taking care of matters that demanded action--relating travel experiences, requesting permission to leave, or resolving disputes, for example. Resolution was reached through consensus in a gradual process directed by the chief or chiefs. Votes were rarely taken, and then only in the more acculturated communities. Agreement was evident when no further contrary opinions were stated. Historically, if an agreement could not be reached the community would split up.

Cuna also held general congresses as frequently as several times per year. Each village sent a delegation; the size varied but typically at least one chief and a chief's spokesperson were included. The rules of procedure were highly formalized. As with local gatherings, the emphasis was on reaching a consensus of the group rather than acquiring the votes necessary for a majority. And, again, agreement was evident when no further contrary opinions were stated or when they were shouted down by the rest of the delegates.

Villages had considerable discretionary powers and they regulated who could settle there. Most refused to accept Colombian Cuna displaced by cattle ranchers. Others expressed disapproval of landless San Blasinos (residents of San Blas) from other villages marrying into their village. The power of villages to grant or withhold travel permits was used as a sanction against misconduct and a weapon in political disputes. Women were rarely permitted to travel outside San Blas, and until the mid-1960s, many villages required an absentee worker to come home for harvest and planting or pay for a substitute.

Villages varied in their willingness to accept innovations. In general, the Cuna of eastern San Blas were more conservative, while those of the western and central parts more readily accepted outside influences. Modernist villages sent more workers to the larger society; conservative communities tended to rely more extensively on agricultural income for their livelihood. Village politics were concerned with questions of inheritance, boundary disputes, land sales, and property theft.

Land was privately held. As population increased, landholding and inheritance were more critical. In theory, all children had an equal right to inherit their parents' fields. In practice, though, most land passed from father to son. Sons, after fulfilling the labor obligations to their in-laws, farmed with their fathers.

Some coconut groves were held in common by the descendants of the original owner; common ownership gave these groups of descendants a strategic importance in controlling resources. Cooperative societies played a significant role in various economic ventures and had a major impact on coconut production, transporting, and selling.

Slash-and-burn farming on uninhabited islands and the mainland was the major economic activity, providing most subsistence. Bananas were the primary subsistence crop; coconuts, the main cash crop. Sources of nonagricultural income included migrant wage labor, the sale of hand-sewn items by Cuna women, and tourism. Most of the tourists were day visitors, but there were several resorts in the San Blas Islands owned by Cuna, United States citizens, and Panamanians. The Cuna also owned retail stores on the San Blas Islands.

Migrant wage labor was the most common source of nonfarm income. The Cuna have a long history as migrant laborers, beginning with their service as sailors on passing ships in the nineteenth century. In the early decades of the twentieth century, Cuna did short stints in Panama City, Colón, and on banana plantations. Later they worked in the Canal Zone. The United Fruit Company banana plantations in Changuinola and Almirante were frequent destinations for Cuna. The company viewed the Cuna as exemplary employees, and a few were promoted to managerial or semi-managerial positions as of the early 1990s. Migrant labor was a part of the experience of almost every young male Cuna in his late teens or early twenties. In contrast with most of rural Panama, however, women left San Blas very infrequently. A mid-1980s survey found that less than 4 percent of San Blas women of all ages were living away.

Missionary activity among the Cuna began with the Roman Catholics in 1907 and Protestant denominations in 1913. Non- Panamanian Protestants were banned in 1925. A small Baptist mission returned with legal guarantees of freedom of confession in the 1950s. The presence of missionaries was a bone of contention between modernist and traditional Cuna for decades. Christianity spread unevenly through the archipelago, and the San Blasinos often resisted it tenaciously. Converts were often lax in their adherence to the new creeds; indigenous belief and practice remained prominent. The Baptist mission, noted one anthropologist, was "thoroughly Kuna-ized."

Ritual was a major focus of Cuna concern and a significant part of the relations between non-kin. It formed the basis for community solidarity and esprit. A man gained prestige through his mastery of rituals and chants. Virtually the entire village took part in female puberty rites, which were held several times each year; much social interaction followed ritualized patterns closely.

Lavish sharing was an esteemed virtue; stinginess was disparaged. Thus, the Cuna continued to celebrate community solidarity through feasting, gift giving, and ritual. The community offered food to visitors and entertained at public expense. The plethora of celebrations in the Cuna calendar offered ample occasions to display their generosity.

Many Cuna recognized the value of literacy, and schools had a long history in the archipelago. In the nineteenth century, some Cuna learned to read and write during periods of migrant labor. By the early 1900s, there were a few primary schools in San Blas. There was some resistance among the more conservative elements in Cuna society, but in general education encountered far less opposition than did missionaries' proselytizing. In the 1990s, most settlements of any size had a primary school; there were also several secondary schools. It was not uncommon for Cuna to migrate to further their education-there was a contingent of Cuna at the University of Panama, and a few had studied abroad. On islands with the longest history of schooling, illiteracy rates among those ten years of age and older were in the range of 15 percent in the late 1970s. The 4 villages that had refused schools until the late 1960s and early 1970s averaged nearly 95 percent illiterate. Overall, more than half the Cuna population over ten years of age was literate, and a comparable proportion of those aged seven to fifteen were in school.

Cuna relations with outsiders, especially the Panamanian government, have frequently been stormy. In general, however, the Cuna have managed to hold their own more effectively than most indigenous peoples. Early in the twentieth century, there were several Cuna confederacies, each under the aegis of the main village's chief. The chiefs negotiated with outsiders on behalf of the villages within their alliance.

In 1930 the national government recognized the semiautonomous status of the San Blas Cuna; eight years later the government formed the official Cuna reserve, the Comarca de San Blas. The Carta Orgánica, legislated by Law 16 of 1953, established the administrative structure of the reservation.

Tensions between the state and the Cuna increased under the rule of Omar Torrijos Herrera (1968-81) as the government attempted to alter Cuna political institutions. Cuna were unhappy over the appointment of Hispanics rather than Cuna to sensitive posts. Relations reached a low point during the controversy surrounding government plans to promote tourism in the region, threatening San Blas's status as a reserve. The conflict ended, however, with the reaffirmation of the reserve's status. The extent of Cuna disagreements with the national government was reflected in their vote in the 1977 referendum on the Panama Canal treaties: San Blas was the only electoral district to reject the treaties. For the Cuna, this action was less a statement about the fate of the former Canal Zone or Panamanian sovereignty than their rather strongly held views about their autonomy. Although many government-sponsored reforms were incorporated into Cuna political institutions, the San Blasinos continued to exercise a significant measure of autonomy.

GUAYMÍ

The Guaymí Indians were concentrated in the more remote regions of Bocas del Toro, Chiriquí, and Veraguas. Because their territory was divided by the Cordillera Central, the Guaymí resided in two sections that were climatically and ecologically distinct. On the Pacific side, small hamlets were scattered throughout the more remote regions of Chiriquí and Veraguas; on the Atlantic side, the people remained in riverine and coastal environments.

Contact was recorded between outsiders and Guaymí in the seventeenth and eighteenth centuries. Spanish colonial policy tried to group the Indians into settlements (*reducciones*) controlled by missionaries. This policy enjoyed only limited success in the area of modern Panama. Although some Indians converted to Christianity and gradually merged with the surrounding rural mestizo populace, most simply retreated to more remote territories.

Roman Catholic missionaries had sporadic contact with the Guaymí after the colonial era. Protestant missionaries--mostly Methodists and Seventh- Day Adventists-were active on the fringes of Guaymí territory on the Atlantic side, beginning in the early twentieth century. The Guaymí were impressed by missionaries because most missionaries, unlike mestizos, did not try to take advantage of them in economic dealings.

Present-day contact was most intense in Veraguas, where the mestizo farmers were expanding into previously remote lands at a rapid rate. Guaymí in Bocas del Toro and Chiriquí were less affected. The entry of these outsiders effectively partitioned Guaymí lands. There was a rise in the proportion of tribal members bilingual in Spanish and Guaymí, substantial numbers of whom eventually abandoned Guaymí and disclaimed their Indian identity.

Government schools, especially along the Atlantic portion of Guaymí territory, attracted Indian settlements. Many parents were anxious for their children to attend at least primary school. They arranged for their children to board as servants with Antillean black families living in town, so that the children could attend classes. The outcome was a substantial number of Guaymí young adults who were trilingual in Guaymí, Spanish, and English.

Guaymí subsistence relied on crop raising, small-scale livestock production, hunting, and fishing. In contrast to the slash-and-burn agriculture practiced by the majority mestizo population, Guaymí agriculture was more similar to the type of exploitation practiced in the pre-Columbian era. It placed less reliance on machete and match, and more emphasis on the gradual selective clearing and weeding of plots at the seedling stage of crop growth. The Guaymí burned some trees (that did not have to be felled), but generally left more vegetation to decay. This strategy did not subject the fragile tropical soils to the intense leaching that often follows clear cutting and burning of the tropical forest. The Guaymí agricultural system relied upon an intimate and detailed knowledge of the forest flora. The Guaymí marked seasons not as much by changes in temperature and precipitation as by differences in plants. They noted the times of the year by observing when various plants matured. As an agricultural system it was highly diversified, and the wide range of crop varieties planted conferred resistance to the diverse pests that afflict more specialized farming systems. As an example, Guaymí banana trees produced fruit for sale during all the years that blight had essentially shut down the commercial banana plantations in the region.

Like much of rural Panama, Guaymí territories were subjected to considerable pressure. The length of time land was left fallow decreased. In addition, there were few stands of even well- established secondary forest, let alone untouched tropical forest. In the more intensively used regions, cultivators noted the proliferation of the short, coarse grasses that are the bane of traditional slash-and-burn agricultural systems.

The decline in stands of virgin and secondary forest led to a decrease in wildlife, which affected the Guaymí diet. Domestic livestock grew in importance as a source of protein because larger animals, such as tapir, deer, and peccary, once plentiful, were available only occasionally. Smaller livestock, such as poultry, was extremely vulnerable to disease and predation. Pigs and cattle were raised, but they were among the most consistently saleable products available; as a result, the Guaymí had to choose between protein and cash income. Overall, the diet was quite starchy, with bananas, manioc, and yams the main food items.

Wildlife was adversely affected by modern hunting techniques, also. Traditional hunting and fishing techniques had a minimal impact on the species involved. However, the small-caliber rifles, flashlights, and underwater gear used by Guaymí in the modern era were far more destructive.

The link of most Guaymí to the market economy was similar to that of many poorer rural mestizos. The Indians bought such items as clothing, cooking utensils, axes, blankets, alcohol, sewing machines, wristwatches, and radios. They earned the money for these purchases through period wage labor and the sale of livestock, crops, and crafts (the most unpredictable source of income).

Most Guaymí young men had some experience as wage laborers, although their opportunities were usually limited and uncertain. Some acquired permanent or semipermanent jobs. A few managed to get skilled employment as mechanics or overseers. Fewer still became teachers. The principal employers for Guaymí were the surrounding banana plantations and cattle ranches. Because government policy after the 1950s limited the hiring of foreign laborers on the plantations, Guaymí formed a major part of the banana plantation work force. A number of Indian families settled in towns to work on the plantations. Nonetheless, the wages Guaymí earned proved illusory since most, if not all, of their earnings were spent on living expenses while away from home.

The Guaymí link to the national economy not only provided cash for the purchase of a variety of consumer goods but also acted as a safety valve, relieving the pressure on land. Their dependence on this link was evident during the 1960s, when the Guaymí endured a real hardship because of a decline in demand for labor on banana plantations.

Settlement patterns among the Guaymí were intimately linked to kinship and social organization. Hamlets, each typically representing a single extended family, were scattered throughout the territory. There were no larger settlements of any permanence serving as trading or ceremonial centers. A few mestizo towns on the fringes of Guaymí territory served as trading posts.

Each hamlet was ideally composed of a group of consanguineally related males, their wives, and their unmarried children. Nevertheless, this general rule glossed over residence patterns of considerable fluidity and complexity. At least at some points in an individual's life, he or she resided in a three-generation household. Households, however, took many forms, including nuclear families; polygynous households; groups of brothers, their wives, and unmarried children; a couple, their unmarried children, and married sons and their wives and children; or a mother, her married sons, and their wives and children.

A hamlet defined an individual's social identity, and access to land and livelihood was gained through residence in a specific hamlet. Typically, a person's closest kin resided there. The wide variety of family forms represented in hamlets reflected the diverse ways individual Guaymí used the ties of kinship to gain access to land. Depending on the availability of plots, an individual couple might live with the husband's family (the ideal), the wife's kin, the husband's mother (if his parents did not live together), the husband's mother's kin, or his father's mother's kin.

Guaymí had pronounced notions about which tasks were appropriately male or female; but men would build fires, cook, and care for children if necessary and women would, as the occasion demanded, weed and chop firewood. Women were never supposed to clear forest, herd cattle, or hunt. Nonetheless, a measure of expediency dictated who actually performed the required duties. Because most men migrated to look for employment, a significant segment of the agricultural work force was absent for lengthy periods of time. Consequently, women assumed a larger share of the farmwork during those absences. Their own male kinsmen helped with the heavier tasks. Children began assisting their parents at approximately eight years of age. By the time a girl was fourteen to fifteen years old and a boy seventeen to eighteen, they were expected to do the work of an adult.

Sharing of food and labor was an important form of exchange among kin. If a hamlet needed food, a woman or child would be sent to solicit food from relatives. Kin also formed a common labor pool for virtually all agricultural work. Guaymí did not hire each other as wage laborers. Non-kin assisted each other only for specific festive or communal works. Within the hamlet, all able-bodied family members were expected to contribute labor. Kin from different hamlets exchanged labor on a day-by-day basis. Individuals were careful not to incur too many obligations so as not to compromise their own household's agricultural production. Those who received assistance were obliged to provide food, meat, and *chicha* (a kind of beer) for all the workers. Moreover, there was supposed to be enough food to send a bit home with each worker.

Marriage was the primary means by which Guaymí created social ties to other (non-kin) Guaymí. The ramifications of marriage exchanges extended far beyond the couple concerned. The selection of a spouse was the choice of an allied group and reflected broader concerns such as access to land and wealth, resolution of longstanding disputes, or acquisition of an ally in a previously nonaligned party.

Fathers usually arranged marriages for children. An agreement was marked by a visit of the groom and his parents to the home of the prospective bride and her family. The marriage itself was fixed through a series of visits between the two households involved. No formal ceremony marked the event. Ideally, marriage arrangements were to be balanced exchanges between two kin groups.

Initially the young couple resided with the bride's parents because a son-in-law owed his parents-in-law labor. Thus, a bride usually did not leave her natal hamlet for at least a year. For the husband, persuading his wife to leave her family and join his was a major, and often insurmountable, hurdle. If the marriage conformed to the ideal of a balanced exchange, however, a husband's task was considerably easier in that his wife had to join him or her brother would not receive a wife.

Young men in groups without daughters to exchange in marriage were at a disadvantage. Although they could (and did) ask for wives without giving a sister in return, the fathers of the brides gained significantly. A son-in-law whose family did not provide a bride to his wife's family faced longer labor obligations to his in-laws and uncertainty about when, or if, his wife would join him and his family.

A minority of all marriages were polygynous. Traditionally, a man's ability to support more than one wife was testimony to his wealth and prestige. Co-wives were often sisters. A man could marry his wife's younger sister after he had established a household and acquired sufficient resources to support two families. Wives lived together until their sons matured and married. At that time, an extended household would reconstitute itself around a woman and her married sons and their wives and children. Younger wives in polygynous marriages had a tendency to leave their husbands as they aged. A reasonably successful Guaymí man might expect to begin his married life in a monogamous union, have several wives as he grew more wealthy, and finish his life again in a monogamous marriage.

In general, there were few external indications of differences in wealth, and there was no formal ranking of status in Guaymí society. Prestige accrued to the individual Guaymí male who was able to demonstrate largesse in meeting his obligations to kin and in-laws. A young man began to gain the respect of his in-laws by providing them well with food and labor. He further demonstrated his abilities by farming his own plots well enough to provide for his family and those of his kin who visited.

An individual might also gain prestige through his ability to settle differences. Historically, disputes between Guaymí were settled at public meetings chaired by a person skilled in arbitration. An individual's prestige was in proportion to his ability to reach a consensus among the parties involved in the dispute. In present-day Guaymí society, a government-appointed representative decided the case. Guaymí gained prestige by proposing settlements more acceptable to the disputants than those of the government representative. As an individual's reputation spread, other disputants sought him out to arbitrate. The entire process emphasized the extent to which indigenous political structures were acephalous and loosely organized. There were no durable, well-organized, non-kin groups that functioned in the political sphere; decision making was largely informal and consensual.

In the 1980s, government plans to develop the Cerro Colorado copper mine, along the Cordillera Central in eastern Chiriquí Province, gave impetus to the efforts of some Guaymí to organize politically. Most of the mining project as well as a planned slurry pipeline, a highway, and the Changuinola I Hydroelectric Project were in territory occupied by the Guaymí. Guaymí attended a number of congresses to protect their claims to land and publicize their misgivings about the projects. The Guaymí were concerned about the government's apparent lack of interest in their plight, about the impact on their lands, and their productivity, and about the effect of dam construction on fishing and water supplies. Guaymí were also worried that proposed cash indemnification payments for lands or damages would be of little benefit to them in the long run.

SOCIAL STRUCTURE

RURAL SOCIETY

The opening of the trans-isthmian railroad in the mid- nineteenth century and the Panama Canal early in the twentieth century reinforced the distinctions basic to Panamanian society: the dichotomies between rural and urban inhabitants; small-scale, mixed agriculturalists and larger cattle ranchers; the landless and landowners; and mestizos and whites. By the late 1980s, urban-based control over rural lands was considerable. The metropolitan elite not only had substantial rural landholdings, but monopolized pivotal political posts as well. Wealthy city dwellers also controlled food-processing and transportation facilities. For the bulk of the mestizo peasants, though, limited population and ample reserves of land made elite control of resources less onerous than it might have been, as did the fact that urban elites tended to view their holdings less as agricultural enterprises than as estates in the countryside.

Traditional slash-and-burn agriculture was the basis of rural livelihood for most human settlement on the isthmus. All able-bodied household members were expected to contribute to the family's support. The peasant family was a single production and consumption unit. There was a marked division of labor by sex, and most of the work associated with crops and planting was done by men. Mestizos recognized the significant contribution children made to the agricultural output of a household. Boys and girls gradually assumed responsibilities for assisting with the duties deemed appropriate to their gender. As children, especially boys, grew older, they received part of the income from the sale of crops or part of a field that was "in their name."

Agricultural production was geared to the household's consumption. A family typically kept some livestock and planted a variety of foodstuffs, of which maize was the principal crop. Peasants gained temporary access to land by entering an agreement to clear and maintain cattle pasture for absentee landowners. A family would agree to clear a stand of forest (ideally secondary growth) and plant it in crops for one to two years. At the end of the cycle, they would often seed the plot with grasses before moving on to a new site. Peasants also owed landowners a minimal number of days in labor each year. They faced further demands on their labor to build and maintain communal buildings, such as churches and schools, and to assist with certain public works required by the government.

Since the 1950s, however, traditional slash-and-burn farming and the system of social relations it supports have been in the throes of change. Increasing population pressure, the rapid expansion of cattle ranching, and production of a variety of other cash crops in the interior provinces have put pressure on the land base necessary to maintain slash-and-burn agriculture while preserving the tropical forest. Improved transportation has been accompanied by a rapid expansion in cattle ranching in regions hitherto inaccessible. The process as a whole has meant an increasing consolidation of landholdings and displacement of traditional small-scale farmers engaged in mixed crop and livestock production. The number of farms classified as family owned and operated has declined, in favor of larger units worked by agricultural laborers. This pattern has been accompanied by an increase in and intensification of land disputes.

The consolidation process has been particularly intense in the lowlands of the Pacific coast and in Colón Province southwest of the city of Colón. In these regions, the expansion of the road network and the increasing number of all-weather roads have given potential cattle ranchers access to the large urban beef markets in Colón and Panama City. Cattle ranches grew five-fold in size in the hinterlands of Colón Province in the 1960s. Similar forces had a comparable impact on the Pacific coast, where cattle ranching increased by more than 400 percent from the 1950s through the 1970s, and land values tripled.

The increased demands on the land base affected peasant farmers on many levels. Growing population pressure and the felling of most untouched stands of tropical forest meant a decrease of hunting and, therefore, of animal protein in the family diet. Peccary, deer, and iguana, once relatively common supplements to the mestizo diet, were less available. The same process limited the forest products available for home construction and firewood. Ironically, the expansion in cattle ranching limited the ability of small-scale farmers to keep larger livestock. The purchase price of cattle rose; and, because increased planting meant that animals could not forage as freely as before, they had to be penned or fenced. Finally, where drought-resistant pasture grasses were seeded, the forest itself regenerated much more slowly-limiting still further the land's ability to support an expanding population of both cattle ranchers and small farmers.

The decline in the land available for slash-and-burn agriculture and the increase in cash cropping also drew peasants more deeply into commercialized agriculture in the 1980s. At the same time that small farmers faced declining harvests and increased pressure on the family's subsistence base, they were forced to compete in markets for cash crops where the price was largely determined by larger-scale producers. Most of their production of cash crops was sporadic and in response to unpredictable situations. Difficulties in marketing placed small producers at a further disadvantage.

Sugarcane provides an instructive example. Farmers often planted sugarcane as a second-year crop in the fields they had cleared. The crop was pressed on the draft-animal presses some families owned and used for home consumption. As transportation improved, more small farmers gained access to large-scale, commercial sugarcane mills and had the option of growing sugarcane on contract for the mills. Although this opportunity offered the cultivator a possible source of more reliable income, small farmers were disadvantaged in a number of ways. Planting cane precludes using a plot for foodstuffs during the second year of cultivation. In addition, it requires hired labor, and small-scale producers were hard pressed to offer wages competitive with those that larger farmers or the mills themselves could pay. Finally, small farmers were unable to control the timing of their harvesting, which is essential for gaining optimal yields, because producers had to cut and transport their harvest whenever they were able to contract laborers and truckers for hauling the crop to the mill.

By the late 1980s, peasant families had become vastly more dependent on the money economy. In many regions, consumer goods replaced the traditional craft items produced at home, and hired labor was used in preference to labor exchange among households. Neighbors previously linked through myriad ties of exchange and interdependence were now bound by their common link with external markets. The amount of cash purchases families had to make rose dramatically: corrugated roofing replaced thatch, metal cookware replaced gourds and wooden utensils, nails served instead of vines as fasteners, and, in rare instances, gas stoves were used instead of wood-burning ranges.

Peasant families had a variety of subsidiary sources of income at their disposal. Men and women alike had opportunities to earn a little cash income. Women husked and cleaned rice for neighbors who could afford to pay, sewed, made hats, cooked, and washed clothes, while men made furniture. Those fortunate enough to own draft animals or trucks hauled goods for other farmers. Depending on location, season, and a variety of other factors, there was occasional demand for casual laborers. Such options represented a "safety net" that farmers took advantage of when crops failed or harvests were short. Nevertheless, nonfarming sources of income did not represent a viable alternative to agriculture for most families.

The general increase in cash in circulation affected various segments of the rural population differently. Younger or more highly educated and trained workers were able to compete for better-paying jobs and thus outearn their parents. Despite this, the impact on family life was cushioned because parents never counted on controlling their grown children. In one sense, families were better off because well-employed children were better able to assist their elderly parents. Where the increased cash purchases included milled rice, women were spared the arduous task of husking and milling rice themselves. Educational opportunities benefited all able to take advantage of them. Women gained in particular from the increase in employment opportunities for primary-school teachers.

In addition to peasant farmers and ranchers, Panama had the core of a rural educated middle class by the mid-twentieth century. Frequently educated at the teachers' college in Santiago, in the province of Veraguas, these educated sons and daughters of more prosperous agriculturalists and small merchants were of marginal influence in comparison with the urban elite. Long excluded from any effective role in the nation's politics, they proved a bulwark of support for the Torrijos regime.

Land reform legislation drafted under the influence of the Alliance for Progress in the early 1960s recognized the peasants' right to land. Nevertheless, the law's consequences in the countryside were often unforeseen. The plots allocated under the law were usually too small to support slash-and-burn agriculture; they did not allow sufficient land for fallowing. And, for a substantial portion of peasant families, the cash outlay required to purchase land was prohibitive. Although the relatively poor were unable to assume such debts, the more prosperous were. Some of the more successful emigrants to the city managed to acquire land through land reform and rented it to farmers under terms equivalent to those previously available through larger absentee owners.

In the late 1960s and early 1970s, the government attempted to model its land reform efforts on a collective farming system borrowed from Chile. The government acquired tax-delinquent properties and set up a variety of collectively operated agro-enterprises. The collectives enjoyed mixed success, however. They tended to be heavily mechanized and dependent on outside infusions of technical assistance and capital, while they generated only minimal employment. The most dramatic successes were achieved in regions like Veraguas Province where small farmers competed with cattle ranchers for land. Collectives were less successful in areas where smallholdings predominated.

Where small farmers held title to their lands-an infrequent pattern in traditional rural Panama--they often sold their lands to the larger, more heavily capitalized cattle ranches. The numbers of landless, or nearly landless, cultivators in search of plots to "borrow" for a season's planting rose. Substantial numbers of these displaced small farmers chose migration as an alternative.

Mestizo migrants from regions where cattle ranching was expanding entered the lowlands of the Atlantic coast and the Darién Peninsula in increasing numbers. Migrants arrived and cleared forest land (generally away from the rivers favored by the region's earlier black, Indian, Hispanic Indian, and Hispanic black settlers). The process then repeated itself: the new settlers remained for a few years until improved roads brought more cattle ranchers; the *colonos* (internal migrants) who originally cleared the forest then sold their lands and moved yet deeper into the tropical forest.

MIGRATION

Migration has played an increasingly significant role in the lives of Panamanians and has followed a distinct pattern throughout the twentieth century. Population movement has been into those districts and provinces enjoying a period of economic prosperity, typically associated with the canal. As the economic boom peters out, the migrant population moves back to the primarily agricultural districts, to be reabsorbed into subsistence farming or small-scale businesses and services in the country's predominantly rural interior. The pattern has been repeated several times with the ebb and flow of economic activity. In the late 1980s, it remained to be seen what adaptations migrants would make given the shrinking rural land base.

The 1911 census provides a baseline for population movements throughout the century. At that time, the provinces of Chiriquí and Panamá accounted for nearly 40 percent of the total population. Chiriquí's growth was the result of migrants from Colombia in the nineteenth century; Panamá's came as a result of the canal construction begun just after the turn of the century. The central provinces-Veraguas, Coclé, Los Santos, and Herrera (in order of population)-accounted for slightly more than 40 percent of the total. The entire region had been populated along the coasts since the colonial era and had grown in response to increased demand for foodstuffs in Panama City and Colón in the second half of the nineteenth century. The decade following the census saw dramatic population growth in response to the United States presence and the building of the Panama Canal. The need to feed the massive numbers of black Antillean laborers who came to work on the construction project generated a boom in agriculture.

Subsequent censuses revealed a specific pattern of rural-rural and rural-urban migration. Some rural districts of a province lost population, while others even relatively close grew rapidly. The pattern reversed itself during periods of economic stagnation. Then, migrants retreated into subsistence agriculture in regions that had enjoyed limited participation in the previous boom. Between 1910 and 1920, for example, the Chepigana District in Darién was in the midst of a boom and enjoyed a significant influx of population, while the neighboring Pinogana District lost population. Their roles were reversed in the following decade.

The 1920s represented such a period of stagnation. The regions of highest growth in the previous decade grew much more slowly-if they grew at all. Colón and Bocas del Toro were the most heavily affected. Panamá Province continued to grow at rates slightly in excess of the national average; nonetheless, a large number of foreign workers left, as did a significant portion of the small business owners who had provisioned them and who were ruined by the decline in clientele.

Rural regions absorbed these surplus laborers and served as centers of population growth throughout the 1920s. Some such as Veraguas and Darién grew in excess of 5 percent annually during the intercensal period. District capitals in predominantly rural provinces tended to enjoy significant growth as well, probably as a result of their administrative functions, and the rise of banana plantations in Chiriquí attracted workers from throughout Central America.

The pattern reversed again in the late 1930s and mid-1940s. The immediate pre-World War II period as well as the war itself were times of significant economic expansion for the country as a whole. The province of Panamá headed the country in population growth, and the entire western portion of the province was a region of economic expansion. Colón, by contrast, lost in importance. Its annual rate of increase, 1.44 percent, was barely half the national average. The decline in Colón's fortunes reflected the centralization of economic and administrative activity in Panama City. Furthermore, Colón's importance as a port on the Atlantic diminished with the construction of the Trans-isthmian Highway (also known as the Boyd- Roosevelt Highway).

The economic expansion accompanying World War II eliminated problems associated with the increase in large-scale agro- enterprises in the interior. Although substantial numbers of small farmers were displaced, they were readily absorbed by the demand for labor in cities and the countryside. Even in the period of economic contraction following the war, cities in predominantly rural provinces enjoyed significant growth. The war fueled the development of small-scale industrial and processing activities throughout the country. The dimensions of this growth were such that large numbers of rural youngsters-sons and daughters of small farmers-remained in the provinces in which they were born rather than migrating to Panama City or the Canal Zone.

World War II also saw Panama's last major influx of foreign workers. Most of these workers left with the economic slowdown at the war's end. As in previous periods of economic contraction, increasing numbers of displaced migrants took refuge in subsistence farming. The late 1940s was a time of growth for the rural regions of the country.

Overall, population grew at an annual rate of 2.9 percent in the 1950s; Panama was in the midst of a demographic transition as birth rates remained high while death rates dropped. The press of the population on the land base reached critical proportions. Peasants, displaced by the spread of large-scale agro-enterprises in the country, found it more and more difficult to find unoccupied land to put into production. At the same time, rural-urban migrants found it increasingly difficult simply to return home and resume farming during periods of economic contraction.

The pressure on the land base was acute enough to precipitate significant conflict over holdings in the 1950s and 1960s. In the province of Panamá, peasants invaded and seized the land around Gatun Lake as well as some regions of the districts of La Chorrera, Capira, and Chaime. Although many of these squatters were successful in maintaining their claim on the holdings, most peasants in other parts of the country were not so fortunate. The expansion of large cattle ranches in much of Los Santos and Veraguas continued the migratory process begun earlier, and peasants were pushed farther and farther along the agricultural frontier.

Substantial numbers of these displaced peasants migrated to less settled regions in Chiriquí, Los Santos, and Veraguas. Likewise, banana plantations in Chiriquí and Bocas del Toro drew significant numbers of migrants. The principal destination for much of the rural populace, however, was Greater Panama City.

Nearly two-thirds of all migrants had as their destination the heavily urban province of Panamá--a proportion that has remained roughly constant since the 1950s. In terms of absolute numbers, Los Santos and Veraguas were the major contributors to the migration stream: together they accounted for one-third of all migrants. The relatively depressed districts around Colón contributed large numbers of migrants, as did a number of districts in Chiriquí and Bocas del Toro. Based on rates of out-migration rather than absolute numbers, Los Santos, Darién, and Coclé were the main places of origin.

Within the province of Panamá, the greater metropolitan area of Panama City attracted most migrants. The districts surrounding the city averaged a growth rate of more than 10 percent per year in the 1960s and 1970s. Panama City played a significant role in the migration patterns of virtually every other province in the country. Over 90 percent of the migrants from Darién went there, as did roughly 80 percent of those from Coclé, Colón, Los Santos, and Veraguas. In the relatively prosperous mid-1960s to mid-1970s, most migrants managed to find employment. Many joined the ranks of peddlers and other small-scale self-employed individuals.

The manufacturing sector expanded significantly during the 1960s, resulting in a doubling of the industrial labor force. The service sector-traditionally the country's most dynamic-was fueled by the expansion of manufacturing as well as Panama's pivotal position as a transit zone. The service sector absorbed more than half the increase in the economically active population and grew at a rate of more than 6 percent annually. For the city- bound migrant, that meant jobs in public and domestic service and construction. Nevertheless, some observers expected the rate of migration to the metropolitan region to decline with economic reverses in the 1980s and the increase in opportunities in other regions, such as the Cerro Colorado copper project in Chiriquí.

Overall, the migration stream in the 1970s was composed of three components: rural-urban migrants (accounting for more than half of all migrants), urban-urban migrants (roughly one-quarter of all migrants), and urban-rural migrants (nearly 20 percent of those questioned about their place of residence five years earlier had been living in a city). The exact proportion and significance of urban-rural migration were difficult to judge. Approximately half the migrants were former residents of the smaller cities of the interior and presumably had left their farms for seasonal work in a nearby city or to attend school. Nearly one-third of these return migrants had lived in Panama City and its environs. Many were specialized workers; others were peasants unable to find permanent employment in the city; still others were children sent home to be cared for by kin.

Those people who migrated were, as a whole, young. In the 1970s nearly 75 percent of them were under 35 years of age; among rural- urban migrants, the percentage rose to more than 80 percent. School-age migrants represented a significant group in the migration stream. Although many simply accompanied their parents on moves, a significant minority were sent by their rural families for education in nearby cities. Men formed the majority among rural- urban migrants to Colón; women, however, accounted for a slight majority of all rural-urban migrants. This tendency was most marked in migration of women to cities in the interior, but was also found among migrants to Panama City. In general, observers attributed the high rate of female migration to the metropolitan region to the opportunities for employment available for young women there. Unemployment was lower among urban females than among their rural counterparts, whereas the reverse was true for males.

URBAN SOCIETY

Since the 1950s, Panama has been in the midst of massive urban expansion. In 1960 slightly more than one-third of the total population was classified as urban; by the early 1990s, the figure had risen to 58 percent. Between 1970 and 1980, overall population increased by 2.5 percent per year, urban population by 2.8 percent, and the metropolitan population surrounding Panama City by 3.7 percent. Regional cities shared in the general urban expansion: the number of people in Santiago grew at 4.1 percent annually; David, 3.7 percent; and Chitré, 3.3 percent. Economically depressed Colón lagged with an annual increase of less than 0.5 a percent. Economic activity and population density in Panama were concentrated along two main axes: the Pan-American Highway (also known as the the Inter-American Highway) on the Pacific corridor from La Chorrera to Tocumen and the Trans-isthmian Highway from Panama City to Colón.

Far and away the most significant focus of urban development was the path following the former Canal Zone that stretches from Colón on the Atlantic coast to Panama City on the Pacific. In the mid-1980s, the region accounted for more than half the total population of the country and over two-thirds of all those classified as inhabitants of cities. It also included most nonagricultural economic activity: 76 percent of manufacturing, 85 percent of construction, 95 percent of transportation, and 84 percent of communications. Growth was not spread evenly throughout the region, and since the 1950s, Panama City and its environs had eclipsed Colón. Colón remained the only significant urban center on Panama's Atlantic coast, but by the early 1980s, substantial numbers of that city's business and professional community had emigrated in response to Panama City's expanding economy.

In terms of sheer numbers, most of the urban expansion was concentrated in slum tenements and, since the 1950s, in squatter settlements around the major cities. As was the case in most urban trends, Panama City led the way. In 1958 there were 11 identifiable slums or squatter settlements housing 18,000 people associated with the city; by the mid-1970s, there were some 34 slum communities and their population had mushroomed more than five-fold. Surveys indicated that 80 percent of slum and squatter settlement inhabitants were migrants to the city.

Many of the tenements took the form of two-story frame houses built as pre-World War I temporary housing for the canal labor force. They continued to be occupied, although in the early 1980s they were in an advanced state of decay. When one part of a building collapsed, slum dwellers continued to live in those sections of the building that remained standing. The structures were frequently condemned, which merely added to their attractiveness for impoverished city dwellers, because the rent therefore dropped to nothing. Squatter settlements offered their own inducements. If squatters were able to maintain their claims to land, the settlements tended to improve and gained amenities over time. Because they were essentially rent-free, they gave their inhabitants considerable advantages over costly and over-crowded, if more centrally located, tenements. A substantial portion of the squatters settled on government land, and there were numerous programs to permit them to purchase their housing sites. The Torrijos regime allocated funds for low-income housing projects, and there were efforts to upgrade the amenities available to the urban poor. By the 1980s, about 96 percent of the urban population had access to potable water and nearly 70 percent had electricity. Despite indications of some slowing in the rate of rural-urban migration in the 1980s, migrants represented a major strain on public services and the economy's ability to generate employment.

Although rural society was relatively homogeneous and simple in the social distinctions it made, urban Panama was not. It was ethnically and socially diverse and highly stratified. City dwellers took note of ethnic or racial heritage, family background, income (and source of income), religion, culture, education, and political influences as key characteristics in classifying individuals.

But, in the early 1990s, the boundaries among the elite, the middle class, and the lower class were neither especially well defined nor impervious. The ambitious and lucky city dweller could aspire to better significantly his or her social and economic status. Neither were the distinctions between rural and urban inhabitants absolute. City and countryside were linked in numerous ways; given the frequency with which migrants moved, this year's urban worker was last year's and (not uncommonly) next year's peasant. There was considerable social mobility, principally from the lower to the middle class and generally on an individual rather than a group basis. Wealth, occupation, education, and family affiliation were the main factors affecting such mobility.

THE ELITE

Urban society in the early 1990s included virtually all members of the elite. Centered mainly in the capital, this class was composed of old families of Spanish descent and a few, newer families of immigrants. All elite families were wealthy, but the assets of the immigrant families were more tightly linked with commerce and Panama's twentieth-century development as a transit zone. Older families were inclined to think of themselves an aristocracy based on birth and breeding. Newer families, lacking such illustrious antecedents, had less prestige and social status. Until the advent of Torrijos, whose power base was the National Guard, an oligarchy of older elite families virtually controlled the country's politics under the auspices of the Liberal Party.

The upper class was a small, close-knit group that had developed strong ties of association and kinship over the years. Prominent family names recurred frequently in the news of the nation: Arias, Arosemena, Alemán, Chiari, Goytía, and de la Guardia. People without a claim to such a family background could gain acceptance, at least for their children, by marriage into an elite family.

Since colonial times, education had been recognized as a mark of status; hence, almost all men of elite status received a university education. Most attended private schools either at home or abroad, and many studied a profession, with law and medicine the most favored. The practice of a profession was viewed not as a means of livelihood, but as a status symbol and an adjunct to a political career. The elite maintained a dual cultural allegiance, because families usually sent their sons to Western Europe or the United States to complete their education. Increasing numbers of women also attended college, but most families did not see such education as essential.

Politics was the quintessential career for a young man of elite background. The old, aristocratic families had long provided the republic's presidents, its cabinet ministers, and many members of the legislatures. Young women were increasingly finding employment in public administration and commerce in the 1990s.

Older elite families were closely interrelated and were careful to avoid racially mixed unions. Antillean blacks enjoyed little success in attaining elite status, although a wealthy, Spanishspeaking, Roman Catholic black could gain acceptance. There was an increasing degree of admixture with mestizo and more recent immigrant elements. Many such families entered the elite and intermarried with members of the older families. In a sense, commercial success had in large measure become a substitute for an illustrious family background. "Money whitens everyone" was a popular saying describing the phenomenon.

THE MIDDLE CLASS

The middle class was predominantly mestizo, but it included such diverse elements as the children and grandchildren of black Antilleans, the descendants of Chinese laborers on the railroad, Jews, more recent immigrants from Europe and the Middle East, and a few former elite families fallen on hard times. Like the elite, the middle class was largely urban, although many small cities and towns of the interior had their own middle-class families. The middle class encompassed small businessmen, professionals, managerial and technical personnel, and government administrators. Its membership was defined by those who, by economic assets or social status, were not identifiably elite but who were still markedly better off than the lower class. As a whole, the middle class benefited from the economic prosperity of the 1960s and early 1970s, as well as the general expansion in educational opportunities in the late twentieth century.

Members of the middle class who had held such status for any length of time were rarely content to remain fixed on the social scale. Emulating elite norms and attitudes, they exerted great effort to continue their climb up the social ladder. They were aware of the importance of education and occupation in determining status and the compensatory role these variables could play in the absence of family wealth or social background. Middle-class parents made great sacrifices to send their children to the best schools possible. Young men were encouraged to acquire a profession, and young women were steered toward office jobs in government or business. In contrast with the elite, the middle class viewed teaching as an appropriate occupation for a young woman.

Nationalist sentiment served to unify the diverse elements of the middle class in the decades following World War II. University students, who were predominantly middle class in family background, typified both the intense nationalism and the political activism of the middle class. Political observers noted a sharp class cleavage in the political consciousness of the Spanish-speaking natives and the more recent, unassimilated immigrant families. Middle-class immigrants tended to be preoccupied with commercial pursuits and largely conservative or passive in their politics.

THE LOWER CLASS

The lower class constituted the bulk of the country's urban population. As a group, it was stratified by employment and race. In terms of livelihood it was made up of unskilled or semiskilled workers, including artisans, vendors, manual laborers, and servants. The basic cleavages were between those who were wage earners and the self-employed, and those employed in the former Canal Zone, who constituted a "labor elite" earning twice the average of the metropolitan region as a whole.

Self-employment offered a precarious existence to most who pursued it, but served as an alternative for those unable to find other work when the economy contracted in the late 1970s and 1980s. Unemployment ran in excess of 10 percent in the late 1970s and early 1980s, and much of it was concentrated in the metropolitan region, which accounted for approximately four-fifths of the country's jobless. In poorer neighborhoods, the rate ran closer to 25 percent, and among low-income families, roughly 40 percent were unemployed.

Because the majority of rural-urban migrants to the metropolitan region were women, women outnumbered men in many larger urban areas. Many came in search of work as domestics. Young, single mothers constituted a significant proportion of the urban population; in Colón, for example, they represented one-third of all families. Women suffered higher unemployment rates than did men, and their earnings, when they were employed, averaged less than half those of males.

Ethnically, the lower class had three principal components: mestizo migrants from the countryside, children and grandchildren of Antillean blacks, and Hispanicized blacks-descendants of former slaves. The split between Antillean blacks and the rest of the populace was particularly marked. Although there was some social mixing and intermarriage, religious and cultural differences isolated the Antilleans. They were gradually becoming more Hispanicized, but the first generation usually remained oriented toward its Caribbean origins, and the second and third generations were under North American influence through exposure to United States citizens in the former Canal Zone where most were employed. Although some Antillean blacks were middle class, most remained in the lower class.

Increasing numbers of urban lower-class parents were sending their children to school. A secondary-school diploma, in particular, served as a permit to compete for white-collar jobs and elevation to middle-class status. This kind of mobility was on the rise throughout the 1960s and 1970s. Mestizos were better able to take advantage of these opportunities than most, but Antilleans who were educated and conformed to Hispanic cultural norms enjoyed considerable mobility as well. The National Guard, and later the FDP, have been an avenue of advancement for both Hispanic and Antillean blacks. A substantial portion of the enlisted personnel have come from the ranks of the black urban poor and, increasingly, the rural mestizo population. Enlisted personnel could hope to advance to the officer corps. Under the Torrijos regime, many troop commanders were promoted from the ranks.

EDUCATION

Public education began in Panama soon after independence from Colombia in 1903. The first efforts were guided by an extremely paternalistic view of the goals of education, as evidenced in comments made in a 1913 meeting of the First Panamanian Educational Assembly, "The cultural heritage given to the child should be determined by the social position he will or should occupy. For this reason education should be different in accordance with the social class to which the student should be related." This elitist focus changed rapidly under United States influence.

By the 1920s, Panamanian education subscribed to a progressive educational system, explicitly designed to assist the able and ambitious individual in search of upward social mobility. Successive national governments gave a high priority to the development of a system of (at least) universal primary education; in the late 1930s, as much as one-fourth of the national budget went to education. Between 1920 and 1934, primary-school enrollment doubled. Adult illiteracy, more than 70 percent in 1923, dropped to roughly half the adult population in scarcely more than a decade.

By the early 1950s, adult illiteracy had dropped to 28 percent, but the rate of gain had also declined and further improvements were slow in coming. The 1950s saw essentially no improvement; adult illiteracy was 27 percent in 1960. There were notable gains in the 1960s, however, and the rate of adult illiteracy dropped 8 percentage points by 1970. According to 1990 estimates, only 8 percent of Panamanians over 10 years of age were illiterate. Men and women were approximately equally represented among the literate. The most notable disparity was between urban and rural Panama; 94 percent of city-dwelling adults were literate, but fewer than two-thirds of those in the countryside were-a figure that also represented continued high illiteracy rates among the country's Indian population.

From the 1950s through the early 1990s, educational enrollments expanded faster than the rate of population growth as a whole and, for most of that period, faster than the school-aged population. The steepest increases came in secondary and higher educational enrollments, which increased ten and more than thirty times respectively. By the early 1990s, primary school enrollment rates were roughly 113 percent of the primary school -aged population. Male and female enrollments were relatively equal overall, although there were significant regional variations.

Enrollments at upper levels of schooling had increased strikingly both in relative and absolute terms since 1960. Between 1960 and early 1990s, secondary-school enrollments expanded some four-and-a-half times and higher education, nearly twelve-fold. In 1965 fewer than one-third of children of secondary school age were in school, and only 7 percent of people aged 20 to 24 years. In the late 1980s, almost two-thirds of secondary-school-aged children were enrolled, and about 20 percent of individuals aged 20 to 24 years were in institutions of higher education.

School attendance was compulsory for children from ages six through fifteen years, or until the completion of primary school. A six-year primary cycle was followed by two types of secondary school programs: an academic-oriented program and a vocational-type program. The academic program, which represented nearly three-quarters of all secondary-school enrollment, involved two three-year cycles. The lower cycle was of a general or exploratory nature, with a standard curriculum that included Spanish, social studies, religion, art, and music. The upper cycle consisted of two academic courses of study: in arts and sciences, leading to entrance to the university, or a less rigorous course of study, representing the end of a student's formal education.

In addition to the academic program, there was a vocational type secondary-school program that offered professional or technical courses aimed specifically at giving students the technical skills needed for employment following graduation. In the mid-1980s, roughly one-quarter of all secondary students pursued this type of course. Like the more academic-oriented secondary school program, the vocational-type program was divided into two cycles. Students could choose their studies from a variety of specializations, including agriculture, art, commerce, and industrial trades.

Admission to the university normally required the *bachillerato* (graduation certificate or baccalaureate), awarded on completion of the upper cycle of the academic course of studies, although the University of Panama had some latitude in determining admissions standards. The *bachillerato* was generally considered an essential component of middle-class status. Public secondary schools that offered the baccalaureate degree also offered the lower cycle. They were generally located in provincial capital cities. The oldest, largest, and most highly regarded of these was the National Institute in Panama City. The University of Panama grew out of it, and the school had produced so many public figures that it was known as the Nest of Eagles (Nido de Aguilas). It tended to draw its student body from upwardly mobile rather than long-established elements of the elite. Its students were well known for their political activism.

Higher education on the isthmus dates from the founding of a Jesuit university in 1749; that institution closed with the order's expulsion from the New World in 1767. Another college, the Colegio del Istmo, was started early in the nineteenth century, but the school did not prosper, and Panamanians who wished to pursue a higher education were required to go abroad or to Colombia until 1935, when the University of Panama was founded. In the mid-1980s, most postsecondary schooling took place within the university. Other institutions, such as the School of Nursing and the Superior Center for Bilingual Secretaries, accounted for less than 3 percent of enrollment at this educational level.

Nearly three-quarters of all university students attended the University of Panama in the mid-1990s. The university had, as well, a number of regional centers and extensions representing a small portion of the school's enrollment and faculty. The University of Santa María la Antigua, a private Roman Catholic institution established in 1965, enrolled another 5,000 to 6,000 students in the mid-1990s. A third university, the Technical University, was founded in 1981. It accounted for approximately 7,000 students. A substantial portion of the well-to-do continued to study abroad.

Most education was publicly funded and organized. In addition to the University of Santa María la Antigua, there were some private primary and secondary schools. Typically located in cities and considered very prestigious, they accounted for 5 to 7 percent of primary-school enrollment and approximately 25 percent of secondary-school students in the mid-1990s.

Education continued to claim a large share of government budgets. It represented 15 to 20 percent of the national government's expenditures in the early to mid-1990s. Most funding went to primary schooling, although both secondary and higher education received proportionately higher funding per student. Primary schools received roughly one-third of government education spending, secondary and higher education approximately 20 percent each.

The growth in enrollment was accompanied by a concomitant (if not always adequate) expansion in school facilities and increase in teaching staff. Teacher education was a high priority in the 1980s and 1990s, a reflection of the generally poor training teachers had received in the past. Schools increased at every level during the early 1990s; secondary schools made the most notable gains, more than doubling. Pupil-teacher ratios for all levels were in the range of nineteen to twenty-six pupils per teacher in the mid-1990s.

RELIGION

The Constitution prescribes that there shall be no prejudice with respect to religious freedom, and the practice of all forms of worship is authorized. However, the Constitution recognizes that the Roman Catholic faith is the country's predominant religion and contains a provision that it be taught in the public schools. Such instruction or other religious activity is not, however, compulsory .

The Constitution does not specifically provide for the separation of church and state, but it implies the independent functioning of each. Members of the clergy may not hold civil or military public office, except such posts as may be concerned with social welfare or public instruction. The Constitution stipulates that senior officials of the church hierarchy in Panama must be native-born citizens.

The majority of Panamanians in the late 1990s were at least nominal Roman Catholics. The Antillean black community, however, was largely Protestant. Indians followed their own indigenous belief systems, although both Protestant and Catholic missionaries were active among the various tribes. Roman Catholicism permeated the social environment culturally as well as religiously. The devout regarded church attendance and the observance of religious duties as regular features of everyday life, and even the most casual or nominal Roman Catholics adjusted the orientation of their daily lives to the prevailing norms of the religious calendar. Although some sacraments were observed more scrupulously than others, baptism was almost universal, and the last rites of the church were administered to many who during their lives had been indifferent to the precepts of the faith or its religious rituals.

In the mid-1980s, when nearly 90 percent of the population was Roman Catholic, there were fewer than 300 priests in the country. Virtually every town had its Roman Catholic church, but many did not have a priest in residence. Many rural inhabitants in the more remote areas received only an occasional visit from a busy priest who traveled among a number of isolated villages.

Religious attitudes, customs, and beliefs differed somewhat between urban and rural areas, although many members of the urban working class, often recent migrants from rural regions, presumably retained their folk beliefs. According to one anthropologist, the belief system of the campesinos centered on God, the Devil, the saints, and the Virgin. Christ was viewed as more or less the chief saint, but as peripheral to the lives of men. The Virgin Mary served as an inspiration and model to women, but there was no comparable model for men.

Although the campesinos believed that each individual "is born with a destiny set by God," they also believed that the destiny could be altered if the individual succumbed to the constant blandishments and enticements of the Devil. The rural dwellers possessed a clear sense of reward and punishment that centered on All Souls' Day. On that day all who died during the previous year are summoned to judgment before God and the Devil. The life record of each person is recited by Saint Peter, and the good and bad deeds are weighed out on a Roman balance scale, thus determining the person's afterlife.

Throughout the society, birth and death were marked by religious rites observed by all but a very few. One of the first social functions in which newly born members of the family participated was the sacrament of baptism, which symbolized their entry into society and brought them into the church community. In the cities, church facilities were readily available, but in rural areas families often had to travel some distance to the nearest parish center for the ceremony. The trip was considered of great importance and was willingly undertaken. In fact, baptism was generally considered the most significant religious rite.

If the family lived near a church that had a priest in regular attendance, children received an early exposure to the formal teachings of the church and were usually taken to mass regularly by their mothers. As they grew older, they took an increasing part in church liturgy and by the age of ten were usually full participants in such activities as catechism classes, communion, and confession. As they approached manhood, boys tended to drift away from the church and from conscientious observation of church ritual. Few young men attended services regularly, and even fewer took an active part in the religious life of the community, although they continued to consider themselves Roman Catholics.

Girls, on the other hand, were encouraged to continue their religious devotions and observe the moral tenets of their faith. Women were more involved in the church than men, and the community and clerics accepted this as a basic axiom. There was social pressure on women to become involved in church affairs, and most women, particularly in urban areas, responded. As a rule, they attended mass regularly and took an active part in church and church-sponsored activities. Religious gatherings and observances were among the principal forms of diversion for women outside the home, and to a great extent these activities were social as much as devotional.

POLITCAL AND GOVERNMENT SYSTEM

THE CONSTITUTIONAL FRAMEWORK

In the 1990s Panama was governed under the Constitution of 1972 as amended by the Reform Acts of 1978 and the Constitutional Act of 1983. This was Panama's fourth constitution, previous constitutions having been adopted in 1904, 1941, and 1946. The differences among these constitutions have been matters of emphasis and have reflected the political circumstances existing at the time of their formulation.

The 1904 constitution, in Article 136, gave the United States the right to "intervene in any part of Panama, to reestablish public peace and constitutional order." Reflecting provisions of the Hay-Bunau-Varilla Treaty, this confirmed Panama's status as a de facto protectorate of the United States. Article 136, along with other provisions of the Hay-Bunau-Varilla Treaty, such as that giving the United States the right to add additional territory to the Canal Zone whenever it believed this was necessary for defensive purposes, rankled Panamanian nationalists for more than three decades.

In 1939 the United States abrogated its right of intervention in internal Panamanian affairs with the ratification of the HullAlfaro Treaty. The 1941 constitution, enacted during Arnulfo Arias's first, brief presidential term, not only ended Panama's constitutionally mandated protectorate status, but also reflected the president's peculiar political views. Power was concentrated in the hands of the president whose term, along with that of members of the legislature, was extended from four to six years. Citizenship requirements were added that discriminated against the nation's English-speaking black community and other non-Hispanic minorities.

In October 1941, President Arias was deposed by the National Police (the predecessor of the National Guard and FDP), and the presidency was assumed by Ricardo Adolfo de la Guardia. In 1946 President de la Guardia promulgated a new constitution, which was basically a return to the 1904 document without the offensive Article 136. The 1946 constitution lasted for twenty-six years. Following the 1968 military coup, eleven constitutional guarantees, including freedom of speech, press, and travel, were suspended for several months, and some were not restored fully until after the adoption of the 1972 Constitution. The 1972 Constitution was promulgated by General Torrijos and reflected the dominance of the political system by the general and the military.

Article 277 of the 1972 Constitution designated Torrijos as the "Maximum Leader of the Panamanian Revolution," granting him extraordinary powers for a period of six years, including the power to appoint most government officials and to direct foreign relations. On October 11, 1978, this and other temporary provisions of the

1972 Constitution expired, and a series of amendments, ratified by the Torrijos-controlled National Assembly of Municipal Representatives, became law. These amendments called for a gradual return to democratic political processes between 1978 and 1984 and were designed, in part, to assuage United States concerns over the undemocratic nature of the Panamanian political system.

In 1983 a commission representing various political parties was created to amend further the Constitution in preparation for the 1984 elections. The sixteen-member commission changed nearly half of the Constitution's articles, producing several significant alterations. Article 2 had given the military a special political role, but all mention of this was omitted in the revised draft. The legislature was also revamped. The National Legislative Council was eliminated, and the unwieldy, government-controlled National Assembly of Municipal Representatives, which had 505 representatives, one from each *corregimiento* (municipal subdistrict), became the Legislative Assembly, with 67 members apportioned on the basis of population and directly elected. The independence of the judiciary and the Electoral Tribunal were strengthened, the term of the president was reduced to five years, and two vice presidents were to be elected. Guarantees of civil liberties were strengthened, and official support for candidates in elections was, at least in theory, severely restricted.

The amended Constitution contains 312 articles. Power emanates from the people and is exercised by the three branches of government, each of which is "limited and separate," but all of which, in theory, work together in "harmonious collaboration." The national territory is defined as "the land area, the territorial sea, the submarine continental shelf, the subsoil, and air space between Costa Rica and Colombia." Any ceding, leasing, or other alienation of this territory to any other state is expressly forbidden. Spanish is the country's national language.

Citizenship may be acquired by birth or naturalization. Articles 17 through 50 guarantee a broad range of individual rights, including property rights, but Article 51 gives the president power to suspend many of these by declaring a "state of emergency." Articles 52 through 124 establish the role of the state in protecting the family, regulating labor conditions, promoting education and culture, providing assistance for health and other areas of social security, promoting agriculture, and protecting the environment.

After the elaboration of the composition, powers, and duties of the various organs of the governmental system, the Constitution ends with descriptions of the state's responsibilities with respect to the national economy, public administration, and national security. Engaging in economic activities, for example, is primarily the function of private individuals, but the state will "orient, direct, regulate, replace, or create according to social necessities . . . with the object of increasing national wealth and to ensure its benefits for the largest possible number of the nation's inhabitants." Article 308 provides for amending the Constitution, either through approval of amendments without modification by an absolute majority of two successive elected assemblies or approval with modifications by two assemblies and subsequent ratification of the modified text by a national referendum.

Panama's successive constitutions have been respected in varying degrees by the republic's governments. Since the 1968 coup, opponents of various governments have accused them of violating the spirit and, at times, the letter of the Constitution and of invoking the state of emergency provisions for purely political purposes. Creating public confidence in the rule of law established by the Constitution presented the government with one of its major challenges in the late 1980s.

THE GOVERNMENTAL SYSTEM

THE EXECUTIVE

President of Panama: Mireya Elisa Moscoso Rodríguez

As is the case throughout most of Latin America, constitutional power in Panama-although distributed among three branches of government-is concentrated in the executive branch. The 1978 and 1983 amendments to the Constitution decreased the powers of the executive and increased those of the legislature, but the executive branch of government remains the dominant power in the governmental system as defined by the Constitution.

The executive organ is headed by the president and two vice presidents. They, together with the twelve ministers of state, make up the Cabinet Council, which is given several important powers, including decreeing a state of emergency and suspending constitutional guarantees, nominating members of the Supreme

Court, and overseeing national finances, including the national debt. These officials, together with the FDP commander, attorney general, solicitor general, president of the Legislative Assembly, directors general of various autonomous and semiautonomous state agencies, and president of the provincial councils, make up the General Council of State, which has purely advisory functions.

The president and the two vice presidents, who must be native born Panamanians and at least thirty-five years of age, are elected to five-year terms by direct popular vote. Candidates may not be related directly to the incumbent president or have served as president or vice president during the two preceding terms. Should the president resign or be otherwise removed from office, as was the case with President Ardito Barletta in 1985, he was replaced by the first vice president, and there was no provision for filling the vacancy thus created in the vice presidential ranks.

Under the Constitution, the president has the exclusive right to appoint or remove ministers of state, maintain public order, appoint one of the three members of the Electoral Tribunal, conduct foreign relations, and veto laws passed by the Legislative Assembly. In theory a veto may be overridden by a two-thirds majority vote of the assembly. In addition, many powers are exercised by the president jointly with the appropriate individual cabinet member, including appointing the FDP high command, appointing and removing provincial governors, preparing the budget, negotiating contracts for public works, appointing officials to the various autonomous and semiautonomous state agencies, and granting pardons. The president's power to appoint and remove cabinet members would seem to make the requirement for operating with the consent of the cabinet largely a formality, but the FDP and its allies in the PRD frequently have dictated the composition of the cabinet, using this as a means to exercise control over the president.

The two vice presidencies are relatively powerless positions, but since three vice presidents have succeeded to the presidency during the 1980s, the posts are not insignificant. The first vice president acts as chief executive in the absence of the president, and both have votes in the Cabinet Council.

The ministers of state include the ministers of agriculture, commerce and industries, education, finance, foreign relations, government and justice, health, housing, labor and social welfare, planning and economic policy, presidency, and the public works. There is no ministry directly representing or having jurisdiction over the FDP. Nevertheless, the minister of government and justice has nominal authority over the FDP's police functions, along with control over prisons, civil aviation, and internal communications, making this one of the most powerful cabinet posts. This ministry also supervises local government in the Comarca de San Blas as well as in the nine provinces, thus exerting central government control over local affairs.

THE LEGISLATURE

The 1983 amendments to Panama's Constitution created a new legislative organ, the Legislative Assembly, a unicameral body with sixty-seven members, each of whom has an alternate. Members and alternates are elected for five-year terms that run concurrently with those of the president and vice presidents. To be eligible for election, an individual must be at least twenty-one years of age and be a Panamanian citizen either by birth or by naturalization with fifteen years of residence in Panama subsequent to naturalization. The legislature holds two four-month sessions each year and may also be called into special session by the president.

In theory, the assembly has extensive powers. It can create, modify, or repeal laws, ratify treaties, declare war, decree amnesty for political offenses, establish the national currency, raise taxes, ratify government contracts, approve the national budget, and impeach members of the executive or judicial branches. There are, however, significant limitations on these powers, both in law and in practice. Members are nominated for election by parties, and the parties may revoke their status as legislators. This gives the official government party, the PRD, and its allies the power to ensure conformity with government policy and prevent defections from its ranks. Moreover, there are no provisions for legislative control over the military. The legislature also is severely limited in its ability to control the budget. Under Article 268 of the Constitution, the assembly is prohibited from adding to the budget submitted by the executive without the approval of the Cabinet Council. It may not repeal taxes included in the budget unless, at the same time, it creates new taxes to make up any revenue lost.

Differences in practice are also important. Since its creation, the assembly has never rejected an executive nomination for a government post, refused to ratify a treaty, or turned down an executive request for grants of extraordinary powers or for the establishment or prolongation of a state of emergency. The opposition, which held twenty-two seats in late 1980s, has used the assembly as a forum to attack government policies and to criticize the role played in the administration by the FDP, but it has been unable to block or even seriously delay any government project. Assembly debates normally are broadcast live, but during the disturbances of June 1987, speeches by opposition members frequently were not carried on the radio.

The lack of institutional independence also has inhibited the development of local or special interest representation within the assembly. The tight control over the selection of candidates and their subsequent performance as legislators by their respective parties works against such representation, as does the dominance of the executive branch. This control is further strengthened by the fact that elections are held only every five years and occur in conjunction with presidential elections.

Should political conditions change in Panama and the dominant role of the military be significantly reduced, the Legislative Assembly has the potential to emerge as a significant participant in the national political process, but its powers would still be less extensive than those exercised by the executive branch. Under the circumstances existing in late 1987, it lacked both the power and the will to block, or even significantly modify, government projects and served largely as a public debating forum for government supporters and opponents.

THE JUDICIARY

The Constitution establishes the Supreme Court as the highest judicial body in the land. Judges must be Panamanian by birth, be at least thirty-five years of age, hold a university degree in law, and have practiced or taught law for at least ten years. The number of members of the court is not fixed by the Constitution. In the early 1990s, there were nine justices, divided into three chambers, for civil, penal, and administrative cases, with three justices in each chamber. Judges (and their alternates) are nominated by the Cabinet Council and subject to confirmation by the Legislative Assembly. They serve for a term of ten years. Article 200 of the Constitution provides for the replacement of two judges every two years. The court also selects its own president every two years.

The Constitution defines the Supreme Court as the guardian of "the integrity of the Constitution." In consultation with the attorney general, it has the power to determine the constitutionality of all laws, decrees, agreements, and other governmental acts. The court also has jurisdiction over cases involving actions or failure to act by public officials at all levels. There are no appeals from decisions by the court.

Other legislation defines the system of lower courts. The nation is divided into three judicial districts: the first encompasses the provinces of Panamá, Colón, and Darién; the second, Veraguas, Los Santos, Herrera, and Coclé; the third, Bocas del Toro and Chiriquí. Directly under the Supreme Court are four superior tribunals, two for the first judicial district and one each for the second and third districts. Within each province there are two circuit courts, one for civil and one for criminal cases. The lowest regular courts are the municipal courts located in each of the nation's sixty-five municipal subdivisions. In the tribunals, the judges are nominated by the Supreme Court, while lower judges are appointed by the courts immediately above them.

The Constitution also creates a Public Ministry, headed by the attorney general, who is assisted by the solicitor general, the district and municipal attorneys, and other officials designated by law. The attorney general and the solicitor general are appointed in the same way as Supreme Court justices, but serve for no fixed term. Lower-ranking officials are appointed by those immediately above them. The functions of the Public Ministry include supervising the conduct of public officials, serving as legal advisers to other government officials, prosecuting violations of the Constitution and other laws, and arraigning before the Supreme Court officials over whom the Court "has jurisdiction." This provision pointedly excludes members of the FDP.

Several constitutional provisions are designed to protect the independence of the judiciary. These include articles that declare that "magistrates and judges are independent in the exercise of their functions and are subject only to the Constitution and the law;" that "positions in the Judicial Organ are incompatible with any participation in politics other than voting;" that judges cannot be detained or arrested except with a "written order by the judicial authority competent to judge them;" that the Supreme Court and the attorney general control the preparation of the budget for the judicial organ; and that judges "cannot be removed, suspended, or transferred from the exercise of their functions except in cases and according to the procedures prescribed by law."

The major defect in the judicial system lies in the manner in which appointments are made to the judiciary. Appointments of judges and of the attorney general are subject to the approval of the Legislative Assembly, but that body has functioned as a rubber stamp for candidates selected by the executive. Lower-level appointments, made by superiors within the judicial organ, are not subject to assembly approval. In addition, the first two Supreme Court justices appointed after the 1984 elections were both former attorneys general, closely associated with the government and even involved in some of its most controversial actions, such as the investigation of the murder of opposition leader Spadafora. As a result, the opposition has denounced regularly the judicial system for being a political organ controlled by the FDP and the PRD. Numerous external observers, including the Inter-American Commission on Human Rights of the Organization of American States (OAS), the United States Department of State, and various human rights organizations, also have criticized the lack of independence of the Panamanian judiciary and of the Public Ministry.

PROVINCIAL AND MUNICIPAL GOVERNMENT

The nine provincial governments are little more than administrative subdivisions of the central government. Article 249 of the Constitution states that "in each province there shall be a Governor freely appointed and removed by the Executive who shall be the agent and representative of the President within his jurisdiction." In addition, each province has a body known as the Provincial Council, composed of district (*corregimiento*) representatives. The governor, mayors, and additional individuals "as determined by the law" also take part in each council, but without voting rights. The powers of these councils are largely advisory, and they lack actual legislative responsibility. The Comarca de San Blas, inhabited largely by Cuna Indians, has a distinct form of local government headed by caciques, or tribal leaders.

In contrast, the nation's sixty-five municipal governments are "autonomous political organizations." Although closely tied to the national government, municipal officials, under Article 232 of the Constitution, may not be removed from office by the national administration. In each municipality, the mayor, the director of municipal administration, and their substitutes (*suplentes*) are directly elected for five-year terms. There is, however, an additional constitutional provision that the Legislative Assembly may pass laws requiring that officials in some or all municipalities are to be appointed by the president rather than elected.

Municipalities are divided further into districts, from each of which a representative is elected to the Municipal Council. Should a town have fewer than five districts, five council members are chosen in at-large elections. These districts, in turn, have their own form of local government, headed by a *corregidor*, and including a *junta communal* made up of the *corregidor*, the district's representative to the Municipal Council, and five other residents "selected in the form determined by law."

The major concern of municipal and district officials is the collection and expenditure of local revenues. These local politicians have some control over public works, business licenses, and other forms of local regulations and improvements, but many functions that fall within the jurisdiction of local governments in other nations, such as educational, judicial, and police administration, are left exclusively to the jurisdiction of the central government. Local administrations do contribute to the cost of schools, but the amount of their contribution is determined at the national level, based on their population and their state of economic and social development.

ADMINISTRATION OF JUSTICE

For the first several years of its existence, Panama depended on the legal code inherited from Colombia. The first Panamanian codes, promulgated in 1917, were patterned on those of Colombia and other Latin American states that had earlier broken away from the Spanish Empire; therefore, Panama's legal heritage was based on Roman law as passed on through Spain and its colonies. Nevertheless, several features of Anglo-American law have also been accepted in Panama. Habeas corpus, a feature of Anglo-American legal procedure that is not found in many Latin American codes, has been constitutionally guaranteed in Panama. Judicial precedent, another Anglo-American practice, has also made some headway; however, judges and magistrates usually have had little leeway in matters of procedure, delays, and degrees of guilt.

The Public Ministry provided for in the Constitution has defended the interest of the state; fostered the enforcement and execution of laws, judicial decisions, and administrative orders; supervised the official conduct and the performance of duty of public officials; prosecuted offenses of constitutional or legal provisions; and served as legal adviser to administrative officials. The functions of the Public Ministry were fulfilled by the attorney general of the republic, the solicitor general, the district attorneys, and the municipal attorneys. There were two alternates for each official of the ministry; all were appointive positions. The attorney general, the solicitor general, and their alternates were executive appointees; district attorneys and municipal attorneys were appointed by their immediate superiors in the judicial system. They in turn appointed subordinate personnel in their own offices.

In addition to the stipulations of "free, prompt, and uninterrupted" administration of justice and the establishment of the Public Ministry, the Constitution has several other statements about the application of laws, the treatment of citizens under the law, and the handling of prisoners. Article 21 guarantees freedom from arbitrary arrest, and Article 22 provides for habeas corpus. Article 29 prohibits the death penalty. Article 42 provides that "In criminal matters, a law favorable to the accused always has priority and retroactivity, even though the judgement may have become final." Article 163 gives the president power to grant pardons for political offenses, to reduce sentences, and to grant parole. Article 187 states that a person convicted of an offense against public order may not hold any judicial office in the future. Article 197 establishes trial by jury.

Under a section of the Constitution headed "Individual and Social Rights and Duties," private citizens are assured that they can be prosecuted by government authorities only for violations of the Constitution or the law. The procedure for arrests is also described, stating that arrests may result from response to complaints made to the police or from direct action on the part of police or DENI agents at the scene of the crime or disturbance. The validity of citizen's arrest is recognized: "An offender surprised may be apprehended by any person and must be delivered immediately to the authorities." No person may be held for more than twenty-four hours by the police without being brought before competent authority. The Constitution forbids arrest or detention for violation of purely civil obligations or for debts.

During the course of an investigation, the accused and all witnesses are questioned, the latter under oath. The Constitution guarantees that no accused person may be forced to incriminate himself or herself, and the authorities are forbidden to force testimony from any close relative, whether related by blood or marriage, that is, "within the fourth degree of consanguinity or the second degree of affinity." Investigators may enter a person's home only with consent or a written order (search warrant) from a competent authority or to assist victims of crime or natural disaster. In general, all testimony must be presented in written form and be signed by investigators, accused, and witnesses. If a case warrants prosecution, it is referred to the appropriate court. Although bail is permissible in some cases, it is a privilege subject to many restrictions and may be denied at the request of the prosecutor if a judge concurrs.

FOREIGN RELATIONS

Panama is a member of the UN General Assembly, most major UN agencies, and has served three terms as a member of the UN Security Council. It maintains membership in several international financial institutions, including the World Bank, the Inter-American Development Bank, and the International Monetary Fund.

Panama is a member of the Organization of American States, and was a founding member of the Rio Group. Although it was suspended from the Latin American Economic System (known informally both as the Group of Eight and the Rio Group) in 1988 due to its internal political system under Noriega, Panama was readmitted in September 1994 as an acknowledgment of its present democratic credentials.

Panama also is one of the founding members of the Union of Banana Exporting Countries and belongs to the Inter-American Tropical Tuna Commission. Panama is an active participant in Central American regional meetings, although it is not a formal participant in integration activities. Panama is a member of the Central American Parliament (PARLACEN) as well as the Central American Integration System (SICA). Panama joined its six Central American neighbors at the 1994 Summit of the Americas in signing the Alliance for Sustainable Development known as the Conjunta Centroamerica-USA or CONCAUSA to promote sustainable economic development in the region and participates in some Miami summit follow-on meetings.

Panama strongly backed efforts by the United States to implement UN Security Council Resolution 940, which was designed to facilitate the departure of Haiti's de facto authorities from power. Panama offered to contribute personnel to the Multinational Force, which restored the democratically elected government to Haiti in October 1994, and granted asylum to some former Haitian military leaders. Also in 1994, Panama agreed to accept 9,000 Cuban "rafters," who were housed temporarily on U.S. military range areas until 1995.

U.S.-PANAMANIAN RELATIONS

The Panama Canal Treaties provided the foundation for an enduring partnership. The U.S. and Panama implemented the treaties by preparing for the transfer to Panama of the Canal and the U.S. base properties. Headquarters of the U.S. Southern Command transferred to Miami in 1997. U.S. development assistance through USAID in FY 1997 was $3 million. Panama does not have a military;

therefore, the United States provides no bilateral military assistance to the country. However, civic action projects, direct, and indirect military spending pump several $100 million annually into the Panamanian economy.

The United States cooperates with the Panamanian Government in promoting economic, political, and social development through U.S. and international agencies. Cultural ties between the two countries are strong, and many Panamanians come to the United States for higher education and advanced training. About 6,000 Americans reside in Panama, most of whom are retirees from the Panama Canal Commission and individuals who hold dual nationality. The number of U.S. visitors to Panama from July 1995 to June 1996 averaged around 3,600.

Panama continues to fight against illegal narcotics. The country's proximity to major cocaine-producing nations and its role as a commercial and financial crossroads make it a country of special importance in this regard. Although money laundering remains a problem, a new banking law of 1998 [should help--**helps**?] combat this crime. Panama has worked closely with the U.S. Treasury Department's Financial Crimes Enforcement Network.

THE PANAMA CANAL TREATIES

The 1977 Panama Canal Treaties entered into force on October 1, 1979. They replaced the 1903 Hay/Bunau-Varilla Treaty between the United States and Panama, and all other U.S.-Panama agreements concerning the Panama Canal which were in force on that date. The treaties comprise:

- A basic treaty governing the operation and defense of the Canal from October 1, 1979, to December 31, 1999 (Panama Canal Treaty); and
- A treaty guaranteeing the permanent neutrality of the Canal (Neutrality Treaty). The details of the arrangements for U.S. operation and defense of the Canal under the Panama Canal Treaty are spelled out in separate implementing agreements.

PURPOSE OF THE TREATIES

In negotiating the Panama Canal Treaties, four successive U.S. administrations acted to protect a fundamental national interest in long-term access to a secure and efficient Canal. Panama's cooperation is fundamental to this objective. By meeting Panamanian aspirations for eventual control of the Canal, the United States sought a new relationship with Panama based on friendship and mutual respect. The treaties make Panama a partner in the continued safe and efficient operation of the Canal. In serving the best interests of both nations, the treaties serve the interests of all users of the Canal.

HISTORY OF THE NEGOTIATIONS

Our bilateral relationship with Panama has centered on the Panama Canal since the beginning of the century. Under the 1903 treaty, the United States acquired unilateral rights to build and operate a canal in perpetuity. It also acquired the Canal Zone--a 553-square mile area in which the United States exercised the rights, power, and authority of a sovereign state. In January 1964, Panamanian dissatisfaction with this relationship boiled over into riots that resulted in the deaths of four U.S. Marines and more than 20 Panamanians. A 3-month suspension of diplomatic relations followed.

The growing bilateral tension in the 1960s gave weight to the views of those who believed that a new Canal Treaty was needed to replace the 1903 treaty and to establish a new relationship with Panama. In June 1967, United States and Panamanian negotiators completed draft treaties dealing with the existing Canal, a possible sea-level Canal through Panama, and defense matters. Neither country ratified the treaties, however, and they were publicly rejected by the new Torrijos government in 1970.

A resumption of treaty negotiations led to a declaration of principles signed in 1973 by Secretary of State Henry Kissinger and his Panamanian counterpart, Juan Antonio Tack. On September 7, 1977, President Carter and General Torrijos signed the Panama Canal Treaties at the headquarters of the Organization of American States in Washington, DC. The Panamanian people approved the new treaties in a plebiscite held on October 23, 1977. The U.S. Senate ratified the Neutrality Treaty on March 16, 1978, and the Panama Canal Treaty on April 18, 1978. The treaties entered into force on October 1, 1979. The protocol to the Neutrality Treaty is open to accession by all nations, and more than 35 have subscribed.

BASIC PROVISIONS OF THE TREATIES

The United States had primary responsibility for the operation and defense of the Canal until December 31, 1999. After that date, the United States and Panama will maintain a regime of neutrality for the Canal, including nondiscriminatory access and tolls for merchant and naval vessels of all nations. A U.S. Senate condition attached to the instruments of ratification allows the U.S. and Panama to negotiate a post-1999 defense-sites treaty, if both countries find such a treaty in their mutual interest. Negotiations for a possible post-1999 U.S. presence in Panama in a proposed multinational counter-narcotics center (MCC) ended in September 1998, and no further negotiations are planned.

In order to meet its treaty responsibilities, the United States has the right to use specified land and water areas and facilities in Panama necessary for the operation, maintenance, and defense of the Canal until December 31, 1999.

After that date, U.S. warships will be entitled to expeditious passage through the Canal at all times, and the United States will continue to have the obligation to ensure that the Canal remains open and secure.

The United States operated the Canal through the Panama Canal Commission (PCC), which was a U.S. Government agency supervised by a Board of Directors consisting of five American and four Panamanian members, appointed by the President (the Panamanian members are initially nominated by their government). Until 1990, the Canal Administrator was an American, and the Deputy Administrator was Panamanian; these nationalities reversed for the final decade of the treaty on September 20, 1990, when Gilberto Guardia was installed as the first Panamanian Administrator.

He was succeeded in 1996 by another Panamanian, Alberto Aleman Zubieta. Pursuant to treaty obligations, the PCC trained Panamanians in all areas of Canal operations prior to the transfer of the Canal in 1999. In 1997 President Perez Balladares named the members of the Panama Canal Authority (PCA), the successor agency to the PCC.

During the life of the treaty, Panama received the following payments from Canal revenues:

- A fixed annual payment of $10 million;
- An annual payment of $10 million, adjustable for inflation, for public services provided to Canal operating areas by the Government of Panama (the Canal Zone and its government ceased to exist when the treaties entered into force, and Panama assumed jurisdiction over Canal Zone territories and functions);
- An annual percentage of toll revenues assessed at $0.39 (since October 1, 1996) per Panama Canal net ton transiting the Canal, worth $84.6 million in 1996; and
- A payment of up to $10 million in the event that revenues exceed PCC expenditures in a given year.

Under U.S. implementing legislation (the Panama Canal Act), the PCC was required to be self-sustaining; its costs could not exceed its revenues, nor could U.S. taxpayer funds be used for Canal operations or payments to Panama.

DEMOCRACY AND HUMAN RIGHTS[2]

BESIC SITUTATION

Panama is a representative democracy with an elected executive composed of a president and two vice presidents, an elected 71-member legislature, and an appointed judiciary. In May voters elected President Mireya Moscoso, who replaced former President Ernesto Perez Balladares on September 1. Although the Constitution provides for an independent judiciary, the judicial system is subject to corruption and political manipulation.

Panama has had no military forces since 1989. In 1990 the Government created the Panamanian Public Forces, which consist of the Panamanian National Police (PNP), the National Maritime Service (SMN), the National Air Service (SAN), and the Institutional Protection Service (SPI). In 1994 a constitutional amendment formally prohibited the establishment of a permanent military, although it contains a provision for the temporary formation of a " special police force " to protect the borders in case of a " threat of external aggression. " The Ministry of Government and Justice oversees the PNP, SMN, and SAN, while the Ministry of the Presidency supervises the SPI. The PNP are responsible for law enforcement. The Judicial Technical Police (PTJ) perform criminal investigations in support of public prosecutors. The PTJ is a semiautonomous body with leadership appointed by the Supreme Court. Police forces respond to civilian authority, have civilian directors, and have internal review procedures to deal with police misconduct. There were reports of instances of abuse by some members of the security forces.

The service-oriented economy uses the U.S. dollar as currency, calling it the Balboa. Gross domestic product grew by 4.6 percent in 1998, but growth for 1999 was projected to be below 4 percent. The Ministry of Economy and Finance expects modestly higher growth in 2000 as the effects of economic liberalization and the Panama Canal transfer become evident. Poverty persists and income distribution remains extremely skewed, with large disparities between rich and poor. Unemployment is estimated at 13 percent.

The Government generally respected the human rights of its citizens; however, there continued to be serious problems in several areas. Police and prison guards on occasion used excessive force against detainees and prisoners, and on occasion police used force against protesters. Credible reports of corruption within both the PNP and PTJ contributed to some police dismissals. Despite

[2] Bureau of Democracy, Human Rights, and Labor U.S. Department of State

some modest improvements, overall prison conditions remained harsh, with occasional outbreaks of internal prison violence. Prisoners were subject to arbitrary and prolonged pretrial detention. The judiciary was subject to political manipulation, and the criminal justice system was inefficient and often corrupt. The Government began implementation of a $27 million program to reduce case backlogs, inefficiency, and corruption in the judiciary. There were instances of illegal searches and political pressure on the media. Violence against women remained a serious problem, and discrimination against women persisted. Discrimination against indigenous people and blacks is a problem. Child labor also is a problem. Worker rights were limited in export processing zones. Trafficking in persons, particularly Asian immigrants, also was a problem.

RESPECT FOR HUMAN RIGHTS

RESPECT FOR THE INTEGRITY OF THE PERSON

A. POLITICAL AND OTHER EXTRAJUDICIAL KILLING

There were no reports of political or other extrajudicial killings.

A Public Ministry investigation concluded in August 1998 that three PNP guards accused of the March 1997 beating death of detainee Jose Luis Alvarado at the Tinajitas prison should stand trial. The guards remain separated from the PNP pending the outcome of the trial, but as of year's end there had been no further action in this case.

There was no further action in the PNP investigation into the June 1997 shooting death of Ngobe-Bugle tribe member Juan Santos Chobra.

In September President Moscoso rescinded pardons granted by former President Perez Balladares for 33 former civilian and military collaborators of former ruler General Manuel Noriega, in order to allow the Government to continue prosecutions of officials for abuses committed during the dictatorship--from 1968 to 1989. One such official reportedly was involved in the execution of nine persons following a failed coup attempt against Noriega in 1989.

In September the authorities discovered an unmarked grave containing two bodies on the grounds of a former military base near Panama City. One of the bodies was believed to be that of Hector Gallego, a Colombian priest who disappeared in 1971 during the Torrijos dictatorship. In 1992 after the return of civilian rule, three former military officers were tried for his murder and given lengthy prison sentences. There was also speculation that the other body was that of Eber Quintanar, an accused guerrilla reportedly killed by the National Guard in 1969. After several DNA tests, investigators determined that the remains belonged to neither Gallego nor Quintanar. As of year's end, the identity of the corpses was still unknown. During the investigation, longstanding rumors of other gravesites scattered around the country reemerged in the press. Investigators initiated excavations at several sites but did not achieve any results by year's end.

B. Disappearance

There were no reports of politically motivated disappearances.

Guerrillas from the Revolutionary Armed Forces of Colombia (FARC) reportedly kidnaped persons in the Darien region along the border with Colombia. At year's end, they had abducted three persons and held them for ransom; there were reports that the FARC harassed citizens and even killed some persons, but there were no confirmed killings.

The Hector Gallego Committee for Disappeared Relatives maintains a list of 120 people who disappeared during the military dictatorships of 1968-89.

C. Torture and Other Cruel, Inhuman, or Degrading Treatment or Punishment

The Constitution prohibits the use of measures that could harm the physical, mental, or moral integrity of prisoners or detainees; however, while the public security forces generally performed in a professional and restrained manner, there were some reports of excessive use of force or inhuman punishment, particularly against prison inmates. There also were reports that police used physical violence and psychological threats to control detainees during the initial arrest, interrogation, and holding phases.

The legislation providing the legal basis for the PNP, promulgated in June 1997, includes specific guidelines for use of force, including deadly force; requires that police officers respect human rights; and prohibits instigation or tolerance of torture, cruelty, or other inhuman or degrading behavior. However, there is no follow-on training in the use of force provided to the PNP.

The PTJ and the PNP have offices of professional responsibility that act as internal affairs organs to hold officers accountable for their actions. Both have staffs of independent investigators as well as administrative authority to open internal investigations. In both organizations, a defined legal process is followed where, upon completion of the process, the respective director has the final authority to determine the disposition of each case. Penalties include reduction in rank, dismissal, and in severe cases, criminal prosecution. The PNP deputy director and secretary general address human rights issues that arise in the police force.

Corruption among police officers remained a problem, but in some cases, PNP and PTJ directors enforced disciplinary measures against officers shown to be involved in illicit activities. However, both organizations only react to egregious abuses, due to a lack of staff, independence, and institutional priority. Credible reports of corruption within both the PNP and PTJ contributed to some police dismissals.

According to residents of the Pueblo Nuevo neighborhood, in March police shot a minor who was lying on the ground in handcuffs. The authorities placed a sergeant and three officers on administrative duty while the PNP's Office of Professional Responsibility investigated, and sent the case to the PNP's disciplinary committee. At year's end, the investigation continued, and the officers remained on administrative duty.

In April the Office of Professional Responsibility stated that it was investigating 50 police officers for poor conduct, including the use of excessive force and violations of citizens' human rights. In addition to the Pueblo Nuevo shooting, the office sent the case of an alleged police attack on two sisters in San Miguelito to the Disciplinary Committee of the PNP.

There were several instances in which police responded with force to demonstrations. For example, in February and in August the police used tear gas and bird shot to disperse protesters (see Section 2.b.).

Police arrested and detained children for minor infractions during neighborhood sweeps (see Section 5).

The FARC guerrillas and the paramilitary forces of the United Self-Defense Forces of Colombia (AUC) share a long history of spillover of violence from Colombia into the border area on the Darien peninsula, including killings, kidnaping, robbery, and other forms of harassment of innocent bystanders. In November the AUC reportedly forced the evacuation of the San Blas town of La Bonga and burned it to the ground.

Prison conditions throughout the country remained harsh and a threat to prisoners' health and safety. Most prisons are dilapidated and overcrowded. Medical screening and care is inadequate, with tuberculosis and other communicable diseases common among the prison population. Frequent gang battles injured or killed numerous inmates. Many of the problems within the prisons stem not only from overcrowding but also from the lack of separation of inmates by classification according to the type or severity of the crime committed. Gang violence, insufficient budgets, and abuse by prison guards also are problems of the prison system.

The General Penitentiary Directorate (DGSP) largely depends on PNP officers, who are trained inadequately for prison duty, to supply its guard force. Civilian corrections officers or " custodians " handle inmates within La Joya, El Renacer, and the central women's prison (which uses only female guards). The DGSP has authority to discipline prison guards with criminal or civil sanctions.

President Perez Balladares' Minister of Government and Justice attempted to introduce some reforms of the penal system. He changed the prison management structure in June and replaced the Department of Corrections with the DGSP, but substantive reform was lacking. In September President Moscoso's Minister of Government and Justice, Winston Spadafora, promised to make prison reform a top priority. PNP Director Carlos Bares also promised reform, stating in September that prison guard responsibilities should fall to civilian corrections officers and not the PNP. However, at year's end, PNP members continued to provide perimeter security at the prisons. Prison directors supervise " custodians " who provide internal security.

Prison conditions on Coiba Island Penal Colony remained harsh and dangerous. In January 1998, a prison gang reportedly beheaded four of five prison escapees who belonged to a rival gang. The authorities accused 14 prisoners of participating in the killings, but these prisoners continued to maintain their innocence. The lone survivor and witness is in a maximum security cell. Both guards and prisoners have been implicated in the investigation into the other eight murders discovered in 1998, but the authorities had brought no one to trial by year's end. Although national prison authorities had planned to close Coiba, they continued to use the island prison colony to relieve overcrowding at the two largest prisons, La Joya and La Joyita. Prison officials also had attempted to establish order in the other prisons by moving dangerous prisoners to Coiba. However, after completion of two new compounds, La Joya became the primary maximum security facility and houses most prisoners accused of serious crimes. This enabled the authorities to use Coiba to hold prisoners accused of lesser crimes and to relieve overcrowding in the prisons of the central provinces (i.e., outside Panama City and Colon). The Government acknowledges that it must keep Coiba open, but it has not made adequate provisions for health, security, and other basic needs of prisoners there.

The authorities have not yet brought to trial many of the 361 prisoners on Coiba Island. Geographic isolation and lack of communications separated detainees from their attorneys and caused many to miss trials. Prisoners suffer from malnutrition and shortages of potable water, and medical care is practically nonexistent. Coiba has a civilian administrator, but its guard force still consists of police guards instead of civilian corrections officers. Escapes from Coiba reportedly are common.

According to unverified press reports, eight inmates at Coiba have AIDS. The prisoners told reporters that they are isolated in small cells and that medical attention is provided once a year. At La Joya prison, 22 inmates with AIDS went on a hunger strike in June to protest their lack of access to medical treatment and their need for special permits to receive medicine. La Joya has a planned capacity of 1,250, yet houses over 2,000 inmates.

Prison conditions in Colon province also are harsh. According to the Human Rights Commission of the Legislative Assembly, prisoners at the Women's Prison of Colon must contend with overcrowding, semidarkness day and night, constantly wet floors, and virtually no health care. The Commission also described the Public Prison of Colon as a " time bomb, " which fails to provide the most basic health needs. The prison frequently has no running water or functioning sewage system. In June approximately 150 inmates at the Colon women's prison refused to return to their cells in order to force a dialog with the Corrections Director and Minister of Government and Justice. The inmates complained about the food, the failure to release inmates who had served two-thirds of their sentences with good behavior, the lack of rehabilitation or skills programs, and the sudden absence of Prison Director Cristina Torres. Then-Corrections Director Maritza Grifo acknowledged the overcrowding problem; 576 inmates were housed in a facility for 325 persons, and 61 persons eligible for conditional release still were incarcerated. The inmates' protest ended without violence after officials promised to investigate the complaints. As of year's end, there had been no substantive reform of the prison.

Conditions at women's prisons in Panama City and Chiriqui province and at the Juvenile Detention Center were noticeably better than at adult male prisons. However, female prisoners, especially those in the primary detention area, reportedly suffered from overcrowding, poor medical care, and lack of basic supplies for personal hygiene. Juvenile Detention Centers throughout the country suffer from inadequate resources to provide for education or adequate supervision of children, many of whom spend a majority of their time in an empty cell.

The current prison system has over 8,600 prisoners with only 6,843 allotted positions. Prison administrators plan to close both the Colon Women's Prison and the Public Prison of Colon and shift those inmates to Nueva Esperanza prison. The new inmates are to be housed in separate sections of Nueva Esperanza, where construction was quite advanced at year's end, with some of the new cells already outfitted with bunks and toilets. However, inmates from the rapidly deteriorating Public Prison reportedly were apprehensive about being moved to Nueva Esperanza, where their access to the outdoors will be limited.

In July 1998, the authorities introduced organizational reforms of the prison system, including a conditional release program for inmates charged with minor offenses who have served a substantial part of their sentence. The new government continued to implement the conditional release program, and released some 60 inmates by year's end, with new rounds expected for early 2000. The release program has already helped relieve pressure on the country's overcrowded prisons. In June former National Penitentiary Director Enriqueta Davis filed an 80-page criminal complaint against then-Minister of Government and Justice Mariela Sagel. The complaint alleged that Sagel knew about prisoners buying furloughs, funds being mismanaged, and other abuses, yet refused to take action. Davis attributed other problems to the lack of modern administrative procedures. For example, because records are kept manually at each location, there is no central archive or census of inmates. The National Council for Private Enterprise (CONEP) publicly asked then-President Perez Balladares to look into Davis's allegations. CONEP expressed concern over the disappearance of materials and food that were destined for the penitentiary system. Several other reports of corruption and misallocation of prison resources appeared in the media throughout the year.

The Government generally allows prison visits by independent human rights monitors. However, the authorities arrange appointments ahead of time, and monitors generally speak to prisoners in the presence of guards or administrators. Prisoners may not feel comfortable speaking freely under such conditions, and they have expressed fear of retaliation if they complain. Officials from the Ombudsman's Office occasionally had trouble gaining immediate access to some prisons, but various procedural details were worked out and it appeared that the situation had improved by year's end.

D. ARBITRARY ARREST, DETENTION, OR EXILE

The Constitution stipulates that arrests must be carried out with a warrant issued by the appropriate authorities, and the Government generally respected this provision; however, the authorities often violated the provision that suspects are to be brought promptly before a judge. Exceptions are permitted when an officer apprehends a person during the commission of a crime, or when disrespect by an individual towards an officer prevents the officer from carrying out his duty. The law requires the arresting officer to inform the detainee immediately of the reasons for arrest or detention and of the right to immediate legal counsel, to be provided to the indigent by the State.

The Constitution also provides for judicial review of the legality of detention and mandates the immediate release of any person detained or arrested illegally. The Constitution prohibits police from detaining suspects for more than 24 hours without bringing them before a competent judicial authority. In practice, the authorities often violated the 24-hour time limit by several days. Under law the preliminary investigation phase may last 8 days to 2 months, and the follow-on investigation phase another 2 to 4 months, depending on the number of suspects. The courts frequently grant extensions of these limits, leaving the accused in detention for a long period without having been charged formally.

Extended pretrial detention continued to be one of the most serious human rights problems, in part a consequence of the elaborate notification phase in criminal cases. Many legal authorities (including court officials) criticized judges for excessive use of this measure. According to government statistics, there were 4,687 pretrial detainees, who constituted about 59 percent of the prison population, down from 65 percent in 1998. The average period of pretrial custody was 16 months, and pretrial detention in excess of the maximum sentence for the alleged crime was common. A legal mechanism exists to hold the Government financially accountable in cases where a detainee spends more than 1 year in jail but subsequently has all charges dismissed at a preliminary hearing. The dismissal must be either because the act of which the detainee was accused is not ruled a crime or because there is no evidence to link the suspect to the crime. Although this redress procedure is not complicated, few former detainees have employed it.

Legal alternatives to prison exist but are not widely implemented. Options such as house arrest have been used in some cases involving the elderly or minors, but require that the defendants have access to and understanding of their legal options.

The Constitution prohibits exile; there were no reports of forced exile.

E. DENIAL OF FAIR PUBLIC TRIAL

The Constitution provides for an independent judiciary; however, the judiciary is susceptible to corruption and outside influence, including from other branches of government.

The President appoints nine Supreme Court magistrates to 10-year terms, subject to Legislative Assembly confirmation. New allegations of executive tampering with the judiciary arose with the creation of the Fifth Chamber of the Supreme Court. In July the Assembly passed a law that created a fifth chamber, which allowed then-President Perez Balladares to appoint three additional Supreme Court Justices before leaving office. In October the Assembly approved a Moscoso administration proposal to repeal the law, eliminate the three additional magistrate positions, and abolish the Fifth Chamber.

The Supreme Court magistrates appoint appellate (Superior Tribunal) judges, who, in turn, appoint circuit and municipal court judges in their respective jurisdictions. Judicial appointments are supposed to be made under a merit-based system, but the top-down appointment system lends itself to political tinkering and undue interference by higher-level judges in lower-level cases in which they have no jurisdiction. The Attorney General, who heads the Public Ministry, appoints the superior and circuit-level prosecutors.

In December 1998, the Legislative Assembly passed a law that gave the Supreme Court the power to appoint the Director and Sub-Director of the PTJ for 7-year terms and requires Supreme Court approval for their removal. Previously, the Attorney General appointed these two officials. The law also gave these two officials the power to name other PTJ officials without consulting the Attorney General. Opposition and media critics charged that this law increased the influence of the Supreme Court over the criminal investigators, removed the generally positive oversight of the Attorney General, and made cooperation between prosecutors and the police much more difficult. Tensions between the Attorney General and the PTJ arose in July when PTJ officers and the Attorney General, accompanied by his PNP bodyguards, exchanged shouts with guns drawn before both sides finally backed down. The incident was followed by charges by both sides of abuse of authority.

At the local level, mayors appoint administrative judges who exercise jurisdiction over minor civil and criminal cases in which they may impose fines or sentences of up to 1 year. This system has serious shortcomings: Defendants lack adequate procedural safeguards; judges need not be (and normally are not) attorneys; and some engage in corrupt practices. In reality, appeal procedures are nonexistent. More affluent defendants tend to pay fines while poorer defendants go to jail, one of the chief factors leading to prison overcrowding.

In May 1998, the Inter-American Development Bank (IDB) loaned the Government $18.9 million to reform the judicial system. The loan is to be used at national and local levels to provide better conditions for the court system, including better information management, training for personnel, revision of judicial procedures, and construction of administrative offices for judges and prosecutors in two locations, San Miguelito and David. Program implementation began during the year, with funding allocated to temporary courts to clear backlogs, for training additional judges, and for working with the judicial college to create a curriculum that encourages the merit-based hiring and promotion of judges. In September the IDB began work on a database linking prison population data with prosecutors and the courts, which is intended to facilitate the systematic release of prisoners who have served time beyond their potential maximum sentence but still are awaiting trial.

The two commissions established during the Endara administration and resurrected by the Perez Balladares administration to evaluate the justice system never presented publicly any results of their work.

The Constitution provides that persons charged with crimes have the right to counsel, to be presumed innocent until proven guilty, to refrain from incriminating themselves or close relatives, and to be tried only once for a given offense. If not under pretrial detention, the accused may be present with counsel during the investigative phase of the proceeding. Judges can order the presence of pretrial detainees for the rendering or amplification of statements, or for confronting witnesses. Trials are conducted on the basis of evidence presented by the public prosecutor, and the accused person is not necessarily present. The Constitution and the Criminal Procedure Code provide for trial by jury at the defendant's election, but only in criminal cases where at least one of the charges is murder.

The Constitution obliges the Government to provide public defenders for the indigent. However, many public defenders are not appointed until after the investigative phase of the case, a serious disadvantage for the defendant since it is during this stage that the prosecutor produces and evaluates the bulk of the evidence and decides whether to recommend trial or the dismissal of charges. Public defenders' caseloads remained staggering, averaging 540 cases per attorney in 1998. Only 3 new public defenders have been hired since 1992, making a total of 38 nationwide, with a similar number of assistants. This heavy workload undermined the quality of representation, with many prisoners meeting their public defender for the first time on the day of trial.

The Legislative Assembly passed legislation in 1998, popularly known as the " Faundes Law, " which requires judges and other public officials to retire at age 75. The law was designed to remove former Supreme Court magistrate Jose Manuel Faundes after attempts to impeach him failed to muster the necessary two-thirds majority vote in the Assembly. The law required the 82-year-old Faundes to retire, making the impeachment proceedings moot. The National Bar Association challenged the constitutionality of the law's retroactive nature. However, in July the Supreme Court ruled that the law did not violate the Constitution.

There were no reports of political prisoners.

F. ARBITRARY INTERFERENCE WITH PRIVACY, FAMILY, HOME, OR CORRESPONDENCE

The Constitution provides for the inviolability of the home, private papers, and telephonic communications, and the Government generally respected these rights; however, there were complaints that in some cases police failed to follow legal requirements and conducted unauthorized searches of private residences. The authorities may not enter private residences except with the owner's permission, or by written order from the appropriate authority for specific purposes. These may include entry to assist the victims of crime or disaster, or to conduct lawful health and safety inspections. The authorities may not examine private papers and correspondence, except as properly authorized by competent legal authority and in the presence of the owner, a family member, or two neighbors.

Although the Constitution prohibits all wiretapping, the Government maintains that wiretapping with judicial approval is legal, and that the Attorney General may authorize a wiretap when confronted with probable cause in a serious crime. Under the guidelines established by antinarcotics legislation passed in July 1994, the Public Ministry may engage in undercover operations, including " videotaping and recording of conversations and telephonic communications. " In March a dispute arose when critics charged Attorney General Sossa with illegally wiretapping a judge. The Attorney General countered that he was operating within his authority to pursue a criminal investigation. Although then-Chief Justice Arturo Hoyos publicly criticized Sossa, the Supreme Court has not issued a definitive ruling on whether wiretapping is constitutional and, if so, under what circumstances.

RESPECT FOR CIVIL LIBERTIES

A. FREEDOM OF SPEECH AND PRESS

The Constitution provides for freedom of speech and of the press, and the Government generally respects these rights in practice.

There is an active and often adversarial press and a broad range of print and electronic media outlets, including foreign newspapers, radio and television broadcasts, and cable stations. Six national daily newspapers, 3 commercial television stations, 2 educational television stations, and approximately 100 radio stations provide a broad choice of informational sources; all are privately or institutionally owned. While many media outlets took identifiable editorial positions, the media carried a wide variety of political commentaries and other perspectives, both local and foreign. There is a noticeable concentration of control of television outlets in the hands of close relatives and associates of former President Perez Balladares.

In June the National Assembly passed a bill that made newspaper companies ineligible for radio and television concessions and vice versa. The bill was proposed after the La Prensa Corporation, the publisher of a newspaper of the same name, sought to acquire the Channel 8 frequency.

Panamanian and foreign journalists worked and traveled freely throughout the country. The Perez Balladares Government never fulfilled its informal promise to seek revocation of the 1978 law that requires directors and deputy directors of media outlets to be citizens. In June then-Minister of Government and Justice Mariela Sagel recommended the revival of the Noriega-era system of issuing journalist licenses to Panamanian citizens graduating from journalism schools. Working journalists and human rights groups criticized this suggestion, and it was dropped.

Under " gag laws " dating from the military dictatorship, the Government had legal authority to prosecute media owners and reporters for criminal libel and calumny. A special executive branch authority had discretionary powers to administer the libel laws, which provide for fines and up to 2 years in prison. Under the statute, opinions, comments, or criticism of government officials acting in their official capacity are exempted specifically from libel prosecution, but a section of the law allows for the immediate discipline of journalists who show " disrespect " for the office of certain government officials. In December President Moscoso ratified the National Assembly's decision to eliminate these gag laws. Although this action improved the legal status of the media, legal actions against many journalists remained pending at year's end.

Human Rights Ombudsman Italo Antinori criticized the Perez Balladares administration's use of libel laws to intimidate journalists who reported on government corruption. Approximately 85 journalists who had been charged with libel met with Antinori to describe the case they have submitted to the Inter-American Court of Human Rights. Other international free press and human rights bodies had criticized the continued use of the laws against journalists.

In 1998 then-PNP Director Jose Luis Sosa used the libel laws to bring charges against National University law professor (and now an adviser to the Moscoso administration) Miguel Bernal for statements about the decapitations of the prisoners on Coiba Island (see Section 1.c.). Bernal had said on television that " the only ones who have decapitated others in this country are the National Police and the National Guard of the now defunct Defense Forces. " Bernal clarified that he had not said that the PNP had carried out the decapitations at Coiba, rather that the PNP, through acts of omission, allowed the decapitations. Bernal, an advocate of prison reform, repeated his charges in follow-up interviews and opinion pieces. He claimed that the PNP Director's charges amounted to a limit on freedom of expression. There was a preliminary hearing on Sosa's charges against Bernal in November, but no trial date had been set by year's end.

In another 1998 case, a prosecutor acting on behalf of Attorney General Jose Antonio Sossa charged La Prensa journalists Gustavo Gorriti and Rolando Rodriguez with a " crime against the honor of the authorities " for defaming a government official and allegedly falsifying evidence. Gorriti and Rodriguez refused to reveal sources for a story they wrote in 1996, which alleged that the Attorney General accepted checks of dubious origin in his unsuccessful 1994 campaign for a seat in the Legislative Assembly. Subsequent press reports suggested that the story was erroneous. The charges remained pending at year's end, and the Attorney General sued the two journalists for $1 million. In December 1998, police officers attempted to escort journalist Herasto Reyes from his office at the La Prensa newspaper to a court appearance. Newsroom staffers prevented the police from taking Reyes into custody. Then-President Perez Balladares had filed libel charges against Reyes, after he published a story in August 1998 accusing the Perez Balladares administration of trying to cover up a government embezzlement scandal. The case was still pending at year's end.

The Electoral Tribunal must approve election polling results before publication. In April the Tribunal fined the newspaper Panama America $10,000 for failing to follow the approval procedure before printing Gallup poll results.

The press laws provide for the establishment of a censorship board. The board monitors radio transmissions and has the authority to fine stations that violate norms regarding vulgar and profane language.

The law provides for academic freedom, which generally was respected in both public and private universities. However, the Faundes Law forced the retirement of dozens of professors at the public universities.

After protesters turned to violence in December 1998 (see Section 2.b.), then-Governor of Panama Province Eduardo Herrera ordered the police to enter and temporarily close the University of Panama. In August then-President Perez Balladares issued a pardon for Herrera, who was accused of abuse of authority for violating the university's autonomy. President Moscoso rescinded that pardon in September.

B. FREEDOM OF PEACEFUL ASSEMBLY AND ASSOCIATION

The Constitution provides for the right of peaceful assembly, and the Government generally respects this right in practice. No authorization is needed for outdoor assembly, although prior notification for administrative purposes is required. In 1998 the Legislative Assembly considered, but did not enact, legislation that would have tightened restrictions on public demonstrations.

Police response to public protests was mixed. Throughout much of the year, police showed restraint and professionalism while monitoring large protests by students, political activists, prisoners, and workers. In February residents of the San Joaquin area protested the power company's cutting off electricity to 400 families that had fallen behind on payments. The move touched off 2 days of protests, during which demonstrators barred a section of the highway leading to the airport. In response, the police used tear gas and bird shot and arrested about 30 persons. Paramedics attended residents affected by the gas and injured by the bird shot. Eventually the residents and the electric company reached an agreement. On August 31, the police used similar methods to disperse bus drivers who blocked traffic in Panama City, as well as at smaller protests throughout the year.

In December 1998, a mix of student and worker groups protesting the privatization of the state-owned water utility, the changing of the date to celebrate a national holiday, and fee changes at the university engaged in a week of protests and confrontations. The demonstrators used Molotov cocktails and hurled stones at police. The police response to the at-times violent protests included the use of bird shot, tear gas, and rubber bullets. There were reportedly dozens of beatings and instances of abusive treatment, particularly against those taken into custody (also see Section 2.a.).

The Constitution provides for the right of association, and the Government generally respects this right in practice. Citizens have the right to form associations and professional or civic groups. They may form and organize political parties freely, although new parties must meet strict membership and organizational standards in order to gain official recognition and participate in national campaigns.

C. FREEDOM OF RELIGION

The Constitution, although recognizing Catholicism as " the religion of the majority of Panamanians, " provides for free exercise of all religious beliefs, provided that " Christian morality and public order " are respected. The Government imposes no limitations in practice, and there is a broad diversity of religions. The Constitution prohibits clerics from holding public office, except as related to social assistance, education, or scientific research.

d. Freedom of Movement Within the Country, Foreign Travel, Emigration, and Repatriation

The Constitution provides for these rights, and the Government respects them in practice. The Government enforced exit permit requirements for foreigners who overstayed their initial visas. A 9:00 p.m. curfew for minors under 18 years of age in the Panama City and San Miguelito districts of Panama province, imposed in 1992, remained in effect. Police enforcement of the curfew was uneven, with strictest compliance focused on high-crime areas.

During the year, between 300 and 500 Colombians fled the violence in Colombia and entered the country by crossing the border. At year's end the refugees were still living in the Darien town of Jaque and refused to return to Colombia until the Colombian Government could guarantee their safety in Jurado municipality. The Government, along with local NGO's and the United Nations, provided the refugees with protection and humanitarian assistance. At year's end, the Ministry of Foreign Affairs had not taken an official stance on policy towards the Colombians.

The law has provisions for granting refugee status in accordance with the 1951 U. N. Convention Relating to the Status of Refugees and its 1967 Protocol. The Government generally cooperates with the office of the United Nations High Commissioner for Refugees and other humanitarian organizations in assisting refugees. The issue of first asylum did not arise during the year.

There were no reports of the forced return of persons to a country where they feared persecution. However, throughout the year, there were unconfirmed reports that the police along the border, on an ad hoc basis, required Colombians to return to Colombia.

RESPECT FOR POLITICAL RIGHTS

THE RIGHT OF CITIZENS TO CHANGE THEIR GOVERNMENT

Citizens have this right and exercised it in the May general elections. The Constitution provides for a representative democracy with direct popular election by secret ballot of the President, two vice presidents, legislators, and local representatives every 5 years. While the Constitution provides for independent legislative and judicial branches, in practice the executive dominates. The independent Electoral Tribunal arranges and supervises elections. The Government respected the rights of its citizens to join any political party, propagate their views, and vote for candidates of their choice.

In the May 2 general elections, Arnulfista candidate Mireya Moscoso defeated Democratic Revolutionary Party (PRD) candidate Martin Torrijos and Christian Democratic Party candidate Alberto Vallarino, winning 44.8 percent of the popular vote. The PRD won 35 seats in the National Assembly; the Arnulfistas, 18; Solidarity, 4; the National Liberal Party, 2; MOLIRENA, 3; Democratic Change, 2; MORENA, 1; the Christian Democratic Party, 4; and the Civic Renewal Party, 2.

Domestic and international observers characterized the elections as generally free and fair; however, several local contests were marred by reports of vote buying and in extreme cases, voter intimidation. Legislative District 9-3, in Veraguas province, was criticized widely for such electoral interference.

There are no legal barriers to participation by women, members of minorities, or persons of indigenous descent, but they generally are underrepresented in government and politics. At year's end, women held 7 of 71 Legislative Assembly seats, and a woman served as its vice president. Women also held 3 of 13 cabinet positions. In May voters elected the first female President, and an indigenous person was elected President of the National Assembly. There are two female members of the Supreme Court, one of whom was elected Chief Justice in October.

The Government provides semiautonomous status to several indigenous groups in their homelands, including the Kuna, Ngobe-Bugle, Madugandi, and Embera-Wounaan reserves. The Kuna of San Blas have two representatives in the Legislative Assembly, proportionate to their share of the population. Locally, tribal chiefs govern each reserve; they meet in a general congress at regular intervals. Neither the Madugandi nor the Embera-Wounaan reserve has its own dedicated legislators, but each has a separate governor. The Government continued the process of demarcating electoral districts within a new reserve created for the Ngobe-Bugle. May elections allowed many Ngobe-Bugle to choose their own local representatives in these newly created electoral districts.

The law prohibits discrimination against any social, religious, or cultural group; however, naturalized citizens may not hold certain categories of elective office.

Section 4 Governmental Attitude Regarding International and Nongovernmental Investigation of Alleged Violations of Human Rights

Human rights organizations, including both religious and secular groups, operated without government restrictions. These organizations carried out a full range of activities, including investigations and dissemination of their findings. Organizations generally had access to government officials while conducting investigations. Some organizations were particularly active in encouraging voter turnout for the May general elections and in assisting election observers.

The legislature created the office of Human Rights Ombudsman in December 1996, but initially did not provide funding, and the office did not open until January 1998, when it began to handle cases. In February 1998, the Supreme Court stripped the Ombudsman of his authority to investigate human rights violations involving the administration of justice.

Human Rights Ombudsman Italo Antinori, the first to fill the position, sparred with the Perez Balladares Government until it left office. The Ombudsman received 15 to 20 complaints daily. With the authority only to investigate and publicize, Antinori handled several high-profile cases, although he failed to develop close links with other domestic human rights organizations. This highly personalized approach may have limited the overall institutional development of the ombudsman's office. Nonetheless, the office handled some 4,000 complaints since its founding in 1998, and Antinori's activities were well-publicized in the press. The Ombudsman also conducted a high profile " get out the vote " campaign prior to the general elections, consisting of public information messages on radio and television.

DISCRIMINATION BASED ON RACE, SEX, RELIGION, DISABILITY, LANGUAGE, OR SOCIAL STATUS

The Constitution prohibits either special privileges or discrimination on the basis of race, birth status, social class, sex, religion, or political views. Nevertheless, societal prejudices persist, based primarily on social status. Cases of discrimination are difficult to prove, and legal remedies for victims are complicated, time-consuming, and costly.

WOMEN

Domestic violence against women continued to be a serious problem. The Center for the Development of the Woman estimated that victims report as few as 20 percent of sexual assaults to judicial or law enforcement authorities. However, statistics indicate a greater willingness by women to report incidents of abuse. The PTJ registered 959 cases of domestic violence through August, compared with 582 through August 1998 and only 35 for all of 1997. The PTJ also registered 514 cases of rape and 135 cases of attempted rape. The Foundation for the Promotion of the Woman, among other women's advocacy groups and government agencies, operated programs to assist victims of abuse, and to educate women on their legal rights. The 1995 Family Code criminalized family violence, including psychological, physical, or sexual abuse, although convictions are rare unless a death occurs. A widely acknowledged characteristic of rape is that it frequently occurs in the home.

In addition to domestic violence, sexual harassment is a threat to the equal status of women in society. According to a report by the Latin American Committee for the Defense of Women, in 1995, the latest year statistics were available, about 70 percent of female government employees reported having endured sexual harassment in the workplace, 42 percent by their immediate supervisors and 18 percent by more senior supervisors. Since a bill to criminalize sexual harassment failed to pass the legislature in 1995, no further legislation has been introduced.

The 1995 Family Code recognizes joint or common property in marriages. However, insufficient resources hampered government efforts to enforce the code's provisions effectively.

The Constitution mandates equal pay for men and women in equivalent jobs, but wages paid to women are on average 20 percent lower and increase at a slower rate. Although statistics are lacking, there are credible reports of irregular hiring practices based upon age and " attractiveness. " In December 1998, the Legislative Assembly passed a law that reiterated protections laid out in the Constitution and prohibited all discrimination on the basis of sex.

A number of private women's rights groups, including groups for indigenous women, concentrate on disseminating information about women's rights, countering domestic abuse, enhancing employment and other skills, and pressing for legal reforms. The Foundation for the Promotion of the Woman stated that it provided legal assistance, counseling, and skills training to over 750 women during the year.

In January 1998, the Government created the Ministry of Women, Youth, Family, and Childhood, appointing Leonor Calderon as the Minister. Although the new Ministry is largely a consolidation of departments previously operating in other government ministries, its creation raised the profile of social issues.

Children

Minors (under 18 years of age) represent 48 percent of the population. The PTJ registered 171 cases of child abuse during the year. Education of children is compulsory through the equivalent of ninth grade. However, in remote areas children do not always attend school due to a lack of transportation, traditional attitudes, and insufficient government resources to enforce the requirement. The Government furnishes basic health care for children through local clinics run by the Ministry of Health. A central children's hospital in Panama City operates on government funds as well as private donations.

The Superior Tribunal for Minors and Superior Tribunal for Families are judicial authorities charged with overseeing the protection and care of minors. The Minister of Women, Youth, Family, and Childhood acts much like an ombudsman, and the office proposes and reviews laws and monitors government performance. Many children continue to suffer from malnutrition, neglect, and inadequate medical care. Malnourishment is lowest in urban areas and highest among rural indigenous groups. Child labor is a problem (see Section 6.d.).

Juvenile courts report a high incidence of juvenile delinquency in major urban areas. The authorities report an increase in crimes attributed to juvenile gangs, including drug trafficking, armed robberies, kidnapings, car thefts, and murders. In March the Minister of Women, Youth, Family, and Childhood charged the police with violating the human rights of minors by arresting and detaining them for minor infractions following periodic neighborhood sweeps.

PEOPLE WITH DISABILITIES

The Workers with Disabilities Office of the Department of Labor and Social Welfare is responsible for government policy and support for citizens with disabilities and for placing qualified disabled workers with employers. The office was in charge of implementing a June 1993 executive order that provided employers with tax incentives for hiring the disabled but has had only minimal success. Although some public buildings and retail stores have access ramps for the disabled, no national law compels the installation of facilitated access features in public or private buildings. In July the Panama City government began enforcing municipal building codes passed in 1998 that require such access to be included in new construction.

INDIGENOUS PEOPLE

Indigenous people number approximately 194,000 (8 percent of the population) and have the same political and legal rights as other citizens. The Constitution protects the ethnic identity and native languages of indigenous people, requiring the Government to provide bilingual literacy programs in indigenous communities. Indigenous people have legal rights and take part in decisions affecting their lands, cultures, traditions, and the allocation of natural resources. The Family Code recognizes traditional indigenous cultural marriage rites as the equivalent of a civil ceremony.

The Ministry of Government and Justice maintains a Directorate of Indigenous Policy. The Legislative Assembly also has an Indigenous Affairs Commission to address charges that the Government has neglected indigenous needs. Despite legal protection and formal equality, indigenous people generally endure relatively higher levels of poverty, disease, malnutrition, and illiteracy than the rest of the population. Discrimination against indigenous people, although generally not overt, is widespread.

Since rural indigenous populations infrequently master Spanish well enough to use appropriate legal terminology, they often have difficulty understanding their rights under the law and defending themselves in court. The indigenous population has grown increasingly vocal in requesting that the Government grant it more autonomy by creating more indigenous reserves or expanding existing ones. The Government continued the process of demarcating electoral districts within a new reserve created for the Ngobe-Bugle. May elections allowed many Ngobe-Bugle to choose their own local representatives in these newly created electoral districts. National/Racial/Ethnic Minorities

There is some evidence that a constitutional provision reserving retail trade to Panamanian citizens originally was directed at Chinese immigrants, but government officials have stated that it serves as a barrier to prevent foreign retail chains from operating in the country. The measure is not enforced in practice. Chinese, Middle Eastern, and Indian legal residents, as well as citizens of Chinese and Indian descent, operate much of the retail trade, particularly in urban areas. Leaders of the over 100,000-member East Asian and South Asian communities credibly claimed that Panamanian elites treat Panamanian-resident Chinese and Indians as well as citizens of Asian origin as second-class citizens.

Although such practices are illegal, clubs and restaurants often discriminate against blacks by denying them admission. After student protests at several nightclubs, Ombudsman Italo Antinori investigated and found racial discrimination at four nightclubs. Racial discrimination also is found in the workplace, particularly in jobs involving dealing with the public, where light-skinned persons are disproportionately represented.

WORKER RIGHTS

A. THE RIGHT OF ASSOCIATION

Private sector workers have the right to form and join unions of their choice, subject to registration by the Government. A labor code reform package signed in 1995 significantly increased workers' ability to establish unions. The reforms streamline the accreditation and registration process for unions, reduce the minimum size from 50 to 40 workers, and cut the Government's required response time on applications from 2 months to 15 days. In the event the Government does not respond within this time frame, the union automatically gains recognition and is accorded all rights and privileges under the law.

According to Ministry of Labor statistics, approximately 10 percent of the total employed labor force are organized. There are over 250 active unions, grouped under 7 confederations and 48 federations representing approximately 80,000 members in the private sector. Neither the Government nor the political parties control or financially support unions.

The 1994 Civil Service Law permits most government workers to form public employee associations and federations and establishes their right to represent members in collective bargaining with their respective agencies. It also provides civil servants (but not other government workers) with the right to strike, except for those in areas vital to public welfare and security, such as the police and health workers and those employed by the U.S. military forces and the Panama Canal Commission.

The Labor Code reforms addressed some longstanding concerns of the International Labor Organization (ILO). The code no longer makes labor leaders automatically ineligible to keep their union positions if they are fired from their jobs.

As is general practice in the country's public offices after elections, newly elected politicians and appointees began dismissing public workers immediately upon taking office to free up positions for loyal followers. The authorities discharged up to several thousand government employees by year's end. Public workers do not benefit from union protection, Labor Code standards, or minimum wage provisions. The Civil Service Law has proven insufficient to protect public workers. Under the law, public workers may be promoted into the civil service and thus enjoy some right to bargain collectively, strike, and evade summary dismissal. The Perez Balladares administration promoted some 10,000 public workers into the civil service during its final weeks in office, but the incoming Moscoso administration responded to this last minute influx by suspending the promotions of the new civil servants " for review. " Only a small percentage of the 150,000 public workers truly enjoy job security by virtue of their status as civil service employees.

The ILO's Committee of Experts has observed for some years that the prohibition of public servants' associations is inconsistent with obligations under ILO Convention 87 (The Right to Organize and Freedom of Association). The ILO made a second request that the Government amend labor laws with regard to public workers, but no changes had been made at year's end.

Union organizations at every level may and do affiliate with international bodies.

B. THE RIGHT TO ORGANIZE AND BARGAIN COLLECTIVELY

The Labor Code provides most workers with the right to organize and bargain collectively, and unions exercise it widely. The law protects union workers from antiunion discrimination and requires employers to reinstate workers fired for union activities. The Ministry of Labor has mechanisms to resolve complaints against antiunion employers. The Civil Service Law allows most public employees to organize and bargain collectively and grants some of them a limited right to strike. While the right to strike applies to some 10,000 civil servants, it does not apply to the approximately 140,000 other government workers. The Labor Code establishes a conciliation board in the Ministry of Labor to resolve labor complaints and provides a procedure for arbitration. A March ruling by the Supreme Court declared unconstitutional Article 452 of the Labor Code, which obligated private sector strikers to submit to binding arbitration after a given period.

Employers commonly hire temporary workers to circumvent onerous labor code requirements for permanent workers; such temporary workers receive neither pensions nor other benefits. The practice of blank contracts is, according to union sources, becoming more widespread. Labor law addresses this problem by requiring all companies to submit copies of all labor contracts for permanent workers to the Labor Ministry and by requiring the Labor Ministry to conduct periodic inspections of companies' work forces and review all contracts to ensure that they are in order. The code also authorizes the Labor Ministry to levy fines against companies not in compliance with the law.

In January and February 1996, the Government issued cabinet decrees governing labor relations in export processing zones (EPZ's) as a means of attracting investment into areas vacated under the terms of the Panama Canal Treaty. The original decree limited a broad range of labor rights, including the right to strike and to bargain collectively. The second decree modified the first and restored most worker rights in EPZ's. However, it provides for collective bargaining with " representatives of employees " but makes no specific mention of trade unions; it requires mandatory arbitration of disputes; and it allows for the participation of an unrepresentative worker delegate in the tripartite (government, labor, and industry) arbitration commission.

A 1997 decree further modified the EPZ labor regulations, stipulating that a strike may be considered legal only after 36 workdays of conciliation are exhausted. If this requirement is not met, striking workers can be fined or fired. A 1998 ILO ruling noted that the 1997 regulations do not mention arbitration or specify procedures to resolve disputes in the courts. The ILO ruling stated that the Government should amend the EPZ labor regulations to conform with international norms, but the Government did not respond. Minimum wage provisions do not apply in the EPZ's.

C. PROHIBITION OF FORCED OR COMPULSORY LABOR

The Labor Code prohibits forced or compulsory labor, including that performed by children, and neither practice was reported.

D. STATUS OF CHILD LABOR PRACTICES AND MINIMUM AGE FOR EMPLOYMENT

The Labor Code prohibits the employment of children under 14 years of age as well as of those under age 15 if the child has not completed primary school; children under age 16 cannot work overtime; those under age 18 cannot perform night work. Children between the ages of 12 and 15 may perform farm or domestic labor as long as the work is light and does not interfere with their schooling. The Ministry of Labor enforces these provisions in response to complaints and may order the termination of unauthorized employment. However, the Government acknowledges that it is unable to enforce other child labor provisions in rural areas, due to insufficient staff. The law prohibits forced or bonded labor by children, and the Government enforces this provision (see Section 6.c.).

The Permanent Committee Against Child Labor asserts that 11 percent of all children between the ages of 10 and 17 are working or actively are seeking employment. Most of these children, both rural and urban, are believed to be working at their parent's insistence. Some of these children may be providing a substantial part of their family income.

Child labor violations occur most frequently in rural areas during the harvest of sugar cane, coffee, and tomatoes. Farm owners usually pay according to the amount harvested, leading many persons to bring their young children to the fields to help with the harvest. In many small rural communities, the entire able-bodied population participates in a harvest, and parents are not willing to leave their children behind unattended. Many children also are involved extensively in subsistence agriculture.

Urban supermarkets employ an estimated 1,500 children, who work for tips bagging groceries. Some supermarket managers claim that these children are not employed by their firm, but these " baggers " often have schedules, uniforms, and must comply with company codes of conduct. In addition, many children work as domestic workers or sell items and wash cars in the streets.

The Government has not developed an effective strategy to address the problem of children working as street vendors and car washers, and has been unwilling to challenge the larger supermarket chains where large numbers of children work.

E. ACCEPTABLE CONDITIONS OF WORK

The Labor Code establishes minimum wage rates for specific regions and for most categories of labor. The minimum wage ranges from $0.77 per hour to $1.33 per hour, depending on the sector. This wage is not sufficient to provide a decent standard of living for a worker and family. Most workers formally employed in urban areas earn the minimum wage or above. An estimated 39 percent of the population who work in the large informal sector earn far below the minimum wage. The Government does not enforce labor laws in most rural areas, where laborers earn $5 or $6 per day, with no benefits. In December a tripartite commission comprising representatives from government, the private sector, and labor convened to negotiate an increase in the minimum wage, which would go into effect in July 2000. If the commission fails to reach consensus, the President has the power to raise the minimum wage by decree.

Unions repeatedly have alleged that contractors operating in the Panama Canal area pay less than the required minimum wage. The Ministry of Labor does not enforce the minimum wage law adequately, due to insufficient personnel and financial resources.

The Labor Code establishes a standard workweek of 48 hours and provides for at least one 24-hour rest period weekly.

The Ministry of Labor is responsible for enforcing health and safety standards and generally does so. The standards are fairly broad and generally emphasize safety over long-term health hazards, according to organized labor sources. An occupational health section in the social security system is responsible for conducting periodic inspections of especially hazardous employment sites, such as those in the construction industry, as well as inspecting health and safety standards in response to union or worker requests. Worker complaints of health problems continued in the banana industry as well as in the cement and milling industries.

The law protects from dismissal workers who file requests for health and safety inspections. Workers also have the right to remove themselves from situations that present an immediate health or safety hazard without jeopardizing their employment. They generally are not allowed to do so if the threat is not immediate, but may request a health and safety inspection to determine the extent and nature of the hazard.

F. TRAFFICKING IN PERSONS

The law prohibits alien smuggling, but does not prohibit specifically trafficking in persons. However, the authorities held several persons in custody for trafficking; they awaited trial at year's end.

The country is a transit point for aliens, primarily from other countries in South America (particularly Colombia and Ecuador) seeking to reach the United States, some of whom are trafficked into indentured servitude. An estimated 30,000 aliens transit the country annually, generally posing as tourists. Their travel is facilitated by a network of alien smugglers, travel agents, hotels, and safe-houses. The majority of aliens transiting through Panama originate in South America but a significant and increasing number come from India and China. Panamanians themselves represent only a small percentage of illegal aliens transiting through Central America.

Anecdotal evidence indicates that illegal aliens transiting through Panama overland are subject to frequent hardship. They commonly are deprived of adequate food and shelter. Chinese aliens are particularly vulnerable to poor treatment. South Americans pay approximately $5,000 in their country of origin for the entire trip. For the Chinese, $5,000 constitutes only the down payment on a total fee that could reach $30,000. Once in the United States, many Chinese are coerced into working off their debt as indentured servants in the Chinese community.

Corruption, legal technicalities, and lack of resources and staff contribute to the Government's inability to combat the problem fully.

INTERNATIONAL ASSISTANCE TO PANAMA

THE WORLD BANK IN PANAMA

Panama aims to become a globally integrated economy and to have a more equitable society, driven by sustainable private sector growth. Following years of frustration, prospects for meaningful reform of the Panamanian economy brightened considerably with the September 1, 1994, inauguration of President Ernesto Perez Balladares. During its first three years, the government has reversed many of the previously enacted populist measures that blocked economic progress, and it has been successfully taking the measures necessary to set Panama on a path toward sustainable growth with poverty reduction.

Panama's current economic program emphasizes: (i) private sector development and employment creation; (ii) fiscal adjustment and public sector modernization; (iii) poverty alleviation and human resources development; and (iv) environmental conservation. Economic growth is showing definite signs of recovery, social services are expanding, and unemployment is beginning to decline.

The World Bank has supported the Government's program through six loans that are under active implementation, and two that have recently closed, for a total of US$333 million. The two fully disbursed loans financed some of the main economic reform initiatives, and a commercial debt buy-back program helped to reduce debt and debt service obligations, thereby restoring Panama's creditworthiness and improving the climate for private investment. The six ongoing projects focus on poverty reduction, especially in rural areas, and on expanding and improving the efficiency of the country's basic infrastructure and utilities.

In addition, the Bank's sister organization, the International Finance Corporation (IFC), which lends to the private sector in developing countries, maintains a portfolio of US$30 million, and is involved in 3 projects.

While the emphasis in this period has been on helping Panama reorient its economic policies and regulatory framework, the Bank's support is increasingly directed toward meeting Panama's social, environmental, and infrastructure needs.

POVERTY AND INEQUALITY IN PANAMA

The incidence of poverty in Panama is high relative to its per capita income—about one-third of Panamanians live in poverty. Moreover, during the 1980s, the income of the poor declined sharply, as policy distortions prevented per capita output from increasing, inhibited job creation and redistributed income from the poor to the wealthy. Although Panama has allocated a relatively high share of its budget to social sector spending, many social programs have been inefficient, and historically there has been a strong bias in favor of urban and higher income groups.

The present Government has a strategy for mitigating poverty and inequality consists of four chief elements. The *first* is to revive sustainable growth. In this context, the economic program emphasizes the reform of policies such as a Labor Code that contributes to high unemployment, and tariffs that contribute to the high cost of consumer goods. Policy changes emphasize agricultural production and employment opportunities in the countryside, where most of the poor are located. *Second* is the introduction of new mechanisms to protect those persons most susceptible to malnutrition and infectious diseases. The *third* element is improving efficiency and equity in social expenditures through sector reforms, especially in education and health; curbing growth in the wage bill; instituting cost recovery, and targeting subsidies to the most vulnerable group. The *fourth* is institutional modernization and capacity building.

PANAMA AND THE WORLD BANK GROUP

The World Bank Group is supporting Panama's efforts to stem poverty through sustainable growth in several ways:

Policy and regulatory reform. In the past, Panama's traditional sources of growth have been constrained by heavy government intervention. Consolidating the economic recovery into sustainable growth and employment creation will depend on the elimination of domestic distortions and measures to enable the private sector to adjust efficiently to changing international economic conditions. The public sector wage bill is still high and there is a mounting deficit of the social security system. The tax burden is also relatively high and hinders private sector development.

Through a US$120 million **Economic Recovery Loan**, the Bank supported the Government's efforts to achieve fiscal stability, improved public finances, tariff reduction and a tax structure that encourages private sector development— and the jobs that come with it.

Giving the poor a chance. Panama's high poverty incidence occurs despite a high allocation of resources to the social sectors. But the impact of social spending is reduced by resource misallocation and wastage, and by a strong bias of social programs in favor of urban and higher income groups. The bulk of the spending in Panama's integrated health care system is devoted to expensive curative— rather than preventive— care, and the system is beset by inefficiency. Tertiary education receives a disproportionate and rising share of the education budget, but the educational system is not responsive to the demand for skilled labor, technicians, professionals and managers, and the overall quality of education is poor. Many primary schools lack educational materials and a large majority of primary school students are ill-prepared because of the low coverage of preschools and the fact that a relatively large proportion of students suffer from malnutrition.

The World Bank places a heavy emphasis on reducing such inequalities through several programs:

- The US$25 million **Rural Health Project** is helping 75,000 people living in remote rural communities gain access to primary health care services, including nutrition. An estimated 20,000 pregnant and breast-feeding women and 95,000 children under the age of 5 are enrolling in complementary feeding programs through the project. It is also increasing the coverage of water supply from about 62 to 80 percent and basic sanitation from about 72 to 88 percent of all of Panama's rural areas.
- The US$35 million **Basic Education Project** is improving the quality of basic education available to lower income children in the 185 poorest townships in the country, expanding coverage of pre-school education through community-based models, and reinforcing the planning and supervision capacity of the Ministry of Education.
- And the US$28 million **Social Investment Fund Project** is benefiting disadvantaged communities and population groups by addressing their demands for priority infrastructure and services and providing support for productive activities of micro-entrepreneurs. This project is notable as well in that it encourages community involvement in poverty alleviation, through direct participation in decisions concerning micro-projects to be funded.

Rural Poverty and Environmental Degradation. Poverty in Panama is largely a rural phenomenon. In 1990, 47 percent of the population resided in rural areas, and over one-half of rural Panamanians lived in poverty. The indigenous populations (about 8 percent of the total) is the most destitute group in Panama's society. The high incidence of rural poverty in Panama is not a consequence of scarcity of natural resources— arable land and water are abundant relative to the population. Natural resource management and conservation, however, is highly deficient. Some 45 percent of the forest cover has been eliminated by the encroachment of extensive cattle ranching and subsistence agriculture. In fragile areas indigenous peoples gradually are being displaced from the flat land rain forests by cattle ranchers who are overexploiting these resources. In the past 30 years, the surface affected by severe erosion has climbed from 0.5 million to 1.3 million hectares, or 18 percent of total land area.

The World Bank is supporting Panama's efforts to address the interconnected problems of rural poverty and environmental degradation through a US$22.5 million **Rural Poverty Alleviation and Natural Resources Management Project**. This project, covering 910,000 hectares (the Panamanian portion of the Mesoamerican Biological Corridor) will channel financial resources to rural communities and promote sustainable productive systems, and will promote the sustainable use and conservation of selected priority diversity areas.

Improving basic infrastructure. Lack of basic infrastructure exacerbates Panama's other problems. For example, periodic water shortages, the lack of wastewater treatment, and the lack of sewerage systems has resulted in an increase in the level of morbidity from water-borne diseases and diarrhea is the leading cause of death in the countryside.

Through its US$12.7 million **Utilities Restructuring Technical Assistance Project**, the Bank is helping Panama improve the quality and coverage of its infrastructure services. The project is creating an enabling environment for mobilizing private sector expertise and capital on a competitive basis, within an appropriate policy and regulatory framework.

THE INTERNATIONAL FINANCE CORPORATION IN PANAMA

The IFC, a member of the World Bank Group, is the largest multilateral source of equity and loan financing for private sector projects in developing countries. IFC has worldwide experience in the privatization of state-owned entities and plays a crucial role in providing comfort to prospective private investors while ensuring protection of the host country's interests. In Panama, the IFC is involved in three activities:

- *The Manzanillo International Terminal.* The IFC is providing loans totaling up to US$25 million for its own account and has arranged syndicated loans with international financial institutions for the Manzanillo International Terminal, located on Manzanillo Bay near the Atlantic coast entrance to the Panama Canal. Because of its strategic location the port will enable shipping lines to serve Latin America and the Caribbean more efficiently by providing them a hub for their regional operations with minimum deviation from current shipping lanes through the Panama Canal.
- *Banco Continental de Panama.* The IFC also has a US$5 million line of credit for a Panamanian private bank, *Banco Continental de Panama* (BCP) for on-lending to local small and medium-sized private sector companies. The credit

line provides loans of up to US$750,000 with maturities as long a 7 years to enterprises seeking to enhance their international competititveness in the context of Panama's economic liberalization program.

- *Instituto de Recursos Hidráulicos y Electrificación (IRHE).* In addition, the IFC has recently agreed to act as the principal adviser to the government of Panama in the privatization of the country's state-owned electricity utility, the *Instituto de Recursos Hidráulicos y Electrificación.* The sale of IRHE is an important element of Panama's modernization and restructuring program. A new electricity law, enacted in 1997, promotes competition, private investment, and service improvements by splitting IRHE into eight new companies: four for generation, three for distribution, and one for transmission. The distribution companies are targeted for privatization in the third quarter of 1998, with the generation companies to be sold in the fourth quarter and the transmission company remaining state-owned.

WORLD BANK PROJECTS IN PANAMA

1	**Panama - Country assistance strategy**	1998-10-29	Country Assistance Strategy Document
3	**Panama - Public Policy Reform Adjustment Project**	1998-11	Project Information Document
4	**Panama - Utilities Restructuring Technical Assistance Project**	1997-10-07	Project Information Document
5	**Panama - Health Sector Reform Project**	1997-10-29	Project Information Document
6	**Community organization, values and social capital in Panama**	1998-04	Departmental Working Paper
7	**Panama - Utilities Restructuring Technical Assistance Project**	1997-12-19	Project Appraisal Document
8	**Panama - Rural Poverty and Natural Resources Project**	1997-04-14	Staff Appraisal Report
9	**Panama - Basic Education Project**	1996-02-29	Staff Appraisal Report
10	**Community organization, values and social capital in Panama**	1998-04	Departmental Working Paper
11	**Panama - Social Investment Fund Project**	1997-09-05	Project Information Document
12	**Panama - Rural Poverty and Natural Resources Project (Proyecto de Pobreza Rural y Recursos)**	1997-09-05	Project Information Document
13	**Panama - Power system loss reduction study**	1983-06	ESMAP Paper
14	**Panama - A dual economy in transition**	1995-07-20	Economic Report
15	**Panama - Issues in basic education**	1995-03-17	Sector Report
16	**Panama - Rural Health Project**	1994-12-16	Staff Appraisal Report

US ASSISTANCE TO PANAMA

	FY 1998 Actuals	FY 1999 Estimate	FY 2000 Request
Development Assistance	$3,182,000	$4,598,000	$3,500,000
Economic Support Funds	---	---	$1,000,000

U.S. assistance to Panama contributes to the achievement of U.S. foreign policy objectives in the areas of economic growth, environment and democracy. Specifically, the assistance supports the successful implementation of the Panama Canal Treaties, which is clearly in the U.S. national interest. Under the Treaties, Panama will assume full ownership, control and operation of the Canal on December 31, 1999. U.S. assistance focuses on assuring effective protection and management of the Panama Canal Watershed, productive uses of reverted military and other properties, and on substantial improvements in the criminal and commercial justice systems of Panama.

Substantial amounts of U.S. (13%-14%) and world (4%) ocean-going cargo transit the Panama Canal. The protection of the watershed's natural environment is vital to safeguarding the fresh water resources upon which canal hydrology depends. Additionally, a democratic, transparent, prosperous and stable Panama will help ensure smooth transfer of Canal ownership and control, contributing to efficient Canal operations well into the 21st Century. Finally, well-planned, productive uses of U.S. military bases and other properties scheduled to revert to Panama can help offset the loss of income from the closure of the bases, contribute to political stability and help preserve the ecology of the canal watershed.

DEVELOPMENT CHALLENGE

Fresh water powers the Panama Canal. The Panama Canal Watershed (PCW) is the only source of water to meet the needs of the Canal as well as the fast growing population in the area. During the past 50 years, massive deforestation has reduced the forest cover in the Watershed by 60% and in the process eroded its river valleys and lake shores. As a result, the fresh water supplies of the watershed are increasingly vulnerable to agricultural and industrial pollution, siltation, sedimentation and the reduction of storage capacity of the lakes. Increasing rates of population migration into the watershed, with concomitant urbanization and economic activities, threatens its environmental health. With USAID assistance, the Government of Panama (GOP) has provided essential infrastructure and equipment, and has developed management plans for the five national parks located in the watershed. USAID has also supported GOP efforts to establish a comprehensive monitoring program to measure changes in forest cover, hydrology, biodiversity and human settlements in the watershed. An Ecological Trust Fund that provides a permanent source of funds which finances environmental education and awareness activities by local NGOs, as well as related management and protection activities, was successfully established with USAID's assistance. USAID will continue to provide assistance to improve the management and technical capabilities of key responsible GOP institutions, local governments, non-governmental organizations and communities in the area, to better protect and conserve the natural resources of the watershed.

Development in Panama, including the environmental sector, is affected by a justice system that is inherently slow, complex and non-transparent. The system is difficult to understand or access for both Panamanians and non-Panamanians, and is highly susceptible to manipulation. USAID will provide assistance to support the consolidation of ongoing efforts by the GOP to implement critical reforms of its criminal and civil systems. The assistance complements a larger effort supported by the IDB in criminal justice. It will also provide additional resources to address issues in commercial justice, an area in which the IDB is not involved. In an effort to modernize the justice system, selected technical assistance and training will focus on the application of internationally recognized commercial law and legal practices, enforcement of environmental regulations, and on the active participation of an organized civil society.

The reversion of the Panama Canal is based upon the 1977 Torrijos-Carter treaty, which established that the United State would progressively give back to Panama by December 31, 1999 all the lands, water resources, and infrastructural installations (including the military bases) necessary to administer, operate and defend the Panama Canal. The Regional Interoceanic Authority, established in 1993 to oversee the reversion process, aims to ensure that the uses of the reverted areas do not impair the proper functioning of the canal and the reverted properties make maximum contribution to Panama's economic and social development. USAID is providing resources to assist the GOP in the development of policies and administrative options for the management of reverted properties. Assistance is financing studies, selected technical assistance, training and computer equipment and software to help the GOP in the efficient conversion and management of reverted properties. Due in part to USAID assistance, the GOP has been fairly successful so far in converting seven military bases or other installations already transferred to productive uses.

Currently the GOP's external public debt is $5.0 billion. Servicing of the external debt is 33.4% of the public sector budget. The U.S. Government has no plans for debt relief.

OTHER DONORS

Currently, USAID is the major donor active in the watershed. Under the Common Agenda Initiative, the Government of Japan (GOJ) has indicated interest in assisting the GOP in the conservation and protection of the watershed, with activities complementary to the USAID program. To date, GOJ assistance has been modest. It recently awarded a $240,000 grant to a local NGO to establish a training center. However, Japan plans to expand its training and technical assistance activities and to assist in significant reforestation beginning in FY 2000 and beyond. The World Bank (IBRD) anticipates a lending program to Panama of $130-225 million over the 1999-2001 period. This support will concentrate on poverty reduction, economic growth policies, and selective activities focused on environmentally sustainable development. Planned activities in land administration will complement watershed conservation.

The IDB is currently assisting the GOP to develop a National Environmental Strategy. Assistance is also planned for the productive reconversion of areas in conflicting land use in the watershed. The IDB is also the lead donor supporting a major GOP effort in the improvement of its administration of criminal justice systems. USAID administration of justice activities complement this effort.

FY 2000 PROGRAM

USAID will focus resources on: 1) the protection of the canal watershed; 2) assisting on-going efforts of the GOP to implement critical reforms of its criminal and commercial justice system; and 3) resolving issues related to effective and productive use of the reverted areas adjacent to the Panama Canal. During CY 1999, USAID will develop a Strategic Plan that outlines the range of activities to be implemented beyond FY 2000 within the framework of the three objectives indicated above. In FY 1999, USAID will continue to support the institutional strengthening of GOP institutions responsible for the protection of the watershed. To enhance the sustainability of the protection of the watershed, USAID will encourage the participation of civil society, the private sector, local governments and residents of the watershed in this effort and provide appropriate financial and technical support. USAID will also provide assistance to the court systems, prosecutors and civil society to effect fundamental changes in the justice sector. Finally, USAID will continue to support GOP efforts in planning and implementing privatization and productive uses of the reverted areas.

PANAMA FY 2000 PROGRAM SUMMARY ($000s)

USAID Strategic and Special Objectives	Economic Growth & Agriculture	Population & Health	Environment	Democracy	Human Capacity Developmnt	Humanitarian Assistance	TOTALS
S.O. 1 Improved	---	----	2,500	---	---	---	2,500

Management and Protection of Panama Canal Watershed -D.A.							
S.O. 2 To facilitate Legal and Policy Changes Required to Sustain Fair, Fast and Independent Criminal and Commercial Justice Systems - ESF	---	---	---	1,000	---	---	1,000
Sp.O. Efficient Transfer of the Panama Canal and Facilitate Productive Use of Reverted Areas -D.A.	1,000	---	---	---	---	---	1,000
Totals -D.A. -ESF	 1,000 ---	 --- ---	 2,500 ---	 --- 1,000	 --- ---	 --- ---	 3,500 1,000

USAID Mission Director: Lars Klassen

SELECTED PROJECTS

PROGRAM: Panama
TITLE AND NUMBER: Improvement in the Institutional Capacity to Manage and Protect the Panama Canal Watershed, 525-SO01
STATUS: Continuing
PROPOSED OBLIGATION AND FUNDING SOURCES: FY 2000: $2,500,000 DA
INITIAL OBLIGATION: FY 1995 **ESTIMATED COMPLETION DATE:** 2006

Summary Numerous studies, including one conducted by USAID in 1994, have demonstrated the link between the environmental protection of the Panama Canal Watershed and the effective long-term operation of the Panama Canal. Protection of the environment helps assure the availability of adequate volumes of water for canal operations by maintaining an increasing forest cover where possible, and by minimizing sedimentation and drainage of contaminants into the Canal. Efficient operation of the Panama Canal relies on the freshwater provided by rain across the 326,000 hectare watershed, as each ship passage requires 52 million gallons of fresh water. As the GOP assumes responsibility for the operation of the Canal on December 31, 1999, the mandate of the newly created Panama Canal Authority (PCA) will extend beyond the management of the Canal itself to include, in coordination with other competent Panamanian authorities, the protection, conservation, and maintenance of the water and natural resources of the watershed. The purpose of this Strategic Objective is to assist Panama in assuming this responsibility for management of the watershed and to serve the U.S. interests in the sustainable operation of the Canal. The direct beneficiaries of this objective will be the Canal watershed ecosystem, the 143,000 residents of the watershed, and the operators and users of the Canal and watershed. The indirect beneficiaries will be the 1.4 million people along the transisthmian corridor on the east bank of the Canal, the population of Panama as a whole, and the global economy.

Key Results: USAID has determined that four key intermediate results are necessary to achieve this objective: (1) Institutional arrangements for effective watershed management and protection adopted; (2) watershed monitoring and evaluation system institutionalized; (3) Protected areas management systems functioning effectively; and (4) Local capacity to protect and manage the watershed increased.

Performance and Prospects: Performance over the past year has been as expected, with successes in all aspects of the portfolio.

The GOP, with USAID assistance, made progress during FY 1998 in improving the institutional arrangements for effective management of the watershed through drafting of alternative organizational structures for the legally mandated Inter-Institutional Commission for the Canal Watershed (IIC), passage of a framework law for the newly created National Environmental Authority (ANAM), and appointment of the members of the newly created PCA's Board of Directors. To finance watershed protection activities, the USAID-created Ecological Trust Fund (FIDECO) provided more than half a million dollars to the GOP for operation and maintenance of protected areas, and an equivalent amount for NGO projects including sustainable agriculture, biodiversity conservation, and watershed management. Over the next two years, USAID expects to support the establishment of the IIC, and assist the GOP in developing policies, regulations, and sustainable financing systems for watershed protection activities.

Continued support to the Smithsonian Tropical Research Institute's watershed monitoring program resulted in a functioning unit of scientists and technicians collecting monitoring information on biotic and abiotic conditions in the watershed including forest cover, hydrology and soils, biodiversity, and human settlements. This monitoring team has provided useful information to decision makers. The identification of an appropriate institutional home for the unit has been moving slowly with continuing discussions between USAID and appropriate GOP institutions. Over the next two years, USAID expects the monitoring unit and its information to become an invaluable resource for managers in the watershed.

Over the past year, USAID has supported the GOP with multiple activities to strengthen the functioning of protected areas within the watershed. USAID is supporting the development and improvement of park-use plans and construction of infrastructure facilities. Over the next two years, USAID will complete these activities and work with the GOP to implement co-management arrangements in the protected areas in accordance with the new environmental law.

Local capacity to conserve natural resources and to manage the watershed was increased through pilot agroforestry activities and support for the institutional consolidation of the Association of Panamanian Municipalities (AMUPA). Activities over the next two years will assist AMUPA to play a lead role in helping local governments implement the regional land-use plan, and help communities solve environmental problems such as solid waste disposal.

Possible Adjustments to Plans: USAID will dedicate significantly more resources toward the development and strengthening of civil society organization and encourage their increased participation, together with local and national government entities and the private sector, in watershed conservation and protection activities.

Other Donor Programs: The IDB and the WB have begun developing projects that will improve management of the watershed. Both entities anticipate activities in land management and watershed conservation as part of their planned $130-$225 million lending program. The IDB has ongoing activities which support the establishment of an institutional and operational framework to promote the development of a modern national environmental strategy and strengthen comprehensive watershed management programs elsewhere in the country. Under the Common Agenda Initiative, Japan is considering establishing a training center in the watershed to provide environmental education and awareness as well as training in forestry and agroforestry techniques. USAID is working closely with all of these donors to ensure complementarity of projects.

Principal Contractors, Grantees or Agencies: Current grantees and contractors include the Smithsonian Tropical Research Institute (STRI), the Academy for Educational Development (AED), the International Institute for

Education (IIE), the International Executive Service Corps (IESC), and Technoserve.

Major Results Indicators:

	Baseline 1997	Target 2000
Land use in the Panama Canal Watershed compatible with the approved Regional Plan	57%	63%
Community-based, pilot agro-forestry activities on-going	1	5
The Inter-Institutional Commission (IIC) to strengthen coordination among public and private institutions in the PCW established and decision-making mechanisms functioning	No	Yes
Note: End-of-Activity Targets to be Developed		

PROGRAM: PANAMA
STRATEGIC OBJECTIVE: To Facilitate Legal and Policy Changes Required to Sustain Fair, Fast and Independent Criminal and Commercial Justice Systems, 525-SO02
STATUS: Continuing
PROPOSED OBLIGATION AND FUNDING SOURCE: FY 2000: $1,000,000 ESF
INITIAL OBLIGATION: FY 1991 **ESTIMATED COMPLETION DATE:** FY 2006

Summary: The Panamanian justice system is a mixed inquisitory/accusatory one which is inherently slow, complex and non-transparent, is difficult to understand or access for both Panamanians and non-Panamanians, and is highly susceptible to manipulation. Recently, an increasing number of policy formulators and opinion leaders have spoken out against the systemic slowness and inefficiency of justice in Panama. Most of the negative remarks have been confined to the criminal system, but the same criticisms apply to commercial law.

Notwithstanding past Panamanian, USAID and other donor efforts, the criminal justice system continues to suffer serious, systemic weaknesses that have produced delayed, flawed, or simply wrong decisions. Major consequences of these weaknesses are increasing backlogs in cases, and a prison population in which 65% of the prisoners held in preventive detention have never even appeared before a judge. Just as worrisome, the courts appear subject to manipulation, corruption and political influence. The civil system, including its commercial component, is similarly lacking. Court productivity is low and slow: approximately 60% of all cases in the system (the majority in civil courts) have been pending over a year, and 40% have been waiting for over three years.

The purpose of this SO is to support GOP efforts in facilitating fundamental change in the justice sector. A fair, timely and transparent justice system is necessary to ensure the economic health and political stability of the country. In particular, fundamental change to the justice system will improve the confidence of Panamanian citizens and U.S. and international businesses and investors which, in turn, will facilitate the productive uses of formerly owned U.S. properties. Additionally, it will contribute to improving and strengthening the legal foundation upon which the institutional framework for sustainable Panama Canal Watershed management and protection is based.

Key Results: USAID has concluded that four key intermediate results are required to achieve this objective: (1) An informed civil society (NGOs) working with other sectors to improve the justice system; (2) An improved prosecution and public defenders system on a sustained basis; (3) Effectively functioning court systems, and alternative dispute resolution systems; and (4) improved police organization and capabilities (through the Department of Justice).

Performance and Prospects: Since Panama's return to democracy in 1990, efforts have been undertaken to re-establish independent Panamanian judicial institutions, strengthen operations and modernize laws. When 1995 budget stringencies forced USAID to reduce its presence worldwide, the Mission was instructed to eliminate its Democracy and Governance Strategic Objective, and phase out its successful Administration of Justice project in 1997. After a year's hiatus, USAID has reinitiated its work in the justice sector with relatively modest financial resources. In returning, a USAID sector assessment has determined that major problems persist. However, because other donor assistance in this area has increased considerably with the advent of the IDB's large justice sector loan, USAID will work to complement IDB efforts and focus in particular areas not being covered by the IDB (e.g., NGO development and strengthening, commercial justice issues and police training (with the Department of Justice).

Possible Adjustments to Plans: The objective is to enable the GOP and civil society organizations to formulate, institutionalize and implement activities designed to ensure fundamental sustainable systemic change in the justice systems. A top priority will be to ascertain receptivity to change, and results of research here could result in changes to USAID's approach in the future. Further research will be undertaken to understand better the constraints to justice and the appropriate means to address them. USAID will continue to coordinate and collaborate closely within the U.S. Government and with the IDB.

Other Donor Programs: The IDB is the major donor in the sector with an $18.9 million loan to the GOP. Other donors include the United Nations Development Program (UNDP), the Organization of American States (OAS) and the European Union (EU) with very modest programs. The British, Germans, French and Spanish have small bilateral programs.

Principal Contractors, Grantees or Agencies: Since this is a new SO, there are no contractors or grantees in place. Thus, USAID is considering accessing support through an existing Agency Indefinite Quantity Contract mechanism, Cooperative Agreements, and Participating Agency Service Agreements, supplemented with local and third country expertise where feasible.

Major Results Indicators:

	Baseline 1998	**Target 2000**
Number of local NGOs actively involved in justice issues	8	10
Number of judges and prosecutors trained in aspects of new penal code	0	200
Note: End-of-Activity Targets to be Developed		

PROGRAM: Panama
TITLE AND NUMBER: Efficient Transfer of the Panama Canal and Productive Use of the Reverted Properties, 525-SpO01
STATUS: Continuing
PROPOSED OBLIGATION AND FUNDING SOURCE: FY 2000 $1,000,000 DA
INITIAL OBLIGATION:FY 1995 **ESTIMATED COMPLETION DATE:** FY 2003

Summary: This activity supports U.S. foreign policy objectives aimed at successful implementation of the Panama Canal Treaties of 1977. According to the Treaties, the ownership, management and operation of the Panama Canal will be transferred from the United States to the Republic of Panama on December 31, 1999. The Treaties also call for the closure of all U.S. military bases and the reversion to Panama of related properties.

With USAID assistance, the GOP seeks to offset the negative impact on the Panamanian economy, in terms of lost jobs and income, resulting from the progressive closure of U.S. military bases. Compared with the base year of 1994, some 12,300 jobs will have been lost, along with $95 million in annual wages and $250 million in other annual expenditures that accrue to the Panamanian economy. In addition, given that approximately 12% to 14% of U.S. international maritime trade transits the Canal, USAID, acting as facilitator in those areas where it possesses a particular comparative advantage, will continue to provide selective technical assistance and short-term training to the newly established Panama Canal Authority (PCA) during the next two years to ensure a smooth and seamless transition.

Key Results: To achieve this Special Objective USAID has defined two key intermediate results: **(1)** selected policies and procedures for Canal operations adopted; and **(2)** enabling conditions established for generating investment and employment in the reverted areas.

Performance and Prospects:USAID-funded technical assistance has contributed to significant improvement in the Inter-Oceanic Regional Authority's (ARI) ability to market reverted properties. Policies for investment development have also been adopted and procedures streamlined with USAID assistance.

As a result, there have been successes in converting for productive use the seven military bases or installations already reverted to Panama: Espinar (1995), Davis (1995), Rodman Tank Farm (1997), Amador (1997), Curundu Flats (1997), Albrook (1997) and Quarry Heights (1998). Conversion of these properties to other uses ranges from 50% of Quarry Heights to 100% of the Rodman Tank Farm. Successes are also evidenced by the sale of 1,186 houses and 80 planned and on-going investment projects implemented in 1998. These projects have been primarily in tourism (hotel and eco-tourism development); plus commercial (fuel tank farm, tanker port) and maritime (overhauling existing ports i.e., Balboa and Cristobal and two new port concessions, Manzanillo and CocoSolo) activities.

Contributing to improvements in the investment climate, USAID-supported activities have led to a number of other accomplishments: new industrial property rights law, amendments to the labor code, legal stability for investment law, streamlining of customs operations and new GOP financial management integrated system.

Given the PCA's recent creation, the focus of USAID assistance has been institutional strengthening, including the introduction of labor mediation (following the model of the U.S. Federal Mediation and Conciliation Service (FMCS)), public information, and financial management.

Possible Adjustments to Plans: To address additional needs in the reconversion and transition process, institutional contractors will be used to address organization and management issues at ARI and PCA. USAID plans to assist ARI in project development for reconverted properties. Emphasis will be technical assistance in urban planning, economics and architecture, maritime industry, tourism, including a School for Tourism Education and master plan development. Technical assistance in business negotiations, customer service, plus public affairs and relations is also contemplated. The institutionalization of the mediation and conciliation system to resolve labor conflicts, using alternate dispute resolution, will be a key element for ensuring continued smooth operation of the Panama Canal.

Other Donor Programs: The IDB has been the major donor in the reversion process. The Bank financed the technical studies that led to the General and Regional Plan (adopted by Law 21). The United Nations Development Program (UNDP) was instrumental in building nation-wide consensus for the passage of Laws 21 and 19 (PCA organic law).

Principal Contractors, Grantees, or Agencies: International Executive Service Corps (IESC), Federal Mediation and Conciliation Service (FMCS), Free Market Development Advisors Program (FMDAP), and Fundación ANDE.

Major Results Indicators:

	Baseline 1995	Target 2000 (a)
Jobs created in the reverted areas (cumulative #)	12,300	6150
Total wages of the newly employed in the reverted areas ($ million/yearly)	95	48.5
Value added of new economic activity in reverted areas ($ million/yearly)	250	125.0
Toll revenues ($ million/yearly)	462.8	503.0
Transits	13,631	14,050
(a) Equivalent to 50% of level attributable to U.S. military presence on December 31, 1994.		

ECONOMY AND ECONOMIC DEVELOPMENT

Taking advantage of Panama's key location, the Government and business community have long promoted it as an international trading, banking, and services center. Recent trade liberalization and privatizations have added substance to these assertions. Panama's dollar-based economy offers low inflation and zero foreign exchange risk for American companies. Panama's Government actively seeks foreign investment and there are real opportunities available in the former Canal Zone properties being transferred to Panamanian jurisdiction in connection with the transfer of the Canal itself in 2000. Ongoing privatization of state-owned enterprises also offers an opening for foreign investors.

Due to the evolution and composition of Panama's economy, which is largely based on services, the extent and nature of local competition is very limited in most of the non-service sectors. Although the United States is Panama's most important trading partner with 58% of the market, and U.S. products have a high degree of acceptance in Panama, competition from third countries is strong in certain sectors including: telecommunications equipment, automobiles, heavy construction equipment, consumer electronics, computers, apparel, gifts and novelty products.

Panama's merchandise imports grew in 1997 by 4 percent over 1996 to a total of $2.65 Billion. The value of Panama's total merchandise exports in 1997 climbed 15 percent over 1996 to a total of US$ 657 million.

The Colon Free Zone is a much bigger market than the country of Panama. Free Zone imports amounted to $5.5 billion in 1997. These were mostly luxury goods, electronic products, clothing, and other consumer products. Because of this product mix, U.S. market share is lower in the Zone than in Panama. Hong Kong is the Free Zone's biggest supplier, while Colombia and Ecuador arethe major final destinations for Zone reexports.

Panama's economy is based primarily on a well-developed services sector that accounts for 73 percent of GDP. Services include the Panama Canal, banking, the Colon Free Zone, insurance, container ports, and flagship registry. Manufacturing, mining, utilities, and construction together account for 20 percent of GDP. Manufacturing is principally geared to production of items such as processed foods, clothing, chemical products, and construction materials for the domestic market. The manufacturing sector developed under a sixties style import substitution high tariff regime. Panama reduced duties on manufactured items from up to 100% to a maximum of 15% in 1998.

Panamanian manufacturers may now have difficulty in maintaining their market share vis-à-vis imports in many sectors. Agriculture, forestry and fisheries make up the remaining 10 percent of GDP.

BUSINESS TRENDS AND OPPORTUNITIES

Consumer attitudes and some brand preferences are similar to the U.S. American television and radio programs, and U.S. magazines are all available and popular in Panama. Panamanians frequently travel to the U.S. for vacation, medical treatment, study, and business. Their buying patterns and tastes are similar to ours.

U.S. products and services are well accepted and highly competitive in most product sectors. Panama has the highest per capita GDP in the region. Income distribution is skewed to the benefit of a relatively small, consumer goods-oriented, economically powerful class. These families have high levels of disposable income. They buy good quality trend-setting goods and price is not the major determinant in their purchasing decisions. The majority of the population has much less disposable income and price and availability of credit loom large when they decide what to buy.

Sharply lower import duties have made U.S. products more competitive with locally manufactured items in recent years. The U.S. share of market in Panama was 58% in 1997 up from 54% the preceding year. The U.S. also had 14% of the larger Free Zone market in 1997.

Panama has potential for substantial growth in the areas of electric power generation, health care services, mining exploration and operations, port services, land development, road construction, telecommunications, and tourism.

TRADE AND INVESTMENT CLIMATE

Panama has no restrictions on the outflow of capital or outward direct investment. The Government has demonstrated its commitment to trade liberalization since taking office in 1994. President Ernesto Perez Balladares has pressed for trade liberalization in the National Assembly and completed negotiations in 1997 for Panama to join the World Trade Organization (WTO). Panama s antiquated, Labor Code was mildly reformed in 1995 but political opposition prevented the sweeping revision needed. The Perez Balladares government has moved forward with reforms but continues to face formidable opposition from some industrial, agricultural, and labor organizations.

TheGovernment in conjunction with its WTO entry has enacted legislation to lower tariffs, reduce non-tariff barriers, eliminate producer subsidies, prohibit anti-competitive and monopoly practices, and strengthen intellectual property protection. Government regulation and occasional intervention in the Panamanian economy have tended to reduce transparency, hinder competition and hamper the efficient allocation of investment.
Bid procedures for certain privatizations and Government-financed major projects have been questioned over transparency and there have been some seemingly unjustified rebids. The Government's economic liberalization program has been designed to reduce these distortions and increase competition and competitiveness, but has fallen short in some areas.

The combination of relatively high costs for both utilities and labor makes unit production costs higher than average for the region. Also, investors complain of burdensome and excessive product registration requirements.

The most interesting sectors for new foreign investment are privatizations and investments in the former Canal Zone. The Government is actively looking investment in the fields of tourism, marine services, and in-bond assembly and manufacturing. The privatization program started with the sale of a state cement company and a state-owned fruit company. The Government awarded concessions for a private toll road in 1994, cellular phone service and another private toll road in early 1996, and two ports in mid-1996. Intel, the Panamanian telephone company, was partially (49%) privatized in mid-1997 and is now being managed by the British firm Cable and Wireless. The previously government-owned Casinos and Race Track were privatized in 1998. The power company has been restructured and converted into 8 companies. The shares will be partially sold to the private sector, starting in August 1998. Two sugar mills will also be sold. Other announced privatizations include a large convention center, the international airport, and water utility operations.

ECONOMIC TRENDS AND OUTLOOK

Approaching the completion of four years in office, the Perez Balladares government has implemented economic policy reforms to restructure the debt, liberalize the trade regime, privatize state-owned enterprises, lower tariffs, and attract foreign investment. These measures appear to be bearing fruit.

According to the Comptroller General's office, Panama's economy grew 4.4% in real terms in 1997, an improvement over 2.4% growth in 1996. However, population growth continues to pressure general economic growth with per capita GDP increasing only 2.4% in 1997. The Ministry of Economic Policy and Planning predicts 5.0 - 5.5% growth for 1998.

Growth notwithstanding, unemployment remains relatively high at 13.7%, falling only slightly in 1997. Although Panama's 1997 per capita GDP is among the highest in the region at $3198, this statistic is misleading, because Panama has one of the most highly skewed income distributions in Latin America. According to a 1989 study, the poorest 40 percent of the population owned 7.5 percent of the wealth, while the richest 10 percent owned 49 percent of the wealth. The Government estimates that 48% of Panamanians live in poverty, with 9.6% in severe poverty.

Panama continues to suffer from a lack of transparency in its bidding procedures as well as political influence and apparent corruption in the judicial system. Unorthodox bidding procedures on two major investment projects in 1996 raised questions of corruption. These cases and several other instances of questionable practices have soured some large international firms on doing business in Panama. The judicial system also has come under question. One example of the extra-judicial pressures that arise is the impeachment proceeding against a Supreme Court Justice accused of accepting bribes from narco-traffickers. Another example is the November 1997 acquittal on murder charges of Pedro Miguel Gonzalez, son of the President of the Legislative Assembly. Gonzalez was charged with murdering an American soldier and his arrest and trial were characterized by political influence and pressure applied by his powerful father.

Foreign investment, capital goods spending, and regulatory reform will be keys to growth in the near-term. The Government passed banking code reform in March 1998, and it is preparing to privatize more state-owned industries. These actions, and previous reforms, could lay the foundation for sustainable, long term growth. Panama's accession to the World Trade Organization in mid-1997 resulted in lower tariffs, which was followed by further reductions, giving Panama the lowest average tariff rate in Latin America. The 1995 "Universalization of Fiscal Incentives to Production Law" removed some of the mechanisms that Panama's protected, monopolistic industry used to exclude foreign competition. The bill reformed the tax subsidy and incentives regimes, and granted any producer, regardless of size, the same tax breaks on imports of inputs and capital goods. It created tax breaks for investments in high technology fields and for investment in infrastructure improvements and training of the workforce.

In addition to the Government of Panama's ongoing economic reform program, two other major challenges face the Perez Balladares administration: finding profitable uses for the 70,000 acres of land and roughly 4800 buildings which are reverting to Panama from the U.S. military; and preparing to take full control of the Panama Canal on December 31, 1999.

STRUCTURE OF ECONOMY/PRINCIPAL GROWTH SECTORS

Panama's economy is based primarily on a well-developed services sector that accounts for approximately 73 percent of GDP. Services include the Panama Canal, container port activities, flagship registry, banking, insurance, government, and the Colon Free Zone. Manufacturing, mining, utilities, and construction together account for 19 percent of GDP. Manufacturing is principally geared to production of processed foods, clothing, chemicals, and construction materials for the domestic market. Agriculture, forestry and fisheries account for the remaining eight percent of GDP. Principal primary products include bananas, shrimp, sugar, coffee, meat, dairy products, tropicalfruits, rice, corn, and beans. The sectors of the Panamanian economy with the greatest potential for growth in the medium term are ports, maritime services, mining, telecommunications, tourism, and energy.

THE PRIMARY SECTOR

The agriculture sector saw mixed results in 1997. Fisheries output rose 13.9% led by shrimp production which increased by 8%. Shrimp is Panama's second most important merchandise export (after bananas), earning $84 million in 1997. Shrimp farming in Panama is growing rapidly, with new aeration and cultivation techniques proving successful. Panama signed in May 1998 the International Dolphin Conservation Program Agreement which paves the way for the lifting of the embargo on Panamanian tuna exports. The Government privatized a tuna cold storage/processing plant at the port of Vacamonte and the plant was subsequently renovated.

Sugar production increased 14% in 1997, earning $22.3 million. The increase was largely due to increased acreage and productivity improvements. Vegetable production also increased 11.2% in 1997, earning $21.9 million. Both crops are poised for continued growth considering a planned privatization of the state sugar operation, recent investments in irrigation, and diminishing effects of El Nino. Chicken and chicken byproduct output rose 19.5% in 1997, earning $48.8 million. The increase resulted from capacity expansion permitted by tariff reductions on feed inputs.

On the other hand, beef and pork production fell slightly; milk production fell 9%; rice production was down 30%; and corn production fell 40%. All suffered as a result of the harmful effects of El Nino.

Banana production, Panama's largest export crop, fell for the third consecutive year, down by 5.6%, earning $109 million. The continued production decrease is attributable Banana Framework Agreement which restricts entry of Latin American bananas into Europe, a market on which Panama relies. Prospects for growth in the banana sector brightened in 1997 when the WTO ruled against the trade practice, though a final resolution to the case is still pending. However, a two-month strike in Chiquita's Pacific Division and the period necessary to rehabilitate the plantations could cut banana exports by as much as 25% in 1998.

Exports of non-traditional products, especially melons, have increased substantially in percentage terms, and continue to show significant potential for growth. Production is, however, on a small scale and suffers from lack of significant capital investment.

Although production in the mining sector rose 17.3% in 1997, earning $9.5 million, the gain was largely due to domestic demand for construction materials. Low world market prices continued to discourage gold, silver, copper, and manganese production, all of which are present in Panama. Only one such mine, a gold mine, is presently operating in Panama, though two world class copper mines are poised to begin extraction operations when pricesrecover. Four other projects are in various stages of development, while over 200 applications for exploration are pending. Mining investment in Panama is encouraged by a favorable mining law, drafted in 1988, which provides incentives to investors.

Mining sector growth has been limited in the past by excessive bureaucracy in authorizing exploration; opposition by Indian groups; and slow implementation of a mining master plan.

MANUFACTURING AND CONSTRUCTION

Industrial activity grew 4% in 1997 following low 0.7% growth in 1996. Growth was led by processed fish for export which increased by 37.1% and construction materials which grew 15%. Panama's manufacturing sector, previously highly protected, is geared for domestic consumption in food products, beverages, construction materials, clothing, consumer products, andintermediate goods. With much lower tariff protection after last year's reductions,Panamanian industry will face significant import competition in the coming year. Manufacture of cement, wood products, clothing, tobacco products, shoes, paper, and similar products should face the greatest challenges. Panama has relatively high labor and electricity costs, exacerbating the competitive challenges ahead.

Construction activity rose 5.0% in 1997 (compared to a decrease of 7.0% in 1996), due primarily to large infrastructure projects in both the private sector and public sector. Private projects included the Colon Port Terminal, a

Taiwanese (Evergreen) container port; an expansion of the Manzanillo Port Terminal, a joint U.S./Panamanian container facility; and two private tollroads, the Corredor Norte and the Corredor Sur. Other large private projects included mine site development, a thermal electricity plant, and the rehabilitation of a transisthmian highway in western Panama.

Major public infrastructure projects also benefited the construction industry in 1997. These included the widening of substantial portions of the Inter-American Highway and the road to the tourist center of El Valle. Also underway is a new road in northwestern Panama which will, for the first time, offer landaccess to parts of the fastest growing province in Panama, Bocas del Toro. Many other smaller projects are also underway including new and rehabilitated bridges in the interior of the country and widened and newly surfaced streets in the capital. All of these projects are expected to fuel demand for cement, steel rebar, concrete block, asphalt and related products over next two years.

Residential housing construction fell 13.6% as the private housing market anticipates the thousands of units which will become available with the U.S. base reversions. Non-residential construction rose 6.9%, with the completion of four luxury hotels and several office towers.

BANKING AND FINANCE

In June, 1998, Panama's banking sector came under a new legal regime which includes a strong, well-financed Superintendent. Other features of the new law include: Basel Accord standards for capital adequacy, enhanced authority to liquidate banks, higher minimum capital requirements, limits on lending to related parties, etc. Three types of licenses will be permitted: a "general license" with the right to operate in the Republic of Panama and internationally; an "international license" with the right to conduct off-shore transactions; and a "representational license" to handle the interests of foreign institutions without conducting banking operations. There is no deposit insurance. New securities legislation should surface in the legislative process later this year, as well.

U.S. banks with general licenses include Chase, Citibank, Bank of Boston and Nationsbank. American Express Bank and Core States Bank are licensed to carry out representational activities. Total bank assets of Panama's 104 licensed banking institutions increased from $33.5 to $36.2 billion from 1996 to 1997, driven by an expanding domestic economy. Growth in the Colon Free Zone and consumer lending, especially in the automobile market, were key factors underlying the numbers. System-wide banking capital and reserves tracked assets, and increased by nearly $400 million to $2,822 million. Similarly, total deposits increased from $25.2 billion to $27.5 billion, regaining ground lost in 1996.

From 1996 to 1997, Panama's foreign public debt increased marginally to $5.1 billion. Twenty-eight percent of the debt is held by foreign official creditors and seventy-two percent by the private sector. Of the private sector debt, 56 percent is in Brady Bonds, 33 percent in Eurobonds and the balance in other instruments. From another perspective 96 percent of the public foreign debt was issued by the central government, and the remainder by decentralized state institutions.

The investigation of Banco Agro-Industrial (Banaico), which failed in early 1996, continues. A major figure in the case was expelled to the U.S. and is being charged with money laundering.

PANAMA CANAL

Panama Canal traffic continues at near capacity rates. In FY 1997, 14,857 ships transited the Canal, down 1.4% from 15,069 in 1996. While net tonnage, on which tolls are assessed, fell 2.5%, toll revenue rose 6.0% to $512 million in FY 1997, this as a result of an 8.2% toll rate increase which effective January 1,1997. An additional toll increase of 7.5% went into effect January 1, 1998. There are two main purposes for the toll increases: a) to fund purchase of millions of dollars of new equipment, and b) to complete the widening the Gaillard cut which will permit two-way traffic of Panamax vessels (largest which can fit into the locks of the Canal). According to the Panama Canal Administrator, the cut-widening will be completed in 2002 and will increase Canal capacity by 20%.

The Legislative Assembly approved in May 1997 a law creating a successor to the U.S. Panama Canal Commission (PCC). The "Panama Canal Authority" (PCA), a Panamanian government agency, will take over the duties of the PCC the Canal transfers to Panamanian control. The PCC operates the Canal on a break-even basis (although this includes an annual payment of about $110 million to the Government of Panama). The successor PCA plans to run the Canal more along commercial lines.

At present, over 92 percent of the Canal's employees are Panamanian, as is the Canal's Administrator. The U.S. Government is confident that the predominantly Panamanian workforce, along with massive investment in new equipment over the next year, will help assure a "seamless transition" of U.S. to Panamanian control of the Canal on December 31, 1999.

COLON FREE TRADE ZONE

Established in 1948 at the Atlantic entrance to the Panama Canal, the Colon Free Zone (CFZ) is the largest of its kind in Latin America. Worldwide, it is second only to Hong Kong in overall activity. Total CFZ imports rose to $5.5 billion in 1997, up 18.3% from $4.67 billion in 1996. Total re-exports rose to

$6.3 billion in 1997, up 13.5% from $5.5 billion in 1996. Imports from January-March, 1998 totaled $1.35 billion, up 17.25% from the same period in 1997, while re-exports of $1.5 billion were up 6%.

CFZ growth in 1997 was due largely to strong growth in Latin America, lower shipping costs, the elimination of a tax on profits, and an increase in the number of businesses in the CFZ. The significant growth in adjacent container ports (MIT and Colon Port Terminal) and the planned revitalization of Panama's transisthmian railroad linking the Pacific and Atlantic ports, should provide for continued CFZ competitiveness. CFZ contributions to the Panamanian economy (re-exports less imports) fell 12% from $862 million in 1996 to $754 million in 1997.

Complaints of intellectual property rights (IPR) violations continue to plague the CFZ. A newly established Intellectual Property Department for the CFZ is viewed as a positive step demonstrating Panama's will to improve enforcement.

TOURISM

The number of visitors to Panama in 1997 increased 9.1% to 483,000, while overall visitor spending rose 7.4% to $368 million. The tourism industry in Panama has substantial growth potential; however, a lack of infrastructure and poor marketing have hampered its development. The National Assembly passed in 1994 a law granting incentives to investors in the sector (primarily tax exemptions and long leaseholds.)

In 1997, the Legislative Assembly approved a General Use Plan and a Regional Use Plan, which provide a blueprint for developing the areas reverting to Panamanian control. The Government's detailed tourism development plan contemplates massive investment in Canal-related eco-tourism, to take advantage of Panama's rainforest, bird-watching, etc. This industry will likely develop slowly over the next ten years.

Following Fort Amador's reversion to Panamanian control in October 1996, a Korean/American consortium signed a deal with the Government to invest nearly $400 million in hotels, a yacht club, a cruise ship landing, a golf course, an aquarium center, etc. Financing for this project may be threatened by the Asian financial crisis. Other more modest projects have a better chance of being completed. Another group has plans to build a shopping mall and cruise ship pier. Basic infrastructure development is presently underway.

GOVERNMENT ROLE IN THE ECONOMY

From 1968 until 1989, Panama was governed by a military regime which took a statist approach to economic development. While price controls were applied to many goods, government involvement was generally less pervasive than that in other countries that pursued import substitution development policies. In 1990, under the Endara government, Panama embarked on a policy reform program to liberalize trade and modernize government operations. Political opposition from entrenched special interest groups, however, diluted the substance of reforms.

An even more ambitious program of reforms was begun under the Perez Balladares administration which took office in September, 1994. This administration has passed reforms in banking, labor regulation, tax code, and fiscal management (funding a near bankrupt government pension program). The Government also negotiated WTO accession, re-negotiated Panama's $3.5 billion foreign commercial bank debt, privatized state-owned enterprises, and lowered tariff protection to the lowest average rate in Latin America.

The use of the U.S. dollar as Panama's currency means that fiscal policy is the government's principal macro-economic policy instrument. Because Panama does not issue its own currency, government spending and investment are strictly bound by tax and non-tax revenues (including payments by the Panama Canal Commission) and the government's ability to borrow.

According to a Department of Defense estimates, the U.S. military in Panama contributed about $265 million into the local economy in 1996 and $239 million in 1997. In addition, the military constructed numerous roads, schools, medical clinics, and wells. Withdrawal of U.S. forces through 1999 will result in a significant loss.

BALANCE OF PAYMENTS

Panama's goods and services export earnings have traditionally been among the largest in the region relative to GDP (35-40%). This is because the country has profited from its geographical location and dollar-based economy to develop a strong services sector. Net services surpluses have traditionally financed large merchandise trade deficits.

Services: Growth of services exports was strong in 1997. The Canal had an excellent year; activity in the Colon Free Zone was up; and maritime services continued to grow as did tourism revenue. As well, banking services were up strongly.
Merchandise: Panama's merchandise imports totaled $2.65 billion in 1997, up 4.2% from $2.55 billion in 1996. Panama's total merchandise exports,

meanwhile, totaled $657 million in 1997, up 15.5% from $569 million. (Note: these statistics do not include Colon Free Zone trade.)

Debt: From 1996 to 1997, Panama's foreign public debt increased marginally to $5.1 billion. Twenty-eight percent of the debt is held by foreign official creditors and seventy-two percent by the private sector. Of the private sector debt, 56 percent is in Brady Bonds, 33 percent in Eurobonds and the balance in other instruments. From another perspective 96 percent of the public foreign debt was issued by the central government, and the remainder corresponded to decentralized state institutions.

Panama has successfully returned to international capital markets. Moody's Investors Service rates Panama government debt Ba1; Standard and Poor's rates Panama BB+. Both are among the highest ratings for third world debt. In February, 1997 the Treasury issued $500 million in five-year, Government-backed notes. The offering was heavily oversubscribed, a testament to the success of the restructuring. A September 1997 issuance of $700 million in Global Bonds was also considered a success. Bond offerings have continued during the first half of 1998.

INFRASTRUCTURE

In comparison to many lesser developed countries, Panama has relatively well-developed infrastructure. Inter-city highways are generally good, allowing goods and services to move with relative ease. With new and soon-to-be completed roads offering access to Bocas del Toro province, that area should see significant growth in the next few years. Roads remain relatively poor in the sparsely populated Darien province. Planned investment in highways, ports, and the railroad in the Panama-Colon corridor should prove very beneficial.

Panama relies heavily on hydroelectric power generation and suffered as a result of an El Nino related drought in 1997 and early 1998. With electricity demand forecast to grow at 6% annually for the next several years, new power plants will need to be constructed. An April 1997 bid awarded to ICA/GE(Mexican/Canadian consortium) to build two hydroelectric plants (total capacity: 132 megawatts) on the Esti River in Western Panama has been voided. To date there are no plans to re-bid the project. Upcoming privatizations in electricity generation and distribution should aid in fulfilling future demand.

Shipping infrastructure has improved greatly over the past year. Colon Port Terminals, an $80 million investment by Taiwan-based Evergreen, opened on the north coast in 1997. Meanwhile, Hutchison Whampoa of Hong Kong has initiated its plan to invest $150 million in the ports of Balboa and Cristobal, at opposite entrances to the Canal. Manzanillo International Terminal, already the largest container port in Latin America, completed a $100 million expansion of its facility in Colon. In February 1998, the government approved a contract with Kansas City Southern Industries to invest over $50 million to rehabilitate the transisthmian railroad, linking the ports at each end of the Canal.

The sale in May 1997 of 49% of the shares of the state telecommunications company to Cable & Wireless (U.K.) guarantees multimillion dollar on investment. Its concession grants monopoly rights until 2003 when telecommunications services will open to competition. At market opening, licenses will be unlimited and issued gratis, while prices will be dictated by themarketplace.

Many of Panama's biggest companies, especially those in the banking sector, have programs in place to handle the year 2000 problem. While the Government has begun a campaign to inform all agencies of the existence of this difficulty, it is not clear that it is being addressed adequately.

POLITICAL ENVIRONMENT

Formal U.S.-Panamanian relations date to 1903, when a bilateral treaty gave the U.S. the right to build and unilaterally control the transisthmian canal that was completed in 1914. Those relations were altered by mutual agreement in the 1977 Panama Canal Treaties, signed by President Jimmy Carter and General Omar Torrijos, which stipulate that Canal administration passes toPanama and all U.S. troops withdraw by December 31, 1999. U.S.-Panama relations are generally cooperative and businesslike as both prepare for U.S. withdrawal and Panamanian takeover of the Canal and U.S. base properties. Managing the Treaty implementation process is one of the prime challenges of the administration of President Perez Balladares.

President Ernesto Perez Balladares is a U.S.-educated businessman. Foreign Minister Ricardo Alberto Arias, a lawyer, is the former Panamanian Ambassador to the U.S. Both understand the U.S. political system and speak fluent English.

Relations between the U.S. and the Panamanian administration of Perez Balladares have been generally positive, with both countries cooperating well on important law enforcement and other international issues. Panama is a major transit point for illegal drugs.

Tensions have arisen, however, over the lack of transparency in the port privatization process, over the political manipulation of the trial of the killers of an

American serviceman, and over the Panamanian Government's handling of negotiations to create a Multinational Counternarcotics Center (MCC) in Panama which would include a reduced U.S. military presence beyond 1999. There are widespread concerns in Panama and among foreign investors that a complete withdrawal of the U.S. military presence would have destabilizing effect on the confidence of investors and financial markets. The talks on the MCC have entered into an impasse created by the complex internal politics of the governing PRD party.

A major feature of the political environment at this writing is the President's effort to amend the constitution to allow his immediate re-election. The amendment will go to a popular referendum on August 30, and the outcome remains uncertain.

Major Political Issues Affecting Business Climate

During the years leading up to the transfer of the Canal and the bases, the government of Panama faces two interrelated problems, attracting foreign investment and managing the vast properties that Panama will receive as the U.S. withdraws. In 1993 the Endara government established the semi-autonomous Inter-Oceanic Region Authority (ARI) to manage the reversion process. Perez Balladares, who had criticized the ARI for ineffectiveness and inefficiency, pushed through legislation in early 1995 that provided for Presidential oversight of the Board's more important personnel and ARI policy decisions. He approved the board's selection of former Panamanian PresidentNicolas Ardito Barletta as administrator of the ARI. Barletta took office in June 1995. Expressing dismay over the government's lack of preparations for reversion and concern for the security and maintenance of the properties the U.S. was preparing to transfer to Panama, Barletta asked for some delays in reversions to give the government more time to decide how best to protect and promote the properties. ARI hired Nathan Associates to prepare a "Master Plan" for use of the properties.

Fort Davis and Fort Espinar on the Atlantic coast reverted to Panama in 1995. Taiwanese companies are establishing export processing zones in the Fort Davis area. The Evergreen company from Taiwan has opened a container terminal at Coco Solo North, and ARI has been selling some of the houses at Fort Espinar on the retail market. Fort Amador on the Pacific coast reverted toPanama in October 1996, and a fuel depot at Arraijan (near Panama City) in January, 1997. In September 1997, the Southern Command vacated its headquarters at Quarry Heights. In the following two months, the military also transferred to Panama Albrook Air Station and Gorgas Hospital. The Government has invested considerable money into Albrook and hopes to open it as a commuter airfield by the end of 1998.

The Government of Panama devoted considerable effort in 1995 to amending the labor code to make it more attractive to investors. After months of heated deliberation, culminating in a highly-disruptive strike, the Government of Panama on August 13, 1995, adopted a package of reforms which made marginal changes but did not lower Panama's relatively high labor costs. In 1996, a special labor regime for export processing zones was created by executive decree and was immediately challenged as a violation of international labor standards in several areas. Although the regime was modified later, the constitutionality of the decree is being challenged by organized labor in Panama's Supreme Court.

The Government of Panama has made progress in decreasing protectionism, promoting structural economic reforms, job creation, protecting intellectual property rights, curbing money laundering, and the partial privatization of parastatals. As noted above, bidding procedures for privatization of ports,however, proved less than fully transparent. Narcotrafficking, domestic drug consumption and alien smuggling remain challenges to the government and are areas of considerable cooperation with the United States.

LEADING SECTORS FOR U.S. EXPORTS AND INVESTMENT

Telecommunications Equipment (tel)
Electrical Power Systems (elp)
Computers and Peripherals (cpt)
Automotive Parts and Service Equipment (aps)
Automobiles and Light Trucks/Vans (aut)
Medical Equipment (med)
Air Conditioning and Refrigeration (acr)
Management Consulting Services (mcs)
Hotel and Restaurant Equipment (htl)
Financial Services (fns)

BEST PROSPECTS FOR AGRICULTURAL PRODUCTS

Consumer Oriented Agricultural Products
Bulk Agricultural Products
Intermediate Agricultural Products

SIGNIFICANT INVESTMENT OPPORTUNITIES

Reverted Areas
Electric Power Generation

Mining Exploration and Operation
Water and Sewage
Forestry

BUSINESS AND INVESTMENT CLIMATE

Based on Panama's central geographic location and its limited manufacturing and agricultural sectors, the Government of Panama and the business community actively promote this country's long-standing reputation as an international trading, banking, and services center, and as a site for foreign direct investment (FDI). Panama's dollar-based economy offers low inflation and no foreign exchange risk. The Panamanian Trade Development Institute (IPCE) and the President's export promotion office (PROPANAMA) provide investors with information, expedite specific projects, lead investment-seeking missions abroad, and support foreign investment missions in Panama.

U.S. companies own many of the largest investments in Panama. Major U.S. investments include Panama's only refinery (Texaco), the largest container port in Latin America (Stevedoring Services of America), Chiriqui Land Company (Chiquita Brands International), a cellular telephone concession (Bell South), and the transisthmian oil pipeline (moth-balled) and container port at Chiriqui Grande (60% owned by Northville Industries and Chicago Bridge and Iron). A U.S. partnership (Kansas City Southern Industries and Mi-Jack Products) plans to invest over $50 million to rebuild and operate the transisthmian railroad. Large non-U.S. foreign investments include the local telecommunications company (Cable and Wireless of the U.K., 49% owner with management rights), the ports of Balboa and Cristobal, (Hutchison Port Holdings of Hong Kong), and a container port (Evergreen of Taiwan).

The Perez Balladares government, which took office September 1, 1994, has embarked upon a vigorous campaign to improve Panama's international image and attract FDI. A major challenge for the government is its development of the U.S. military areas being reverted under the Carter-Torrijos treaties. Projects already underway include a Taiwanese investment in an industrial "exportprocessing zone" (EPZ) in the former U.S. base Fort Davis and the former Arraijan fuel tank farm which was immediately handed over to a U.S./Saudi partnership when it reverted in January 1997. Several other projects are on the drawing board, including a major tourist complex at the former Fort Amador at the Pacific entrance to the Canal.

The former Albrook Airfield will replace Paitilla Airport in the fall of 1998 as the city's commuter airstrip, freeing the Paitilla site for residential development. Gorgas Army Hospital remains idle after an American company backed out of a plan to administer the facility which reverted in 1997. The largest U.S. bases, Howard AFB, Fort Clayton, Fort Sherman, and Rodman Naval Base, revert in

1999. In that year, Panama also obtains control of the Canal and holds presidential elections.

Neglected throughout the Torrijos-Noriega years, basic public infrastructure development is a priority for the current administration. One major new urban highway is complete and another is under construction. As well, both the Inter-American and the Transisthmian Highways are being widened. Otherinfrastructure development includes Cable and Wireless' plans to invest over $500 million in the newly privatized (1997) telecom within five years and upcoming privatizations of the water and power utilities.

While these infrastructure improvements will help to attract investors, the government has come under fire for its failure to establish and follow clear rules in public bidding and procurement practices. Several badly managed public tenders and concession awards have led to suggestions of corruption and soured some American companies on doing business in Panama, undermining the image the Government has tried to create with its policy reforms.

The tax system promotes savings and investment by giving a wide variety of incentives and maintaining rates which are comparable to those in the U.S. The maximum personal income tax rate is 30% and the maximum corporate rate is 34% of domestically produced earnings. Although tax collection methods have been strengthened lately, the overall regulatory and supervisory framework is weak. In April 1993, a law was passed granting tax incentives for the creation of voluntary pension funds (IRA's) by individuals or corporations.

Panama has privatized a number of state-owned enterprises. To date, completed privatizations include the state telecom, the transisthmian railroad, ports at both entrances to the Canal, casino operations, the state cement company, a state-owned fruit company, and a horse racetrack. Water and electricity utilities, the national airport, a major convention center, and the state sugar companies are scheduled for privatization in 1998 or 1999.

Inflexible labor laws have been cited as a problem by local businessmen. Excessive regulation of hiring and firing practices reduces labor mobility and flexibility. The combination of high electricity and telecommunications costs and the highest minimum wage in Central America deters some investors. It is not clear what effect privatization will have on electricity rates.

The Panamanian Constitution forbids certain kinds of monopolistic behavior. The Government of Panama passed in February, 1996 an Antimonopoly Law, designed to prevent monopolistic practices and create a consumer protection regime. As well, Panama has lowered overall tariff protection to one of the lowest average rates in Latin America. Consumers are protected by an aggressive consumer protection division of the Ministry of Commerce and

Industry which has instituted fines for practices ranging from selling expired products to price-gouging. Panama does not have a bankruptcy law to facilitate the restructuring of firms, such as Chapter 11 in the U.S., although the new banking law gives the Superintendent of Banks considerable powers in this regard for the banking sector.

PRIVATE OWNERSHIP AND ESTABLISHMENT

With the exception of retail trade and certain professions, foreign and domestic entities have the right to establish, own, and dispose of business interests in virtually all forms of remunerative enterprise. Foreigners need not be legally resident or physically present in Panama to establish corporations or to obtain local operating licenses for a foreign corporation. Business visas (and even Panamanian passports) are readily obtainable for significant investors. Banking, legal and financial services and the legal regime are strongly oriented toward attracting foreign business and banking activity.

Panama's privatization framework law does not distinguish between foreign and domestic investor participation in prospective privatizations. The law calls for pre-screening of potential investors or bidders in certain cases to establish technical viability, but nationality and Panamanian participation are not criteria. Foreigners have participated actively and successfully in all privatizations to date.

PROTECTION OF PROPERTY RIGHTS

Business, corporate, and banking laws are relatively modern and sophisticated and in general are enforced so as to create a favorable business climate, although there is no modern bankruptcy law. Mortgages, liens, and other security interests are recognized. There is a public property registry which is undergoing expansion and modernization. Unique features of Panamanian law and practice in specific areas (including but not limited to banking, accounting requirements, formation and functioning of corporations, and taxation) make retention of local legal counsel highly advisable.

Intellectual Property Rights: Panama is a member of the World Intellectual Property Organization (WIPO), the Geneva Phonograms Convention, the Brussels Satellite Convention, the Universal Copyright Convention, the Bern Convention for the Protection of Literary and Artistic Works, and the Paris Convention for the Protection of Industrial Property.

Protection for intellectual property rights in Panama has in the past been less than adequate in several areas, but the situation has shown signs of improvement. Representatives of some U.S. firms allege that Panama provides inadequate copyright and trademark protection. For this reason, Nintendo of America and associated video game manufacturers petitioned the U.S. TradeRepresentative (USTR) in 1995 to remove Panama's benefits under the Generalized System of Preferences (GSP) program. The case is still pending.

In April 1997, USTR placed Panama on the Special 301 "Watch List" for failure to provide adequate and effective protection of intellectual property rights. In October 1997, USTR removed Panama from the "Watch List" in an out-of-cycle review, upgrading its status to the "Other Observations" category. USTR has cited inadequate border measures to combat transshipment of counterfeited goods through Panama and lack of enforcement in the Colon Free Zone (CFZ) as critical problems. The March 1998 creation of an Intellectual Property Department in the CFZ is viewed as a positive step demonstrating Panama's will to improve enforcement. In its April 1998 review, USTR placed Panama once again in the "Other Observations" category.

In August 1994, the Legislative Assembly passed a Law 15 (the Copyright Law) to help modernize copyright protection. Implementing regulations for the new copyright law were passed in October 1995. A new Industrial Property Law (Law 35) entered into force in November 1996, with implementing regulations issued by decree in 1997. The Government also passed an Anti-Monopoly Law in early 1996 calling for the creation of four commercial courts to hear anti-trust, patent, trademark, and copyright cases exclusively. Two courts and one superior tribunal began to operate in mid-1997, but establishment of the other courts hasbeen delayed. Some U.S. intellectual property owners have experienced significant delays when they have sought infringement remedies in the Panamanian judicial system.

In 1997, Panamanian authorities conducted numerous raids against large video piracy operations, with several cases pending in the courts. Since October 1997, there have been several raids against CFZ companies accused of trafficking in counterfeit trademarked goods. The operating permits of some CFZ companies have been suspended as a result, but transshipment of such goods remains a serious problem.

Patents: Panama's new Industrial Property law provides 20 years of patent protection in place of the former period of 5 to 15 years for foreigners and 5 to 20 years for Panamanians. The law grants patent protection from the date of filing. Pharmaceutical patents are granted for only 15 years, but can be renewed for an additional ten years, if the patent owner licenses a national company (minimum of 30% Panamanian ownership) to exploit the patent. The law also provides for protection of trademarks, simplifying the process of registering trademarks and making them renewable for ten-year periods. The Industrial Property Law provides specific protection for trade secrets.

Copyrights: The National Assembly in 1994 passed a comprehensive copyright bill, based on a World Intellectual Property Organization model. The law modernizes copyright protection in Panama, provides for payment of royalties, facilitates the prosecution of copyright violators, protects computer software, and makes copyright infringement a felony. There is public support for the improvement of copyright protection in Panama, but some domestic interests opposed the new law and have sought to undermine it.

In a July 1996 decision, the Supreme Court suspended the Copyright Office's authority to seize counterfeit merchandise as a result of a legal challenge to the Copyright Law. The Court restored that authority in an October 1997 decision. Although the Attorney General's Office has taken a vigorous enforcement stance, especially against video piracy, the Copyright Office has been ineffective, and Panama's judicial system has not provided speedy and effective remedies for private civil litigants under the law. Panama is in the process of modernizing its copyright registration and patent and trademark registration capabilities. The Government also plans to propose legislation to consolidate copyright, patent, and trademark functions into a single autonomous entity, and to create a specialized Prosecutor's Office for IPR.

EXPROPRIATION AND COMPENSATION

There are no large enterprises at apparent risk of expropriation. There is no de jure discrimination against U.S. or other foreign investors in most areas. There is a constitutional prohibition against foreign land ownership within ten kilometers of the national border or on an island. Neither Panamanian citizens nor foreigners may own beaches or the shores of rivers or lakes. Builders and investors generally rent the land for 20-30 years, via the Ministry of Finance. The tourism incentives law expands this period for up to 40 years.

DISPUTE SETTLEMENT

Panama has a court and judicial system built around a civil code, rather than the Anglo-American system of reliance upon case law and judicial precedent. Fundamental procedural rights in civil cases are broadly similar to those available in U.S. civil courts, although some notice and discovery rights, particularly in administrative matters, may be less extensive than in the U.S. Judicial pleadings are not always a matter of public record, nor is the process always transparent. Many U.S. investors lack confidence in the Panamanian judicial system as an objective, independent arbiter in a legal or commercial dispute, especially when the case involves powerful local figures with political influence. When disputes with foreign investors arise, as they do from time to time, the investors often choose not to pursue remedies available to them via the court system. The decision by investors to avoid the court system is understandable, given massive case backlogs and the aforementioned political influence in case outcomes.

Panama became a member of the International Center for the Settlement of Investment Disputes (ICSID) in 1996. The United States and Panama are near to signing an amendment to the Bilateral Investment Treaty to incorporate Panama's membership.

POLITICAL VIOLENCE

Political violence in Panama is rare. The 1994 national election, which international and domestic observers agree was the cleanest and fairest in three decades, was a model of the democratic political process. Peaceful elections were followed by a calm and coordinated transition as the Endara administration stepped aside to let its political rival take over the reins of the government.

Concentration of wealth, and the high unemployment rate (officially 14% but believed to be higher)and illicit drugs have been cited as the chief causes of crime. This is especially true in Panama's second largest city, Colon, where unemployment among young people is close to 50%, there is a lack of housing, and extreme poverty is commonplace. Although attempts are being made to reform the criminal justice system, it is overloaded, cumbersome, inefficient and at times inequitable.

Previous acts of violence in Panama include a June 1994 grenade used to bomb the car of a prominent Jewish businessman. No arrests have been made in case. In July, 1994, a Panamanian domestic commuter aircraft traveling between Colon and Panama City exploded, killing 21 people, including three American citizens. The attack, which killed several well-known members of Panama's Jewish community remains under investigation and the motive is still unknown. The two incidents prompted the government to tighten airport security and to promise increased police vigilance against terrorists and their alleged support networks.

BILATERAL INVESTMENT AGREEMENTS

Panama has bilateral investment agreements with the United States, the United Kingdom, France, Switzerland, Germany and Taiwan. Panama is not a party to any agreements providing for completely free trade, but does have bilateral preferential trade agreements with Costa Rica, El Salvador, Honduras, Guatemala, Nicaragua, Colombia, Dominican Republic, Mexico, Germany, Bulgaria, Czech Republic, Hungary, Romania, Russia, and Poland. Panama has committed to negotiate a free trade agreement with the Andean Pact and is negotiating agreements with Mexico and Chile.

OPIC AND OTHER INVESTMENT INSURANCE PROGRAMS

OPIC currently supports only one U.S. investment in Panama. In previous years, OPIC has supported over 30 projects in Panama. In general, modest expansion of OPIC programs would be possible, if Panama facilitated approval for any OPIC-insured investment and if Panama lifted the restriction on foreign government ownership of land. OPIC has no desire to own land in Panama, but typically collateralizes loans with land, as is standard worldwide.

MAJOR FOREIGN INVESTORS

- Adrian Resources
- Alireza Mobil
- American Airlines
- American Hospital Supply Co.
- American Life Insurance Co.
- AOKI Corporation
- AT&T
- Banco Do Brasil
- Banco Exterior, S.A.
- Becton Dickinson & Co.
- Bell South Corp.
- Black and Decker International Corp.
- Borden Co.
- Braswell Service Group
- Bristol Laboratories International Corp.
- Cable and Wireless (U.K.)
- Challenge Air Cargo
- Chase Manhattan Bank, N.A.
- Cheesebrough Pond's Int. Ltd.
- Chiriqui Land Company (Chiquita)
- Chevron Corp.
- Citibank, N.A.
- Coca-Cola Bottling Co.
- Colgate Palmolive (Central America), Inc.
- Cyprus Minerals Co.
- Del Monte Corporation
- Dole Foods Co.

- Eastman Kodak Company
- Environmental System Research Institute
- Exxon Corp.
- Esso Standard Oil, S.A.
- First National Bank of Boston
- Freeport Exploration Co.
- General Mills Inc.
- Georgia Pacific Corp.
- Gillette Co.
- Glidden - Durkee
- Greenstone Resources
- Griffith Laboratories, Inc.
- Grupo Carvajal
- Goldstar Corp.
- GTE
- Hong Kong Shangai Bank
- Hospital Corporation of America
- Hutchison Port Holdings (Hong Kong)
- IBM
- ICA
- International Proteins Corp.
- Jenny Manufacturing, Inc.
- Johnson and Johnson
- Kansas City Southern Industries
- Kendall Company
- Ketchum Public Relations
- Kimberly-Clark International, S.A.
- Kraft Foods, Inc.
- Lanier Worldwide, Inc.
- Lykes Line
- Marine Midland Bank
- McDonald's Corporation
- Merrill Lynch, Pierce, Fenner & Smith Int'l
- Mi-Jack Products
- Minnesota, Mining & Manufacturing
- Nabisco Brands Inc.
- Nestle Company
- Northville Industries Corp.
- Otis Elevator Company
- Chas. Pfizer & Company, Inc.
- Panasonic Latin America
- Phelps Dodge Corp.
- Phillip Morris, Inc.
- PYCSA, S.A.
- Revlon Inc.

- Rubbermaid Inc.
- Samsung Electronics
- Schering Corp. International
- Seaboard Marine Ltd.
- Sears, Roebuck & Co.
- Sherwin Williams
- Shell Co. (WI) Ltd.
- Sony Corporation
- Sterling Drugs International
- Stevedoring Services of America
- Swift and Company
- Swiss Bank Corp.
- Syntex Corporation
- Technoserve Inc.
- Texaco Inc.
- TRT Telecommunications Corp.
- Twentieth Century Fox
- United Brands
- United Parcel Service
- UNYSIS USA
- Warner Lambert Co.
- Xerox Corp.

PANAMA OFFSHORE SECTOR

The term 'offshore' is not used in Panama legislation; since taxation is on a 'territorial' basis, ie only Panama-sourced income is taxed, an entity which has its activities or assets outside Panama will automatically escape taxation. There are more than 120,000 corporate entities in Panama, of which the majority are 'offshore'.

BASIC INFORMATION

FORMS OF OFFSHORE OPERATION

Offshore entities may take the following forms:

- Corporation (Sociedad Anonima)
- Foreign Corporation
- General or Limited Partnership
- Civil Partnership
- Foundation
- Trust

Licenses are required only for financial institutionsCorporations do not have to disclose beneficial ownership, and Trusts and Foundations need not disclose the names of their beneficiaries. Limited Partnerships do however need to disclose the names of their members.

PANAMA'S INCLUSION ON FATF BLACKLIST

In June 2000, Panama was identified by the FATF as a non-cooperative tax haven in the global fight against money-laundering. The result of this is that Panama was one of fifteen tax jurisdictions placed on an FATF blacklist. Each offending tax haven has a year in which to correct its regulations and legislation

The FATF released an annual report in June 2001, in which the organisation revised its list of countries and territories deemed non-cooperative. Only four were removed from the list, including Panama (the other three being the Cayman Islands, Liechtenstein and the Bahamas). Panama was praised by the FATF for its substantial efforts to conform to forty recommendations set out by the FATF in a code of good practice governing money laundering.

TAX TREATMENT OF OFFSHORE OPERATIONS

Income tax is levied only on income derived from operations within Panama. A Panama business entity can direct its offshore activities from Panama without becoming liable for tax. The Fiscal Code (Article 694) excludes the following types of income from the tax net:

- the profits of re-invoicing external goods or services;
- the profits of operations that are directed from Panama but carried out externally;
- the distribution of dividends derived from external income, including the above types of income.

Interest on deposits with Panamanian banks is exempt from taxation whatever the source of the cash.

An entity with both external and Panamanian business activities is taxed only on the Panama-derived income, and is subject to withholding tax only on that income

Panama business entities with only external operations are exempt from the Dividends (Withholding) Tax, the Undistributed Profits Tax, the Business Tax, and from Stamp Duty on contracts executed in Panama to be performed elsewhere.

Companies in the Colon Free Zone, or in Export Processing Zones, are treated in the same way as companies with external operations, as described above.

Taxation of Foreign Employees of Offshore Operations

This section refers to the taxation of foreign employees of offshore operations, There are no statutory residence rules as such, but an individual is considered resident if he is present in Panama for more than 180 days in any one tax year. Residence has to be officicially recognised by the Government.

There is no distinction between foreign and Panamanian employees, whether or not the business is 'offshore'. The territorial basis of taxation applies to individuals as it does to business entities, so that individuals pay income tax on Panama-source income. 'Panamanian-source' means, that the services rendered are deemed to be provided within Panama - if a Panamanian entity pays an employee for services rendered abroad, tax will not be due.

Exchange Control

There are no exchange controls in Panama, which in effect uses the US dollar as its currency other than for very small transactions in the Balboa, which is at parity with the dollar. There is no Central Bank.

Offshore Activities

'Offshore' entities are not prohibited from carrying on business activities in Panama, other than banks with International or Representation Licenses but will be taxed on income arising from domestic trading, and will need to segregate such trading in their accounts.

Shipping Registry Fees

Provisional registration for 6 months costs $500, and $50 for renewal; the renewable provisional 3-month radio licence costs $150 per quarter.

Under Law no. 4 of 1983 (as amended) ongoing annual registration fees and duties (Consular Tasa) are based on tonnage as follows:

Tonnage, GRT	Registration Fee, $
Up to 2,000	500
Over 2,000 up to 5,000	2,000
Over 5,000 up to 15,000	3,000
Over 15,000	plus $0.10 per GRT to a maximum of $6,500

Tonnage, GRT	Consular Tasa, $
Up to 1,000	1,200
Over 1,000 up to 3,000	1,800
Over 3,000 up to 5,000	2,000
Over 5,000 up to 15,000	2,700
Over 15,000	3,000

There are also annual Tasa charges dependent on tonnage covering inspection and regulatory costs.

There is a separate scale of duties for barges, pontons and vessels operated other than for profit.

There is also a separate regime for pleasure vessels under which registration is on a renewable 2-year basis; a single fee of $1,500 ($1,000 for a Panamanian individual or corporation) is payable every two years. Pleasure vessels are exempt from duties and other Tasa charges.

EMPLOYMENT AND RESIDENCE

The employment market is quite closely regulated: the law sets maximum percentages for the employment of foreigners in a business according to its sector. However, foreign companies are allowed to fill senior and/or sensitive positions with expatriates.

Long-stay working residents are issued with Immigrant visas if their employment is permitted. Short-stay visas are issued freely. The Tourist-Pensioner visa is given to those who can demonstrate a monthly income of not less than $750 from interest on time-deposits in a Panamanian bank; the Investor's visa is for those who invest their own capital into local business activity.

CORPORATE TAXES

Taxation in Panama, which is governed by the Fiscal Code, is on a territorial basis; this is to say, that taxes apply only to income or gains derived through business carried on in Panama itself. The existence of a sales or administration office in Panama, or the re-invoicing of external transactions at a profit, does not of itself give rise to taxation if the underlying transactions take place outside Panama. Dividends paid out of such earnings are free of taxation.

In addition to the taxes described below, employers pay social security contributions in respect of employees

SCOPE OF INCOME TAX

Income tax is payable on the income of a Panama or foreign corporation or other entity derived from business carried on within Panama; a corporation carrying on business both inside and outside Panama will pay tax on the proportion of its income that arises within the country. Capital gains are counted as income after deduction of allowances.

RATES OF INCOME TAX

The rate of income tax in Panama is 30% on chargeable income; a higher rate of 34% applies to income over PAB 500,000 for companies that are registered with the Official Registry of National Industry or that have government contracts. Companies with gross income below PAB 200,000 pay lower rates on the first PAB 100,000 of their taxable income.

There is a withholding tax of 10% on dividends paid out of taxed income. If less than 40% of taxed income is distributed, then Undistributed Profits Tax of 10% becomes payable on the undistributed balance; this therefore amounts to a maximum of 4% tax. In effect this is an advance withholding tax, and it is creditable against the 10% tax on later distributions of the taxed profit.

CALCULATION OF TAXABLE BASE

Taxable income is Panama-source income less allowable deductions, except that transportation sector companies may choose to calculate their taxable income as 3% of gross revenue; telecommunications companies need pay tax on only 50% of their normally taxable income.

Dividends are not included in taxable income (either because, if Panama-sourced they will have been subject to withholding tax at 10%, or because, if they are foreign, they are exempt). Expenses associated with receipt of dividends are not deductible. Interest received from time-deposits in Panama banks or from Government securities is exempt.

Stocks are valued at cost, with several different bases being allowed, including FIFO and average cost. 'Cost' means purchase price including import duties, or the cost of manufacturing including direct overhead.

Allowable deductions include:

- Expenses paid or incurred for the production of income or the maintenance of a source of income;
- Depreciation of capital assets is mandatory, usually by the straight-line method. The life of assets is at the tax-payer's discretion, subject to a minimum of 3 years (30 years for immovable property).
- Interest on loans employed for the production of income, but not if they are made on the security of a term deposit;
- Bad debt provisions are allowable up to 1% of sales, with a maximum reserve of 10% of receivables;

Losses can be employed over 5 years forward at 20% per year, but only to offset up to 50% of taxable income; any losses not so employed are lost. There is no group or consortium relief, although it is sometimes possible to assign tax credits between companies.

NB: This brief summary of some of the more important aspects of Panama income tax law is given for general information only; it should not be relied upon in actual situations, for which professional tax advice is necessary.

FILING REQUIREMENTS AND PAYMENT OF TAX

The tax year is the calendar year, ending 31st December, although a different year can be agreed with the tax authorities. A tax return is due within three months (can be extended to six). The previous year's tax return must be accompanied by a forecast of the current year's tax, which is then payable in three instalments after six, nine and twelve months after the end of the previous year.

Any under-payment of tax must be paid along with submission of the previous year's return.

WITHHOLDING TAX

Dividends paid out by Panamanian companies are subject to 10% withholding tax; the rate is 20% for dividends on bearer shares. Dividends paid to a Panamanian holding company however are not subject to withholding.

If less than 40% of taxed income is distributed, then Undistributed Profits Tax of 10% becomes payable on the undistributed balance; this therefore amounts to a maximum of 4% tax. In effect this is an advance withholding tax, and it is creditable against the 10% tax on later distributions of the taxed income.

Branches of foreign corporations pay the 10% 'deemed dividend tax' on their full taxed income (making their effective taxation rate equal to 37%); but they are not subject to withholding tax on eventual distributions.

REAL ESTATE TAXES (CAPITAL GAINS TAX)

There are annual taxes on the value of real estate, plus capital gains tax on profits from the sale of real estate, and a transfer tax arising on sale.

The annual tax, under Article 766 of the Fiscal Code, is based on official valuations, and is levied on a sliding scale, starting from 1.4% on the first PAB 10,000 of value, and rising to 2.1% on value in excess of PAB 75,000.

Capital Gains Tax is levied on real estate gains under Article 701 of the Fiscal Code and Articles 89 and 90 of the Income Tax Regulations. The rate of tax is 30% on the taxable gain after deductions, but the calculation basis is quite complex, at least for persons not otherwise paying much tax.

The tax on the transfer of real estate (not new homes) is 2%, payable by the seller, which is credited against capital gains tax.

STAMP DUTY

Most official and public documents in Panama require stamping, including sales invoices, receipts, legal submissions and contracts. Fiscal stamps are on sale in various denominations; pre-stamped paper can be bought at PAB 4 the sheet.

It is possible to account for stamp duty on a quarterly or half-yearly basis to the tax authorities.

COMMERCIAL LICENSE TAX

Companies carrying on business in Panama (not Free Zone companies or offshore companies) need to pay an annual Commercial License Tax of 1% of the net worth of the business (minimum PAB 10, maximum PAB 20,000). Certain rural and/or small business are exempt from the tax. In addition to the national business license tax, municipalities also levy similar taxes on businesses.

PERSONAL TAXATION

RESIDENCE AND TAXATION

There are no statutory residence rules as such, but an individual is considered resident if he is present in Panama for more than 180 days in any one tax year. Residence has to be officially recognised by the Government.

As regards taxation, there is no distinction between foreign and Panamanian individuals. The territorial basis of taxation applies to individuals as it does to business entities, so that individuals pay income tax on Panama-source income. 'Panamanian-source' means, that the services rendered are deemed to be provided within Panama - if a Panamanian entity pays an employee for services rendered abroad, tax will not be due.

INCOME TAX

Income is defined as the aggregate of income from Panamanian sources after deduction of allowable expenses and losses and ignoring exempt income. Income includes income from employment and from rendering independent personal services, income from business activities, and investment income.

Employment income in respect of work done in Panama is taxable regardless of where the payment is made or received. Dividends are not included in income (they will have been subject to the final withholding tax of 10%.)

Capital gains are included in taxable income. The taxpayer has a choice of methods in computing the taxable gain on sales of real estate; gains on sales of securities issued by Panamanian companies and other personal property are taxable without adjustment; however, gains on the sale of securities listed with the National Securities Commission are exempt from tax.

Individuals have a personal allowance of PAB 800 (1,600 for a married couple filing together), plus PAB 250 for each dependent. Mortgage interest is deductible up to PAB 15,000 per year; medical expenses incurred in Panama are deductible, as are health insurance premiums and some charitable donations.

The rates of tax on taxable income are as follows:

Band of Income, PAB	Rate of Tax, %
Up to 3,000	nil
3,001 to 3.250	52
3,251 to 4,000	4
4,001 to 6,000	6.5
6,001 to 10,000	11
10,001 to 15,000	16.5
15,001 to 20,000	19.0
20,001 to 30,000	22
30,001 to 40,000	27
40,001 to 50,000	30
50,001 to 200,000	33
over 200,000	30

SOCIAL SECURITY TAXES

Employers and employees make social security contributions in Panama: the employer pays 10.75% of salaries and wages, plus 1.5% educational tax; the employee pays 7.25% plus 1.25%. The employer deducts the social security contribution along with income tax. The self-employed also make contributions.

STAMP DUTY

Most official and public documents in Panama require stamping, including sales invoices, receipts, legal submissions and contracts. Fiscal stamps are on sale in various denominations; pre-stamped paper can be bought at PAB 4 the sheet.

REAL ESTATE TAX

There is an annual tax on the value of real estate, under Article 766 of the Fiscal Code. It is based on official valuations, and is levied on a sliding scale, starting from 1.4% on the first PAB 10,000 of value, and rising to 2.1% on value in excess of PAB 75,000.

A tax on the transfer of real estate (not new homes) is 2%, payable by the seller, which is credited against capital gains tax (see Income Tax, above).

VALUE ADDED TAX

VAT (impuesto a la transferencia de bienes corporales muebles) is a tax on consumers imposed on transfers of personal property by sale or otherwise, and also applies to imports. The taxable value is the price paid plus ancillary charges, or in the case of imports, the customs value plus customs charges. The rate is generally 5%, but it is 10% for imports, alcohol and tobacco.

DOUBLE TAX TREATIES

Since Panama does not levy taxes on foreign source income, it has no double tax treaties.

OTHER INTERNATIONAL AGREEMENTS

Mutual Assistance Treaties: Panama has concluded mutual legal assistance treaties with the US, Costa Rica, El Salvador, Guatemala, Honduras, Nicaragua and Colombia. The treaties operate at the administrative level: in other words, Court procedures are not required, although there is an appeal procedure. The treaties cover serious crime, but do not include fiscal crime. The Panamanian authorities do not entertain requests for information on fiscal matters.

Panama's Inclusion on FATF Blacklist: In June 2000, Panama was identified by the OECD as a non-cooperative and harmful tax haven. The result of this is that Panama is one of fifteen tax jurisdictions placed on an FATF blacklist.

Panama, as with the other blacklisted tax havens, will be given a year to conform. Those who do not conform within the year will be dealt with by measures set out in a US Anti-Money Laundering Bill. The Bill is currently in the draft stage, but it aims to give sweeping powers to the US, which will prevent US financial institutions from dealing directly with errant jurisdictions or with specified institutions in those jurisdictions.

SELECTED BUSINESS CONTACTS

ACCOUNTING AND AUDITING

Offshore Solutions Inc

Calle Elvira Mendez #10, Banco do Brasil Building 1st Floor, Ofic #1 P O Box 85-0070, Panama 5 Republic of Panama	Telephone +507 223 2027	Fax +507 264 3224

Banking Services and Asset Management

Fortress Management Group		
P.O. Box 0832-0817 World Trade Center, Panama City, Rep. Of Panama	Telephone + 507 315 1073	Fax +507 315 1074
The Harris Organisation		
P O Box 0832-0795, World Trade Center Panama, Republic of Panama	Telephone +507 263 6900	Fax +507 263 6964
O.P.M. Corporation		
Apartado 55-0382 Panama, R. of P.	Telephone +809 221 6984	Fax +809 221 8678
Trust Services, S.A.		
Apartado 6-2495, Estafeta El Dorado, Panama, Rep. Of Panama	Telephone +507 269 2438	Fax +507

Offshore Company and Ship Registration

American Finance & Development Group SA		
Calle 61 #23A, P O Box 871047 Panama 7, Republic of Panama	Telephone +507 223 3172	Fax +507 223 3899
Arias Fabrega & Fabrega		
Edificio Plaza Bancomer, Calle 50 y Calle 53 Apartado 6307, Panama 5, Republic of Panama	Telephone +507 263 9200	Fax +507 263 8919
Arosemena Noriega & Contreras		
Calle Elvira Mendez #10, Banco do Brasil Building 2nd Floor, Panama City, P O Box 5246 Republic of Panama	Telephone +507 265 3411	Fax +507 264 4569

Trust Management

American Finance & Development Group SA		
Calle 61 #23A, P O Box 871047 Panama 7, Republic of Panama	Telephone +507 223 3172	Fax +507 223 3899
Arosemena Noriega & Contreras		
Calle Elvira Mendez #10, Banco do Brasil Building 2nd Floor, Panama City, P O Box 5246	Telephone +507 265 3411	Fax +507 264 4569

TRAVELING10 REASONS WHY PANAMA IS A GREAT TOURIST DESTINATION

There are many new and excellent tourist destinations in Panama. You can be one of the first to discover them. You will understand why the Americans who lived in the former Panama Canal Zone (now reluctantly leaving) refer to Panama as "Paradise Lost."

1. Panama is the best place for ecotourism today.
Panama has some of the world's most beautiful and biodiverse rainforests. As one indicator of biodiversity, Panama has more bird species than the US and Canada combined: 934. Furthermore, all that great nature is very accessible. Some of the best locations are just 30 minutes from Panama City. There is a saying that in Costa Rica, there are 20 tourists to look at one bird, while in Panama there are 20 birds for one tourist to look at. There is much truth to this. An article in an Audubon Society Magazine rates Panama's Canopy Tower as one of the top eight nature lodges in the world.

It is interesting to contrast Panama today with Costa Rica today. Costa Rica has seen an upsurge in tourist-related crime, and prices. It has become more difficult to do on your own. Panama is friendlier, easier to get around with much better roads, less touristy and with many of the counterparts to Costa Rica (rainforests, volcanoes, Indians, tropical forest, beaches) plus the Canal and more historic attractions at a lower cost with less commercial hassle.

2. Panama is economical.
Because tourism is just beginning, prices are still modest and you can really stretch your tourist dollar. Within Panama City, taxis and meals and hotel prices in all categories are particularly pleasing. Yet, even though it is economical, you will find that Panamanians know how to do things right. They want you to be happy and come back again.

3. Panama is safe.
In fact, it is one of the safest tourist destinations anywhere. According an article on tourist safety in Newsweek (Feb. 22, l999), Panama was rated by the prestigious Pinkerton Intelligence Agency in the highest category for tourist safety. The crime rate is very low. Unlike other places in Latin American, most taxi drivers are honest and crimes that plague foreigners in other countries like purse-snatching and pick pocketing are rare. You are safe in Panama- just relax and enjoy!

4. Panama is tourist friendly.
This may be Latin America, but you don't need Spanish. Most people here speak English as a second language. Calculating the value of the local currency versus the American dollar? No problem! The currency of Panama IS the American

dollar! Panamanians have been working closely with foreigners - the Americans in the Canal Zone - for nearly a hundred years. They are accustomed to us, understand us, like us and have a sense for what Americans appreciate.

5. Panama is a first-world country in many ways.
Panama has a sophisticated service-based economy, tap water you can drink, high quality services, excellent roads and highways. There is a long tradition of service to foreigners as an international crossroads and the educated populace speaks English as a second language. Serious political difficulties are a thing of the past and Panama now has one of Latin America's most exemplary democracies.

6. Panama has a wide selection of beaches, island venues and activities.
With two coasts, countless islands and Caribbean style beaches ,there is much to choose from for beach vacations: full service resorts (Coronado, Contadora, Banana Village) exotic off-the-beaten-track getaways (Bocas del Toro), Indian reservation islands (San Blas) etc.

7. Panama has some of the best and most accessible places in the world for bird watching and nature observation.
Pipeline Road, the scene of a world record (350 bird species counted in one day) is scarcely a half an hour from Panama City. In Panama, you can get very close to the best of tropical nature without traveling long distances, giving up your creature comforts or putting yourself in any kind of danger.

8. Panama has an unusual variety of attractions.
Panama has exotic tropical rainforests, cool gorgeous mountain refuges, Caribbean-style beaches, Indian tribes, a pretty Miami- style capital city, historic venues (Balboa and Columbus left their mark in Panama) adventure tours, kayaking, white water rafting, not to mention one of the engineering marvels of the world- the Panama Canal. There is so much to do and see in Panama that the prestigious Lonely Planet just published (1999) an entire guide book on Panama.

9. Panama has world-class fishing, diving, snorkeling and sailing.
One place in Panama, Bahia Pina, holds 170 world fishing records. There are five world-class diving and snorkeling areas- Bocas del Toro, Coiba Island, the Pearl Islands, Isla Grande and for historical diving, the Panama Canal itself.

10. Panama is a great place for ethnotourism.
Panama has not one, but 6 colorful Indian tribes right out of the pages of National Geographic. Each of them has preserved its own fascinating life lifestyle. Many live in accessible locations and happy to share their life and culture with visitors.

US STATE DEPARTMENT SUGGESTION

COUNTRY DESCRIPTION: Panama has a developing economy. The capital is Panama City. Outside the Panama City area, which has many first class hotels and restaurants, tourist facilities vary in quality. U.S. currency is valid in Panama, and it is exchangeable on a one-to-one basis with the Panamanian Balboa. As of January 1, 2000, all U.S. military facilities in the Panama Canal Zone have been transferred to Panamanian control.

ENTRY REQUIREMENTS: U.S. citizens are encouraged to obtain a U.S. passport before traveling to Panama. Although entry into Panama is permitted with any proof of U.S. citizenship (such as a certified birth certificate or a naturalization certificate) and official photo identification (such as a driver's license), travelers may experience difficulties entering Panama or returning to the U.S. when not in possession of a valid U.S. passport. Panamanian law requires that travelers must either purchase a tourist card from the airline serving Panama or obtain a visa from a Panamanian embassy or consulate before traveling to Panama. Further information may be obtained from the Embassy of Panama, 2862 McGill Terrace, N.W., Washington, D.C. 20009, telephone 202/483-1407, or from the Panamanian consulates in Atlanta, Chicago, Houston, Los Angeles, Miami, New Orleans, New York, Philadelphia or Tampa.

U.S. citizens transiting the Panama Canal as passengers do not need to obtain visas, report to customs, or pay any fees. U.S. citizens piloting private craft through the canal should contact the U.S. Embassy in Panama City for details on required procedures.

SAFETY/SECURITY: Travel toward Colombia beyond Yaviza in Darien Province and Punta Carreto in Comarca de San Blas Province may be dangerous. There is limited Panamanian police presence in these areas, which are known to be frequented by Colombian guerrillas and paramilitary groups, drug smugglers, and undocumented aliens. Travel beyond Yaviza towards the Colombian border is possible only by foot and is risky for individual travelers or small groups. This information also pertains to the Ancon Nature Preserve at Cana in the Darien National Park, due to its proximity to the Colombian border and possible cross-border activity by Colombian rebels.

From time to time, there may be demonstrations or other manifestations of anti-American sentiment by small but vociferous groups. While there is no evidence that U.S. citizens might be targeted (most demonstrations often have nothing to do with the U.S., but relate to labor disputes or other local issues), and while such protests are typically non-violent, it is nonetheless a good security practice to avoid demonstrations. Should further information be required, please contact the U.S. Embassy Consular Section.

On the Pacific coast, boaters should steer clear of Coiba Island, which houses a penal colony, and be wary of vessels that may be transporting narcotics northward from Colombia; similarly, boaters should avoid the southeastern coast of Comarca de San Blas, south of Punta Carreto. With the 1999 departure of the U.S. military from Panama, local maritime search and rescue capabilities are greatly diminished.

CRIME INFORMATION: There is a moderate level of crime in the Panama City and Colon areas. Crimes there are typical of those that plague metropolitan areas and range from armed robberies to rape, muggings, purse-snatchings, petty theft, and narcotics possession, use, and trafficking. The Consular Section of the U.S. Embassy regularly receives reports about incidents of crimes from U.S. tourists, business people, and residents. Many incidents are reported to have occurred in the following neighborhoods: Veracruz Beach, Chorrillo, Ancon, Curundu, Panama Viejo, San Miguelito, Rio Abajo and Madden Dam. U.S. citizens should be aware of their surroundings, especially at night.

A curfew for minors under 18 years of age has been in effect throughout Panama City since October 1996. Under the law, students attending night classes must have a carnet issued by the school or, if employed, a Certificate of Employment. Minors who are picked up for a curfew violation are subject to detention at a police station until parents or legal guardians can arrange for them to be released into their custody. Parents or legal guardians may be fined up to $50.00 (U.S.) for the violation.

The loss or theft abroad of a U.S. passport should be reported immediately to the local police and the nearest U.S. embassy or consulate. Travelers can refer to the Department of State's pamphlet, A Safe Trip Abroad, for ways to promote a more trouble-free journey. This publication and others, such as Tips For Travelers to Central and South America, are available by mail from the Superintendent of Documents, U.S. Government Printing Office, Washington, DC 20402, via the Internet at http://www.access.gpo.gov/su_docs, or via the Bureau of Consular Affairs home page at http://travel.state.gov.

CRIMINAL PENALTIES: While in a foreign country, a U.S. citizen is subject to that country's laws and regulations, which sometimes differ significantly from those in the U.S. and may not afford the protections available to the individual under U.S. law. Penalties for breaking the law can be more severe than in the U.S. for similar offenses. Persons violating Panamanian laws, even unknowingly, may be expelled, arrested or imprisoned. Penalties for possession, use, or trafficking in illegal drugs in Panama are strict, and convicted offenders can expect jail sentences and heavy fines.

MEDICAL FACILITIES: Although Panama City has some very good medical facilities, outside the capital these facilities are limited. Serious medical problems requiring hospitalization and/or medical evacuation to the United States can cost thousands of dollars or more. Doctors and hospitals often expect immediate cash payment for health services. Most hospitals accept credit cards for hospital charges, but not for doctors' fees.

MEDICAL INSURANCE: U.S. medical insurance is not always valid outside the United States. U.S. Medicare and Medicaid programs do not provide payment for care outside the United States. Uninsured travelers who require medical care overseas may face extreme difficulties. Please check with your own insurance company to confirm whether your policy applies overseas, including provision for medical evacuation. Please ascertain whether payment will be made to the overseas hospital or doctor or whether you will be reimbursed later for expenses that you incur. Some insurance policies also include coverage for psychiatric treatment and for disposition of remains in the event of death. Useful information on medical emergencies abroad, including overseas insurance programs, is provided in the Department of State's brochure Medical Information for Americans Traveling Abroad, available via the Bureau of Consular Affairs home page or via autofax at (202) 647-3000.

OTHER HEALTH INFORMATION: Information on vaccinations and other health precautions may be obtained from the Centers for Disease Control and Prevention's hotline for international travelers at 1-877-FYI-TRIP (1-877-394-8747); fax 1-888-CDC-FAXX (1-888-232-3299), or via their Internet site at http://www.cdc.gov.

TRAFFIC SAFETY AND ROAD CONDITIONS: While in a foreign country, U.S. citizens may encounter road conditions that differ significantly from those in the United States. The information below concerning Panama is provided for general reference only, and may not be totally accurate in a particular location or circumstance.
Safety of Public Transportation: Poor
Urban Road Conditions/Maintenance: Good
Rural Road Conditions/Maintenance: Poor
Availability of Roadside Assistance: Fair

Flooding during the rainy season, which lasts from April to December, washes out some roads in the interior and renders others impassable by car. Roads in the interior are often poorly maintained and lack illumination at night. Road travel is more dangerous during the rainy season and in the interior from Carnival through Good Friday (Carnival starts the Saturday prior to Ash Wednesday and goes on for four days; from Ash Wednesday there are 40 days to Good Friday). On roads where poor lighting and driving conditions prevail, night driving is difficult, and should be approached with caution. Buses and taxis are not always maintained in safe operating condition due to lack of regulatory enforcement.

Driving is often hazardous and demanding due to dense traffic, undisciplined driving habits, poorly maintained streets, and a lack of effective signs and traffic signals. Auto insurance is not mandatory, and many drivers are uninsured. If an accident occurs, the law requires that the vehicles remain in place until a police officer responds to investigate.

TRAVELING ON THE PAN AMERICAN HIGHWAY: The Pan American Highway ends at Yaviza in the Darien Province of Panama, and the final portion from Chepo to Yaviza is reasonably passable only during the dry season (January-April). If destined for South America, automobile travelers may wish to ship their cars on a freighter. (The auto/passenger ferry service "Crucero Express" ceased operations in early 1997.)

AVIATION SAFETY OVERSIGHT: The U.S. Federal Aviation Administration (FAA) has assessed the Government of Panama's Civil Aviation Authority as Category 1 -- in compliance with international aviation safety standards for oversight of Panama's air carrier operations. For further information, travelers may contact the Department of Transportation within the United States at telephone 1-800-322-7873, or visit the FAA's Internet web site at http://www.faa.gov/avr/iasa/index.htm. The U.S. Department of Defense (DOD) separately assesses some foreign air carriers for suitability as official providers of air services. For information regarding the DOD policy on specific carriers, travelers may contact the DOD at telephone (618) 256-4801.

DOMESTIC AIR TRAVEL: Only Tocumen International Airport employs airport security measures known to meet international standards. Security measures at domestic commuter fields that serve popular travel destinations such as the Colon Free Zone, Contadora Island and the San Blas Islands, including Albrook Airport, are lax. The U.S. Embassy has received anecdotal information that maintenance and pilot safety procedures on small carriers flying only domestic routes do not meet U.S. standards.

CHILDREN'S ISSUES: For information on international adoption of children and international parental child abduction, please refer to our Internet site at http://travel.state.gov/children's_issues.html, or telephone (202) 736-7000.

EMBASSY LOCATION/REGISTRATION: U.S. citizens living in or visiting Panama are encouraged to register at the Consular Section of the U.S. Embassy in Panama and obtain updated information on travel and security within Panama. The Consular Section of the U.S. Embassy is located on Panama Bay, Panama City, at Balboa Avenue and 39th Street. The international mailing address is Apartado 6959, Panama 5, Republic of Panama. The U.S. mailing address is U.S. Embassy Panama, Department of State, Washington, D.C. 20521-9100. The telephone number of the Consular Section is 011-507-225-1495/6988 (after hours, 011-507-227-1377); fax 011-507-225-1495; web site http://www.orbi.net/usispan/ and e-mail is usispan@pty.com.

Foreign visitors should use the same precautions while traveling in Panama as in any metropolitan U.S. city.

BUSINESS CUSTOMS

Business practices and customs in Panama are a unique blend of North American methods and traditional Latin style. Foreign corporations operating in Panama are important in shaping the style and manner of doing business.

Most private business offices are open from 8:00 a.m. until 5:00 p.m., Monday through Friday, and Saturdays from 8:00 a.m. to 12 noon. Banks are open from 8:00 a.m. to 1:00 p.m., Monday through Friday. Most government offices are open from 8:30 a.m. to 4:30 p.m., Monday through Friday.

TRAVEL ADVISORY AND VISAS

U.S. Citizens are subject to Panamanian law when visiting Panama and penalties for possession, use and trafficking in illegal drugs are severe.

In 1987, the State Department's Bureau of Consular Affairs established the Consular Affairs Bulletin Board (CABB), as a means to keep the international business community informed about security and crime problems abroad. Access to the CABB is free of charge to anyone with a computer and a modem. Callers dial 202-647-9225 from their modem. Consular Affairs and the Bureau of Diplomatic Security update the CABB daily.

The Travel Advisory Service of the Department of State provides foreign travel information and, when appropriate, warnings. Phone: (202)647-5225 or Fax: (202)647-3000.

U.S. citizens may enter Panama with a passport or a certified copy of a U.S. birth certificate and an official picture I.D., (e.g. driver's license) and a Tourist Card purchased for $ 5.00 from an airline serving Panama. The Tourist Card is valid for 30 days and may be extended for two more 30-day periods. The following are three types of Visas available to businesspersons wishing to spend extended periods of time in Panama:

1. Inversionista (Investor): A minimum of $ 100,000 must be invested and $ 600 must be deposited in advance ($ 500 with the Ministry of Government and Justice and $ 100 with the Ministry of Treasury).

2. Visa de Visitante Temporal (Temporary Visitor's Visa): For executives or technicians working with a company in Panama for a limited time. The Visa is valid for one year and is renewable.

3. Temporal Especial (Working Permit): For professional or skilled personnel transferred from an overseas office to work in Panama temporarily. The applicant must prove his earnings will come from outside of Panama. The Visa is valid three to six months.

Further information can be obtained from the Consular Section of the U.S. Embassy in Panama, Unit 0945, APO AA 34002, Tel: (507) 227-6988, Fax: (507) 227-0239.

HOLIDAYS

All private, government, municipal and U.S. Embassy offices are closed during local holidays. In addition the U.S. Mission observes all U.S. holidays.

The national holidays for 1999 are:

January 1 New Year's Day
January 9 Mourning Day (observed, January 11, Monday)
February 15 Carnival
April 2 Good Friday
May 1 Labor Day (observed, January 3, Monday)
November 3 Independence Day from Colombia
November 4 Flag Day
November 10 The Uprising of Los Santos (observed, November 8, Monday)
November 28 Independence Day from Spain (observed, November 29, Monday)
December 8 Mother's Day (observed, December 6)
December 25 Christmas Day

There are a large number of Jewish owned businesses, which observe Jewish holidays.

BUSINESS INFRASTRUCTURE

Panama's official language is Spanish. However, English is widely spoken as a second language in the main cities. Panama has excellent local and international telephone services. Direct dialing is available to more than 150 countries worldwide. There are 170 radio stations and 5 television stations in Panama.

Health conditions in Panama are good, especially in the urban centers. Running water is available in almost all parts of the country and is usually potable. Use of bottled water or boiling before use is necessary only in some rural areas and small towns in the provinces.

There are several international level hotels. Facilities usually include swimming pools, tennis courts, fitness centers, clothing and souvenir shops, casinos, restaurants, coffee shops and bars.

Furnished apartments are available for longer stays. A wide variety of restaurants offer international cuisine, including Chinese, Italian, Mexican, Indian, Spanish and Japanese. Several specialize in seafood. All large hotels offer American, European, and local cuisine. There are some hotel coffee shops that are open around the clock.

Transportation from the International Airport into Panama City is by a special taxi service, and the price ranges from $ 12 per trip for small taxis to $ 20 for large taxis. There is no bus service, however, taxis may be shared with other passengers. Car rentals are also available.

Buses and Taxis are readily available in urban areas. Taxi fares are low and usually range from one to five dollars depending on the trip's length.

The official currency of Panama is the Balboa (symbol B/.) which is the same as the U.S. Dollar. The Balboa exists only in coin form of the same denomination and size as U.S. coins. Both U.S. paper currency and coins are legal tender and circulate freely.

The U.S. system of weights and measures and the metric system are both used in Panama. Speed limits are posted in miles per hour in some places and kilometers per hour in other places. Some signs have both mile and kilometer speed limits.

GETTING THERE

AIR

Panama's national airline is *Compaña Panaomeña de Aviación (COPA).*

Approximate flight times: From Panama City to Miami is 2 hours 45 minutes.

International airport: *Panama City (PTY)* (Tocumen) is 27km (17 miles) northeast of the city (travel time – 30-60 minutes). Airport services include a bank, car hire, restaurant and full duty-free facilities. Buses and taxis go to the city.

Departure tax: B20. Children under two years are exempt.

SEA

The Panama Canal is the major route from the Atlantic to the Pacific Ocean, and Panama (Balboa) is a port of call for many cruise lines and ocean vessels for both passenger and freight. Cruise lines include *Sitmar, Cunard, Royal Viking, Princess, Delta, Norwegian American* and *P&O.*

TRAIN

There is currently no rail link betwen Panama and other international destinations.

ROAD

The principal route to Panama is the Pan-American Highway from Costa Rica to Panama City. The Trans-Isthman Highway links Panama City and Colón. Visitors are advised not to use the route to Colombia via the Darién for personal safety reasons.

GETTING AROUND

Air

Smaller airports for internal flights are: *Aeropuerto Marcos A. Gelabert* in Albrook and *Enrique Maleck* in David, Chiriquí. Internal air services are operated by *Aeroperlas, Aviatur* and *Aeropaelidades* which link Panama City with all centres in the interior of the country.

Train

The *Ferrocarril de Panamá* currently only operates freight trains and is in the process of selling the national rail service. Further information can be obtained from the Instituto Panameño de Turismo (see address section).

Road

The Trans-Isthman Highway links Panama City and Colón.

Bus

Traffic drives on the right. There are services between most large towns, but they can be very slow.

Taxi

Not metered, and fares, though varying considerably, are generally very low. Fares should be agreed in advance.

Car rental

Available in city centres and airport.
Documentation
A national driving licence is sufficient.

Urban

Extensive bus and minibus services run in Panama City. There is a flat fare with coin-operated turnstiles at the entrances of most buses.

MONEY

CURRENCY

Balboa (B) = 100 centavos. There is no Panamanian paper currency; coins exist in denominations of B10 and 1, and 50, 25, 10, 5 and 1 centavos. US currency circulates freely: B1 = US$1.

CURRENCY EXCHANGE

Banks and *cambios* are available for changing currency. There is no need to exchange US Dollars.

CREDIT CARDS

Visa and American Express are the most commonly used, but MasterCard and Diners Club are also accepted. Check with your credit card company for details of merchant acceptability and other services which may be available.

TRAVELERS' CHECKS

To avoid additional exchange rate charges, visitors are advised to take travellers cheques in US Dollars.

Currency restrictions

There are no restrictions on the import and export of either foreign or local currency.

Banking hours 8AM-1.30PM Monday to Friday, 8.30AM-12PM Saturday.

WHAT TO SEE IN PANAMA CITY AND NEARBY

Panama La Vieja
Fascinating, 16th century ruins of the original Panama City sacked by pirate Henry Morgan. Also has a good museum with a scale model of the original city and an artisans' market. Unfortunately, all the signs and exhibits at this time are in Spanish, so if you don't speak Spanish, this site is best seen with a tour operator or a bi-lingual friend.

Casco Viejo
The second Panama City of Spanish colonial days. Many historical buildings and churches including an excellent Panama Canal Museum in a beautifully restored building that once served as the French headquarters during their effort to build the Canal. Take a walking tour using Lonely Planet as your guide or go with a tour operator. Pesantez and Iguana Tours offer reasonable half day tours that cover Panama La Vieja, Casco Viejo and the Canal.

Canopy Tower
Whether you go for a day trip or an overnight, Canopy Tower is a must. Just 30 minutes from Panama City in a national park and acclaimed by the Audubon Society as one of the top nature lodges in the world. Fantastic nature and bird watching in a pristine rainforest ,spectacular views and excellent food.

Ancon Hill and Los Pueblitos
A prominent hill in Panama City overlooking the mouth of the Canal and the city. A stairway on the bottom of the hill leads up to a road to the top. About half an hour walk in a rain forest with birds and animals along the way, leads to a stunning double view at the summit: on one side, the entire city of Panama old and new and on the other side, a bird's eye view of the Canal and all its workings.

Also at the foot of Ancon Hill are three miniature villages recently built to represent Panama's three cultures- the Spanish, the West Indian and the native Indian San Blas. Have a meal and enjoy the view.

Summit Gardens
A Zoo containing animals and birds unique to Panama's rain forests and jungles

set in a magnificent botanical garden. In the former Canal Zone, about 45 minutes from downtown Panama City: 40 minutes from downtown Panama City. You can take a taxi and see this for yourself.

Taboga Island

A trip to the "Island of Flowers" is the perfect day trip from Panama City. The boat ride itself is worth the trip. The one-hour trip offers you enjoyable ocean breezes, an unforgettable view of Panama Citys' striking skyline and the activity at the entrance to the Panama Canal. The Island has pretty beaches, history, (the second oldest church in the Western Hemisphere -1550) and some good walks. You can make this an overnight getaway by staying at one of the islands two hotels.

Boats leave to and from Taboga everyday. Call Argo Tours at 232-5395 for schedule information.

Pipeline Road

This road in the former Canal Zone is considered by experts as one of the best places in the world for nature observation and bird watching. Unless you are an expert yourself, you will want to hire one of Panama's fascinating nature guides to take you on this trail. The cost is very reasonable. Lonely Planet says " the country's finest nature guides work for Ancon Expeditions." Call them at 269-9414 or click on below.

Handicraft and Souvenir Shopping

Panama's handicrafts are unique and of excellent quality. You can't leave Panama without buying at least one mola (an intricate decorative embroidery that comes in many forms) You will be much tempted by other items - like the hand-woven baskets of the Embera Indians similar to baskets woven by Navajo Indians in the States but much less expensive.

Right near your hotel, there is a Gran Morrison variety store with a large handicraft department.

To buy directly from the Indian artisans themselves, take a taxi to the huge and fascinating Artisans' Market in Balboa near the old YMCA.

Cerro Azul

Panama City is the tropics but amazingly less than an hour away in the direction of the International Airport is Cerro Azul (Blue Mountain), a cool refuge of pine tree covered mountains. Before or after your trip, renew yourself and stay at Casa Del Campo a lovely bed and breakfast offering a variety of spa and health treatments.

WHAT TO SEE OUTSIDE OF PANAMA CITY

San Blas Islands
Ethnotourism at its best. The Kuna Indians of the San Blas Islands have preserved a unique culture which you can observe and be a part of as you stay at one of their San Blas-style hotels. At the same time, the scenery and seas of the San Blas Islands compare favorably to anywhere in the Caribbean. Excellent diving and snorkeling. To get the most out of San Blas, a trip with a tour operator is recommended.

Contadora Island
Contadora Island is part of the Pearl Island Archipelago and is just a 15-minute plane ride from Panama City. These islands have everything- idyllic beaches, great fishing, diving, and snorkeling. Prices at the Contadora Resort are very reasonable and include 3 meals. You can also sail to Contadora on a yacht and fish on the way! Click on Ocean Fun below.

Bocas del Toro Archipelago
Tourism to Bocas just began about 5 years ago and it is now a popular destination for Americans and Europeans who seek unusual, off-the beaten track destinations. These friendly and peaceful islands feature great nature observation, diving, snorkeling, attractive if not fancy lodging and just being truly away from it all. The prices on everything are unbeatable. An hour flight from Panama City.

Posada del Cerro la Vieja
La Posada features unusual mountain scenery, picturesque cabins, a splendid 100-ft. waterfall you can bath beneath, horseback riding in the mountains, nature walks and for the really adventurous, a hot, herbal mud bath. Just a two and half-hour trip from Panama City by car.

El Valle
A lovely mountain town nestled in a 10,000 year volcano crater; El Valle can be done as a day trip from Panama City or a delightful overnight. Majestic mountains, fantastic bike riding, hot springs, a zoo, Indian hieroglyphics, an Indian Handicrafts market on Sunday mornings and a thrilling Canopy Adventure ride are some of the things to do.

Pacific Coast Beaches
Less than two hours from Panama City is a string of lovely Pacific Coast beaches. Among the attractions is the Coronado Hotel and Resort, the only 5 star Beach resort in Panama which features a golf course. You can also rent a beach cabin like Pacific Hideaway and from there visit El Valle less than an hour away.

Boquete
Boquete feels as much like Europe as Latin America, a picturesque mountain town full of flowers, coffee and orange farms. Up on the mountain side, you can enjoy the peaceful beauty at the cabins of La Montana y El Valle which features gourmet food or the newly built Villas Maritza with simpler fare.

Los Quetzales
Los Quetzales is a must! Famous for its beauty, it is located in the cloud forest of La Amistad National Park near the Costa Rican border. You can stay up in the lovely mountain cabins or in the nicely appointed nature lodge which features a complete a health spa, on-premise bakery and pizzeria. From both places you can arrange nature walks, bike and horseback riding. You will definitely see among other things the "resplendent" Quetzal, a bird whose sighting is a lifetime experience. You'll love the prices too.

Isla Grande
In Panama, you can travel from the Pacific Ocean to the Atlantic Ocean in only an hour.When you do, the place to land is Isla Grande, a pretty isle that features Bananas Village Resort, a very attractive beach venue with gourmet food. Also, once on the Atlantic Coast, you can easily visit from here the historic Spanish forts of Portobello and San Lorenzo.

San Lorenzo/Portobello
For history buffs, Panama has much to offer. A major crossroads in the time of the Spanish conquerors, both Columbus and Balboa left their mark here.For sites outside Panama City,on the Atlantic Coast, the 16th century Spanish forts of San Lorenzo and Portobello are both easy to reach in a day trip from Panama City.

The Darien Jungle
The only gap in the Panamerican Highway is the Darien Jungle, a stretch of jungle too dense to be conquered by man. The talk of the birdwatching world are the trips Panama's renowned Ancon Expeditions has set up to its location in the Darien Biosphere Reserve at Las Canas. The biosphere is just a one hour plane ride from Panama City and not to be missed by serious nature lovers.

SPORT & ACTIVITIES

Boat trips

Boat trips on the Panama Canal are one of Panama's major tourist attractions and there are various types of tours available. Crocodiles, frigate birds and other animals living along the banks and in the surrounding jungle can be observed. Canal tours often aim to provide visitors with a chance to observe one of the many large vessels moving through the canal locks. For further details, contact the Panamanian Institute of Tourism *or* the Panamanian Embassy (see address section).

Watersports

There are some excellent locations for **diving** and **snorkelling** in Panama, the best of which include *Isla Grande* near Portobelo, where there are a number of dive centres offering excursions to the best reefs; the *Bocas del Toro* archipelago; *Tabboga Island* (20km/12 miles south of Panama City); and the *San Blas Islands* (off the northeast coast). **Whitewater rafting** is becoming increasingly popular on the *Chiriqui* and *Chiriqui Viejo* rivers (not possible during the rainy season, from April to mid-December). For further details on some of these destinations, see also the *Resorts & Excursions* section.

Fishing

Fish are abundant in the Panamanian waters of the Pacific and the Caribbean. Locations include Piñas Bay, Coiba Island, Contadora Island and Taboga on the Pacific side and the San Blas Islands and the Chiriquí Lagoon off the archipelago of Bocas del Toro in the Caribbean.

Golf

There are six golf courses on the isthmus. *Panama Country Club*, *Summit* and *Fort Amador*'s courses are all open to tourists. Guest cards are needed to play the 18-hole course at Coronado Beach Country Club.

HORSE RIDING

This is popular in the mountainous Chiriqui province, whose wild landscapes provide a natural habitat for cattle and horses. There are numerous horse-breeding farms, some of which can be visited. Horse trips to the Baru Volcano are also available.

SUPPLEMENTS

U.S. AND COUNTRY CONTACTS - PANAMA

U.S. EMBASSY CONTACTS

The Commercial Service
U.S. Department of Commerce
Commercial Attache, Richard Benson;
Senior Trade Specialist: J.Enrique Tellez;
Commercial Assistant, Jilma A. De Robles;
Commercial Secretary, Diana Lozano;
Commercial Clerk, Jeane A. De Zu?curren;iga
Tel: (507) 227-1777
Fax: (507) 227-1713
http:\\www.ita.doc.gov
E-mail: fcspanam@sinfo.net

Economic Unit, U.S. Department of State
(Trade Policy, Industry Specialists)
Chief, Economic Section, Edward Goff;
Economic Officer, John Warner
Tel: (507) 227-1777
Fax: (507) 227-1964

Foreign Agricultural Service,
U.S. Department of Agriculture
Agricultural Specialist, Hugo Salazar;
Secretary, Maria Victoria Guardia
Tel: (507) 227-1777
Fax: (507) 225-4209

Embassy Mailing Address in the U.S.:
Unit 0945
APO AA 34002
Tel: (507) 227-1777
Fax: (507) 227-1964

WASHINGTON-BASED USG COUNTRY CONTACTS

U.S. Department of Commerce,
International Economic Policy
Panama Desk Officer, Matt Gaisford
14th & Constitution Ave.
Washington, D.C. 20230
Tel: (202) 482-4464
Fax: (202) 482-4157

U.S. Department of State
Desk Officer, David Noble
ARA (Inter American Affairs)/CEN-PAN
2201 C St. NW
Washington, DC 20520
Tel: (202) 647-4986
Fax: (202) 647-2901

U.S. Department of the Treasury
Desk Officer, Rachel Barrell
Office of Latin America & Caribbean
1500 Pennsylvania Ave. NW
Washington, D.C. 20220
Tel: (202) 622-1266
Fax: (202) 622-1273

U.S. Department of Commerce,
Liaison Office of Inter-American Development Bank
Director, Eric Weaver
1250 H Street, NW, 10th Floor
Washington, D.C. 20005
Tel: (202) 623-3821
Fax: (202) 623-2039

U.S. Department of Commerce,

Liaison Office to the International Bank
for Reconstruction and Development
U.S. Executive Director's Office
1818 H St., NW, Room D-13004
Washington, D.C. 20433
Tel: (202) 458-0118
Fax: (202) 477-2967

U.S. Department of Commerce,
Office of Multilateral Development Banks
Director (Acting), Janet Thomas
Room 1107
Washington, D.C. 20230
Tel: (202) 482-3399
Fax: (202) 273-0927

U.S. Department of Agriculture,
Foreign Agricultural Service
Trade Policy, Marsha Moke
12th and Jefferson Drive, SW
Washington, DC 20250
Tel: (202) 720-6010
Fax: (202) 690-2079

Overseas Private Investment Corporation
1100 New York Avenue, N.W.
Washington, DC 20527
Insurance Officer, Ray Ruga
Tel: (202) 336-8472 (x8602)
Fax: (202) 408-5142
Finance Officer, Adrien Seaton
Tel: (202) 336-8472, Fax: (202) 408-9866

Export-Import Bank of the U.S.
811 Vermont Avenue, NW
Washington, DC 20571
Business Development, Lee Ann Wetterhan
Tel: (202) 565-3921
Fax: (202) 565-3931
http:// www.exim.gov

U.S. Trade and Development Agency
Country Manager,Latin America & Caribbean, Nathan Younge
1621 N. Kent St., Suite 300
Arlington, VA 2209-2131
Tel: (703) 875-4357
Fax: (703) 875-4009
E-mail: nyounge@tda.gov

Office of U.S. Trade Representative
Deputy Assistant USTR, Peter Allgeier,
Director for Caribbean Basin Affairs, Sue Crunin
Office of the U.S. Trade Representative
600 17th Street, NW
Washington, D.C. 20506
Tel: (202) 395-5190
Fax: (202) 395-3911

U.S. - BASED MULTIPLIER ORGANIZATIONS RELEVANT FOR COUNTRY

Embassy of Panama
Ambassador Eloy Alfaro
2862 McGill Terrace NW
Washington, DC 20008
Tel: (202) 483-1407
Fax: (202) 483-8413

MINISTRIES AND GOVERNMENT OWNED AGENCIES IN PANAMA

Ministerio de Comercio e Industrias,
(Ministry of Commerce and Industry)
Minister, Ra?pound;l Hern?nbsp;ndez
P.O. Box 9658
Panama 4, Republic of Panama
Tel: (507) 227-4222
Fax: (507) 227-4134

Ministerio de Comercio e Industrias, Direccion General de Registro de la Propiedad Industrial,
(Industrial Property Registry Administration)
Director General, Luz Celeste R. de Davis
P.O. Box 9658
Panama 4, Republic of Panama
Tel: (507) 227-3987
Fax: (507) 227-2139

Ministerio de Desarrollo Agropecuario,
(Ministry of Agricultural Development)
Minister, Eng. Carlos Sousa Lennox
P.O. Box 5390
Panama 5, Republic of Panama
Tel: (507) 232-5043
Fax: (507) 232-5044

Ministerio de Hacienda y Tesoro,
(Ministry of Treasury)
Minister, Miguel Heras Castro
P.O. Box 7304
Panama 5, Republic of Panama
Tel: (507) 227-4998
Fax: (507) 227-2357
http://www.mhyt.gob.pa/
E-mail: mhyt@mhyt.gob.pa

Ministerio de Hacienda y Tesoro
Direccion Nacional de Aduanas,
(Customs Service)
Director General, Carlos Icaza
P.O. Box 1671 Balboa, Ancon
Panama, Republic of Panama
Tel: (507) 232-5355
Fax: (507) 232-6494
http://www.mhyt.gob.pa

Ministerio de Salud, (Ministry of Health)
Minister, Dr. Aida M. de Rivera
P.O. Box 2048
Panama 1, Republic of Panama
Tel: (507) 225-6080
Fax: (507) 227-5276

Ministerio de Obras Publicas,
(Ministry of Public Works)
Minister, Luis Blanco
P.O. Box 1632
Panama 1, Republic of Panama
Tel: (507) 232-5572
Fax: (507) 232-5776
http://www.mop.gob.pa/
E-mail: infomop@sinfo.net

Autoridad de la Region Interoceanica (ARI),
(Interoceanic Regional Authority)
Administrator, Nicolas Ardito Barletta
P.O. Box 2097, Balboa
Panama, Republic of Panama
Tel: (507) 228-8044
Fax: (507) 228-8988
http://www.ari-panama.com
E-mail: ari@ns.sinfo.net

Autoridad Mar?iexcl;tima Nacional,
(National Maritime Authority)
Administrator, Ing. Ruben Reyna
P.O. Box 8062
Panama 7, Rep. of Panama
Tel: (507) 232-5553/5528
Fax: (507) 232-5527

Administracion de la Zona Libre de Colon,
(Colon Free Zone Administration)
General Manager, Ricardo Alem?nbsp;n
P.O. Box 1118
Colon, Republic of Panama
Tel: (507) 445-5794/5114
Fax: (507) 445-2165
http://www.zonalibre.com

E-mail: david@zolicol.org

Direccion de Aeronautica Civil (DAC),
(National Aeronautics Authority)
Director General, Eustacio Fabrega
P.O. Box 7615
Panama 5, Republic of Panama
Tel: (507) 226-1142
Fax: (507) 226-3860

Instituto Panameno de Turismo (IPAT),
(Tourism Institute of Panama)
Director General, Cesar Tribaldos
P.O. Box 4421
Panama 5, Republic of Panama
Tel: (507) 226-7414 or 226-3751
Fax: (507) 226-3483
http://www.ipat.gob.pa
E-mail: webmaster@ipat.gob.pa

Instituto Panameno de Comercio Exterior (IPCE),
(Panama Trade Development Institute)
Director General, Kenia Jaen
P.O. Box 6-1897
Panama 6, Republic of Panama
Tel: (507) 236-0550/0347
Fax: (507) 236-0495

Instituto de Recursos Hidraulicos y Electrificacion (IRHE),
(National Power and Light Company)
Director General, Fernando Aramburu Porras
P.O. Box 5285
Panama 5, Republic of Panama
Tel: (507) 227-2240
Fax: (507) 262-9294
http://www.irhe.com
E-mail: dei@sinfo.net

Instituto de Acueductos y Alcantarillados Nacionales (IDAAN),
(National Water Works Company)
Director General, Elida Diaz
P.O. Box 5234
Panama 5, Republic of Panama
Tel: (507) 223-8640
Fax: (507) 264-0034

Inter-American Development Bank,
(In-country office and representative)
Representative, Dra. Camille Gaskin-Reyes
Apartado Postal 7297
Panama 5, Rep. of Panama
Tel: (507) 263-6944
Fax: (507) 263-6183
http://www.iadr.org

TRADE ASSOCIATIONS

American Chamber of Commerce and Industry
Executive Director - Gina Latoni
P.O. Box 168, Balboa
Panama, Republic of Panama
Tel: (507) 269-3881
Fax: (507) 223-3508
http://www.panamcham.com
E-mail: amcham@sinfo.net

Asociacion de Distribuidores de Automoviles de Panama (ADAP),
(Automobile Distributors Association)
Executive Director - Simon de la Rosa
P.O. Box 476
Panama 9A, Republic of Panama
Tel: (507) 261-1264
Fax: (507) 261-0906
E-mail: analmo@sinfo.net

Asociacion de Usuarios de la Zona Libre de Colon,
(Colon Free Zone Users Association)

Executive Director - Galo Pinto de la Ossa
P.O. Box 3118, Zona Libre de Colon
Colon, Republic of Panama
Tel: (507) 441-4244
Fax: (507) 441-4347
E-mail: au@sinfo.net

Asociacion Panamena de Exportadores (APEX),
(Exporters Association)
Executive Director - Daniel Vega
P.O. Box 6-6527
Panama 6, Republic of Panama
Tel: (507) 230-0284 or 230-0169
Fax: (507) 230-0805
E-mail: sip@sinfo.net

Camara de Comercio, Industria y Agricultura de Panama,
(Chamber of Commerce, Industry and Agriculture of Panama)
Executive Director - Jose Ramon Varela
P.O. Box 74
Panama 1, Republic of Panama
Tel: (507) 227-1285 or 227-1445
Fax: (507) 227-4186 or 225-3653
http://www.panacamara.com
E-mail: cciap@panama.phoenix.net

Camara Panamena de la Construccion (CAPAC),
(Construction Chamber)
Executive Director - Eduardo Rodriguez
Apartado 6793
Panama 5, Republic of Panama
Tel: (507) 264-2255
Fax: (507) 264-2384
E-mail: capac@pty.com

Sindicato de Industriales de Panama (SIP),
(Industrialists Association of Panama)
Executive Director - Daniel Vega
P.O. Box 6-4798
Panama 6, Republic of Panama
Tel: (507) 230-0284 or 230-0169
Fax: (507) 230-0805
E-mail: sip@sinfo.net

COUNTRY COMMERCIAL BANKS

Asociacion Bancaria de Panama,
(Banking Association of Panama)
Executive Director, Mario de Diego
P.O. Box 4554
Panama 5, Republic of Panama
Tel: (507) 263-7044
Fax: (507) 263-7783

Banco del Istmo
General Manager, L.J. Montague Belanger
P.O. Box 6-3823, El Dorado
Panama 6A, Republic of Panama
Tel: (507) 270-0015
Fax: (507) 270-0861

Banco General
General Manager, Raul Aleman
P.O. Box 4592
Panama 5, Republic of Panama
Tel: (507) 265-0303
Fax: (507) 265-0206
http://www.banco-general.com

Banco Comercial de Panama
General Manager, Emmanuel Gonzalez Revilla
P.O. Box 7659
Panama 5, Republic of Panama
Tel: (507) 263-6800 or 263-4433
Fax: (507) 263-8033

Banco Nacional de Panama

General Manager, Lic. Jose Antonio de la Ossa
P.O. Box 5220
Panama 5, Republic of Panama
Tel: (507) 269-2966/269-2966
Fax: (507) 264-7155

The Chase Manhattan Bank, N.A.
General Manager, Olegario Barrelier
P.O. Box 9A-76
Panama 9A, Republic of Panama
Tel: (507) 263-5855 or 263-5877
Fax: (507) 263-6009

Citibank, N.A.
General Manager, Julio Bonifacino
P.O. Box 555
Panama 9A, Republic of Panama
Tel: (507) 236-4044
Fax: (507) 236-1025

PRIBANCO, Primer Banco de Ahorros
General Manager, Robert J. Boyd III
P.O. Box 7322
Panama 5, Republic of Panama
Tel: (507) 265-3444
Fax: (507) 265-3838

The First National Bank of Boston
General Manager, Luis Navarro
P.O. Box 5368
Panama 5, Republic of Panama
Tel: (507) 264-2244 or 64-2146
Fax: (507) 223-4089

COUNTRY MARKET RESEARCH FIRMS

Ditcher & Neira - Marketing Consultant
Director General, Leopoldo Neira
P.O. Box 6-7373, El Dorado
Panama, Republic of Panama
Tel: (507) 264-3466
Fax: (507) 223-1174
E-mail: d&n@pananet.com

Jaime Porcell & Asociados
President, Jaime A. Porcell
P.O. Box 4760
Panama 5, Rep. of Panama
Tel: (507) 226-0438/0452
Fax: (507) 226-7390

Grupo Ariston
Maria Nela Galvez, General Manager
P.O. Box 944
Panama 9A, Republic of Panama
Tel: (507) 226-1276
Fax: (507) 226-5275
E-mail: mthalass@pan.gbm.net

PANAMANIAN BANKS WITH CORRESPONDENT U.S. BANKS

Banco Comercial de Panama, S.A. (BANCOMER)
P.O. Box 7659
Panama 5, Republic of Panama
Tel: (507) 263-6800
Fax: (507) 263-8033
General Manager: Emmanuel Gonzalez-Revilla

U.S. Correspondents:
Citibank N.A., New York
The Bank of New York, New York

The Chase Manhattan Bank, N.A., New York
Marine Midland Bank, N.A., New York
Barnett Bank of South Florida, N.A., Miami

Banco Continental de Panama, S.A.
P.O. Box 135
Panama, 9A, Republic of Panama
Tel: (507) 263-5955
Fax: (507) 264-3359
General Manager: Paul Smith

U.S. Correspondents:
Chemical Bank, New York
Citibank, New York and Miami
Credit Suisse, Miami
Nations Bank, Miami
Standard Chartered Bank PLC, Miami

Banco de Latinoamerica, S.A. (BANCOLAT)
P.O. Box 4401
Panama 5, Republic of Panama
Tel: (507) 264-0466
Fax: (507) 263-7368
General Manager: Rafael Arias

U.S. Correspondents:
Banco Atlantico, New York
The Chase Manhattan Bank, New York
Extebank, New York
AmTrade Bank International, Miami
Barclays Bank PLC, Miami
Capital Bank N.A., Miami
Hamilton Bank N.A., Miami
The International Bank of Miami, Miami
Republic National Bank of Miami, Miami
Popular Bank of Florida, Miami

Banco del Istmo, S.A.
P.O. Box 6-3823, El Dorado
Panama, Republic of Panama
Tel: (507) 270-0015
Fax: (507) 270-0861
General Manager: J. Montague Belanger

U.S. Correspondents:
Capital Bank, Miami
Nations Bank, Miami
Standard Chartered Bank, Miami
Banco Atlantico, Miami
Barclays Bank PLC, Miami
The Chase Manhattan Bank N.A., New York
Brown Brothers Hamman & Co., New York

Banco del Pacifico, S.A.
P.O. Box 6-3100, El Dorado
Panama, Republic of Panama
Tel: (507) 263-5833
Fax: (507) 263-7481
Operations Manager: Jose Chung

U.S. Correspondent:
First Chicago International Bank, New York

Banco Disa, S.A.
P.O. Box 7201
Panama 1, Republic of Panama
Tel: (507) 263-5933
Fax: (507) 264-1084
http://www.bdisa.com
Manager: Rafael Endara J.

U.S. Correspondents:
The Chase Manhattan Bank N.A., New York and Miami
Marine Midland Bank, New York
Nations Bank International, New York

Dadeland Bank, Miami
National Westminister USA International, Miami

Banco General, S.A.
P.O. Box 4592
Panama 5, Republic of Panama
Tel: (507) 265-0303
Fax: (507) 265-0210
http://www.banco-general.com
General Manager: Raul Aleman Z.

U.S. Correspondents:
Citibank N.A., New York
The Chase Manhattan Bank N.A., New York
Marine Midland Bank, New York
Bank of America N.T. & S.A., San Francisco
Nations Bank, Atlanta
Dadeland National Bank, Miami
First Union Bank, Miami

Banco Internacional de Costa Rica, S.A. (BICSA)
P.O. Box 600
Panama 1, Republic of Panama
Tel: (507) 263-6822
Fax: (507) 263-6393
General Manager: Jose Francisco Ulate

U.S. Correspondents:
Citibank N.A., New York
BankAmerica International, New York
Banco Atlantico, New York
The Bank of New York, New York

Banco Internacional de Panama, S.A. (BIPAN)
P.O. Box 11181
Panama 6, Republic of Panama
Tel: (507) 263-9000
Fax: (507) 263-9514
General Manager: Rene A. Diaz A.

U.S. Correspondents:
Nations Bank International, Miami
Barclays Bank, Miami
Banco Internacional de Costa Rica, Miami

Banco Latinoamericano de Exportaciones, S.A. (BLADEX)
P.O. Box 6-1497, El Dorado
Panama, Republic of Panama
Tel: (507) 263-6766
Fax: (507) 269-6333
Chief Executive Officer: Jose Castaneda

U.S. Correspondents:
The Chase Manhattan Bank N.A., New York
Citibank N.A., New York
Credit Lyonnais, New York
Swiss Bank Corporation, New York
Barclays Bank PLC, Miami

Banco Panamericano, S.A. (PANABANK)
P.O. Box 1828
Panama 1, Panama
Tel: (507) 263-9266
Fax: (507) 269-1537
E-mail: panabank@sinfo.net
General Manager: Guido Martinelli

U.S. Correspondents:
American Express Bank, New York
Marine Midland Bank, New York
Hong Kong and Shanghai Bank, New York
Popular Bank of Florida, Miami
Hamilton Bank N.A., Miami
Barclays Bank PLC, Miami
Nations Bank International, Miami

PANAMA CONSULATE OFFICES ABROAD

NORTH AMERICAN REGION

CONSULATE OF PHILADELPHIA, PENNSYLVANIA, U.S.A.
Ms. Georgia Athanasopulos - Consul Honoraria
Address 2207 Chesnut Street
Philadelphia, Pa 19103
Tel: 215-564-6333
Fax: 215-564-6334

CONSULATE OF HOUSTON, TEXAS, U.S.A.
Mr. Julio Sosa - Consul
Address 24 Greenway Plaza
Suite 1705
Houston, Texas
Tel: 713-622-4451 / 713-622-4459
Fax: 713-622-4468

CONSULATE OF LOS ANGELES, CALIFORNIA, U.S.A.
Mr. Alfred Marohl - Consul Honorario
Address 435 North Roxbury Drive
Suite 207, Beverly Hills
California 90210
Tel: 310-859-7583
Fax: 310-273-5339

CONSULATE OF MIAMI, FLORIDA, U.S.A.
Mr. Rodrigo Gonzalez - Consul
Address Rivergate Plaza
444 Brickell Avenue
Suite 729
Miami, Florida 33131
Tel: 305-371-7031
Fax: 305-371-2907

CONSULATE OF MONTREAL, CANADA
Mr. Luis E. Uribe - Consul
Address 1425 Blvd. Rene Levesque W
Suite 904 Montreal
Quebec H3g 1t7
Tel: 514-767-6280
Fax: 514-874-1929

CONSULATE OF NEW ORLEANS, LOUISIANA, U.S.A.
Ms. Elizabeth Martinez - Consul
Address World Trade Center
Suite 1324
New Orleans, La 70130
Tel: 504-525-3458
Fax: 504-524-8960

CONSULATE OF NEW YORK, N.Y., U.S.A.
Mr. Francisco Iglesias - Consul
Address 1212 Ave. Of The Americas
1oth Floor
New York, N.Y. 10036
Tel: 212-840-2450
Fax: 212-8402469

CONSULATE OF SAN FRANCISCO, CALIFORNIA, U.S.A.
Mr. Rolando Paredes - Consul
Address Flood Bldg. 870 Market St.
Suites 551-553
San Francisco, Ca 94102
Tel: 415-391-4268
Fax: 415-391-4269

CONSULATE OF TAMPA, FLORIDA, U.S.A.
Mr. Jose Hooker - Consul
Address Galeria Office Bldg.
Consulado De Panama
4326 El Prado Blvd. Suite 4
Tampa, Fl. 33629
Tel: 813-831-6685
Fax: 813-831-6685

CONSULATE OF WASHINGTON D.C., U.S.A.
Mr. Federico Boyd - Consul
Address 2862 Mcgill Terrace N.W.
Washington, Dc 20008
Tel: 202-483-1407
Fax: 202-387-6141

CONSULATE OF MEXICO
Mr. Fabriciano Lopez Tirone - Consul
Address Schiller No.326 8vo. Piso
Colonia Chapultepec Morales
Mexico, D.F.
Tel: 52-5250-4229
Fax: 52-5250-4045

CENTRAL AMERICAN REGION

CONSULATE OF PORT AU PRINCE, HAITI
Mr. Antonio Puello, Jr. - Consul
Address Rue Lamarre, No.43
Petion, Ville
Republic Of Haiti
Tel: 509-57-4504
Fax: 509-57-9789

CONSULATE OF SANTO DOMINGO, DOMINICAN REPUBLIC
Ms. Aida Torrijos Herrera - Consul General
Address Ave. Bolivar No.7
Plaza Cornelia, Edificio F
Apartamento F301
Santo Domingo, R. D.
Tel: 1-809-688-1043
Fax: 1-809-689-1273

SOUTH AMERICAN REGION

CONSULATE OF BUENOS AIRES, ARGENTINA
Mr. Carlos Rodriguez - Consul
Address Avenida Santa Fe #1461
Quinto Piso
1060 Buenos Aires
Tel: 541-42-8542 / 541-42-1254
Fax : 541-81-4045

CONSULATE OF BARRANQUILLA, COLOMBIA
Ms. Angela Vasquez - Consul
Address Carrera 49b N.76-240
Piso 2
Panaconsul, Barranquilla
Colombia
Fax: 0057-53-561-503

CONSULATE OF LIMA, PERU
Ms. Maria E. Aramburu P. - Consul
Address Av. Emilio Cavenecia
No.175
Of No.10, Miraflores
Lima, Peru
Tel: 51-40-6516
Fax: 51-40-6592

CONSULATE OF MARACAIBO, VENEZUELA
Mr. Ernesto Quijada - Consul
Address Centro Commercial Las
Tejas
Ave. 20 Con Calle 68 Y 69a
Sector Indio Mara, Planta
Baja Local 1-9, Venezuela
Tel: 58-2061-527-451
Fax: 58-014-610-468

CONSULATE OF RIO DE JANEIRO, BRAZIL
Mr. Severiano Rodriguez - Consul
Address Nossa Sra De Copacabana
1183
Sala 602
Cep 20,000 Rio De Janeiro
Brazil
Tel: 55-21-267-7999
Fax: 55-21-227-7277

CONSULATE OF SAO PAULO, BRAZIL
Ms. Dorothy Nair Pinilla - Consul
Address Rua General Mena Barreto
602
Jardin Paulista -Cep 01433010
Sau Paulo, Brazil
Tel: 11-884-99-46
Fax: 11-884-99-46

CONSULATE OF SANTOS, BRAZIL
Ms. Ofelina De Madeiros - Consul
Address Ave. Ana Costa
482 Sala 1017
Cep 11,100 Santos, Brazil
Tel: 55-132-915373
Fax: 55-132-49379

CONSULATE OF VALPARAISO, CHILE
Mr. Ricardo Moreno V. - Consul
Address Ave. Arturo Prat #865
Sexto Piso, Oficina 603
Valparaiso, Chile
Tel: 56-32-213-592
Fax: 56-32-236-042

EUROPEAN REGION

CONSULATE OF ANTWERP, BELGIUM
Mr. Luis E. Torres - Consul
Address Meirburg 1, B/39
2000 Antwerp
Tel: 0032-3-231-6961
Fax: 0032-3-231-9969

CONSULATE OF ATHENS, GREECE
Mr. Constantino Mataragas - Consul
Address Vassilissis Sofias 21
Athens 139 11

CONSULATE OF BARCELONA, SPAIN
Ms. Itzia P. De Gonzalez - Consul General
Address Paseo De Gracia 20, 4o. 1a.
08007 Barcelona
Tel: 0034-330-0073
Fax: 0034-3268-2738

CONSULATE OF GENOA, ITALY
Ms. Aida De Gonzalez - Consul General
Address Via Assarotti 15/9
Scala B
16122 Genova, Italia
Tel: 0039-10-839-1786
Fax 0039-10-839-3024

CONSULATE OF GENEVA, SWITZERLAND
Mr. Leonardo Kam - Ambasador
Address 72, Rue De Lausanne
1202 Ginebra
Suiza
Tel: 41-22-738-0388
Fax: 41-22-738-0363

CONSULATE OF HAMBURG, GERMANY
Mr. Alberto Castillero - Consul General
Address Gansemarkt 44
20354 Hamburg
Tel: 49-4034-0218
Fax: 49-4035-3771

CONSULATE OF LA CORUÑA, SPAIN
Mr. Jose Luis Lopez - Consul Honorario
Address Ave. Piruleiro 8-1o. Der. B
15011, La Coru-A
Tel: 34-981-251542
Fax: 34-981-251542

CONSULATE OF LAS PALMAS, CANARY ISLANDS
Mr. Leonardo Carrizo - Consul
Address Calle San Juan Rejon 47
35008 Las Palmas De Gran Canarias
Tel: 34-928-463-307
Fax: 34-928-463-317

CONSULATE OF LISBON, PORTUGAL
Mr. Humberto Lopez Tirone - Consul
Address Rua Pedro De Sintra No.15
Restelo, 1,400 Lisboa,
Portugal
Tel: 3511-301-9046
Fax: 3511-301-2086

CONSULATE OF LONDON
Mr. Kevin Lucas Harrington
Address Panama House, Mayfair
40 Hertford Street
London Wiy 7tg
England
Tel: 44-171-409-2255
Fax: 44-171-493-4499

CONSULATE OF MARSEILLES, FRANCE
Ms. Beatriz Fierro Ortiz - Consul
Address 11 Quai Des Belges
13001 Marsella, Francia
Tel: 33-9190-0584
Fax: 33-9350-3206

CONSULATE OF MONTECARLO, MONACO
Mr. Humbert Schurr - Consul Honorario
Address Estrella De Montecarlo
Apto. 65 Blvd. 15 Louis Ii
Montecarlo
Fax: 33-9350-3206

CONSULATE OF NAPLES, ITALY
Ms. Aminta Quijada De Nobili - Consul
Address Centro Direzionale
Isola C-2 Scala A Piano 6
80143 Napoles, Italy
Tel: 39-081-5629107
Fax: 39-081-5629085

CONSULATE OF PARIS, FRANCE
Mr. Jose Manuel Watson - Consul
Address Embajada De Panama
145 Avenue De Suffren
75015 Paris
Tel: 33-1478-32332
Fax: 33-1456-79943

CONSULATE OF PIRAEUS, GREECE
Dr. Pablo Garrido - Consul
Ilas Merarchias Praxitelous 192
185 35 Piraeus, Greece
Tel: 301-428-6441
Fax: 301-428-6448

CONSULATE OF ROME, ITALY
Ms. Mayra Ivankovich - Enc. De Asuntos Consulares
Address Viale Del Vigonia
39 Interno 6
00196 Roma
Italy
Tel: 39-6-321-9587 Embajada / 39-6-321-1692

CONSULATE OF ROTTERDAM, THE NETHERLANDS
Mr. Valentin Escobar - Consul
Address Groothandelsgebouw
Ingang C, Weena 723
Rotterdam
Tel: 31-10-414-3530
Fax: 31-10-404-8243

CONSULATE OF STOCKHOLM, SWEDEN
Mr. Rene Sinclair - Consul Honorario
Address Erik Dahlbergsallem 15
Stockholm
Tel: 46-8-662-6535
Fax: 46-8-663-0407

CONSULATE OF VALENCIA, SPAIN
Mr. Johnny A. Maizon - Consul
Address Avenida Pais Valenciano
#33 Apto 7, 46016
Tabernes Blanques
Valencia, Spain
Fax: 34-6-3476630

CONSULATE OF VALLETA, REP. OF MALTA
Mr. John Gauci - Consul Honorario
Address 147-1 Stulcia Street
Valleta, Malta Vit 04
Tel: 356-235341
Fax: 356-220101

CONSULATE OF VENICE, ITALY
Ms. Neslin Arce M - Consul
Address Gran Viale Santa Maria
Elizabetta 8/A Lido
Venezia, Italy
Tel: 39-21-2760577
Fax: 39-21-2760577

CONSULATE OF ZURICH, SWITZERLAND
Mr. Rogelio Tribaldos - Consul Honorario
Address Lowenstrasse 40 4to. Piso
Ch-8023, Zurich
Suiza
Tel: 41-71-7-421-420
Fax: 31-72-2-520-426

MIDDLE EASTERN REGION

CONSULATE OF BOMBAI, INDIA
Mr. Gabriel Barrios - Consul
Address C-O Ras Business Centre
Rammini Bldg., Floor No.2
Mandlink Road
Colaba, Mumbai 400001
Tel: 91-22-204-1198
Fax: 91-22-287-1299

CONSULATE OF DUBAI, UNITED ARAB EMIRATES
Mr. Jose A. Maher - Consul
Address Al Abbas Trading Co., Bldg.
Suite 63, Jalid Ibn Walid St
Dubai
Tel: 00971-4-263319
Fax: 00971-4-263315

CONSULATE OF CAIRO, EGYPT
Mr. Victor Barletta - Embajador
Address 5, Chagaret El Dorr St
El Cairo, Egypt
Tel: 202-340-7488
Fax: 202-341-1092

CONSULATE OF ISTAMBUL, TURKEY
Ms. Irma De Firuz - Consul Honorario
Address Kubilay Sitesi
Mimoza Apt. D:4
Tarabya, Istambul
Tel: 90-212-2936981
Fax: 90-212-293900

CONSULATE OF LIMASSOL, CHIPRE
Mr. Eduardo Sol Garrido - Consul
Address Ch Hadjipavlou Str.
Hawaii Royal Gardens
Ier Piso Oficina No.17
Limassol, Cyprus
Tel: 357-05-749-322
Fax: 357-05-749-242

ASIAN REGION

CONSULATE OF BANGKOK, THAILAND
Mr. Jorge Contantino - Consul General
Address Sarasin Bldg. 5th Floor
14 Surasak Road
Bangrak
Bangkok 10500
Tel: 662-237-900
Fax: 662-237-9009

CONSULATE OF HONG KONG
Mr. Silio Galo Ortiz - Consul
Address 1008 Qw Wing On Centre
111 Connaught Road Central
Hong Kong

Tel: 852-2-5452166
Fax: 852-2-5434614

CONSULATE OF JAKARTA, INDONESIA
Mr. Raul A. Eskildsen - Ambassador
Address World Trade Center 8th Floor
J1, Jenderal Sudirman
Kav 29-31, Jakarta,
Indonesia 12920
Tel: 6221-571-1867
Fax: 6221-571-1933

CONSULATE OF KOBE, JAPAN
Mr. Jose A. Sosa - Consul
Address P.O. Box 43 Kobe Port
Kobe 651-01
Fax: 81-078-392-7208

CONSULATE OF MANILA, PHILIPPINES
Mr. Javier Perez A. - Consul
Address Embajada De Panama
Rm. 501, Victoria Bldg.
429 United Nations Ave.
Ermita, Manila 1054
Tel: 632-521-12-33
Fax: 632-521-57-55

CONSULATE OF MOSCOW, RUSSIAN FEDERATION
Mr. Gabriel Sosa - Consul
Address Mosfilmonskaiya
50-1, Moscow Russia
119590
Tel: 7-095-143-0691
Fax: 7-095-956-0730

CONSULATE OF SEOUL, KOREA
Mr. Alfredo Zebede - Ambassador
Address Apartado Postal 3957
Seul, Korea
Tel: 82-2765-0363
Fax: 82-2742-5874

CONSULATE OF SINGAPORE, SINGAPORE
Mr. Ivan Gonzalez - Consul & Ambassador
Address 16, Raffles, Quay #41-06
Song Leong Bldg.
Singapore 0104
Tel: 65-22-18677/8
Fax: 65-22-224-0892

CONSULATE OF TAIPEI, TAIWAN
Mr. Carlos Mendoza - Ambassador
Address 6 Fl. #111
Sung Chiang Road
Taipei, Taiwan
Tel: 88-62-509-9189
Fax: 88-62-509-9801

CONSULATE OF TOKYO, JAPAN
Mr. Mario Medaglia O. - Consul
Address Kowa Bldg. No. 5 R, 802
4-15-23, Nishi Azabu
Minato-Ku, Tokyo 106
Japan
Tel: 81-3-3499-3661
Fax: 81-3-3499-3666

PANAMA LARGEST LAW FIRMS

Aleman, Cordero, Galindo & Lee, Swiss Bank Corporation Building, 2nd Floor, Calle 53 Este, Marbella, P.O. Box 6-1014 El Dorado, Panama, Panama, Tel:(507)264-3111, Fax:(507)264-3133, Contact: Jaime Eduardo Aleman

Alfaro, Ferrer, Ramirez & Aleman, Avenida Federico Boyd No. 33, P.O. Box 951, Panama, Panama, Tel:(507)263-9355, Fax:(507)263-7214, Contact: Alfredo Ramirez Jr.

Arias, Fabrega & Fabrega, P.O. Box 6307, Panama City, 5, Panama, Tel:(507)263-9200, Fax:(507)263-8919, Contact: Francisco Arias G.

Arosemena & Diaz, Comosa Building, 8th Floor, Samuel Lewis Avenue, Panama City, Panama, Tel:(507)69-6027, Fax:(507)63-4472, Contact: Rodrigo Arosemena

Arosemena, Noriega & Contreras, PO Box 5246, Panama 5, Republic of Panama, Tel: (507) 2653411, Fax: (507) 2644569, Contact: Dr. Carlos Arosemena A.

Arosemena, Noriega & Contreras is engaged in general practice in the areas of corporate and commercial law, admiralty, patent and trademark law. Arosemena, Noriega & Contreras is the Panama member of Lex Mundi, a global association of 152 independent law firms.

Benedetti & Benedetti, Comosa Building, 21st Floor, Avenida Samuel Lewis and Manuel M. Ycaza, P.O. Box 850120, Panama, 5, Panama, Tel:(507)263-4444, Fax:(507)269-1474, Contact: Ramon R. Benedetti

Boutin Law Firm, Via Grecia, Nuevo Reparto El Carmen, Edificio Alamanda, 3 piso, Oficina 6-B, Panama, Panama, Tel:(507)264-7975, Fax:(507)264-8002, Contact: Gilberto Boutin I.

Bufete Candanedo, Global Bank Building, 6th Floor, 50th Street Avenue, P.O. Box 1843, Panama, 9A, Panama, Tel:(507)213-0033, Fax:(507)264-2498, Contact: Gabriel Rodriguez Cover

Bufete Illueca, 5th Floor, Deutsch Sudamerikanische Bank Tower, 50th and E. 55th St., P.O. Box 6-3356 El Dorado, Panama, Panama, Tel:(507)269-1333, Fax:(507)269-4698, Contact: Enrique M. Illueca

Cajigas & Co., 7th Floor, Bank of Boston Bldg., Spain Ave. and Elvira Mendez, P.O. Box 6354, Panama, 5, Panama, Tel:(507)264-6111, Fax:(507)264-5749, Contact: Enrique Cajiga S.

Carreira-Pitti, P.C., Attorneys, Samuel Lewis Avenue, Comosa Building, Third Floor, P.O. Box 6-10100 El Dorado, Panama, Panama, Tel:(507)230-1012, Fax:(507)263-8290, Contact: Leonor I. Arauz Silva

Cohen, Vassilopulos & Varela, 55th Street and Via Argentina El Bayano Building, P.O. Box 200, Panama, 1, Panama, Tel:(507)263-4949, Fax:(507)263-4950, Contact: David Cohen S.

De Castro & Robles, 5th Floor, American Int'l Bldg, 50th@Aquilino de la Guardia Streets, P.O. Box 7082, Panama, 5, Panama, Tel:(507)263-6622, Fax:(507)263-6594, Contact: Cesar Mario Escobar G.

De Obaldia & Garcia De Paredes, Proconsa Building, Sixth Floor, Manuel Maria Icaza Avenue & 51 E. St., P.O. Box 55-0761, Panama, Panama, Tel:(507)264-0311, Fax:(507)264-0707, Contact: Carlos Alberto De Obaldia

Dudley & Asociados, Avenida 5a. Norte, Enrique Geenzier, El Cangrejo, P.O. Box 1082, Panama, 9-A, Panama, Tel:(507)263-5400, Fax:(507)269-3589, Contact: Lic. Juan Carlos Dudley Porras

Durling & Durling, Edificio Vallarino, Top Floor Calle 52 y Elvira Mendez, P.O. Box 1450, Panama, 1, Panama, Tel:(507)263-8244, Fax:(507)263-8234, Contact: Orlando Ernesto Lopez Arosemena

Eisenmann & Dutari, Edificio Omega, 2DO Piso, Avenida Samuel Lewis y Calle 53, P.O. Box 9921, Panama, 9, Panama, Tel:(507)269-4320, Fax:(507)263-7458, Contact: Maria Alejandra Eisenmann

Eskildsen & Eskildsen, Calle 50, N. 102, Edificio Universal N. 18, P.O. Box 6978, Panama, 5, Panama, Tel:(507)269-2182, Fax:(507)263-9227, Contact: Ricardo Eskildsen Morales

Fabrega, Barsallo, Molino & Mulino, Samuel Lewis Avenue & 53 Street Omega Building, P.O. Box 4493, Panama, 5, Panama, Tel:(507)263-5333, Fax:(507)264-0181, Contact: Eduardo A. Molino Paz

Franco & Franco, 12th Floor, Torre Universal Building, Federico Boyd Avenue, P.O. Box 8807, 7283, Panama City, 5, Panama, Tel:(507)263-8555, Fax:(507)263-8051, Contact: Joaquin Fernando Franco III

Galindo, Arias & Lopez, Via Espana #200, P.O. Box 8629, Panama City, 5, Panama, Tel:(507)263-5633, Fax:(507)263-5335, Contact: Diego A. De La Guardia

Icaza, Gonzalez, Ruiz & Aleman, Calle Aquilino de la Guardia No. 8, P.O. Box 87-1371, Panama, 7, Panama, Tel:(507)263-5555, Fax:(507)269-4891, Contact: Joel R. Medina

Infante, Garrido & Garrido, Banco Central Bldg, 3d Flr, Samuel Lewis Avenue & Gerardo Ortega's St., P.O. Box 6-7411, El Dorado, Panama, Panama, Tel:(507)269-4416, Fax:(507)223-9415, Contact: Jorge A. Garrido

J.F. Boyd & Associates, Comosa Building Suite 10, Avenida Samuel Lewis, P.O. Box 8699, Panama, 5, Panama, Tel:(507)264-1422, Fax:(507)263-5442, Contact: Maria Del Carmen Gonzalez De Chang

Kuzniecky & Co., Plaza Obarrio Building, Samuel Lewis Avenue, 53rd Street, Office 310, Panama, Panama, Tel:(507)264-4866, Fax:(507)223-2192, Contact: Dani A. Kuzniecky

Lopez, Lopez & Associates, World Trade Center Tower, 53rd Street, Marbella, 5th Floor, Suite 502, P.O. Box 0832-0610, Panama, 9-A, Panama, Tel:(507)263-7670, Fax:(507)264-5052, Contact: Lic. Anibal Vallarino Velarde

Luque-Coronell y Lam, Calle 11 y Ave. Roosvelt, Edificio Sevilla, Ofic. No. 2, P.O. Box 3103, Zona Libre, Colon, Panama, Tel:(507)4415123, Fax:(507)4416243, Contact: Luis Carlos Coronell Morais

Moreno y Fabrega, Edificio Torre Swiss Bank, Calle 53E, Panama, Panama, Tel:(507)269-6412, Fax:(507)264-3933, Contact: Luis Ramon Fabrega

Moreno, Arjona & Brid, Banco Central Bldg, Fifth Floor, Samuel Lewis & Gerardo Ortega Street, P.O. Box 6-4566, Panama, Panama, Tel:(507)269-5566, Fax:(507)263-8005, Contact: Cecilio Roberto Moreno-Arosemena

Moreno, Marquez & Preciado, Cuba Avenue and 40 St., No. 4-91, 1st Floor, P.O. Box 55-2478, Panama, Panama, Tel:(507)227-6700, Fax:(507)227-6703, Contact: Yuri A. Moreno V.

Morgan & Morgan, Torre Swiss Bank Bldg, 16th Floor 53 E Street, Urbanizacion Obarrio, P.O. Box 0832-00232, World Trade Center, Panama, Panama, Tel:(507)265-7777, Fax:(507)265-7700, Contact: Luis Alberto Hincapie V.

Mossack Fonseca & Co., Arango-Orillac Building, Second Floor, East 54th Street, P.O. Box 0832-0886 W.T.C., Panama, 7, Panama, Tel:(507)263-8899, Fax:(507)263-9218, Contact: Ramon Fonseca M.

Pardini, De La Guardia, Ballard & Lachman, Quantum Plaza 2nd Floor, 53rd Street East, P.O. Box 9654, Panama, 4, Panama, Tel:(507)223-7222, Fax:(507)264-4730, Contact: Juan Francisco Pardini

Patton, Moreno & Asvat, Hongkong Bank Building 6th Floor, Samuel Lewis Avenue, P.O. Box 6-4298 - El Dorado, Panama, Panama, Tel:(507)267-8044, Fax:(507)263-7887, Contact: Brett R. Patton P.

Pedreschi & Pedreschi, Federico Boyd Avenue and 51st. Street, No. 20, P.O. Box 4746, Panama, 5, Panama, Tel:(507)269-4966, Fax:(507)264-7622, Contact: Nadia Pedreschi De Halman

Quijano & Associates, Salduba Building, Top Floor, 53rd East Street, Urbanizacion Obarrio, P.O. Box 7284, Panama, 5, Panama, Tel:(507)269-2641, Fax:(507)263-8079, Contact: Julio Antonio Quijano Berbey

Rosas Y Rosas, Via Espana 122 - Oficina 1600, Edificio Banco De Boston, Apartado 8240, Panama, 7, Panama, Tel:(507)649177, Fax:(507)640269, Contact: Jorge Ruben Rosas

Ruben J. Levy & Co., Grecia Building, Ground Floor, 49th Street, Bella Vista, Panama, Panama, Tel:(507)223-1649, Fax:(507)269-1185, Contact: Ruben J. Levy

Shirley & Diaz, Arango Orillac Bldg, 3rd Floor, 54th Street, Nueva Urbanizacion Obarrio, PO Box 5216, Panama, 5, Panama, Tel:(507)692255, Fax:(507)691552, Contact: Luis A. Shirley

Sucre, Arias, Castro & Reyes, Sucre Building, 48 East Street Bella Vista, P.O. Box 6277, Panama, 5, Panama, Tel:(507)264-1355, Fax:(507)264-1168, Contact: Miren A. Ispizua

Tapia,Linares y Alfaro, Bancomer Plaza Via General Nicanor A de Obarrio, (50th Street) PO Box 7412, Panama City, 5, Panama, Tel:(507)63-6066, Fax:(507)63-5305, Contact: Eloy Alfaro

Victor Mendez Fabrega & Associates, Omega Building, First Floor, Samuel Lewis Avenue & 53rd Street Obarrio, P.O. Box 850135, Panama, 5, Panama, Tel:(507)263-3690, Fax:(507)263-3689, Contact: Victor E. Mendez F.

SELECTED LAW FIRMS DEALING WITH PANAMA ABROAD

THE MORGAN & MORGAN GROUP

Main Office:
Torre Swiss Bank Building, 16 th Floor
Calle 53E Urbanización Nuevo Obarrio
P. O. Box 0832-00232
World Trade Center
Panama, Republic of Panama
Ph: (507) 265-7777 / 263-8822
Fax: (507) 265-7700 / 263-9918
E-mail: info@morimor.com

The Morgan & Morgan Law Firm has opened offices for the practice of local and/or international law in the following countries:

LONDON
MORGAN & MORGAN

3rd Floor
Meadows House
20 Queen Street
London W1X 8NE
Tel: (44) (171) 493 1978
Fax: (44) (171) 493 1979
E-mail: morgan@morganuk.btinternet.com

Established in 1982

SPAIN
MORGAN & MORGAN
Ave. del Brasil No. 17, Piso 12, Puerta C
Madrid 28020
Spain
Tel: (34) (1) 555 7736
Fax: (34) (1) 556 3689
E-mail: morgan@morgan-morgan.com
Web Site: www.morgan-morgan.com
Opened since 1989

BELIZE
MORGAN & MORGAN
35 A Regent Street
Jasmine Court, Suite 101
P.O. Box 1777
Belize City, Belize
Tel: (501) 276 687/ 276 688
Fax: (501) 276 689
E-mail: morganblz@btl.net

Opened since 1992

In addition to the practice of law, we also offer from the above mentioned offices, our traditional international services of company and trust formation and administration as well as ship and mortgage registration.

ZURICH
PANAZUR INC.
Löwenstrasse 40
CH-8023, Zurich 1
Switzerland

Telephone: (411) 225 1414
Fax: (411) 225 1400
E-mail: panazur@ibm.net

Contact: Rogelio Tribaldos Alba

GENEVA
MORGAN & MORGAN CORPORATION
SERVICES, S. A.
63, Rue de Lausanne
P. O. Box 2565
1211 Geneva 2, Switzerland
Telephone: (41) (22) 7380630
Fax: (41) (22) 7387321
E-mail: morgan@worldcom.ch
WebSite:http://home.worldcom.ch/~morgan/

Contact: Jorge L. Reyes

LUGANO
MORGAN & MORGAN TRUST CORPORATION LTD.
Succursale Di Lugano
Corso Elvezia, 27
P. O. Box 3138
CH-6901 Lugano, Switzerland
Telephone: (41 91) 923 4040
Fax: (41 91) 923 9346
E-mail: info@morgan-lugano.com

Contact: Susana Reyes

LUXEMBOURG
MORGAN & MORGAN TRUST CORPORATION LTD.
15, Boulevard Royal
L-2449 Luxembourg
Telephone: (352) 46 33 46 1
Fax: (352) 46 33 66

BRITISH VIRGIN ISLANDS
MORGAN & MORGAN TRUST CORP. LTD.
Pasea Estate, P.O. Box 958

Road Town, Tortola
British Virgin Islands
Telephone: (1) (284) 494 2011
Fax: (1) (284) 494 2015
E-mail: morgabvi@caribsurf.com

Managing Director: Marcela Tejeira

Opened since 1988

THE BAHAMAS
MORYMOR TRUST CORPORATION LTD.
50 Shirley St., 2nd Floor
P. O. Box CB 13937
Nassau, The Bahamas
Tel: (1) (242) 326 5859
Fax: (1) (242) 326 5567

E-mail: morymor@bahamas.net.bs

Managing Director: Maria Isabel Doyle

Opened since 1991

HONG KONG
MORGAN & MORGAN
3rd. Fl. Kailey Tower
16 Stanley St.
Central Hong Kong
Tel: (852) 827 1658
Fax: (852) 522 7347

Contact: Lo Tai On

Opened since 1991

BELIZE
MORGAN & MORGAN
TRUST CORPORATION (BELIZE) LTD.

35 A Regent Street
Jasmine Court, Suite 101

P.O. Box 1777
Belize City, Belize
Tel: (501) 276 687/ 276 688
Fax: (501) 276 689

Contact: Naim Musa

Opened since 1992

SPAIN
MORGAN & MORGAN
CORPORATION SERVICES (SPAIN) S. A.
Ave. del Brasil No. 17, Piso 12, Puerta C
Madrid 28020, Spain
Tel: (34) (1) 555 7736
Fax: (34) (1) 556 3689
E-mail: morgan@net64.es

Contact: Bruno Varela Garcia de Paredes

Opened since 1989

SINGAPORE
MORGAN & MORGAN CORPORATE SERVICES
101 Cecil Street
#22-01 Tong Eng Building
Singapore 069533
Telephone: (65) 2244312
Telefax: (65) 2246230

Contact: Allen Walters

OTHER GROUP AFFILIATES

PIRAEUS
PANAMANIAN SERVICES, S. A.
P. O. Box 80697
Central Post Office
185 10 Piraeus, Greece

HONG KONG
PANAMA SHIPPING CONSULTANTS

22nd Floor, Shum Tower
268 Des Voeux Road Central
Hong Kong
Tel: (852) 25438848
Fax: (852) 28153275
E-mail: shipreg@netvigator.com

Contact: William Lui

NEW YORK
INTERNATIONAL CORPORATE CONSULTANTS, INC.
805 Third Avenue, 7th Floor
New York, New York 10022
Tel: (212) 850 2988
Fax: (212) 850 2987
E-mail: dluntz@IDT.net
Contact: David Luntz

MAJOR NEWSPAPERS

El Panama America
Advertising Chief - Margaret de Ucar
P.O. Box B-4
Panama 9A, Republic of Panama
Tel: (507) 230-1666
Fax: (507) 230-1033
Daily Circulation: is 22,000
Format: standard
Advertising prices: US$ 7.00 per columnar inch, each page has 126 columnar inches.

La Estrella de Panama
Advertising Manager - Angie de Ochy
P.O. Box Q
Panama 4, Republic of Panama
Tel: (507) 227-0555
Fax: (507) 227-0723
Daily Circulation: 21,200
Format: standard
Advertising prices: US$ 8.00 per columnar inch, each page has 126 columnar inches.

La Prensa

Advertising Manager - Adela Mendoza
P.O. Box 6-4586, El Dorado
Panama, Republic of Panama
Tel: (507) 221-7222
Fax: (507) 221-7328
Daily Circulation: 38,000
Format: standard
Advertising prices: US$ 11.00 per columnar inch, each page has 126 columnar inches.

INTER-AMERICAN CONVENTION ON INTERNATIONAL COMMERCIAL ARBITRATION

Done at Panama, 30 January 1975;
entered into force 16 June 1976;
Organization of American States, Treaty Series, no. 42.

PREAMBLE

The Governments of the Member States of the Organization of American States, desirous of concluding a convention on international commercial arbitration, have agreed as follows:

Article 1

An agreement in which the parties undertake to submit to arbitral decision any differences that may arise or have arisen between them with respect to a commercial transaction is valid. The agreement shall be set forth in an instrument signed by the parties, or in the form of an exchange of letters, telegrams, or telex communications.

Article 2

Arbitrators shall be appointed in the manner agreed upon by the parties. Their appointment may be delegated to a third party, whether a natural or juridical person.

Arbitrators may be nationals or foreigners.

Article 3

In the absence of an express agreement between the parties, the arbitration shall be conducted in accordance with the rules of procedure of the Inter-American Commercial Arbitration Commission.

Article 4

An arbitral decision or award that is not appealable under the applicable law or procedural rules shall have the force of a final judicial judgment. Its execution or recognition may be ordered in the same manner as that of decisions handed down by national or foreign ordinary courts, in accordance with the procedural laws of the country where it is to be executed and the provisions of international treaties.

Article 5

1. The recognition and execution of the decision may be refused, at the request of the party against which it is made, only if such party is able to prove to the competent authority of the State in which recognition and execution are requested: a. That the parties to the agreement were subject to some incapacity under the applicable law or that the agreement is not valid under the law to which the parties have submitted it , or, if such law is not specified under the law of the State in which the decision was made; or

b. That the party against which the arbitral decision has been made was not duly notified of the appointment of the arbitrator or of the arbitration procedure to be followed, or was unable, for any other reason, to present his defense; or
c. That the decision concerns a dispute not envisaged in the agreement between the parties to submit to arbitration; nevertheless, if the provisions of the decision that refer to issues submitted to arbitration can be separated from those not submitted to arbitration, the former may be recognized and executed; or
d. That the constitution of the arbitral tribunal or the arbitration procedure has not been carried out in accordance with the terms of the agreement signed by the parties or, in the absence of such agreement, that the constitution of the arbitral tribunal or the arbitration procedure has not been carried out in accordance with the law of the State where the arbitration took place; or
e. That the decision is not yet binding on the parties or has been annulled or suspended by competent authority of the State in which, or according to the law of which, the decision has been made.

2. The recognition and execution of an arbitral decision may also be refused if the competent authority of the State in which the recognition and execution is requested finds:

a. That the subject of the dispute cannot be settled by arbitration under the law of the State; or
b. That the recognition or execution of the decision would be contrary to the public policy ("ordre public") of that State.

Article 6
If the competent authority mentioned in Article 5.1.e has been requested to annul

or suspend the arbitral decision, the authority before which such decision is invoked may, if it deems it appropriate, postpone a decision on the execution of the arbitral decision and, at the request of the party requesting execution, may also instruct the other party to provide appropriate guaranties.

Article 7

This Convention shall be open for signature by the Member States of the Organization of American States.

Article 8

This Convention is subject to ratification. The instruments of ratification shall be deposited with the General Secretariat of the Organization of American States.

Article 9

This Convention shall remain open for accession by any other State. The instruments of accession shall be deposited with the General Secretariat of the Organization of American States.

Article 10

This Convention shall enter into force on the thirtieth day following the date of deposit of the second instrument of ratification.

For each State ratifying or acceding to the Convention after the deposit of the second instrument of ratification, the Convention shall enter into force on the thirtieth day after deposit by such State of its instrument of ratification or accession.

Article 11

If a State Party has two or more territorial units in which different systems of law apply in relation to the matters dealt with in this Convention, it may, at the time of signature, ratification or accession, declare that this Convention shall extend to all its territorial units or only to one or more of them.

Such declaration may be modified by subsequent declarations, which shall expressly indicate the territorial unit or units to which the Convention applies. Such subsequent declarations shall be transmitted to the General Secretariat of the Organization of American States, and shall become effective thirty days after the date of their receipt.

Article 12

This Convention shall remain in force indefinitely, but any of the States Parties may denounce it. The instrument of denunciation shall be deposited with the General Secretariat of the Organization of American States. After one year from the date of deposit of the instrument of denunciation, the Convention shall no longer be in effect for the denouncing State, but shall remain in effect for the other States Parties.

Article 13
The original instrument of this Convention, the English, French, Portuguese and Spanish texts of which are equally authentic, shall be deposited with the General Secretariat of the Organization of American States. The Secretariat shall notify the Member States of the Organization of American States and the States that have acceded to the Convention of the signatures, deposits of instruments or ratification, accession, and denunciation as well as of reservations, if any. It shall also transmit the declarations referred to in Article 11 of this Convention.

IN WITNESS WHEREOF the undersigned Plenipotentiaries, being duly authorized thereto by their respective Governments, have signed this Convention.
DONE AT PANAMA CITY, Republic of Panama, this thirtieth day of January one thousand nine hundred and seventy-five.

STRATEGIC STATISTICS

Balance of Payments (Annual)

Million of Dollars

Reporting Country: Panama

Series	Source	Units (Valuation)	1998
CURRENT ACCOUNT: BALANCE (B-C--B)	IDBSTA	USD (C)	-1,211.7
CURRENT ACCOUNT: BALANCE (B-C--B)	IDBCED	USD (C)	-1,211.7
CURRENT ACCOUNT: BALANCE (B-C--B)	IMFBOP	USD (C)	-1,211.7

Reporting Country: Panama

Series	Source	Units (Valuation)	1998
EXPORTS OF GOODS: CREDIT (B-C-G-C)	IDBSTA	USD (C)	6,325.2
EXPORTS OF GOODS: CREDIT (B-C-G-C)	IDBCED	USD (C)	6,325.2
EXPORTS OF GOODS: CREDIT (B-C-G-C)	IMFBOP	USD (C)	6,325.2

Reporting Country: Panama

Series	Source	Units (Valuation)	1998
TRADE: BALANCE (B-C-G-B)	IDBSTA	USD (C)	-1,371.1
TRADE: BALANCE (B-C-G-B)	IDBCED	USD (C)	-1,371.1
TRADE: BALANCE (B-C-G-B)	IMFBOP	USD (C)	-1,371.1

Reporting Country: Panama

Series	Source	Units (Valuation)	1998
IMPORTS OF GOODS: DEBIT (B-C-G-D)	IDBSTA	USD (C)	-7,696.3
IMPORTS OF GOODS: DEBIT (B-C-G-D)	IDBCED	USD (C)	-7,696.3
IMPORTS OF GOODS: DEBIT (B-C-G-D)	IMFBOP	USD (C)	-7,696.3

Reporting Country: Panama

Series	Source	Units (Valuation)	1998
EXPORTS OF GOODS AND SERVICES: CREDIT (B-C-GS-C)	IDBSTA	USD (C)	8,022.6
EXPORTS OF GOODS AND SERVICES: CREDIT (B-C-GS-C)	IDBCED	USD (C)	8,022.6
EXPORTS OF GOODS AND SERVICES: CREDIT (B-C-GS-C)	IMFBOP	USD (C)	8,022.6

Reporting Country: Panama

Series	Source	Units (Valuation)	1998
SERVICE: BALANCE (B-C-S-B)	IDBSTA	USD (C)	524.9
SERVICE: BALANCE (B-C-S-B)	IDBCED	USD (C)	524.9
SERVICE: BALANCE (B-C-S-B)	IMFBOP	USD (C)	524.9

Reporting Country: Panama

Series	Source	Units (Valuation)	1998
ADDENDUM: FREIGHT & INSURANCE BALANCE (B-C-SFI-B)	IDBSTA	USD (C)	-614.3
ADDENDUM: FREIGHT & INSURANCE BALANCE (B-C-SFI-B)	IDBCED	USD (C)	-614.3

Reporting Country: Panama

Series	Source	Units (Valuation)	1998
OTHER SERVICES: BALANCE (INCLUDES	IDBSTA	USD (C	96.2

PROPERTY INCOME) (B-C-SO-B)		)	
OTHER SERVICES: BALANCE (INCLUDES PROPERTY INCOME) (B-C-SO-B)	IDBCED	USD (C)	96.2

Reporting Country: Panama

Series	Source	Units (Valuation)	1998
TRAVEL: BALANCE (B-C-ST-B)	IDBSTA	USD (C)	202.6
TRAVEL: BALANCE (B-C-ST-B)	IDBCED	USD (C)	202.6
TRAVEL: BALANCE (B-C-ST-B)	IMFBOP	USD (C)	202.6

Reporting Country: Panama

Series	Source	Units (Valuation)	1998
TRANSPORTATION SERVICES: BALANCE (B-C-STR-B)	IDBSTA	USD (C)	226.1
TRANSPORTATION SERVICES: BALANCE (B-C-STR-B)	IDBCED	USD (C)	226.1
TRANSPORTATION SERVICES: BALANCE (B-C-STR-B)	IMFBOP	USD (C)	226.1

FOREIGN TRADE OF PANAMA

PANAMA: TOP 50 COMMODITIES EXPORTED IN 1997

Commodity Description					Country Codes											
		Exports in Thousands			Top 5 Trading Partners and their Percentage of World Trade											
Rank	Commodity	WORLD	FTAA	%	1st.	%	2nd.	%	3rd.	%	4th.	%	5th.	%	1-5(%)	
1	08030021	179,841	63,056	35.1	USA	35.1	SWE	30.3	RBL	18.8	DEU	9.6	ESP	3.5	97.3	...
2	03061310	95,736	78,485	82.0	USA	81.8	ESP	16.4	CHN	0.6	FRA	0.6	CHT	0.3	99.7	...
3	17011100	28,669	28,669	100.0	USA	100.0	...	...	...	...	...	...	...	...	100.0	...
4	03021900	24,981	24,660	98.7	USA	98.5	MTQ	0.6	GBR	0.5	HKG	0.1	COL	0.1	99.9	...
5	09011100	22,425	19,309	86.1	USA	67.2	CAN	18.9	DEU	8.4	ITA	3.4	RBL	1.0	98.9	...
6	08071000	20,638	20,638	100.0	USA	100.0	...	...	...	...	...	...	...	...	100.0	...
7	27100061	17,981	17,981	100.0	USA	45.1	HND	44.6	SLV	10.3	...	...	...	...	100.0	...
8	71081200	13,503	13,503	100.0	CAN	86.4	USA	13.6	...	...	...	...	...	...	100.0	...

9	30049099	11,864	10,670	89.9	USA	31.5	HND	14.1	NIC	12.9	CRI	11.1	ZLC	10.1	79.7	...
10	03041090	11,408	11,370	99.7	USA	95.0	GTM	4.0	PER	0.4	ABW	0.2	GBR	0.1	99.7	...
11	01021090	11,130	11,130	100.0	HND	99.9	NIC	0.1	SLV	0.0	...	...	...	...	100.0	...
12	76129092	10,350	10,350	100.0	CRI	47.3	COL	21.6	SLV	10.0	VEN	9.4	NIC	7.5	95.8	...
13	03062391	9,881	9,876	99.9	USA	21.3	COL	18.4	HND	17.7	MEX	11.5	NIC	8.4	77.2	...
14	41042200	8,639	4,906	56.8	ITA	34.3	GTM	27.4	MEX	14.7	CRI	8.1	HKG	4.0	88.6	...
15	62059019	7,718	5,734	74.3	USA	47.0	ZLC	19.1	VEN	4.7	DOM	4.3	PER	4.1	79.3	...
16	02013000	7,220	3,591	49.7	JPN	50.2	COL	46.1	ECU	3.6	CHT	0.0	...	...	100.0	...
17	76020000	6,033	5,830	96.6	USA	95.8	CHT	2.7	MEX	0.8	JPN	0.4	HKG	0.3	100.0	...
18	04029999	5,898	5,898	100.0	CRI	79.4	GTM	9.2	HND	5.1	NIC	3.8	SLV	2.5	100.0	...
19	24022000	5,312	5,302	99.8	USA	99.8	ZLC	0.2	...	...	...	...	...	...	100.0	...
20	96039020	5,295	5,256	99.3	USA	92.0	CAN	3.7	CRI	2.5	COL	1.0	ZLC	0.5	99.7	...
21	07099090	5,009	5,009	100.0	USA	100.0	COL	0.0	...	...	...	...	...	...	100.0	...
22	04029192	4,685	4,685	100.0	BOL	35.2	CRI	29.5	HTI	21.1	GTM	5.4	VEN	2.3	93.5	...
23	03055900	4,658	1,937	41.6	HKG	57.9	USA	28.9	CRI	11.4	MEX	1.1	GBR	0.5	99.7	...
24	21039039	4,604	4,602	100.0	GTM	38.5	SLV	37.9	HND	12.2	CRI	6.4	PER	1.8	96.8	...
25	22084000	4,581	2,473	54.0	ZLC	43.0	CRI	12.6	PER	9.6	BHS	7.9	ECU	7.2	80.2	...
26	23012000	4,549	4,160	91.4	USA	79.9	CRI	9.6	MYS	5.0	JPN	3.6	CHL	0.9	98.9	...
27	03061100	4,399	4,116	93.6	USA	93.0	JPN	4.7	CHE	1.2	GTM	0.6	ESP	0.5	99.9	...
28	15042000	3,854	1,782	46.2	NLD	53.8	USA	46.0	HND	0.3	...	...	...	...	100.0	...
29	27100041	3,808	3,808	100.0	USA	98.8	CRI	1.2	...	...	...	...	...	...	100.0	...
30	27100073	3,182	3,156	99.2	CRI	47.3	SLV	29.9	COL	6.5	NIC	5.2	DOM	5.1	93.9	...
31	40151990	3,182	1,583	49.7	GBR	28.8	USA	28.2	ESP	20.2	CHL	7.5	CRI	4.3	89.1	...
32	21032020	2,898	2,812	97.0	CRI	75.4	SLV	7.2	HTI	6.9	GTM	3.6	ZLC	3.0	96.0	...
33	32041111	2,738	2,733	99.8	CRI	45.3	SLV	20.7	HND	11.9	GTM	6.5	COL	4.4	88.8	...
34	96039041	2,732	2,711	99.2	USA	81.3	CAN	8.9	DOM	3.1	CRI	2.7	COL	2.3	98.4	...
35	62171039	2,571	1,359	52.9	ZLC	38.9	VEN	11.5	USA	10.0	BOL	5.1	CRI	4.2	69.5	...
36	48010000	2,520	2,520	100.0	GTM	76.9	HND	19.6	DOM	2.4	CRI	1.1	...	...	100.0	...
37	04063000	2,341	2,341	100.0	CRI	71.6	SLV	24.1	GTM	4.2	COL	0.1	...	...	100.0	...
38	23099099	2,301	2,301	100.0	NIC	68.1	CRI	30.9	USA	0.5	HND	0.5	COL	0.0	100.0	...
39	48236010	2,177	1,945	89.3	USA	74.1	CRI	13.1	CUR	4.0	NLD	2.5	FRA	1.3	95.0	...
40	21039021	1,986	1,986	100.0	CRI	98.4	COL	1.3	SLV	0.3	ESP	0.0	VEN	0.0	100.0	...
41	48184030	1,984	1,984	100.0	CRI	48.2	SLV	23.0	USA	15.6	GTM	6.6	BOL	2.5	95.9	...
42	48192090	1,944	1,944	100.0	CRI	99.9	USA	0.1	...	...	...	...	...	...	100.0	...

43	96031000	1,922	1,870	97.3	USA	96.3	ESP	1.2	ZLC	1.0	GRL	0.5	JAM	0.5	99.5	...
44	03071010	1,763	1,763	100.0	GTM	71.4	USA	28.4	ECU	0.2	...	...	...	...	100.0	...
45	12071090	1,737	1,737	100.0	CRI	100.0	...	...	...	...	...	...	...	...	100.0	...
46	73231010	1,711	1,711	100.0	USA	95.7	CAN	3.4	JAM	0.5	CRI	0.4	...	...	100.0	...
47	72041000	1,699	1,669	98.2	COL	85.7	USA	12.2	ESP	1.8	BOL	0.2	CRI	0.1	100.0	...
48	07149090	1,622	1,622	100.0	USA	100.0	...	...	...	...	...	...	...	...	100.0	...
49	22071000	1,608	628	39.1	ESP	55.8	COL	21.1	DOM	18.0	UNS	5.2	...	...	100.0	...
50	32089019	1,566	159	10.2	CUB	89.7	CRI	7.0	NIC	2.0	HND	0.6	GTM	0.3	99.7	...

PANAMA CANAL TREATY IMPLEMENTATION:

ISSUES AND UPDATE

August 24, 1998
Vol. IX, No. 8
Bulletin

The treaty implementation process is on track although much remains to be done over the remaining months of the 20-year transition period. Progress is most impressive in joint efforts for a seamless turn over of the operation of the canal--key personnel are in place, including a new Panamanian board of directors that will assume responsibility when the canal is handed over on 31 December 1999. More importantly, steps have been taken to minimize the risk of possible future political interference in the efficient operation of the canal. Progress has been slower in finding commercial uses for transferred property and facilities. Also, many in Panama are concerned about possible environmental risks in the former Canal Zone. Discussions for possible post-1999 U.S. access to former defense facilities in Panama have not produced sufficient common interest to result in an accord. Nevertheless, Panama and the United States are committed to full implementation of the Panama Canal Treaties and the future continuous and neutral operation of the canal

The Canal Transition

The key issue in the Panama Canal transfer is ensuring an independent and non-politicized management. To this end, Panama adopted a constitutional amendment in 1996 providing for "autonomous, apolitical" administration of the canal. Also, in May 1997, the Panamanian National Assembly passed legislation providing for an independent Canal Administration. Together, these initiatives create a Panamanian entity modeled after the structure and procedures of the current Panama Canal Commission (PCC). Strong domestic support for these measures in Panama indicates substantial national resolve to protect and promote the canal.

The leadership of the new Panama Canal Authority (PCA) also is taking shape. Alberto Aleman Zubieta, a U.S.-educated civil engineer and the current Panamanian administrator for the Canal, will continue as administrator of the pca after 1999. In 1998, the Panamanian Legislative Assembly confirmed 10 of the 11-person Panamanian board of directors of the pca, including Minister of Canal Affairs, Dr. Jorge Ritter. These steps indicate progress toward assuring a competent Panamanian administration well before the transition.

Modernization of the canal also is well underway to ensure it will continue to meet demands. This $1 billion effort began with an engineering review of the canal system by the U.S. Army Corps of Engineers, at Panama's request, in the mid-1990s. At the recommendation of the Panamanian board, several respected Panamanian civil engineers also participated in that review, including Alberto Aleman Zubieta, who subsequently became the canal administrator. The most significant improvement is the widening of Gaillard Cut, the narrowest part of the canal, which when completed in 2002 and combined with other improvements, will increase canal capacity by 20 percent, by permitting continuous two-way traffic. Other improvements include new tugboats, improved locomotives and tracks for control of vessels in the locks, modernized machinery and controls, and a new traffic management system employing satellite positioning.

To fund these improvements and to transfer the canal to solid financial footing, canal tolls were raised 8.2 percent in January 1997 and 7.5 percent in January 1998. These rate increases reduce pressure on the pca to adjust rates in the early years of Panamanian administration. However, they also may test the canal's competitiveness relative to alternative routes and modes of shipping such as intermodal shipping across the United States.

Early on, the pca will face additional, challenging decisions to keep the canal competitive. Within 20 years, more than 50 percent of ocean-going cargo vessels are projected tc be too large to pass through the canal's locks, an increase from 15 percent today. Construction of a third set of locks will be needed to accommodate these "post-PANAMAX" vessels. Such an effort would require almost $7 billion, financed by the international community. In addition to the size and related cost of the third locks, concerns include additional water consumption in the gravity-fed canal system and the financial burden imposed by future tolls.

Preserving the canal environment will remain a special challenge. About 52 million gallons of fresh water are used for each ship transit and about 34 ships pass each day or 12,500 transits per year. A severe drought over the past year induced by El Niño forced the pca to limit temporarily ship drafts to 36 feet, down from the normal draft of 39.5 feet. In turn, shippers had to adjust cargoes and incur higher costs. The current climatic phenomenon is passing, but the adjustments in ship drafts required by changes in the water supply illustrate the critical importance of water resources to the canal's future. The canal's viability could be threatened if nearby commercial development were to impose new demands on the fresh water supply of the canal system or if erosion and silt accumulation were to reduce lake capacity.

By law, the pca has jurisdiction to ensure that such problems do not occur and that any use of the canal watersheds is consistent with canal operations. Furthermore, the Government of Panama has undertaken measures to curtail deforestation by squatters and is actively promoting reforestation efforts to reduce erosion and silting.

Development Plans and Prospects

Another major challenge for Panama is conversion of the many U.S. military installations to appropriate commercial use. About 64,000 acres including military reservations and ranges remain to be transferred to Panama before the end of 1999.

Panama established the Inter-Oceanic Regional Authority (Spanish acronym, ARI) in 1993 to manage the transfer and development of reverting properties. ari seeks to ensure that the former Canal Zone properties are developed consistently with canal operations and are integrated into Panama's economic planning.

The ARI strategy focuses on development in four complementary sectors: maritime, light industry, tourism, and education and research. In the maritime sector, ari seeks to make Panama the principal container trans-shipment and maritime services center of Latin America. Modern container port operations operated at Colon on the Atlantic side by U.S. and Taiwanese companies are successful and expanding. In 1996, the Panamanian Port Authority privatized government-owned ports by granting a concession to a Hong Kong firm. Combined with interconnecting rail service awarded to a U.S. firm, investments are intended to provide a diversified and complementary transportation infrastructure. Other growth areas include diverse shore services required by intermodal shippers.

ari also envisions opportunities for light industry and assembly work as an adjunct to maritime trade. The Colon Free Zone is enjoying a renaissance after the addition of a former U.S. airfield. In a related move, ari leased the former Fort Davis to a Taiwan concern for development as an industrial park.

Another focus is tourism. Even though 250,000 passengers transit the canal each year, none stop in Panama. ari has identified several sites, and contracts are under negotiation for hotel construction. However, substantial investment is needed in wastewater treatment, enlarged power and fresh water services, and roads to make these sites viable for tourism.

Education and research represents another development priority for the reverted properties. Plans include using some of the former military bases to develop a "City of Knowledge." Panama hopes to leverage the excellent reputation of the Smithsonian's Tropical Research Institute to attract new public and commercial research activities. For example, convenient access to rich and diverse tropical resources could prove valuable in public and private biomedical research.

However, to date the education and re-search sector has seen the least tangible results.

The most controversial issue in the transfer process is environmental clean-up of military areas. Some observers assert that the U.S. military conducted hazardous tests in Panama and that the military bases are dangerously polluted. U.S. military authorities maintain that the bases, in which U.S. personnel live and work, are very well managed and safe. They acknowledge that the firing ranges, about 25 percent of the total range area, contain unexploded ordnance that cannot be completely nor practicably removed due to the limits of technology and the damage to the environment that would result from cleaning operations. Furthermore, these ranges are mainly within the canal watershed and thus cannot be used for intensive commercial development.

Both governments have strong fiscal and political interests at stake. An objective means is needed to identify risks, evaluate corrective measures, and publicize results to minimize the impact of this issue on future U.S.-Panamanian relations.

Canal Security and U.S. Troop Withdrawal

After the transition, the United States still will have an interest in maintaining access to the canal. In principle, this is guaranteed by the Neutrality Treaty, the second of the two 1977 canal treaties, which provides for "expeditious passage" of U.S. military vessels. In its ratification, Panama expressed a commitment to the continuous and neutral operation of the canal. Ultimately, "continuous operation" depends on sound administration of the canal as well as political and economic conditions in Panama.

Today physical protection of the canal facilities is provided by the pcc Security Division; this function will continue under pca authority after the transition. U.S. forces in Panama currently play no direct role in the physical security of the canal, although they contribute to the overall sense of security.

Panama has been politically stable since the corrupt Noriega regime was overthrown by the U.S. invasion in 1989. The governments of President Guillermo Endara and President Ernesto Perez Balladares pursued pragmatic and reform-minded agendas and promoted economic growth through international investment. Panama also disbanded its military forces which, under Noriega, became a much-hated threat to civilian rule.

A proposal by the government to amend the constitution to permit reelection of a sitting president will face a national plebiscite on 30 August 1998. This initiative may sharpen divisions among Panama's 14 political parties and will set the stage for national elections in May 1999. Nevertheless, Panama's current commitment to international investment and sound administration of the canal is not likely to be challenged by the give and take of party politics.

Stability in Panama also is a function of the economy, so concern has been high about the impact of the withdrawal of U.S. troops. Historically, the U.S. presence contributed about $350 million to the Panamanian economy, out of the GDP of $7 billion, or about 5 percent. This economic loss is being stretched over several years and much of it already has been absorbed through growth in the Panamanian economy.

The troop withdrawal is on schedule. In September 1997, the headquarters of U.S. Southern Command moved to Miami, Florida. The U.S. Army's regional command will transfer to Puerto Rico in 1999, and U.S. operations at Howard Air Force Base will effectively cease in early to mid-1999 to prepare for the final transfer of facilities by year's end. This constitutes a decline from about 10,000 U.S. troops typically stationed in Panama to less than 4,500 this year, to zero in 1999.

The possibility of U.S. access to the former Howard Air Force Base after 1999 was considered as part of a Multilateral Counterdrug Center. U.S. forces would support the counterdrug effort as well as the performance of missions such as disaster response and search-and-rescue. Discussions between Panama and the United States did not, however, result in sufficient convergence of interests to produce an accord.

Outlook

An era is ending in which the canal was managed essentially as a non-profit global public utility by the United States. In contrast, Panama will run the canal as a competitive business enterprise. To accomplish this, a regional dialogue, both public and private, is important to a successful transition in Panama. Recognizing this, in September 1997 Panama hosted the "Universal Congress on the Panama Canal" in an initiative to brief the world community on preparations for canal transition. Also needed is the sustained confidence of canal users, private investors, canal workers and Panamanian voters. Fortunately, the interests of Panama, the United States, the hemisphere and global shippers converge in the long term stability and efficiency of canal operations. These objectives can best be achieved through cooperative and rational solutions in matters of management, commercial development and security.

POLITICAL CONSTITUTION OF THE REPUBLIC OF PANAMA TITLE XVI

Article 309. The Panama Canal constitutes an inalienable patrimony of the Panamanian Nation; it shall remain open to the peaceful and uninterrupted transit of ships of all nations, and its use shall be subject to the requirements and conditions established by this constitution, the Law, and its Administration.

Article 310. An autonomous legal entity by the name of Panama Canal Authority is hereby established under public law, which shall be exclusively in charge of the administration, operation, conservation, maintenance, and modernization of the Panama Canal and its related activities, pursuant to current constitutional and legal provisions in force, in order that it may operate the Canal in a manner that is safe, continuous, efficient, and profitable. This entity shall have its own patrimony, and the right to administer it.

The Panama Canal Authority, in coordination with other government agencies as established by the Law shall be responsible for the administration, maintenance, use and conservation of the water resources of the Panama Canal watershed, which include the waters of the lakes and their tributary streams. Any plans for construction, the use of waters, and the utilization, expansion, and development of the ports, or any other work or construction along the banks of the Panama Canal shall require the prior approval of the Panama Canal Authority.

The Panama Canal Authority shall not be subject to the payment of taxes, duties, tariffs, charges, rates or tribute of a national or municipal nature, with the exception of Panama Social Security payments, educational insurance, workmen's compensation, and public utility rates, except as provided in Article 315.

Article 311. The Panama Canal Authority, and all other institutions and authorities of the Republic related to the maritime sector shall be included in the national maritime strategy. The Executive Branch shall propose to the Legislative Branch the Law to coordinate all these institutions in order to promote the country's social and economic development.

Article 312. The administration of the Panama Canal Authority shall be under a board of directors composed of eleven members designated as follows:

1. One member designated by the president of the Republic, who shall preside over the board of directors and hold the rank of minister of state for canal affairs.
2. One member to be designated or removed freely by the legislative branch.
3. Nine members appointed by the president of the Republic as agreed with the Cabinet Council and ratified by the Legislative Branch by an absolute majority of its members.

The Law shall establish the requirements for the post of board member, guaranteeing the staggered replacement of the board members mentioned in Item 3 of this article, in groups of three, every three years. After the first replacement, all board members shall serve for a period of nine years.

Article 313. The board of directors shall have the following powers and duties, without prejudice to any other as determined by the Constitution and the Law:

1. Appoint and remove the Administrator and Deputy Administrator of the Canal, and establish their duties in accordance with the Law.
2. Set tolls, charges, and fees for the use of the Canal and its related services, subject to final approval by the Cabinet Council.
3. Make loans, with the prior approval of the Cabinet Council and within the limits established by the Law.
4. Grant concessions to provide services to the Panama Canal Authority and transiting vessels.
5. Propose the boundaries of the Canal watershed for approval by the Cabinet Council and the Legislative Assembly.
6. Exclusively approve regulations to implement the general policies issued by the Legislative Branch as proposed by the Executive Branch, on contracts and procurement, and on any matters as may. be required for the best operation, maintenance, conservation and modernization of the Canal within the national maritime strategy.
7. Exercise all the powers established by this Constitution and the Law.

Article 314. The Panama Canal Authority shall adopt a triennial financial planning and management system, according to which it shall approve its annual budget by means of a justified resolution; this budget shall not be included in the general budget of the government of Panama.

The Panama Canal Authority shall submit its draft budget to the Cabinet Council, which in turn shall submit it to the Legislative Assembly for consideration and review, approval or rejection, in accordance with Chapter II, Title IX of this Constitution.

Funds shall be allocated in the budget for Panama Social Security payments, and for the payment of charges for any public utilities provided, as well as for any surplus to be transferred to the Panama National Treasury, once the operating, capital project, management, maintenance, modernization, Canal widening, and the required contingency reserve costs are covered as provided according to the Law and its administration.

The Administrator shall be in charge of the implementation of the budget, which shall be monitored by the Board of Directors or its designee, and only through subsequent control, by the office of the Comptroller General of the Republic.

Article 315. The Panama Canal Authority shall make annual payments to the Panama National Treasury per Panama Canal net ton or its equivalent, from the monies collected from vessels transiting the Panama Canal, which are subject to the payment of tolls. The rates for these payments shall be set by the Panama Canal Authority, and shall not be less than those paid to the Republic of Panama for the same concept on December 31, 1999.

By reason of their transit through the Panama Canal, vessels, their cargo, passengers, owners or operators, or their operation, as well as the Panama Canal Authority may not be subject to any other national or municipal tax.

Article 316. The Panama Canal Authority shall be subject to a special employment regime based on a merit system, and shall adopt a general employment system that maintains, at least, basic employment conditions and rights similar to those existing on December 31,1999.

Permanent employees, and employees who must make use of the special retirement that year, whose positions are deemed necessary according to applicable provisions shall be guaranteed employment with the same benefits and conditions as they enjoyed up to that date.

The Panama Canal Authority shall hire, preferably, Panamanian nationals. The Organic Law shall regulate the hiring of foreign nationals, guaranteeing that there will be no detriment to the conditions or standards of living of Panamanian employees. Considering the essential international public service rendered by the Canal, its operation may not be interrupted for any reason.

Any labor conflicts between the employees of the Panama Canal and its administration shall be resolved by the employees or their unions and the Administration, through the mechanisms established by the Law to resolve such conflicts. Arbitration shall constitute the last administrative instance.

Article 317. The regime contained in this Title may only be implemented by means of laws establishing general policies. The Panama Canal Authority shall regulate these matters and shall forward to the Legislative Branch within a period of fifteen calendar days copies of any regulations it issues in the exercise of this power.

TEMPORARY PROVISIONS. Unless otherwise provided in this Constitution, the Panama Canal Authority shall incorporate into its organization the administrative and operating structure existing in the Panama Canal Commission on December 31, 1999, including its departments, Offices, positions, policies in force, regulations, and collective bargaining agreements, until such time as they are modified according to the Law.

INTERNATIONAL MONETARY FUND

PANAMA

Recent Economic Developments

Prepared by G.A. Mackenzie (Head), G. Bindley-Taylor, M. Gapen, A. Gómez-Oliver, C. Paiva, M. Papaioannou (all WHD) and M. Moore (MAE)

Approved by the Western Hemisphere Department

January 5, 2001

Contents

Page

Text Tables

Statistical Appendix Tables

Panama: Basic Data

I. Social and Demographic Indicators

Area (thousand sq. km)	77,082
Population	
Total (million) (est., 2000)	2.9
Rate of increase (percent a year)	1.6
Density (per sq. km.)	38
GDP per capita (US$) (1999)	3,395
Unemployment (Aug. 2000)	13.3
Population characteristics (1999)	
Life expectancy at birth (years)	75.5
Crude birth rate (per thousand)	19.5
Crude death rate (per thousand)	5.0
Infant mortality (per thousand live birt	20.8
Income distribution (1999)	
By highest 20 percent of households	63
By lowest 20 percent of households	2
Health (1994)	
Per capita calorie intake	2,534
Population	
Per physician (1995)	592
Per hospital bed (1996)	455
Access to safe water (percent of population, 1998)	
Total	84
Urban	92
Rural	72
Education (in percent, 1997)	
Net Enrollment rates	
Primary education	92
Secondary education	62
Higher education	21
GDP (1999)	US$9,545 million

II. Economic Indicators, 1996–2000

	1996	1997	1998	Revised 1999	Proj. 2000
	(In percent change)				
National accounts and prices					
GDP at constant 1982 market prices	2.8	4.5	4.4	3.0	2.3
Agriculture and mining	0.8	1.2	6.8	-0.3	-2.3
Manufacturing and construction	-2.1	6.1	4.7	0.6	-6.7
Services	4.2	4.8	4.7	4.7	4.7
Consumer price index (end-of-period)	2.3	-0.5	1.4	1.5	2.0
Monetary 1/					
Net Domestic assets	5.0	10.3	17.8	18.0	12.0
Credit to the public sector	2.5	-2.0	-1.2	-0.7	-0.1
Credit to the private sector	7.0	12.5	21.9	17.4	13.1
Liabilities to the domestic private sector	8.1	15.4	12.4	7.6	9.1
Real effective exchange rate 2/	86.9	87.7	88.2	89.7	...
	(In percent of GDP) 3/				
Investment and saving					
Gross domestic investment	30.5	31.1	32.8	32.6	30.2
Private investment	26.7	26.6	26.4	27.8	26.5
Gross national savings	26.8	24.3	19.7	18.2	19.8
Private saving	22.8	21.3	17.3	15.3	17.6
Nonfinancial public sector					
Revenue and Grants	28.0	28.7	28.3	29.2	28.7
Expenditure	27.5	28.9	31.3	30.7	29.8
Current	23.7	24.5	25.0	25.9	26.1
Capital	3.8	4.3	6.4	4.8	3.7
Primary balance	3.8	3.5	1.0	2.5	3.0
Overall balance	0.5	-0.2	-3.0	-1.4	-1.1
External current account	-3.7	-6.8	-13.1	-14.4	-10.4
Gross public debt	77.2	71.9	69.7	72.8	72.3
External	62.0	57.8	58.5	58.3	57.9
Domestic	15.2	14.1	11.2	14.4	14.4

Panama: Basic Data

	1996	1997	1998	Revised 1999	Proj. 2000
	(In millions of U.S. dollars)				
Balance of payments					
Trade balance	-644.1	-685.2	-1,361.6	-1,416.5	-1,224.5
Exports, f.o.b.	740.6	843.9	862.5	864.6	1,011.0
Imports, f.o.b.	-2,248.9	-2,462.2	-2,751.9	-2,858.4	-2,836.1
Colon Free Zone (net)	864.2	933.1	527.8	577.3	600.5
Services, income, and transfers (net)	342.2	96.8	159.4	39.0	196.8
Of which :					
Interest on public debt	-243.3	-282.3	-301.9	-368.0	-410.2
Current account	-301.9	-588.4	-1,202.2	-1,377.5	-1,027.8
Capital and financial account balance					
(including errors and omissions)	601.0	731.0	1,008.7	1,286.6	1,121.8
Public (including grants)	-108.4	-564.3	-160.7	-33.9	155.8
Private	863.7	923.5	1,371.6	1,257.9	971.9
Errors and omissions	133.0	298.7	-248.7	61.2	0.0
Overall balance	299.1	142.6	193.5	90.9	94.0
Stock of net foreign assets of BNP	952.1	1,082.3	906.3	824.5	890.5
Stock of external payments arrears	67.8	29.8	0.0	0.0	0.0
Memorandum item:					
Debt-service ratio 4/	15.2	44.1	21.5	24.5	23.8
IMF data (as of November 30, 2000)					
Article VIII status					
Intervention currency and rate					B 1.00 per U.S. dollar
Quota					SDR 206.6 million
Fund holdings of local currency					SDR 271.8 million
From Fund resources (including SBA and EFF)					SDR 77.0 million
Fund holdings as percent of quota					131.6
Arrears with the Fund					None
Special Drawing Rights Department					
Net cumulative SDR allocation					SDR 26.3 million
Holdings of SDRs					SDR 1.3 million

Sources: Panamanian authorities; and Fund staff estimates.

1/ In percent of initial stock of liabilities to the private sector.
2/ Based on the period average.
3/ Reflects the authorities' revisions to nominal GDP.
4/ External debt service as percent of exports of goods and services. In 1997 the increase reflects debt restructuring involving the retirement of Brady bonds.

INTRODUCTION

1. This report provides background information and supporting analyses for the staff report for the 2000 Article IV consultation discussions with Panama. Chapter I presents an overview of economic developments since 1998. Chapter II summarizes the financial and economic aspects of the operation of the Panama Canal and discusses the economic impact of the reversion of the Canal and its adjacent areas to Panama. Chapter III describes the progress of bank supervisory reform. Finally, Chapter IV briefly discusses poverty and poverty alleviation programs.

I. REVIEW OF RECENT ECONOMIC DEVELOPMENTS

A. Summary of Developments

2. Real GDP growth fell to an estimated 2.3 percent in 2000 from 4.4 percent in 1998 and 3.0 percent in 1999. The decline in growth is mainly attributable to the repercussions on the re-exports of the Colón Free Zone (ZLC) of economic difficulties in trading partner countries, and the impact of disease and drought on fishing and agriculture. It does not reflect a decline in the underlying rate of economic growth. Despite the decline in the value added of the ZLC, the service sector, which accounts for about 80 percent of GDP, continued to grow quite steadily at 4.7 percent per year.

3. The unemployment rate fell from 13.4 percent in 1997 to 11.8 percent in 1999 before increasing to 13.3 percent in 2000. The increase in the CPI averaged about 1½ percent per year with little fluctuation despite the increase in world oil prices since March 1999.

4. Public sector finances weakened in the second half of 1998 because of election-related capital spending by the central government. As a result, the borrowing requirement of the nonfinancial public sector (the PSBR) rose from 0.3 percent of GDP in 1997 to 2.9 percent in 1998. Efforts to restrain central government expenditure reduced the PSBR to 1.4 percent of GDP in 1999. Restraint of capital expenditure is projected to lower the PSBR to 1.1 percent of GDP in 2000 despite a slowdown in revenue growth brought on by the decline in economic growth.

5. Substantial progress was achieved in reducing the size of the nonfinancial public enterprise sector in 1996–98, and in establishing regulatory bodies to promote competition. In 1998–00, however—apart from bank regulatory reform (discussed in Chapter III)—the pace of structural reform slackened. In particular, there were no further privatizations, and tax and social security reform did not advance. Nonetheless, the privatized complementary fund for civil servants began operations in 1998 and some progress was achieved in the development of the automated public financial information system, SIAFPA.[1]

---

[1] SIAFPA stands for "*Sistema Integrado Automático Financiero de Panamá.*"

6. Bank credit to the domestic economy grew rapidly in 1998–00, and the domestic business of the general license banks—those allowed to deal with residents—is now greater than their international business. The growth of credit outstripped the growth of deposits, requiring that the banks reduce substantially their net foreign asset position. The credit growth financed private sector investment projects related to the reversion and investments by households in housing and consumer durables. Net bank credit to the public sector declined.

7. The external current account deficit increased from about 6.8 percent of GDP in 1997 to an average of 13.8 percent of GDP in 1998–99 (it is estimated to have declined to 10.4 percent of GDP in 2000). An increase in the trade deficit of 7.0 percent of GDP and an increase in net factor income payments of 2.0 percent of GDP outweighed an increase in the surplus on services. The drop in the net exports of the ZLC and an increase in imports related to the investment boom and easy terms for consumer credit explain most of the deterioration of the trade balance. The increase in the current account deficit in 1997–99 was mirrored by an increase in the private sector's financing requirement of 7.0 percent.

8. The current account deficits were financed entirely by the private sector in 1998–00. Net public capital inflows (including changes in public sector deposits abroad) were negative in these years. Public external debt remained at about 59 percent of GDP.

B. Aggregate Supply and Demand, Employment and Prices

9. The growth of real GDP fell from 4.5 percent in 1997 to 3.0 percent in 1999, and is estimated to have declined to 2.3 percent in 2000. The slowdown was mainly attributable to the impact of economic difficulties in Brazil, Colombia, Ecuador, and Venezuela on net exports of the ZLC.[2] Specifically, the ZLC's net exports fell from US$933 million in 1997 to US$577 million in 1999, and are estimated to have risen to US$600 million in 2000. Severe declines in agriculture and fishing output also contributed.[3] In contrast, the service sector, and in particular financial intermediation and telecommunications grew strongly, construction activity was stimulated by investments in the reverted areas and some large public works projects in 1998–99, and electricity output recovered from the effects of the El Niño-related drought in 1998. The growth rate of the service sector has been relatively constant in recent years and has contributed to the overall stability of economic growth given its large contribution to output.[4]

---

[2] These four countries account for 44 percent of the ZLC's exports.

[3] Primary activity, including agriculture and mining, accounts for approximately 8 percent of GDP. Manufacturing and construction account for 12 percent.

[4] The reversion of the Canal at end-1999 and the closure of the U.S. military bases in the adjacent areas entailed a loss of income from employment on the bases and the sale of goods

(continued)

10. Domestic demand increased much more rapidly than supply from 1997–99, and the deficit on external current account increased from 6.8 percent of GDP in 1997 to 14.4 percent of GDP in 1999, before declining to an estimated 10.4 percent of GDP in 2000. The increase in the current account was mirrored by an increase in the private sector's financing requirement (investment minus saving) of 7 percent of GDP. In particular, private sector saving declined steeply from 21.3 percent of GDP in 1997 to 15.3 percent of GDP in 1999, in part because banks were extending consumer loans on more liberal terms than previously. Private sector investment increased from the already high level of 26.6 percent of GDP in 1997 to 27.8 percent in 1999 because of investment in the reverted areas and other projects already noted. It is estimated to have declined to 26.5 percent of GDP in 2000.[5] Much of the increase in fixed investment since the mid-1990s was financed by direct foreign investment.

11. On the basis of estimates through the third quarter, the rate of growth of GDP fell to 2.3 percent in 2000 compared with the program projection of 3.8 percent. Growth in services remained robust, and the ZLC began to recover from its slump, but construction, farming and fishing, and related food-processing industries experienced unexpectedly large declines. The completion of several large infrastructure projects reduced construction activity by more than expected, while the lingering effects of disease on the shrimp harvest and a change in the European Union (EU) trading preferences on banana production were unexpectedly strong.

12. The rate of unemployment fell from an average of 13.5 percent in 1997–98 to 11.8 percent in 1999 before rising again to 13.3 percent in 2000. From 1997 to 2000, the growth rate of the labor force was 3.5 percent and the growth rate in overall employment was 3.6 percent. The labor force participation rate declined from 61.5 percent to 59.9 percent over the same period.

13. The share of employment in the primary and secondary sectors in total employment continued to decline in 1997–00. Specifically, the share of agriculture and mining employment in the total fell from 18.9 percent in 1997 to 17.3 percent in 2000. Manufacturing employment's share declined from 10.6 percent to 9.1 percent. In contrast, the share of employment in services including commerce, transportation and communications grew from 63.0 percent in 1997 to 65.5 percent in 2000.

14. Despite the impact of increases in world petroleum prices on domestic gasoline and other petroleum products, inflation remained low and stable, reflecting Panama's monetary arrangements. The average annual rates of increase in the consumer price index in 1994–00

---

and other services of about US$130 million (1.4 percent of GDP). However, the phasing out of the U.S. military presence had been expected for some time, and the reversion was already stimulating substantial investment in ports and other facilities (see Chapter II).

[5] The quarterly GDP estimates for the first three quarters of 2000 are product-side only. There are no estimates of the components of demand.

have ranged from 0.6–1.5 percent. The 12-month inflation rate in November 2000 was 1.1 percent.

C. The Nonfinancial Public Sector

The structure of the nonfinancial public sector

15. Panama's monitored nonfinancial public sector (NFPS) comprises the central government, the social security agency (CSS), a number of decentralized agencies, and several public enterprises. Total NFPS revenues and grants are equivalent to about 29 percent of GDP, whereas total expenditures amount to some 30 percent of GDP. The central government is the dominant entity in the NFPS, responding for approximately 65 percent of total revenues and 60 percent of total expenditures of the NFPS. As its second largest entity, the CSS accounts for about 27 percent of total NFPS revenues and expenditures.[6]

16. In addition to all ministries and offices of the direct central administration, the central government is defined to also include the Provincial Councils, the Legislative Assembly, the Supreme Court, and the Electoral Court. The nine Provincial Councils are local administration bodies with largely advisory responsibilities, as provincial governments have little autonomy and are under direct control of the central government.[7] Although they are not included in the monitored public sector, municipalities collect a small share of the public sector revenues through some taxes and fees, and some small municipalities depend on transfers from the national government to finance their expenditures.[8] Many functions that fall within the jurisdiction of local governments in other nations—such as education, the judiciary, and police administration—are the responsibility of the central government in Panama.

17. The CSS administers old-age and disability retirement plans, health insurance, work-related accident and other work benefits. It covers about 60 percent of Panama's population, including some 550,000 active contributors, more than 100,000 pensioners, and about 1 million dependents. About 80 percent of the CSS's revenue currently comes from payroll taxes. Most of the remaining revenue comes from earnings on CSS's accumulated surplus, which is invested in government securities and near-cash instruments, including deposits with the BNP. The CSS also receives some transfers from the central government, amounting to 0.4 percent of GDP to cover administrative costs.

---

[6] In the case of public enterprises, revenues are reported net of operating expenses.

[7] Each Provincial Governor is appointed and can be freely removed by the President.

[8] In 1999, municipalities' revenues and expenditures were about 0.7 percent of GDP.

18. The main decentralized agencies are the University of Panama, the Agriculture Development Bank (BDA), and the National Mortgage Bank (BHN).[9] The decentralized agencies finance their operations mainly by means of transfers from the central government. Although the BDA and the BHN are formally public financial institutions, their role as quasi-fiscal agents justify their inclusion in the NFPS. The University of Panama has the largest budget of the decentralized agencies (corresponding to about 60 percent of the total) and receives most of the government transfers, reflecting a policy of heavily subsidizing tertiary education in public institutions.

19. The privatization program carried out during the second half of the 1990s substantially reduced the size of the nonfinancial public enterprise sector in Panama. The main enterprises remaining in the NFPS are the Electricity Transmission Company (ETESA), the National Water and Sewerage Company (IDAAN), and the Colón Free Zone Operating Agency. Despite some operational inefficiencies, especially at IDAAN, the monitored public enterprise sector has generated consistent—albeit declining—operating surpluses. A large share of these surpluses has been transferred to the central government.

Developments in 1998–99

20. Fiscal performance in 1998–99 was mixed. The overall deficit of the NFPS increased from 0.3 percent of GDP in 1997 to 2.9 percent of GDP in 1998, substantially exceeding the deficit of 0.7 percent of GDP targeted in the program supported under the EFF. The swings in the NFPS basically reflect developments at the central government. In particular, most of the increase in the deficit can be attributed to central government capital expenditure overruns in the run-up to the presidential election of May 1999. A significant fiscal tightening took place in 1999, mainly through cuts in investment and increased tax collection. Although the adjustment reduced the overall NFPS deficit to 1.4 percent of GDP, the target of the EFF-supported program was exceeded by 0.4 percent of GDP. Net public sector debt increased from 47.2 percent of GDP in 1998 to 50.7 percent of GDP in 1999. This increase is attributable to the issuance of bonds by the government to recognize past unfunded civil service pension obligations transferred to the newly formed private plan, SIACAP.[10]

21. The increase in capital expenditures already noted was the main force behind the increase in the deficit of the central government from zero in 1997 to 5.0 percent of GDP in 1998. In addition, pensions and transfer payments increased sharply with the settlement of

---

[9] The remaining decentralized agencies included in the monitored public sector are the *Instituto de Mercadeo Agropecuario* (agriculture support) and the *Instituto para la Formación y Aprovechamiento de los Recursos Humanos* (professional training).

[10] SIACAP stands for *Sistema de Ahorros y Capitalización de Pensiones de los Servidores Públicos.*

arrears to the CSS.[11] The deficit was reduced to 2.4 percent of GDP in 1999, with expenditure retrenchment accounting for most of the adjustment. In addition to the decrease in pension payments from the extraordinarily high levels of 1998, capital expenditures were reduced by about one percent of GDP in 1999. Revenues benefited from a large transfer of profits from the Banco Nacional de Panamá, increased tolls and dividends from the Panama Canal, and higher income tax collection attributable mainly to changes in the legislation that closed loopholes and reduced the exemptions granted to some business activities. Tolls and dividends received from the Canal increased as a consequence of the impending reversion of the Canal to Panamanian administration. American workers had additional benefits for living abroad, and as the work force became increasingly dominated by locals, labor costs declined. These cost savings permitted an increase in the central government's share of Canal revenues.

22. The CSS posted a surplus of about 2.6 percent of GDP in 1998, mostly explained by the extraordinary transfers received from the central government. Nonetheless, the CSS's financial position excluding transfers also improved in 1998, reflecting some administrative gains in the collection of contributions and a slowdown in the increase of benefit payments. In 1999, the overall surplus of the CSS was equivalent to about 0.9 percent of GDP, as central government transfers declined from 1998 levels, but the deficit without transfers remained at about 1.8 percent of GDP. The central government's transfers also accounted for the small surplus of decentralized agencies in 1998–99. Excluding these transfers, the operating deficit of decentralized agencies was fairly stable at about 0.8 percent of GDP during 1998–99.

23. The overall balance of public enterprises declined markedly to a deficit of 1 percent of GDP in 1998. This is explained mostly by the privatizations of electricity companies that took place that year, which effectively transferred operating surpluses from the public sector to the private sector while temporarily increasing expenses associated with the preparations for the sale. As these major privatizations were concluded, the balance of public enterprises shifted into a small surplus in 1999, with both revenues and expenditures being significantly reduced.

24. Substantial progress was achieved with public sector structural reform in 1998 and early 1999. The government privatized a sugar mill in addition to the electricity companies, and granted concessions for the operation of the National Casinos and the Trans-Isthmian Railroad. A comprehensive study of the actuarial soundness of the CSS was prepared with the assistance of the International Labor Organization which will serve as input to the ongoing debate on social security reform. The reform of public administration advanced when the government approved a new job classification scheme and implemented new career streams for some occupational groups. Expenditure control has benefited from the

[11] Certain central government contributions to the CSS had been withheld due to a disagreement over the amount due.

development and gradual implementation of an electronic and integrated system of financial administration and management (SIAFPA). Changes in the tax legislation eliminated some income tax exemptions to investments in tourism and reforestation, and reduced the amount deductible for mortgage interest payments. The pace of reform slowed considerably in 1999, with important advances being limited to the expansion of SIAFPA and the start-up of SIACAP.

Developments in 2000

25. The public sector borrowing requirement during the first nine months of 2000 was contained to US$86 million (approximately 1.1 percent of the estimated GDP), against US$302 million observed in the same period of 1999. Most of the deficit reduction can be attributed to lower capital expenditures, which declined by US$202 million in the comparison between both periods.

26. The central government deficit of US$294 million in the first nine months of 2000 was about US$100 million lower than in the same period of 1999, mainly because of lower capital expenditures. Both current expenditures and current revenues increased marginally. Nontax revenues—and notably revenues associated with the Panama Canal—continued to grow strongly. Import and sales tax collection declined, however, reflecting the slowdown in economic activity.

27. The operating balance of the CSS remained roughly unchanged from 1999, although higher transfers from the central government increased the overall surplus. Public enterprises posted a lower operating current surplus that was more than compensated by lower capital expenses, thus closing the first nine months of 2000 with a slightly lower overall deficit than that observed in the same period of 1999. The surplus of decentralized agencies was reduced to about US$15 million (about US$27 million in 1999), reflecting a reduction in current and capital revenues that offset a decline in current expenditures.

D. The Financial Sector

Overview and structure

28. The financial sector of Panama consists of the banking system, the stock exchange, insurance and reinsurance companies, finance houses, and leasing companies. The banking system is by far the most important component. The creation of the Banking Superintendency in 1998 marked the start of a major effort to reform the regulatory and supervisory framework of the banking system (see Chapter III).

29. At end-September 2000, the banking system consisted of 80 banks, including two publicly-owned banks: the National Bank of Panama (BNP), and the Savings Bank (Caja de

Ahorros).[12] Of these banks, 54 were general license banks, and 26 international license banks. The discussion of commercial banking that follows covers the operations of the general license banks, which are allowed to conduct banking with both residents and nonresidents. International license banks can conduct business only with nonresidents.

30. Finance houses specialize in small business and consumer loans at the lower end of the financial market.[13] At end-September 2000, there were 152 such institutions with assets of approximately US$900 million. Finance houses are not authorized to accept deposits. Instead, their funding comes from bank loans or through equity participation. Several of the larger finance houses are direct subsidiaries of banks or members of large commercial conglomerates. In recent years some finance houses have issued various forms of financial paper to the private sector. These unorthodox operations have raised concerns that they circumvent the law prohibiting the finance companies from funding their operations through deposit taking activities. New regulatory legislation for the finance houses is now being prepared.

Commercial banks

31. Since 1996 both bank liabilities to the private sector and net domestic credit have been growing faster than GDP, with liabilities growing faster than net credit in 1996–97. Since 1997, however, net domestic credit has expanded faster than bank liabilities to the private sector. As a result, net foreign assets of the banking system declined by US$1.5 billion between 1997 and 1999. This fall in net foreign assets reflected strong credit demands by the private sector. In 2000, net foreign assets continued to fall but at a less rapid pace, and although gross foreign assets have increased through September 2000 in part reflecting some recovery in growth in the ZLC—foreign liabilities have grown even faster.[14]

32. Credit to the domestic private sector grew by around 13 percent in 1997. Its rate of growth increased to 22 percent in 1998 before declining to 17 percent in 1999.[15] The major

[12] Apart from its role as a commercial bank, the BNP functions as the financial agent for the Central Government and the official clearing house for the banking system. It also ensures an adequate supply of U.S. currency to the banking system, and has acted at times to supply liquidity to banks that were short of it.

[13] Traditionally finance houses have catered to the market for small business and domestic consumers who do not meet the credit standards of commercial banks.

[14] Many of the foreign based companies in the ZLC borrow from Panamanian banks to finance working capital. In 1998–99 ZLC inventories were higher than desired due to weak demand conditions in several major export markets.

[15] Refers to a 12-month change in relation to liabilities to the private sector at the beginning of the period.

factors affecting this growth in credit was the robust economic activity at first associated with rapid expansion in the ZLC in 1997–98, followed by substantial increases in gross fixed capital formation in 1998–99. At the same time, the sale of properties in the reverted areas stimulated the mortgage loan market, and aggressive competition in the consumer loan market led to rapid growth in that market. As a result, gross credit for personal consumption and mortgages grew by 40 percent and 18 percent respectively, in 1998, and by 9 percent and 36 percent, respectively in 1999.[16] The decline in credit demand from the ZLC in 1999 further strengthened the willingness of banks to expand into the area of domestic installment credit.[17] The growth in credit from the commercial banks to finance houses of 90 percent in 1998 and 38 percent in 1999 implies that finance houses also contributed to the strong growth in credit to the private sector.[18]

33. Competitive pressures also affected the market for credit. Several foreign-owned general license banks attempted to exploit the credit card and lease financing markets, which they viewed as underdeveloped. Domestic banks attempted to match the competition by lowering the minimum income for obtaining a credit card, expanding credit limits and lengthening the repayment period. Banks also reduced the level of their minimum loan requirements and lengthened repayment periods on both commercial loans and mortgages. Although credit growth continued to be strong in 2000, with net credit growing by 15 percent for the 12-month period ending September 2000, the rate of increase has begun to decline.

34. This slowdown reflects several factors. The first is the drop in economic growth and employment. In response, banks have begun to shift, once again, towards the more conservative lending practices of earlier years. Minimum loan amounts have been raised and repayment periods shortened. Moreover, recent large scale repossession of cars has discouraged banks and finance houses from offering lease type arrangements. In addition, the rapid and aggressive market penetration by banks over the last two years was reducing the pool of untapped creditworthy borrowers. As a consequence, gross credit for personal

---

[16] The increase in gross credit refers to the increase in the stock of credit relative to the beginning-period stock of credit.

[17] Installment credit in Panama is highly collateralized. Individuals must meet specific income standards, each loan must have a guarantor, each borrower must assign to the lending agency an irrevocable right to be repaid through automatic payroll deductions, with this right being transferable whenever there is a change in employment. All consumer loans are insured and the legal framework to enforce compliance with respects to guarantors and to seize and sell assets, of those in default, is strong and functional.

[18] The 90 percent growth in credit refers to growth in the category identified in the accounts of the Superintendency of Banks (SB) as Financial and Insurance Enterprises. The Superindendency reports that 70–80 percent of the activity in this group is attributable to finance houses.

consumption and to finance and insurance companies which both grew by around 40 percent by September 1999, on a 12-month basis, had declined to rates of 24 percent and 3 percent respectively, by September 2000. Growth in mortgages, however, continued to be strong growing by 16 percent by end September 2000 compared to 13 percent by end-September 1999. Notwithstanding the rapid growth in credit and the less conservative lending practices of the last two years, the total of loans in arrears and loans written off, as a percent of total loans outstanding, grew from around 2 percent at end-1998 to around 3.2 percent by end-September 2000.

35. Net credit to the public sector in 1998–00 was negative. The CSS has a financial surplus, part of which is invested with the banking system, while the central government has tended to finance much of its deficit through the issue of external debt.

36. Commercial interest rates in Panama following U.S. commercial rates, began to decline in 1997 falling from an average of 10.2 percent for the year to around 9.9 percent in 1998 and have remained relatively unchanged since. At that time the difference between the U.S. prime and Panama's interest rate on commercial loans, which is normally between 200 and 160 basis points, stood at around 200 basis points. During 2000 however, the U.S. prime rate was adjusted upward several times during the year, and the differential between the two rates narrowed to around 40 basis points by September 2000. Average deposit rates have also remained relatively stable between September 1997, when the six-month deposit rate stood at 6.2 percent and September 2000 when the same rate stood at 6.4 percent.

The development banks

37. As noted above, the National Mortgage Bank (BHN) has a mandate to provide housing loans to persons of below-average income. The BHN also provides apartments for rent and sells developed sites, for the purposes of home construction, to persons in this income bracket. The BHN has always run small surpluses on its current operations but these have not been large enough to cover its sporadic, but costly, capital programs. Central government transfers has financed the shortfall. After declining to around US$3.2 million in 1997, operating profits grew to US$7.8 million and US$8.4 million in 1998 and 1999 respectively. The increased surplus in 1998 resulted in part from a strong effort to contain operating expenditure, in part through reductions in staff. In 1999 most of the improved financial performance was due to the sale of houses, and apartments. The BHN has been generally considered to be inefficiently run. In 1996 arrears on loans stood at approximately 24 percent of the loan portfolio. An effort was made in 1997 to forgive interest arrears and the stock of arrears fell to 4 percent of outstanding loans. Since then the arrears portfolio has more than doubled and by end 1999, stood at around 12 percent of total loans. As of end-2000, the government is planning to submit legislation to the assembly to close the BHN and introduce a more transparent budgetary subsidy to assist the less well off in acquiring a home.

38. The BDA is, like the BHN, generally considered to be inefficiently run. Efforts to reform the bank in the past have floundered over the sensitive political issue of how to

subsidize the agricultural sector most efficiently given strong resistance to change from sectoral interests. After averaging operating losses of 0.4 percent of GDP in 1996–97 the operating losses of the BDA fell to around less than 0.1 percent of GDP in 1998–99, reflecting measures taken to contain operating costs and improve collections. The operating losses are covered by transfers from the Special Fund for the Compensation of Interest, (FECI).[19]

39. By the mid-1990s the share of BDA's portfolio in arrears began to grow significantly, and at end 1998 amounted to about 25 percent of the loan portfolio. By September 1999 it had risen to 30 percent, in large part because the bank's new management team decided to apply commercial bank criteria in the classification of the arrears portfolio. In 1998 a new Board was assigned to the BDA ,which quickly installed new management and both have been given the task to reform and restructure the BDA. To this end, beginning in November 2000, an external auditor has begun to review the operations of the BDA. The findings of the auditor will provide the basis for designing a program to restructure the BDA and to promote the efficient functioning of the bank.

E. External Sector

40. The external current account deficit widened from about 6.8 percent of GDP in 1997 to 14.4 percent of GDP in 1999 before declining to an estimated 10.4 percent of GDP in 2000. The increase in the deficit between 1997 and 1999 is attributable to an increase in the trade deficit (including the net exports of the ZLC) of 7 percent of GDP and in net factor income payments of 3 percent which offset an increase in the surplus on services and in current transfers. The increase in the trade deficit is largely attributable to a drop in net exports of the ZLC of 3.5 percentage points of GDP, and an increase in consumer and intermediate goods imports of about 3 percent of GDP. In addition, disease and drought reduced shrimp and farm exports in 1999 by about US$65 million (0.7 percent of GDP). The increase in imports reflects both strong growth in consumer durables and increased demands for intermediate goods used in public works and in construction projects in the newly reverted areas. The increased surplus on services mainly reflected higher transportation revenues (Table 35). The increase in net factor payments is largely a consequence of the increase in the deficit in goods and nonfactor services trade.

41. In the first half of 2000, the current account deficit is estimated to have declined to US$470 million from US$630 million in the first half of 1999. The trade deficit also declined by about US$110 million in the same period. Higher exports—including a recovery in re-exports of the ZLC—offset the impact of higher oil prices on imports. The service surplus

---

[19] This Fund is financed by a tax on bank loans. Its proceeds are earmarked as follows: 50 percent of the collections go towards the subsidization of interest on agricultural loans, 25 percent is use for equity support of the BDA, and the remaining 25 percent utilized in the support of cash flow operations.

also increased by about US$35 million, mainly because of higher revenues in travel services (Table 36).

42. Net private sector capital inflows more than fully financed the current account deficits of 1998 and 1999. Foreign private direct investment financed slightly more than 100 percent of the current account deficit in 1998 and about 38 percent of the deficit in 1999. Acquisitions of privatized enterprises account for much of the FDI in 1998. A reduction in banks' net foreign assets financed about 66 percent of the current account deficit in the latter year. Net external financing of the public sector was negative in both years (Table 35). Although Panama's issued net new external debt of US$578 million in 1998–99, the impact of debt issue on net external financing was largely offset by an increase in deposits abroad due to the operations of the Trust Fund for Development (TFD). The TFD, which is custodian of the proceeds of privatizations, placed US$564 million of these proceeds abroad in cash and near-cash instruments in 1998 and 1999. The overall balance of payments incurred a deficit of US$193 million in 1998 and US$91 million in 1999. Net foreign assets of the National Bank of Panama declined by US$258 million in the two years.[20]

43. In the first six months of 2000, private sector net capital inflows more than financed the current account deficit. In particular foreign direct investment financed about two thirds of the current account deficit. Net public sector capital inflows were again negative. The overall balance of payments recorded a surplus of US$8 million and the net foreign assets of the National Bank of Panama rose by about US$6 million (Table 36).

44. External debt management in the last few years has had two principle objectives: to finance the central government's deficit and to reduce the nominal value of public external debt and the present discounted value of future debt servicing through repurchase operations. In 1998, the government issued US$300 million in ten-year U.S. dollar bonds and repurchased US$43.9 million of Brady bonds issued in 1996, with a face value of US$70 million. In 1999, the government issued US$500 million in 30-year U.S. bonds and repurchased the equivalent of US$163 million of Brady bonds with a nominal value of US$203 million. The government then used the released collateral (US$20.9 million) from the latter operations to repurchase US$20 million of Brady bonds with a face value of US$27.5 million in the first half of 2000. Finally, the authorities issued US$350 million in ten-year U.S. dollar bonds and repurchased the equivalent of US$99.5 million of Brady bonds with a face value of US$127 million in July 2000. While these transactions also led to

[20] The overall balance of payments is defined as the sum of the change in NFA of the BNP, the change in Panama's position with the IMF, and exceptional financing. Panama has no central bank as such. The National Bank of Panama is a publicly-owned commercial bank, and its net foreign assets are not reserves in the conventional sense, since they are not maintained to influence the value of Panama's currency or the operations of the foreign exchange market.

small reductions in the present value of the external debt, they increased debt service in 1999–00 by increasing amortization payments.

45. Despite these repurchase operations and because of net borrowing from the (Inter-American Development Bank (IDB), the World Bank and CAF ("*Corporación Andina de Fomento*"), the stock of the external debt increased by US$552 million from 1997 to 1999 and by a further US$175 million in the first nine months of 2000. In relation to GDP, the external debt of the overall public sector remained at about 59 percent in 1997–00, after falling from 63 percent in 1996 and 76 percent in 1995 (Table 48).

46. The nominal effective exchange rate appreciated by about 15 percent during 1999 and the first nine months of 2000, mainly as a result of the appreciation of the U.S. dollar (Panama's currency) against the other major currencies. However, the real effective exchange rate only appreciated by about 4½ percent in the same period reflecting Panama's relatively low inflation.

47. In 1995–98, trade and tariff reforms substantially liberalized Panama's trade regime. In particular, a 1997 agreement with the World Trade Organization (WTO) established a maximum import tariff of 40 percent for all but a small number of "sensitive" products[21] and eliminated nontariff barriers.[22] The agreement also provided for the elimination of both the remaining export tax on bananas by January 1, 1999 and the phase-out of tax credit certificates granted to nontraditional exports by December 31, 2002.

48. Effective January 1, 1998, the government announced further tariff reductions that lowered the maximum import tariff to 15 percent, except for automobiles (20 percent), lactose products (40 percent), and rice (50 percent). However, in October 1999 and in January 2000, the Moscoso administration reimposed the maximum limits agreed with WTO on a small number of the sensitive products.[23] Until end-2004 these tariffs are to be reduced according to the schedule agreed with the WTO implying a very gradual adjustment. At end-2004 they are to be reduced to a maximum of 15 percent.

[21] Agricultural products and foodstuffs.

[22] The agreement required that procedures for the issue and registration of sanitary permits follow WTO rules by end-1998.

[23] Maximum tariffs for 2000 in the schedule agreed with WTO for these products are the following: boneless and whole hams (83 percent), cabbage, carrots, celery, and lettuce (32.5 percent), kitchen oils made from corn or sunflower (30 percent) and from soy (20 percent), margarines (20 percent), milk (167 percent), onions (73 percent), poultry meat in pieces (300 percent), rice (103 percent), salt (87 percent), and tomato paste (83 percent).

II. The Panama Canal And The Reverted Areas—An Update

1. The Panama Canal Treaty of 1977, which became effective October 1, 1979 awarded Panama general territorial jurisdiction over the Canal and the lands adjacent to the Canal (formerly known as the Canal Zone, and now known as the reverted areas). The two governments agreed on a gradual transfer of land and facilities during the following two decades. Most of the reverted areas and their properties were in fact transferred in the late 1990s. This chapter describes the institutional arrangements that have been put in place to manage the Canal since the reversion, and summarizes some basic features of its operation and finances. It then turns to describe the management of the integration of the reverted areas into the Panamanian economy and to discuss in general terms the implications of the reversion for the economy of Panama.

A. The Canal

2. The Panama Canal Treaty dissolved the Canal Zone Government and replaced the Panama Canal Company by the binational Panama Canal Commission (PCC). The PCC was responsible for management, operation, and maintenance of the Canal until the expiration of the treaty on December 31, 1999 when it was replaced by the **Panama Canal Authority** (PCA). The PCA is an autonomous state entity run by an eleven-member board. Only a minority of board members can be nominated during the five-year term of the President of Panama and the chairperson of the board has cabinet rank in the government. The PCA, unlike the PCC seeks to make a profit on its operations.

3. The Canal, which was inaugurated on August 15, 1914 runs approximately 51 miles from the Caribbean to the Pacific Ocean. The average ship takes 8 to 10 hours to transit the Canal and is raised and then lowered 85 feet by a system of three sets of locks at either end of the Canal. The Canal operates 24 hours per day year round. Each opening and closing of a set of locks uses some 52 million gallons of water. The natural watershed on which the Canal depends faces potential environmental risks due to the changing agricultural patterns in Panama. During periods of drought, the Canal operators are required to conserve water. In extreme periods of drought, like the one in 1998 caused by El Niño, the maximum draught of ships and their transit speed must be reduced to limit ship depth. The restrictions imposed during the recent drought did not reduce noticeably the number of ships traversing the Canal. Nonetheless, the ecological health of the Canal basin has an obvious bearing on the contribution of the Canal to Panama's economy.

4. Canal tolls are based on net tonnage or displacement tonnage if net tonnage is not available. Toll revenue reached US$569 million (roughly 6 percent of GDP) in fiscal year 1999. The sustained economic growth of the United States, a continuing recovery of Asian economies, and continued low commodity prices all increased demand for cargo transit in

1999.[1] The Canal by its nature is not a growth industry—there are physical limits to the number and the size of the ships that can traverse it in a year. At the same time, it is not prone to large swings in activity or revenue.

5. The investment program of the PCA for 1995–02 amounts to approximately US$870 million. Much of the investment budget will be devoted to widening the Gaillard Cut, a section of the Canal whose narrowness prevents two-way traffic. The Canal is currently able to accommodate 35 to 37 vessels a day and has been operating at capacity during the past three years. The widening of the Gaillard Cut, to be completed by end-2002 will increase the average number of daily transits to about 42 vessels per day, a capacity increase of about 15–20 percent. Investments will also be made in the replacement and modernization of Canal equipment (tugboats, towing locomotives, locks machinery, and control systems).

6. The PCA is analyzing the feasibility of building a new set of locks parallel to the existing set to accommodate Post-Panamax vessels. In contrast to the less ambitious project of widening the existing locks, parallel locks would allow the Canal to remain in operation during construction. They would also require less water, since the wider locks would only be used for Post-Panamax vessels. The project is provisionally estimated to take 12 years and to cost US$7.5 billion, or about 75 percent of GDP in 2000. The PCA has commissioned a study of its potential profitability. A project of this size would have significant ramifications for both the finances of the PCA and the general economy.

7. In recent years, the relative importance of the Canal in the economy as a whole has fallen due to the emergence of telecommunications and other transportation and transshipment activities. From 1991–99, the value added generated by the Canal's operation averaged 6.4 percent of GDP. During the period 1980–90, the activities of the Canal accounted for a slightly higher annual average of 7.0 percent of GDP. For the first time since 1987, activities in transportation and communication have accounted for a higher percentage of GDP than the activities directly related to the Canal's operation. In 1998–99, transportation and communication accounted for 7.3 percent of GDP while the operations of the PCC accounted for 6.4 percent. This trend is expected to continue given the strong rate of growth in transportation and communication, which has averaged 16.5 percent annually during 1997–99, as Panama fully develops the interoceanic region.

---

[1] The most recent toll increase of 7.5 percent became effective on January 1, 1998. In 1999, the average net tonnage per oceangoing commercial vessel increased 1.6 percent to 17 percent, 419 tons. There were 13,136 oceangoing transits in fiscal year 1999, 85 percent of which were commercially related—an increase of 0.9 percent over fiscal year 1998.

B. Development Strategy and Economic Impact of the Reverted Areas

8. The process of transferring the former Canal Zone and its infrastructure began in 1979, but intensified in 1997–99. The interoceanic region that reverted to Panama at the end of 1999 stretches from the Caribbean to the Pacific Ocean on both sides of the Panama Canal. Five army installations, two air force bases, and one naval station were located in the reverted areas. The reverted areas contain many houses, residential areas, schools, hospitals, industrial areas, storage facilities, ports, marinas, golf courses, theaters, bowling alleys, and other recreational facilities. In all, 95,000 hectares and 7,000 buildings and installations were transferred. In 1993, the authorities decided to privatize all reverting properties by means of outright sales, or concessions and rentals of the properties.

9. The reversion of the interoceanic region can be expected to increase economic growth. Economic theory suggests that economic growth depends on increases in one or more of the factors of production; land, capital, labor, or technology. The reversion should increase the rate of growth of Panama's economy temporarily if not permanently, because it entails a substantial transfer of land and physical capital.[2] It creates opportunities for investments that can profitably exploit Panama's comparative advantage in services like transshipment, telecommunications, and other associated Canal activities with high marginal productivities.[3] These opportunities did not exist previously because the reverted land could not be devoted to commercial or industrial activities—for example, the expansion of ports and the ZLC into adjacent land previously part of the U.S. military bases. In addition, the residential housing in the reverted areas requires little additional expenditure to make it useable.

10. The **Interoceanic Region Authority** (ARI) is an autonomous government agency created in February 1993 to integrate the reverted areas into the Panamanian economy. ARI is responsible for administering the privatization and use of the reverted areas, and promotes

---

[2] Neoclassical growth theory (with exogenously determined technical progress) implies that a once-off increase in the capital stock will not increase the steady-state rate of growth. However, it will increase the rate of growth temporarily, and conceivably for some time, during the transition to the higher steady state. The reverted areas (the former Canal Zone) were not part of Panamanian territory, and economic activity there was not included in GDP.

[3] A substantial share of the value added generated by the Canal was already accruing to residents in the form of wages and salaries and payments to the government. Consequently, the transfer of ownership of the Canal itself—apart from the reverted areas—does not greatly increase the nation's capital stock. Assuming unchanged revenues in real terms and a discount rate of 7 percent, the staff estimate that the present value of the additional income stream that accrues to residents of Panama (the government in this case) would be approximately US$300 million.

investment in ports, industry, commerce, and tourism. The National Maritime Authority (AMN) coordinates the port projects. ARI (in cooperation with AMN) seeks projects that make a contribution to the Panamanian economy by generating local employment, stimulating exports, and using local materials and inputs when possible. It also requires that investors comply with requirements for the protection of the Panama Canal watershed.

11. ARI receives most of its revenue from the sale of land, housing, and office buildings, but also receives revenue from leasing operations and concessions. ARI's proceeds during 1999 and 2000 from the sale of land, housing, and offices amounted to approximately US$120 million.

The development strategy

12. ARI is promoting investment projects for the reverted areas in maritime facilities and services, other transportation, manufacturing and export industries, education, and tourism. ARI estimates that to date, approximately US$1.8 billion has been invested or committed through 2005 in the interoceanic region. The investment program in maritime facilities and other transportation is particularly significant.

Maritime facilities and services

13. The maritime sector has already developed considerably, and Panama's two major ports have been privatized and modernized. The large number of ships passing through the Canal and the 22 to 24 hours they spend waiting to enter the Canal creates a natural demand for maritime services. In consequence, new enterprises are being established in ship handling, salvage operations, and maritime insurance. Maritime services to be developed further include ship registration, legal and arbitration services, financial and banking services and naval mortgages, and communications and other business-related infrastructure. Specific ship services offered will include hull and tank cleaning, ship and container repairs, crew services, insurance, rescue and towage, brokerage of cargo space, piloting in port, and medical services.

14. The Cristobal and Balboa ports on the Caribbean and Pacific ends of the Canal were privatized in 1997–98, and in 1999–00 an estimated US$143.6 million was invested in their development. The Manzanillo International Terminal (MIT), located on the Caribbean end of the Canal, transports 70,000 TEUs (20 foot container units) per month. Its operative standard is 30 containers per hour, matching the port movement in Miami. MIT has invested US$12.5 million to add an additional 20 hectares of operating space to the 37 currently in usage. Adjacent to the MIT, the recently completed Colón Container Terminal, operated by Evergreen, has an operative standard of 34 containers per hour and storage capabilities for 400,000 containers. On the Pacific end of the Canal, the Panama Ports Company, which is a subsidiary of Hutchinson-Whampoa, plans to invest US$209.2 million in 1999–01 (US$73.2 million was invested in 1999–00) to develop the port at Balboa. The Balboa terminal is divided into three phases, with Phase I having been recently completed. Phases I and II will have an estimated annual capacity of 600,000 containers and Phase III will add

capacity for an additional 300,000 containers. The completion of the Balboa port will require deepening the entrance in order to allow large Post-Panamax ships to enter and unload.[4]

Other transportation investment

15. The **Panama Canal Railway Company**, a subsidiary of Kansas City Southern Railway, is investing US$75 million to develop a railway that will run 47 miles and connect the Colón Free Zone and the ports on the Caribbean to the ports on the Pacific. The railway is expected to begin operations in the first half of 2001. Initially, it will handle only containers. It is expected to add passenger transportation in the medium-term.

16. The railway is part of a proposed multimodal transportation system. The strategy behind the system is to offer a diverse set of transportation modes (maritime, air, rail, and motor vehicle) that improve transportation across the Isthmus and in Panama as a whole. The completion of the multimodal transportation system will require additional investment in the modernization of airports and development of the trucking terminal adjacent to the ZLC. The former military bases of Albrook and Howard contain airport facilities. The Administration of the ZLC has designated 23 hectares of the newly added land at the head of the recently expanded highway from Colón to Panama City for the purpose of developing a modern truck transportation terminal.

17. The ZLC, which is currently situated on 400 hectares of land at the entrance to the Canal on the Caribbean, is adding an additional 885 hectares. This expansion will give it ample room to increase the number of its resident companies, which have already increased from 1,469 in 1990 to 1,944 as of September 2000. The ZLC's expansion will also allow for the expansion of the multimodal transportation system.

Projects in other areas

18. An export processing zone has been established in the former Fort Davis, focusing on manufacturing and assembly. In addition, tertiary educational establishments are being established in the area of the former Fort Clayton. The tourism sector is also a target for development and several international investors have shown interest in eco-tourist resorts and increased cruise ship transit. The country has about 2,000 miles of coastline on two oceans. Major projects are planned or are in partial execution near Fort Amador at the Pacific mouth of the Canal, including the Amador causeway, cruise ship facilities, hotels, and related services.

19. ARI's sale, concessions, or rental of property in the reverted areas has contributed to the development in housing, industry, and tourism. In 1999 and 2000, housing sales started

---

[4] Ships built with the maximum allowable width to pass through the current system of locks on the Canal are defined as "Panamax." Ships that are too wide to pass through the current system of locks are defined as "Post-Panamax."

several months behind schedule, but have been strong, especially in the former base of Clayton which has become a focus of Panama City expansion. Clayton is made up of over 2,057 acres and has 1,392 housing units and 39,000 square meters of warehouse space.

III. Banking Sector Developments[1]

A. Introduction and Background on Recent Events

1. Panama has a well-developed banking system, comprised of established domestic and foreign banks run by experienced management teams. The use of the U.S. dollar as the official currency has limited transfer risk and kept interest rates stable and relatively low. Market discipline continues to be an important force for transparency and high operating standards, as there is no lender of last resort or deposit insurance. The supervisory and regulatory environment has evolved rapidly following the passage of the 1998 banking law and creation of the Superintendency of Banks (SB). Bank indicators, especially among Panama headquartered banks, continue to show fundamental soundness in capital adequacy and asset quality, as well as ample liquidity and good profitability.

2. The following four sections cover the structure of the banking system and current banking conditions (Section B), measures introduced to strengthen the supervisory and regulatory infrastructure (Section C), private banking and anti-money laundering measures (Section D), and key articles and regulations (Section E). Section F presents the chapter's conclusion.

B. Structure of the Banking System and Current Banking Conditions

Structure

3. As of September 30, 2000, Panama's banking system comprised 80 general and international license banks with assets of US$38 billion. (Table 1 provides market share information on Panama's banking system by assets, loans and deposits.) The banking system is largely privately owned, apart from the Banco Nacional de Panama and the Caja de Ahorros, which are government-owned.

4. The banking system plays a major role as financial intermediary for the domestic economy. Only general license banks and the two government-owned banks are authorized to lend to and take deposits from both residents and nonresidents. General license banks may be foreign or locally owned. The major providers of consumer, mortgage and commercial credit to the local market are 10 large general license banks.[2] Most of them are headquartered in Panama, but they also include the foreign-owned HSBC, Citibank and Banco Bilbao Viscaya

[1] Prepared by Michael K. Moore.

[2] The ten large banks active in domestic retail banking are Banco Nacional de Panama, Banco General, Banco del Istmo, Primer Banco, Banco Continental, Banco Bilbao Viscaya Argentaria, Citibank, Caja de Ahorros, HSBC, and Global Bank. Excluded are Banco Latinoamericano de Exportaciones, Dredner, Bank of Tokyo Mitsubishi and Sudameris, which though they are large have limited retail banking activities.

Argentaria. These 10 banks have between 7 and 53 branches and account for about 50 percent of general license bank assets. The two large government-owned banks have traditionally provided short and long term financing for the consumer market and have the most extensive branch networks.[3]

Table 1. Panama: Banking System

(In billions of dollars as of September 30, 2000)

Type of Depository Financial Institution (DFI)	Number of DFIs	Percent of total	Assets	Percent of total	Loans	Percent of total	Deposits	Percent of total
General license banks	54	61.4	31.0	81.8	18.8	86.0	21.4	78.4
- Panama headquartered banks	26	29.5	20.9	55.0	12.9	58.7	12.6	46.1
- Branches of foreign banks	18	20.5	7.3	19.3	4.0	18.4	6.5	24.0
- Subsidiaries of foreign banks	10	11.4	2.9	7.5	1.9	8.8	2.3	8.3
International license banks	26	29.5	6.9	18.2	3.1	14.0	5.9	21.6
Representative offices	8	9.1	N/A		N/A		N/A	
Total Banking System	88	100.0	37.9	100.0	21.9	100.0	27.3	100.0

Source: Superintendency of Banks.

5. Of the 54 general license banks, 26 are headquartered in Panama, and have total assets of US$21 billion (55 percent of the banking system). Families or local economic groups control most of the Panama headquartered banks. There are 28 foreign banks, with assets of US$10 billion that hold a general license and operate as either separately capitalized subsidiaries or as branches.

6. Banks with international licenses can participate in the interbank market, but are restricted in their ability to lend or take deposits from residents. Generally, their activities are limited to providing trade finance or private banking to nonresidents and other services as directed by their head office. The terms of the international license are similar to that provided by most offshore financial centers, with the notable difference that all licensees must have a physical presence with local staff. Consequently, managed banks that operate under the administration of another bank or nonbank institution are not permitted.

[3] The two government-owned banks were created through specific legislation, but are subject to the same regulations and restrictions as general license banks.

7. Besides general and international license banks, there are eight representative offices of foreign banks, which cannot take deposits. Their activities are restricted to performing liaison functions and marketing.

8. The foreign bank presence is substantial. (See Table 2 for a breakdown of assets, loans and deposits by geographic region, as well as the ten largest banks from each region.) Banks from Europe and North America play a major role with Panama assets of US$11.4 billion and represent (30.1 percent of the system total), which compares to US$3.9 billion and 10.3 percent of the system total for banks from Latin America and the Caribbean, which is the next largest region. Banks from Asia and the Middle East hold the smallest share at US$1.7 billion or 4.4 percent of system assets.

Performance

9. Banking conditions are generally sound. Nonperforming loans (NPLs) increased to 2.9 percent of total loans at end-September 2000 from 1.8 percent at end-1998 and 2.4 percent at end-1999, but remain moderately low (Table 3). The provision level for loan losses has stayed relatively constant since 1998, so that provisioning, which was 76 percent of NPLs at end-1998, declined to 62 percent at end-September 2000. At end-September 2000 the local banks reported NPLs equal to 2.5 percent of loans and provisioning of 81 percent. For the system as a whole, provisioning is expected to increase, partly due to growth in NPLs, but also because of a change in the SB's loan classification and provisioning requirements, which comes into effect in stages starting in January 2001. The regulatory change will reduce income because of higher provision expense, but it is not expected to result in losses.

10. The banking system reported net income of US$414 million through end-September 2000 or 1.5 percent annualized return on assets, which compares to 1.4 percent earned for all of 1999 (Table 4). Revenue performance for Panama-headquartered banks was better than for the overall system, with an annualized return on assets of 1.9 percent through end-September 2000, up from 1.7 percent for 1999. Through end-September 2000, eight banks reported net losses; all but one was foreign-owned.[4]

[4] The Panama headquartered bank reporting a loss began operations in 1998; losses are not uncommon for a newly formed bank. The bank remains very small and its capital remains ample.

Table 2. Panama: Bank Presence by Region

(In billions of dollars as of September 30, 2000)

Regional aggregates

Geographic Region 1/	Number of DFIs	Percent of total	Assets	Percent of total	Loans	Percent of total	Deposits	Percent of total
Panama headquartered banks	28	35.0	20.9	55.1	12.9	58.9	12.6	46.2
Europe and North America	20	25.0	11.4	30.1	5.9	27.1	10.4	38.2
Latin America and Caribbean	26	32.5	3.9	10.3	1.8	8.3	2.7	9.8
Asia and Middle East	6	7.5	1.7	4.4	1.3	5.7	1.6	5.8
Total banking system	80	100.0	37.9	100.0	21.9	100.0	27.3	100.0

Ten largest banks from each region

Panama headquartered banks	Assets	Europe and North America	Assets
Banco Latinoamericano de Exportaciones	5.2	Dresdner Bank (Germany)	2.2
Banco Nacional de Panamá	3.4	HSBC (UK) 2/	1.0
Banco General, S.A.	2.3	ABN Amro Bank (Netherlands)	0.9
Banco del Istmo, S.A.	1.9	Banco Bilbao Viscaya Argent (Spain)	0.9
Primer Banco de Ahorros, S.A.	1.4	Banque Nationale de Paris (France)	0.8
Banco Continental de Panamá, S.A.	1.3	Citibank, (USA)	0.8
Caja de Ahorros	0.8	Banque Sudameris (Italy)	0.7
Global Bank Corporation	0.5	Société Generale (France)	0.7
Banco Internacional de Panamá	0.5	HSBC, plc (UK)	0.5
Multicredit Bank, Inc.	0.5	Banco Santander, S.A. (Spain)	0.4
Ten largest banks from region	17.7	Ten largest banks from region	8.9
18 other banks	3.2	10 other banks	2.6
Total 28 banks for region	20.9	Total 20 banks for region	11.4

Latin America and Caribbean	Assets	Asia and Middle East	Assets
Banco Internacional (Costa Rica)	0.6	Bank of Tokyo Mitsubishi (Japan)	0.8
Bancolombia (Colombia)	0.4	Dai-Ichi Kangyo Bank (Japan)	0.3
Banco de la Provincia (Argentina)	0.4	International Commercial Bank (Taiwan Province of China)	0.2
Banco Do Brasil, S.A. (Brazil)	0.4		
Popular Bank (Domincan Republic)	0.3	Korea Exchange Bank (Korea)	0.2
Bancafé (Colombia)	0.2	Bank Leumi-Le Israel, B.M. (Israel)	0.1
Banco Santa Cruz (Bolivia)	0.2	Bank of China (China)	0.1
Banco de Occidente (Colombia)	0.2	-	-
Bancrédito (Domincan Republic)	0.2	-	-
Banco Unión (Venezuela)	0.2	-	-
Ten largest banks from region	3.0	Six banks from region	1.7
16 other banks	1.0	-	-
Total 26 banks for region	3.9	Total 6 banks for region	1.7

Source: Superintendency of Banks.

1/ Includes both general and international license banks (depository financial institutions - DFIs).

2/ Formerly Chase Manhattan Bank (USA).

Table 3. Panama: Trend in Nonperforming Loans

Type of Depository Financial Institution (DFI)	Dec. 1998	Dec. 1999	Jun. 1999	Sep. 2000
	(In millions of dollars)			
General license banks	275.5	461.7	551.0	534.9
- Panama headquartered banks	163.2	216.2	298.7	316.6
- Branches of foreign banks	75.2	178.8	139.0	100.1
- Subsidiaries of foreign banks	37.2	66.8	113.2	118.2
International license banks	132.3	62.4	75.1	93.7
Total Banking System	407.8	524.1	626.1	628.7
	(In percent of total loans)			
General license banks	1.5	2.5	3.0	2.8
- Panama headquartered banks	1.5	1.8	2.5	2.5
- Branches of foreign banks	1.5	3.8	3.4	2.5
- Subsidiaries of foreign banks	2.3	4.0	5.8	6.1
International license banks	2.7	1.7	2.4	3.0
Total Banking System	1.8	2.4	2.9	2.9

Source: Superintendency of Banks.

11. At end-September 2000, the equity to asset ratio for the system was 9.1 percent, up from 8.6 percent at end 1999. Panama headquartered banks reported an equity to asset ratio of 11.8 percent. The higher figure is partly explained by the fact that the foreign banks mostly operate as branches. A branch of a foreign bank is not required to hold as much capital in Panama as a stand-alone bank or subsidiary because it may rely on the capital position of the foreign head office. The SB requires that banks maintain capital funds of at least 8 percent of risk-weighted assets, including off-balance sheet contingencies.

12. The banking system enjoys stable liquidity provided primarily through deposit funding. Liquid assets are defined to comprise cash, government securities, approved private sector securities, and interbank deposits. (See Section E for a fuller description of liquid assets.) The law requires banks to hold a high level of liquid assets. The minimum ratio of liquid assets to deposits is 30 percent, which must be maintained at all times. Liquidity in the banking system remains stable, as loans represent a conservative 58 percent of assets and 80 percent of deposits at end-September 2000. The stable liquidity and interest rate environment has allowed many banks to offer long-term, variable-rate mortgages renewable for up to 25 years. Though the deposit base has proved very stable over time, its comparatively short average

maturity has encouraged banks to match the longer-term lending with more diverse funding provided by long-term, locally raised bonds and term loans from international banks—including from the International Finance Corporation.

Table 4. Panama: Capital Adequacy and Income Indicators

(In percent)

	Equity to Assets		Return on average assets	
Type of Depository Financial Institution (DFI)	Dec. 1999	Sep. 2000	Dec. 1999	Sep. 2000 1/
General license banks	9.6	10.0	1.5	1.5
- Panama headquartered banks	11.3	11.8	1.7	1.9
- Branches of foreign banks	4.1	3.7	1.1	0.5
- Subsidiaries of foreign banks	12.1	13.0	1.0	1.9
International license banks	4.8	5.0	1.1	1.2
Total Banking System	8.6	9.1	1.4	1.5

Source: Superintendency of Banks.

1/ Return on assets annualized for September 2000.

C. Developments in Supervision and Regulation

History and structure of the Superintendency of Banks

13. The origins of the passage of the 1998 banking law and the creation of the Superintendency of Banks (SB) lies in the recognition by both bankers and the authorities that the weak supervisory framework then in place was impeding the continued development of the banking system and limiting the opportunities abroad for local banks. Rating agencies and foreign governments were subjecting Panama-headquartered banks to increased scrutiny and introducing obstacles to their establishing a presence in certain foreign jurisdictions. Similarly, internationally active banks faced difficulties in justifying a presence in Panama to both their home country supervisors and their head office.

14. The 1998 banking law established the SB as an autonomous agency. The SB replaced the National Banking Commission, which was relatively weak. The powers of the Superintendency are divided between the Board of Directors and the Superintendent. The board has five members who are appointed by the President of Panama for a maximum of two eight-year terms. They may not serve as officers or directors of any bank, or hold more than 5 percent of the stock of any bank. The Board of Directors is responsible for approving regulations in connection with the interpretation and implementation of banking laws, and

setting capital adequacy standards. The initial group of board members was appointed with staggered terms ranging from five to eight years so as to not coincide with changes in the executive branch of government.

15. The Superintendent is a salaried, full-time public official who is appointed for a five-year term renewable one time. The term of the Superintendent does not coincide with that of the executive branch. The Superintendent's powers include authority: (i) to approve licensing, mergers and consolidations; (ii) to intervene, reorganize and order the compulsory liquidation of banks; (iii) to supervise economic groups; (iv) to order corrective or preventive measures in the operations of banks; (v) to establish cooperation with foreign supervisory bodies; and (vi) to set salaries, hire, and fire employees of the SB and oversee the implementation of the annual budget. Neither the directors nor the Superintendent may be removed from office except for specific cause as judged by the Supreme Court of Justice.[5]

Onsite inspections and offsite monitoring

16. The SB has a professional staff of about 100 for onsite and offsite supervision. In addition, there are 20 staff devoted to the legal and administrative duties for regulations and reviewing applications and another 10 for information systems. In carrying out its onsite inspections, the SB applies the so-called CAMEL criteria, looking at Capital adequacy, Asset quality, Management, Earnings and Liquidity. In its review of management oversight, the SB places considerable emphasis on the internal control system, including verification of compliance with laws, regulations and banks' own policies. Onsite inspections are not announced in advance. The onsite inspection program is complemented by offsite surveillance by a bank analysis group that looks at monthly prudential indicators and other managerial reports, placing particular emphasis on related party transactions.

17. Through October 2000, the SB has completed consolidated inspections of 30 general and international license banks and is committed to inspect the remaining banks by end-2001, including the government-owned *Banco Nacional de Panamá* and *Caja de Ahorros*. General license and international license banks are subject to the same onsite inspection requirements.

18. To improve both offsite monitoring and system transparency, the SB receives monthly reports from individual banks and publishes an extract of the balance sheet and income information for each quarter on its website. The web-based information is presented both for individual banks and by type of institution, economic sector and region. In addition, the SB makes available all of its regulations and circulars on the website (several of these are in

---

[5] The Supreme Court of Justice may order the dismissal of a director or the Superintendent if the person: (i) is permanently incapacitated; (ii) declares bankruptcy; (iii) no longer meets the requirements for appointment; (iv) demonstrates dishonesty in his or her functions; or (v) fails to comply with the obligations and prohibitions imposed under the banking law.

English). The SB is working to enhance further its information system, for example by requiring that banks use the internet for transmitting information to the SB directly. The new system should help to address two weaknesses related to collection of information on risk-based capital requirements and consolidated financial statements for individual banks and their subsidiaries (see Section E). The IDB is financing this effort to improve the overall quality of information on bank operations.

New regulations

19. In its first 18 months of operation, the SB issued the new regulations dealing with the following activities or areas: (i) accounting and auditing standards, (ii) a Basel-like capital adequacy requirement, (iii) exposure limits on credit to related parties and single obligors (iv) and risk management requirements for liquidity, interest rate and country risk. Most recently, the SB has issued additional regulations for loan classification and provisioning that come into force beginning in 2001, and a know-your-customer regulation that now is in effect. The latter implements a regulation for the banking sector following the passage of anti-money laundering legislation in October 2000 (see below). These regulations conform to standards of accepted international practice. A summary of individual regulations is provided in Section E.

The view of the Financial Stability Forum

20. In May 2000, the Financial Stability Forum (FSF) released its groupings of offshore financial centers, which was based on the views of onshore supervisors in 27 countries. The FSF placed Panama along with 26 others in Group III, the lowest ranking group.[6] Countries in Group III are characterized by the FSF as "generally seen as having a low quality of supervision, and/or being noncooperative with onshore supervisors, and with little or no attempt being made to adhere to international standards."

21. The SB regrets the FSF's characterization, and believes that the FSF has not considered the important advances in Panama's system of regulation and supervision. To counteract the FSF's rating, and to take stock of its progress towards meeting international standards for prudential supervision, the SB completed in October 2000 a self-assessment assisted by a Fund staff member of its compliance with the Basel Core Principles for Effective Banking Supervision (BCP).[7] In April 2001, at the authorities' request, Fund will conduct an

---

[6] The other two groupings are: Group I—jurisdictions generally viewed as cooperative, with a high quality of supervision, which largely adhere to international standards and Group II—would be jurisdictions generally seen as having procedures for supervision and cooperation in place, but where actual performance falls below international standards, and there is substantial room for improvement.

[7] The self-assessment of BCP compliance was assisted by the writer.

independent, BCP assessment. Under the Fund's rules, the authorities may choose to publish the results of that assessment.

22. As already noted the SB has achieved important progress in putting in place a proper system of supervision and regulation, conforming to internationally accepted standards. The independent assessment beginning in April will examine the concerns raised by the FSF.

D. Private Banking and Anti-Money Laundering Measures

23. Panama is a significant regional center for private banking.[8] Both local and foreign-owned banks offer private banking services primarily to Latin American clients, and compete effectively with onshore centers in North America and Europe. There is a tradition of strong bank secrecy provisions that oblige bankers and bank supervisors to keep bank client information strictly confidential. Improper disclosure of information by bankers or supervisors is punishable by fine or imprisonment.

24. The authorities and the banking industry are very aware of the legal, operational, and reputational risks associated with private banking. Cabinet Decree Law number 41, issued in 1990, requires banks and nonbanks to have systems in place to prevent the laundering of proceeds from drug trafficking. In June 2000 the Financial Action Task Force strongly criticized the existing anti-money laundering regime, and listed Panama as "noncooperative" in the fight to combat money laundering.[9] The FATF cited four principal shortcomings: (i) failure to criminalize money laundering for crimes other than drug trafficking; (ii) inefficient reporting of suspicious transaction reports to competent authorities; (iii) overly restrictive rules for international information exchange; and (iv) civil law provisions that impeded the identification of the true beneficial owners of trusts.

25. To address the FATF's criticisms, the authorities, with the strong support of the banking industry, enacted laws 41 and 42 in October 2000. The new laws criminalized the laundering of proceeds from fraud, extortion, embezzlement, corruption of public officials, kidnapping, terrorism and theft or trafficking in vehicles or weapons. In addition, they streamlined the reporting of suspicious transactions to the competent authorities and facilitated the exchange of information with other governments.[10] Lastly, the laws expanded the SB's ability to examine anti-money laundering compliance by trust companies.

---

[8] Private banking is the providing of financial and related services to wealthy individuals (including their closely held companies).

[9] The Financial Action Task Force is made up of 29 member countries and territories, primarily composed of OECD members; the Secretariat is based at the OECD.

[10] Executive Decree No. 163 authorizes the government to exchange information regarding suspicious activity with counterparts in foreign jurisdictions so long as there is a

(continued...)

26. The SB under Decree Law 41 of 1990 and under the recent legislation has the responsibility to enforce compliance with anti-money laundering laws and regulations in the banking sector. The new legislation gives the SB broad authority to use the means necessary to ensure that banks comply with the law, including the authority to issue regulations intended to deter money laundering.[11]

27. The SB's anti-money laundering program has two primary focuses: (i) know your customer (KYC) compliance and (ii) suspicious activity reporting. Compliance with laws, regulations and banks' own policies is verified through onsite inspections. KYC requirements apply to individuals and corporations, including bearer share companies. Other areas reviewed by the SB are records retention practices,[12] the adequacy of anti-money laundering training and banks' own internal anti-money laundering policy. The inspection work papers evidenced that the SB's inspectors are reviewing compliance with KYC and reporting requirements. Instances of noncompliance with Panama's anti-money laundering laws are brought to bank management for prompt correction.

28. Panama is a member of the Caribbean Financial Action Task Force (CFATF) and the Egmont Group. A team from CFATF members has conducted a mutual evaluation of Panama's compliance with the FATF and CFATF anti-money laundering recommendations.[13] The Egmont Group is an association of "financial intelligence units" (FIU). An FIU is responsible for receiving, analyzing and disseminating financial information concerning suspicious transaction reports.

E. New Regulations

Capital requirements for general and international license banks

29. The SB has imposed a risk-based capital framework that is modeled after the original Basle capital standard. The framework is applicable to both general and international license banks. Capital is defined as primary capital plus secondary capital, with primary capital equal to paid-in-common and perpetual preferred shares, declared reserves and retained earnings.

Memorandum of Understanding in place. The authorities are actively seeking an MOU with the United States.

[11] The SB issued Agreement 9–2000 as an implementing regulation for the new law.

[12] By law, banks are required to maintain customer documentation for a minimum of five years. This requirement applies to closed as well as active accounts.

[13] The CFATF is a regional anti-money laundering group modeled after the FATF. Their activities include conducting mutual evaluations of members, training activities and technical assistance programs.

Secondary capital is comprised of qualifying subordinated debentures, other hybrid capital instruments, and general reserves for loan losses. Together, primary and secondary capital must be at least 8 percent of risk-weighted assets, and secondary capital cannot exceed primary capital. Assets are assigned different risk weights that range from a zero weight to 100 percent weight (e.g., cash has a zero weight and loans have a 100 percent weight). Off-balance sheet items are included as assets according to their cash equivalency. The SB does not impose a capital charge for market risk.

30. In addition to the adoption of the risk-based capital requirement, there is a minimum capital level requirement. General license banks are to maintain a minimum capital level of US$10 million and international license banks are to maintain a minimum level of US$3 million. International license banks must deposit US$250,000 in the BNP or invest that amount in bonds held in the custody of the BNP. Those banks not meeting the minimum requirement will have five years from the date of the enactment of the law to reach the required capital level. Those banks not meeting the minimum capital requirement during the five year transition period will not be allowed to pay dividends and may be subject to other sanctions. If after the five years the capital of a bank fails to reach or falls below the minimum level, the bank will not be allowed to continue operations. Branches of foreign banks may have this amount assigned on the books of the head office.

Accounting standards, regulatory reports and transparency

31. The SB requires that banks and economic groups file financial information using either International Accounting Standards (IAS) as issued by the International Accounting Standards Committee or U.S. General Accepted Accounting Principles (US GAAP) as issued by the Financial Accounting Standards Board. The requirement applies to both the general and international license banks. The change affects the reporting of financial statements and other information filed after the start of calendar year1999. Because of the relative conservatism of existing accounting practices, meeting the higher standard did not impose a serious difficulty for the banks. Many of Panama's larger domestic-owned financial institutions were already reporting their financial results using US GAAP. Similarly, adoption of the international standard had little effect on the many foreign banks operating in Panama. They were accustomed to the higher standard because it was already in place in their home countries.

32. The SB requires that banks file various types of condition reports on a weekly, monthly, quarterly and annual basis. Failure to comply with reporting requirements can result in a fine imposed by the SB. Efforts are underway by the SB to provide more financial and structural information on individual banks via its website that already includes monthly, unconsolidated bank-by-bank and system financial information. Once a year, the banks are to provide the financial statements on an audited basis. The five major international accounting firms carry out most accounting and external auditing activity.

33. As already mentioned, the SB is revising its program for collecting prudential information from banks with financial support from the IDB. As the design evolves, it will be

important that the SB ensures collection of key prudential indicators for offsite monitoring. It is noted that the SB collects risk-based capital information only on an annual basis for which at least a quarterly monitoring capability is warranted. Also, the SB will need to ensure that it collects the routine financial reporting on a consolidated basis at the bank level, consolidating the results of both the bank and its subsidiaries.[14] The consolidated reporting at the bank level would be in addition to the consolidated reporting that would occur at the corporate level as required by the International Accounting Standards and U.S. GAAP. The purpose of consolidated reporting at the bank level is to have a view of all of the risks faced by the bank, which may be hidden, without the consolidation of the accounts of the subsidiaries. Consolidated reporting at the bank level will be important to ensuring compliance with limits for loans to related parties and loans to a single borrower.

Consolidated supervision (including cross-border supervision)

34. The SB is empowered to supervise economic groups and their bank and nonbank affiliates on a consolidated basis. Its powers include the right to require audited financial statements and other reporting information as appropriate from the bank and nonbank affiliates of economic groups.[15] Still to be inspected are several of the more complex general license banks, which will pose important challenges given the range of financial and nonfinancial activities in which they are involved. Although the development of the system for consolidated supervision is largely complete, some policy work is warranted with regard to the types of specialized financial and nonfinancial activities that should be permitted within a bank or a bank subsidiary. The policy should consider the appropriateness of the activity for a bank or bank subsidiary, its relative size, the demand it makes on management and the degree to which its accounts obscure the transparency of the bank's operations.

35. As an important regional banking center, the SB requires that all offices of foreign banks be subject to consolidated supervision by their home country supervisor. In addition, several Panamanian banks have subsidiaries in neighboring jurisdictions, primarily in Central America and the Caribbean. To facilitate the cross-border supervision, the SB has pursued memorandums of understanding (MOU) with 16 foreign jurisdictions in the Western Hemisphere. Of these, four have been agreed and signed, one is agreed, but awaiting final signature, two have been deferred, and nine others are under active negotiation.

---

[14] Consolidated financial statements are a combination line-by-line of all like items (assets, liabilities, equity, income, expenses and off-balance sheet items). In conjunction with the combination of like items, intragroup balances and transactions are eliminated.

[15] The applicable regulation is Agreement 3–99, Consolidated Supervision of the Economic Banking Group.

36. The MOUs are intended for the sharing of information for supervisory purposes only, which contrasts with MOUs intended to facilitate information flows for law enforcement or crime prosecution purposes. Though the SB prefers an MOU, it is not a pre-condition to conducting an onsite inspection by a foreign supervisor, which can be arranged on a case-by-case basis. The arrangement will set out guidance on use of information and will stipulate that information obtained be for supervisory purposes only. There is a precedent for allowing an onsite inspection by a foreign supervisor without an MOU being in place. Despite the large number of foreign banks operating in Panama, especially from Europe and North America, the SB reports that it has not received any requests from foreign supervisors to conduct on-site inspections.

Single borrower limit and loans to related parties

37. The 1998 banking law (Article 63) establishes a 25 percent limit relative to bank capital on the level of lending and other exposure that a bank may have to a single borrower. The limit applies only to general license banks. A single borrower is a natural or legal person or an economic group. The definition of an economic group is a group of natural or legal persons whose interests are so interrelated that in the opinion of the SB they are to be treated as a single person. Agreements 1, 7, and 9 for 1999 provide detailed requirements and restrictions on lending or the purchase of securities issued by a single obligor or a single economic group.

38. The 1998 banking law (Article 64) and regulations issued by the SB have established restrictions on credit exposures to related parties and related economic groups (both through loans and the purchase of securities).[16] Credit exposure to any one related party is limited to 10 percent of bank capital, if the exposure is secured by real estate and 5 percent of bank capital if unsecured. In addition, there is a global cumulative limit equal to 75 percent of the bank capital that declines to 25 percent by 2005, with an intermediate limit of 50 percent for 2002. The transition to the cumulative 25 percent limit was needed to allow time for banks to adjust without a serious disruption. These limits once fully in force will be in line with accepted international practice.

Loan classification and provisioning requirement

39. Under the new loan classification and provisioning regulation that comes into force beginning January 2001, general and international license banks are to classify loans according to five categories as follows: Normal, Special Mention, Subnormal, Doubtful and

---

[16] Applicable regulations are Agreements 2, 8, and 10 for 1999. Related parties are bank directors, individuals owning 5 percent or more of a bank's shares, managers, officers, employees and their spouses and any entity for which the bank or its directors or officers control (individually or jointly) a significant influence.

Unrecoverable. Loan classifications need to consider the bank's lending policies and procedures, the borrower's financial condition and repayment capacity, assessment of cash flow and market value and the potential for realizing the collateral.

40. After the phase in period, banks will be required to maintain provisioning equal to the higher of one percent for the whole loan portfolio or the cumulative provisions required according to the individual loan classification. The amount of provisions for individual loans is to reflect the probability of loss, whereby loans with a classification of Special Mention would require a provision of between two and 14 percent, Subnormal between 15 percent and 49 percent, Doubtful between 50 percent and 99 percent, and for Unrecoverable 100 percent.

41. Under requirements in place through end-2000, loans classified as Doubtful must be provisioned at 50 percent and those classified as Unrecoverable at 100 percent. During the phase-in, one half of the increase in provisions under the new regulation must be met by end-June, with the full amount of the increase to be met by end 2001. The SB may instruct banks to establish higher provisions than would be called for by the regulation and provisions may be reduced for particular loans depending on quality of collateral.

Liquidity requirements

42. Minimum liquidity requirements are set by Article 46 to 49 of the 1998 banking law. General license banks must maintain at all times liquid assets equal to at least 30 percent of total deposits. The SB may restrict on a case-by-case basis the share of certain liquid assets in the total qualifying liquidity of a bank. To monitor liquidity, banks must submit weekly liquidity reports. Liquid assets, which must be unencumbered and freely transferable, include the following: (i) gold or currency of legal tender in Panama; (ii) clearing balances due from banks; (iii) demand and time deposits (maturity less than one year) held in Panama banks; and, (iv) treasury bills and other Panamanian government securities with less than one year maturity valued at market value.

43. Liquid assets can include demand and time deposits (maturity less than six months) and other liquid balances held in foreign banks pre-approved by the SB. Also with the approval of the SB, debt instruments of foreign governments, foreign financial institutions and private companies can be allowed. The instruments are to be carried at their market value, must be of investment grade and actively traded on well-recognized exchanges.

F. Conclusions

44. Over several decades, Panama's banking system has evolved into an important regional banking center largely following a model of self-regulation. The banking industry and government came to recognize that self-regulation had its limitations and in tandem worked to adapt an appropriate framework for supervision and regulation to the banking system, which resulted in the passage of the 1998 banking law and the creation of the SB. The SB and its supervisory staff demonstrate a high level of professionalism and integrity and receive high

marks within the banking industry, having established credibility through the rapid pace of reform designed to introduce a modern supervisory and regulatory framework.

45. Panama confronts a new challenge due to concerns raised by the Financial Action Task Force (FATF) and Financial Stability Forum (FSF). The authorities have moved quickly to pass and implement new laws and regulations to deal with the FATF criticism and demonstrate that Panama is working aggressively to combat money laundering. To address the FSF concern, the authorities are continuing their efforts to modernize the supervisory and regulatory environment that have been underway since 1998. The SB is participating in the IMF's initiative for offshore financial centers and has agreed to an assessment under Module 2 of the OFC program beginning in April 2001. This assessment will examine the concerns raised by the FSF.

IV. POVERTY IN PANAMA—FINDINGS OF A RECENT ASSESSMENT

1. Poverty in Panama remains pervasive in spite of the country's comparatively high income per capita of US$3,395 in 1999. The Government of Panama, with assistance from the World Bank, recently completed a comprehensive poverty assessment.[1] This chapter summarizes its major conclusions.

2. About 37 percent of the population, or 1 million people, live below the poverty line and 19 percent of the population, or over half a million people, live in extreme poverty.[2] Over 50 percent of children in Panama live below the poverty line. Poverty is concentrated heavily in rural areas and is most highly concentrated within the indigenous population. Although the indigenous population only accounts for one-eighth of the overall population, an estimated 95 percent, about 197,000 people, fall below the poverty line and 86 percent live in extreme poverty. Although not as pervasive as in rural areas, poverty in urban areas is of concern as 15 percent of the urban population falls below the poverty line. Moreover, many city dwellers live just above the poverty line, making them vulnerable to the effects of job loss, illness and other contingencies.

A. Causes of Poverty in Panama

3. The problems of poverty are the result of the highly unequal distribution of productive assets such as labor, human capital, physical assets, and access to financial markets. Labor is the most abundant asset available to the poor, accounting for 77 percent of total income versus 69 percent for the nonpoor. High rates of unemployment and disparities in educational opportunities often prevent the poor from increasing their skills and know-how. Unemployment is highest among the urban poor, women, and the young. Many of the employed poor work as day laborers in the informal sector. In all, nearly 80 percent of the extremely poor and 70 percent of the poor work in the informal sector. A majority of poor and extremely poor women are employed in the informal sector.

4. Progress has been made in recent years as regards the educational attainment of all economic groups, but gaps remain in literacy, attainment, and coverage. Literacy rates in Panama are relatively high. About 97 percent of the nonpoor and 83 percent of the poor are literate. Nonetheless, less than two-thirds of those over age nine in the indigenous population can read and write, and rates for women are lower than those for men. Enrollment levels

---

[1] *Panama Poverty Assessment: Priorities and Strategies for Poverty Reduction.* The World Bank, Washington, D.C., 2000.

[2] Extreme poverty is defined in the *Panama Poverty Assessment* as the level of per capita annual consumption required to purchase the minimum average daily caloric requirement. The full poverty line includes an allowance for nonfood items. The annual cost of achieving the extreme poverty line was estimated at US$519 and the full poverty line, US$905.

continue to be affected by the high direct costs of schooling, which at the primary and secondary level represent 12 percent and 28 percent of income, respectively, of a household at the poverty line. Even if the poor are able to finance the high direct costs of schooling, the quality of education they receive is deficient, given the dearth of bilingual (Spanish-indigenous languages) learning materials, schools that are close-by, teachers, and basic textbooks. As a result, educational attainment is lowest among the indigenous poor (average of 3.3 years of schooling), followed by the rural poor (5.1 years), and the urban poor (7.0 years). In contrast, the nonpoor have average schooling of 9.5 years.

5. The overall level of public expenditure on education appears adequate at 6 percent of GDP, but its distribution is inequitable and regressive. The poor represent 43 percent of the school aged population, but only receive 28 percent of total spending on education. Education spending is split roughly equally among primary, secondary, and tertiary education. Virtually all of the spending on higher education benefits the nonpoor and over 40 percent of higher education subsidies favor the highest income quintile. Education spending is also tilted in favor of the urban areas despite the fact that the poor are located predominantly in rural areas. In total, the urban areas receive 65 percent of education spending even though their inhabitants account for 53 percent of the population ages 5–24. This compares to 30 percent of spending for rural areas and only 5 percent for the indigenous population even though the rural areas account for 38 percent and the indigenous population 10 percent of those in the 5–24 age group.

6. The unequal distribution of physical assets, such as housing and land, prevents the use of property as collateral for credit. Those poor who own land tend not to have title to their property. The assessment cites the lack of a property title as the principal reason the poor are refused access to credit in the financial system (the size of land holdings and the possession of land titles are the two main factors influencing access to, and volume of, agricultural lending in rural areas). According to the study, 79 percent of poor homeowners and 64 percent of poor land owners lack proper titling. Overall, 50 percent of all homeowners and 51 percent of all land owners lack proper titling. In addition, the study estimates that titling contributes an average of US$456 per hectare in land value, suggesting that the market places a high value on the existence of a title.

7. The characteristics of poverty in Panama are reflected in a dual pattern of historical development. Panama's geographical location combined with the existence of the Canal and a monetary arrangement that uses the U.S. dollar as legal tender has fostered the development of an internationally oriented service sector and financial center. This modern service sector operates side by side with traditional agriculture and manufacturing industries that have been constrained until recently by a protectionist trade regime that fostered low productivity. Because of the specialized nature of Panama's service economy, education reform is necessary to bridge the gap for the poor to move into productive, higher wage jobs. The duality of the economy has resulted in large wage differentials between those employed in the service sector and those in the rest of the economy. In addition, this distortion may have increased the rate of unemployment and encouraged the informal labor market by increasing

the relative price of labor and, therefore, reducing the demand for the poor's most abundant asset.

B. Poverty Reduction Strategy and Reform

8. Poverty reduction is the top priority of the new government, as emphasized in the Social Agenda. This agenda outlines the principles for reducing poverty, strengthening the key assets of the poor, and assessing the geographic differences in the distribution of poverty. The strategy includes: increased efficiency in social spending to improve human capital, specific targeting of resources to the poor, a program to decentralize services and improve efficiency, increased community participation, and comprehensive monitoring of the available indicators of the incidence of poverty and implementation of programs. The study recommends that the government: prioritize among poverty groups; reallocate existing public expenditures in education, healthcare, and other basic services to target key groups among the poor; implement policy reforms to reduce disparities in assets; and improve targeting mechanisms. The *Poverty Assessment* estimates the minimum annual cost of eliminating poverty (bringing all poor Panamanians to the poverty line) at approximately 5 percent of GDP and the cost of eliminating extreme poverty at 1 percent of GDP.[3]

9. The main priority should be a reallocation of existing spending as opposed to additional spending. Investing in education is seen as the principal means for alleviating poverty in the long run and gains can be made at reasonable costs. The *Poverty Assessment* estimates that full enrollment in primary schooling would cost about US$12 million (0.14 percent of GDP). Full coverage in secondary schooling would cost about US$89 million (1 percent of GDP), but coverage in secondary schooling only for the poor would only amount to three quarters of this amount.[4] Given that each year of schooling is estimated to add an additional five percent increase in hourly earnings, such investments should be considered.

10. A key recent poverty reform of the Government of Panama has been to expand the coverage of land titling by modernizing land administration services and launching a streamlined national land titling program that includes air photography land studies. In addition to the 690,000 hectares that have been titled from 1963–99, a US$400 million pilot program, funded by the Government of Panama and the IDB, has been initiated in the province of Veraguas to title over 500,000 hectares. The second phase of this program is to be implemented in the provinces of Herrera and Los Santos and title an estimated 620,000 hectares. Approximately 6,000 titles were granted in September and October of 1999. It is estimated that this expanded program will issue over 60,000 new land titles by

---

[3] These estimates take account only of the direct cost of poverty alleviation. They do not, for example, take account of administrative costs.

[4] These assessments do not take account of the leakage that would result from less than perfect targeting.

2004. However, while ambitious, this program only targets land owners in general, not poor land owners. The poor account for approximately two-thirds of the rural population, but only own one-third of agricultural land. Half the poor in the rural areas are landless and, consequently, will not benefit from a titling program. This underscores the importance of taking other measures, and in particular improving the targeting of social expenditure, especially health and education.

Table 5. Panama: National Accounts by Productive Activity

	1995	1996	1997	1998	1999
	(In millions of balboas at 1982 prices)				
Gross domestic product at market prices	6,198.0	6,372.2	6,657.4	6,947.2	7,152.2
Primary activity	517.8	522.2	528.5	564.2	562.6
Agriculture	509.2	515.0	514.9	547.5	545.4
Mining	8.6	7.2	13.6	16.7	17.2
Secondary activity	874.6	856.2	908.6	951.5	956.8
Manufacturing	615.8	608.1	646.8	672.1	632.8
Construction	258.8	248.1	261.8	279.4	324.0
Services	4,784.2	4,984.2	5,225.9	5,473.8	5,733.1
Public utilities	259.9	305.9	308.2	294.0	348.9
Commerce, restaurants, and hotels	1,280.4	1,267.8	1,381.2	1,411.1	1,371.7
Colon Free Zone wholesale	516.6	490.2	570.7	554.1	473.8
Restaurants and hotels	95.0	100.9	107.7	113.3	117.8
Other	668.8	676.7	702.8	743.7	780.1
Transport and communications	761.3	780.1	824.9	914.7	1,006.2
Panama Canal Commission	419.4	429.9	423.6	442.7	452.3
Other transport and comm.	341.9	350.2	401.3	472.0	553.9
Financial intermediation	641.8	725.4	729.2	809.4	887.1
Housing	841.4	879.2	908.8	937.2	981.6
Public administration	653.5	665.3	690.6	711.3	721.3
Other services	345.9	360.5	383.0	396.1	416.3
Plus: import taxes 2/	249.8	256.5	270.4	294.4	292.8
Less: imputed banking services	228.4	246.9	276.0	336.7	393.1
	(Percent change)				
Gross domestic product at 1982 market prices	1.8	2.8	4.5	4.4	3.0
Primary activity	3.1	0.8	1.2	6.8	-0.3
Agriculture	3.2	1.1	0.0	6.3	-0.4
Mining	-5.5	-16.3	88.9	22.8	3.0
Secondary activity	1.3	-2.1	6.1	4.7	0.6
Manufacturing	0.2	-1.3	6.4	3.9	-5.8
Construction	4.1	-4.1	5.5	6.7	16.0
Services	1.6	4.2	4.8	4.7	4.7
Public utilities	1.9	17.7	0.8	-4.6	18.7
Commerce, restaurants, and hotels	-0.7	-1.0	8.9	2.2	-2.8
Colon Free Zone wholesale	-3.2	-5.1	16.4	-2.9	-14.5
Restaurants and hotels	5.2	6.2	6.7	5.2	4.0
Other	0.4	1.2	3.9	5.8	4.9
Transport and communications	9.4	2.5	5.7	10.9	10.0
Panama Canal Commission	15.7	2.5	-1.5	4.5	2.2
Other transport and comm.	2.5	2.4	14.6	17.6	17.4

Table 5. Panama: National Accounts by Productive Activity (Concluded)

	1995	1996	1997	1998	1999
Financial intermediation	-4.9	13.0	0.5	11.0	9.6
Housing	2.5	4.5	3.4	3.1	4.7
Public administration	3.4	1.8	3.8	3.0	1.4
Other services	1.3	4.2	6.2	3.4	5.1
Plus: import taxes 2/	1.9	2.7	5.4	8.9	-0.5
Less: imputed banking services	-0.5	8.1	11.8	22.0	16.8
	(Percent distribution)				
Gross domestic product at 1982 market prices	**100.0**	**100.0**	**100.0**	**100.0**	**100.0**
Primary activity	8.4	8.2	7.9	8.1	7.9
Agriculture	8.2	8.1	7.7	7.9	7.6
Mining	0.1	0.1	0.2	0.2	0.2
Secondary activity	14.1	13.4	13.6	13.7	13.4
Manufacturing	9.9	9.5	9.7	9.7	8.8
Construction	4.2	3.9	3.9	4.0	4.5
Services	77.2	78.2	78.5	78.8	80.2
Public utilities	4.2	4.8	4.6	4.2	4.9
Commerce, restaurants, and hotels	20.7	19.9	20.7	20.3	19.2
Colon Free Zone wholesale	8.3	7.7	8.6	8.0	6.6
Restaurants and hotels	1.5	1.6	1.6	1.6	1.6
Other	10.8	10.6	10.6	10.7	10.9
Transport and communications	12.3	12.2	12.4	13.2	14.1
Panama Canal Commission	6.8	6.7	6.4	6.4	6.3
Other transport and communication	5.5	5.5	6.0	6.8	7.7
Financial intermediation	10.4	11.4	11.0	11.7	12.4
Housing	13.6	13.8	13.7	13.5	13.7
Public administration	10.5	10.4	10.4	10.2	10.1
Other services	5.6	5.7	5.8	5.7	5.8
Plus: import taxes 2/	4.0	4.0	4.1	4.2	4.1
Less: imputed banking services	3.7	3.9	4.1	4.8	5.5

Sources: Office of the Comptroller General; and Fund staff estimates.

1/ The national accounts for 1980-94 were revised and published in December 1995. The base year for the constant price data was updated to 1982 from 1970 and methodological improvements were implemented.

2/ Includes the sales tax: "*impuesto a la transferencia de bienes muebles.*"

Table 6. Panama: National Accounts by Use

	1995	1996	1997	1998	1999
	(In millions of balboas at current prices)				
Total domestic demand	**8,063.4**	**8,270.6**	**8,984.9**	**9,980.5**	**10,346.5**
Consumption	5,669.2	5,783.2	6,293.8	6,983.3	7,237.3
Public	1,029.7	1,055.4	1,176.2	1,238.6	1,319.5
Private	4,639.5	4,727.8	5,117.6	5,744.7	5,917.8
Gross domestic investment	2,394.2	2,487.4	2,691.1	2,997.2	3,109.2
Public	272.0	313.4	385.4	581.1	457.2
Private 1/	2,122.2	2,174.0	2,305.7	2,416.1	2,652.0
Balance of trade (goods and nonfactor services)	-157.3	-119.5	-327.4	-836.7	-801.1
Balance excluding the Colon Free Zone	-389.8	-459.1	-902.7	-839.6	-763.0
Exports of goods and nonfactor services	7,610.3	7,381.5	8,318.1	8,047.1	7,019.0
Exports excluding the Colon Free Zone	1,176.0	1,265.2	1,201.7	1,387.4	1,480.0
Imports of goods and nonfactor services	7,767.6	7,501.0	8,645.5	8,883.8	7,820.1
Imports excluding the Colon Free Zone	1,565.8	1,724.3	2,104.4	2,227.0	2,243.0
Gross domestic product at current market prices	7,906.1	8,151.1	8,657.5	9,143.8	9,545.4
	(In percent of GDP)				
Total domestic demand	**101.9**	**101.4**	**103.8**	**109.1**	**108.4**
Consumption	71.7	70.9	72.7	76.3	75.8
Public	13.0	12.9	13.6	13.5	13.8
Private	58.7	58	59.1	62.8	62
Gross domestic investment	30.2	30.5	31.1	32.8	32.6
Public	3.4	3.8	4.5	6.4	4.8
Private 1/	26.8	26.7	26.6	26.4	27.8
	(In percent of GDP)				
Balance of trade (goods and nonfactor services)	-2	-1.5	-3.8	-9.2	-8.4
Balance excluding the Colon Free Zone	-4.9	-5.6	-10.4	-9.2	-8.0
Exports of goods and nonfactor services	96.3	90.6	96.1	88	73.5
Exports excluding the Colon Free Zone	14.9	15.5	13.9	15.2	15.5
Imports of goods and nonfactor services	98.2	92	99.9	97.2	81.9
Imports excluding the Colon Free Zone	19.8	21.2	24.3	24.4	23.5
Gross domestic product at current market prices	100.0	100.0	100.0	100.0	100.0
	(Percentage change)				
Total domestic demand	**5.5**	**2.6**	**8.6**	**11.1**	**3.7**
Consumption	-2.5	2.0	8.8	11.0	3.6
Public	2.2	2.5	11.4	5.3	6.5
Private	-3.5	1.9	8.2	12.3	3.0
Gross domestic investment	30.9	3.9	8.2	11.4	3.7
Public	2.0	15.2	23.0	50.8	-21.3
Private 1/	35.9	2.4	6.1	4.8	9.8
Exports of goods and nonfactor services	2.2	-3.0	12.7	-3.3	-12.8
Exports excluding the Colon Free Zone	-43.2	7.6	-5.0	15.5	6.7
Imports of goods and nonfactor services	5.5	-3.4	15.3	2.8	-12.0
Imports excluding the Colon Free Zone	-45.9	10.1	22.0	5.8	0.7
Gross domestic product at current market prices	2.2	3.1	6.2	5.6	4.4

Sources: Office of the Comptroller General; and Fund staff estimates.

1/ Includes changes in inventories.

Table 7. Panama: Savings and Investment

	1995	1996	1997	1998	1999
	(In millions of balboas)				
Gross domestic investment	**2,394.2**	**2,487.4**	**2,691.1**	**2,997.2**	**3,109.2**
Fixed capital formation (gross)	2,057.9	2,059.2	2,295.0	2,624.9	2,831.2
Public sector	272.0	313.4	385.4	581.1	457.2
Private sector	1,785.9	1,745.8	1,909.6	2,043.8	2,374.0
Changes in inventories	336.3	428.2	396.1	372.3	278.0
Gross national savings	**2,025.1**	**2,185.5**	**2,102.7**	**1,795.0**	**1,731.7**
Public sector savings	262.8	323.9	259.9	224.0	273.7
Private sector savings	1,762.3	1,861.6	1,842.8	1,571.0	1,458.0
Foreign savings	**369.1**	**301.9**	**588.4**	**1202.2**	**1377.5**
	(In percent of GDP)				
Gross domestic investment	**30.3**	**30.5**	**31.1**	**32.8**	**32.6**
Fixed capital formation (gross)	26.0	25.3	26.5	28.7	29.7
Public sector	3.4	3.8	4.5	6.4	4.8
Private sector	22.6	21.4	22.1	22.4	24.9
Changes in inventories	4.3	5.3	4.6	4.1	2.9
Gross national savings	**25.6**	**26.8**	**24.3**	**19.7**	**18.2**
Public sector savings	3.3	4.0	3.0	2.4	2.9
Private sector savings	22.3	22.8	21.3	17.3	15.3
Foreign savings	**4.7**	**3.7**	**6.8**	**13.1**	**14.4**

Sources: Office of the Comptroller General; and Fund staff estimates.

Table 8. Panama: Agricultural Production

	1994	1995	1996	1997	1998
	(In millions of balboas at 1982 prices)				
Total	**493.3**	**509.2**	**515.0**	**514.9**	**545.1**
Crops	269.0	262.9	261.6	242.3	244.4
Rice	32.3	33.2	36.0	25.0	40.0
Corn	17.3	17.6	18.2	13.7	16.5
Bananas	136.1	126.6	117.6	112.4	86.0
Sugarcane	19.3	18.2	19.6	21.7	23.9
Coffee	13.2	15.0	15.5	14.6	15.9
Other	50.8	52.3	54.7	54.9	62.1
Livestock	157.3	159.3	167.5	174.2	188.0
Forestry	14.6	12.8	12.0	12.7	12.7
Fish	52.4	74.2	73.9	85.7	100.0
	(Annual percent change)				
Total	**2.7**	**3.2**	**1.1**	**0.0**	**5.9**
Crops	3.7	-2.3	-0.5	-7.4	0.9
Livestock	1.5	1.3	5.1	4.0	7.9
Forestry	-0.7	-12.3	-6.3	5.8	0.0
Fish	2.1	41.6	-0.4	16.0	16.7

Sources: Office of the Comptroller General; and Fund staff estimates.

Table 9. Panama: Value-Added in Manufacturing

	1994	1995	1996	1997	1998
	(In millions of balboas at 1982 prices)				
Total	**614.6**	**615.8**	**608.1**	**646.8**	**673.4**
Food	237.1	245.5	246.4	265.5	295.2
Beverages	53.7	52.7	53.3	58.4	63.2
Tobacco	27.8	27.2	29.2	28.6	8.2
Petroleum products	15.1	10.5	17.3	17.5	19.3
Textiles and garments	38.1	34.4	30.3	27.8	25.8
Leather products and footwear	11.6	13.0	10.9	9.8	8.7
Wood and furniture	31.4	27.6	28.4	31.1	35.8
Paper products	29.9	30.6	27.8	25.9	23.3
Printing and publishing	15.2	16.2	12.0	11.9	16.8
Chemicals, rubber and plastic products	57.6	59.3	55.2	57.3	56.8
Glass and other mineral products	49.9	45.2	41.3	46.3	52.9
Basic metal industries	9.8	10.9	13.7	18.0	20.4
Metal products, machinery, and equipment	21.5	22.7	22.2	26.0	28.0
Other	15.9	20.0	20.1	22.7	19.0
	(Annual percent change)				
Total	**4.3**	**0.2**	**-1.3**	**6.4**	**4.1**
Petroleum products	-28.4	-30.5	64.8	1.2	10.3
Total (excluding petroleum products)	5.5	1.0	-2.4	6.5	3.9
Food, beverages, and tobacco	5.7	2.1	1.1	7.2	4.0
Other products	5.2	-0.4	-6.4	5.7	3.9

Sources: Office of the Comptroller General; and Fund staff estimates.

US FEDERAL GOVERNMENT LIBRARY-2003

ULTIMATE INFORMATION ON US FEDERAL GOVERNMENT AGENCUES

The ultimate handbook with detailed information on US Federal Government Agencies and more

Price: $99.95 each

Title *	ISBN
1. Overseas Private Investment Corporation (OPIC) Handbook	0739731835
2. The White House Handbook	0739731815
3. U.S. House Committee on Agriculture	0739727370
4. U.S. House Committee on Appropriations	0739727389
5. U.S. House Committee on Armed Services	0739727397
6. U.S. House Committee on Education and the Workforce	0739727710
7. U.S. House Committee on Energy and Commerce	0739727435
8. U.S. House Committee on Financial Services	0739727745
9. U.S. House Committee on Government Reform	0739727443
10. U.S. House Committee on House Administration	0739727788
11. U.S. House Committee on International Relations	0739727451
12. U.S. House Committee on Resources	0739727486
13. U.S. House Committee on Rules	073972780X
14. U.S. House Committee on Science	0739727494
15. U.S. House Committee on Small Business	0739727729
16. U.S. House Committee on Standards of Official Conduct	0739727737
17. U.S. House Committee on the Budget	0739727419
18. U.S. House Committee on the Judiciary	073972746X
19. U.S. House Committee on Transportation and Infrastructure	0739727453
20. U.S. House Committee on Veterans Affairs	0739727761
21. U.S. House Committee on Ways and Means	073972777X
22. U.S. House Joint Committee on Printing	0739727699
23. U.S. House Joint Committee on Taxation	0739727362
24. U.S. House Joint Economic Committee	0739727354
25. U.S. House Permanent Select Committee on Intelligence	0739727796
26. U.S. Senate Agriculture, Nutrition, And Forestry Committee	0739727818
27. U.S. Senate Appropriations Committee	0739727826
28. U.S. Senate Armed Services Committee	0739727834
29. U.S. Senate Banking, Housing, And Urban Affairs	0739727842
30. U.S. Senate Budget Committee	0739727850
31. U.S. Senate Commerce, Science, And Transportation	0739727869
32. U.S. Senate Committee On Indian Affairs	0739727990
33. U.S. Senate Energy And Natural Resources Committee	0739727877
34. U.S. Senate Environment And Public Works Committee	0739727885
35. U.S. Senate Finance Committee	0739727893

To order and for additional analytical and marketing information, please contacrt
International Business Publications, USA at:
P.O. Box 15343, Washington, DC 20003, USA. Phone: (202) 546-2103. Fax: (202) 546-3275.
E-mail: rusric@erols.com

Title *	ISBN
36. U.S. Senate Foreign Relations Committee	0739727907
37. U.S. Senate Governmental Affairs Committee	0739727915
38. U.S. Senate Health, Education, Labor And Pensions Committee	0739727931
39. U.S. Senate Joint Committee On Taxation	0739728644
40. U.S. Senate Joint Economic Committee	0739728636
41. U.S. Senate Judiciary Committee	0739727923
42. U.S. Senate Rules And Administration Committee	073972794X
43. U.S. Senate Select Committee On Ethics	0739727982
44. U.S. Senate Select Committee On Intelligence	0739727974
45. U.S. Senate Small Business Committee	0739727958
46. U.S. Senate Special Committee On Aging	0739728628
47. U.S. Senate Veterans' Affairs Committee	0739727966
48. US African Development Fund Handbook	073973184X
49. US AGENCY FOR INTERNATIONAL DEVELOPMENT BUSINESS OPPORTUNITIES HANDBOOK	0739731866
50. US Agency for International Development Handbook	0739731874
51. US Arms Control and Disarmament Agency Handbook	0739739832
52. US CENTRAL INTELLIGENCE AGENCY (CIA) HANDBOOK	0739732757
53. US Civil Rights Policy Handbook	073976201X
54. US Commodity Futures Trading Commission Handbook	0739762028
55. US Congressional Budget Office Handbook	0739762036
56. US Defense Intelligence Agency Handbook	0739711709
57. US Department of Agriculture Business Opportunities Handbook	0739762044
58. US Department of Agriculture Handbook	0739762052
59. US Department of Commerce Handbook	0739762079
60. US Department of Defense Handbook	0739762087
61. US Department of Energy Business Opportunities Handbook	0739762095
62. US Department of Energy Handbook	0739762109
63. US Department of Health and Human Services Handbook	0739762117
64. US Department of Housing and Urban Services Handbook	0739762125
65. US Department of Interior Handbook	0739762133
66. US Department of Justice Handbook	0739762141
67. US Department of Labor Handbook	073976215X
68. US Department of State Handbook	0739762168
69. US Department of the Air Force Handbook	0739762060
70. US Department of the Army Handbook	0739762176
71. US Department of the Navy Handbook	0739762184
72. US Department of the Treasury Handbook	0739762192
73. US Department of Transport Handbook	0739762206
74. US Department of Veteran Affairs Handbook	0739762214
75. US Environmental Protection Agency Handbook	0739762222
76. US Export-Import Bank Handbook	0739762230

Title *	ISBN
77. US FBI ACADEMY HANDBOOK	0739731858
78. US Federal Bureau of Investigation (FBI) Business Opportunities Handbook	0739762370
79. US Federal Bureau of Investigation (FBI) Handbook	073976246X
80. US Federal Communication Commission Handbook	0739733494
81. US Federal Election Commission Handbook	0739762400
82. US Federal Energy Sector Regulations Handbook	0739762419
83. US Federal Executive Government Handbook	0739731823
84. US Federal Maritime Commission Handbook	0739762427
85. US Federal Mine Safety and Health Commission Handbook	0739762435
86. US Federal Reserve System Handbook	0739762532
87. US Federal Trade Commission Handbook	0739762451
88. US Food and Drug Administration Handbook	0739762397
89. US Food Assistance to Russia Handbook	0739762478
90. US Information Agency Handbook	0739762486
91. US Intelligence Policy Handbook	0739762494
92. US Internal Revenue Service Handbook	0739762508
93. US Libraries and Information Science National Commission Handbook	0739762516
94. US National Academy of Science and Research Policy Handbook	0739762524
95. US National Aeronautics and Space Administration Handbook	0739762249
96. US National Drug Control Policy Handbook	0739762389
97. US National Institute of Health Handbook	0739762443
98. US National Science Foundation Handbook	0739762362
99. US National Security Policy Handbook	0739762354
100. US Navy Seals Handbook	0739762540
101. US Office of Management and Budget Handbook	0739762346
102. US Office of Personnel Management Handbook	0739762338
103. US Peace Corp Handbook	073976232X
104. US Postal Service Handbook	0739762311
105. US Science and Technology Policy Handbook	0739762303
106. US Securities and Exchange Commission Handbook	073976229X
107. US Small Business Administration Handbook	0739762281
108. US Special Combat Fources Handbook	0739762001
109. US Submarine Force Hnadbook	0739764136
110. US Trade and Development Agency Handbook	0739762273
111. US Trade Representative Office Handbook	0739762265
112. WORLD BANK BUSINESS OPPORTUNITES HANDBOOK	0739762257

NEW WORLD POLITICAL LEADERS LIBRARY-2003

ULTIMATE INFORMATION ON LOLITICAL AND BUSINESS LEADERS OF FOREING COUNTRIES

The ultimate handbook with detailed information on foreign leaders, including biographic data, position on domestic and international issues, economic policy and more

Price: $89.95 each

TITLE	ISBN
1. Albania President Rexhep Meidani Handbook	07397-2762-8
2. Armenia President Robert Kocharian Handbook	07397-1180-6
3. Austria President Dr. Thomas Klestil Handbook	07397-05997
4. Azerbaijan President Heydar Aliyev Handbook	07397-1072-9
5. Bangladesh Prime Minister Khaleda Zia Handbook	07397-1181-4
6. Belarus President Alexander LUKASHENKO Handbook	07397-1073-7
7. Brunei Sultan Haji Hassanal Bolkiah Mu'izzaddin Waddaulah Handbook	07397-1190-3
8. Canada Prime Minister Joseph Jacques Jean Chrétien Handbook	07397-09488
9. China President Jiang Zemin Handbook	07397-09976
10. Cuba President Fidel Castro Handbook	07397-1183-0
11. Egypt President Hosny Mubarak Handbook	07397-1185-7
12. France President Jacques Chirac Handbook	07397-1188-1
13. Germany President Johannes Rau Handbook	07397-09968
14. Guyana President BHARRAT JAGDEO Handbook	0739764152
15. Iran President Hojjatoleslam Seyed Mohammad Khatami Handbook	07397-1178-4
16. Iraq President Saddam Hussein Handbook	07397-1179-2
17. Israel Prime Minister Ariel Sharon Handbook	07397-1192-X
18. Japan Prime Minister Junichiro Koizumi Handbook	07397-1194-6
19. Korea North General Secretary Kim Jong Il Handbook	07397-1197-0
20. Korea South President Kim Dae-jung Handbook	07397-1198-9
21. Libya President Muammar Muhammad Abd as-Salam al-Gaddafi Handbook	07397-1175-X
22. Norway Queen Sonja Handbook	07397-2699-4
23. Pakistan President Pervez Musharraf Handbook	07397-2735-4
24. Palestine President Yasser Arafat Handbook	07397-2766-0
25. Philippines President Gloria Macapagal Arroyo Handbook	07397-2737-0
26. Poland President Aleksander Kwasniewski Handbook	07397-2738-9
27. Russia President Vladimir Putin Handbook	07397-0999-2
28. Saudi Arabia King Fahd bin Abdul Aziz Handbook	07397-2740-0
29. Syria President Bashar Hafez Al-Assad Handbook	07397-2744-3
30. Taiwan President Chen Shui-bian Handbook	07397-64160
31. Thailand King Bhumibol Adulyadej Handbook	07397-2747-8
32. United Arab Emirates Ruler Sheikh Zayed bin Sultan Al Nahyan Handbook	07397-2736-2
33. United States President George W. Bush Handbook	07397-0998-4
34. Uzbekistan President Islam Karimov Handbook	07397-2764-4
35. Yugoslavia President Vojislav Koštunica Handbook	07397-0995X

To order and for additional analytical and marketing information, please contacrt International Business Publications, USA at:

P.O. Box 15343, Washington, DC 20003, USA.
Phone: (202) 546-2103. Fax: (202) 546-3275. E-mail: IBPUSA@comcast.net

WORLD COUNTRY STUDY GUIDE LIBRARY
2003

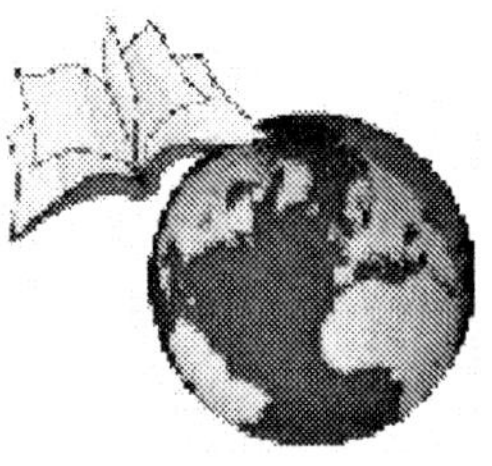

Ultimate guides for a correspondent country. Geography, history, people, language, culture, traditions, foreign and domestic policy, economy, government, constitution, places to visit, info for travelers...and more

Price: $99.95 each

Title
1. Afghanistan Country Study Guide
2. Aland Country Study Guide
3. Albania Country Study Guide
4. Algeria Country Study Guide
5. Andorra Country Study Guide
6. Angola Country Study Guide
7. Anguilla Country Study Guide
8. Antigua and Barbuda Country Study Guide
9. Antilles (Netherlands) Country Study Guide
10. Argentina Country Study Guide
11. Armenia Country Study Guide
12. Aruba Country Study Guide
13. Australia Country Study Guide
14. Austria Country Study Guide
15. Azerbaijan Country Study Guide
16. Bahamas Country Study Guide
17. Bahrain Country Study Guide
18. Bangladesh Country Study Guide
19. Barbados Country Study Guide
20. Belarus Country Study Guide
21. Belgium Country Study Guide
22. Belize Country Study Guide
23. Benin Country Study Guide
24. Bermuda Country Study Guide
25. Bhutan Country Study Guide
26. Bolivia Country Study Guide
27. Bosnia and Herzegovina Country Study Guide
28. Botswana Country Study Guide
29. Brazil Country Study Guide
30. Brunei Country Study Guide
31. Bulgaria Country Study Guide

32. Burkina Faso Country Study Guide
33. Burundi Country Study Guide
34. Cambodia Country Study Guide
35. Cameroon Country Study Guide
36. Canada Country Study Guide
37. Cape Verde Country Study Guide
38. Cayman Islands Country Study Guide
39. Central African Republic Country Study Guide
40. Chad Country Study Guide
41. Chile Country Study Guide
42. China Country Study Guide
43. Colombia Country Study Guide
44. Comoros Country Study Guide
45. Congo Country Study Guide
46. Congo, Democratic Republic Country Study Guide
47. Cook Islands Country Study Guide
48. Costa Rica Country Study Guide
49. Cote d'Ivoire Country Study Guide
50. Croatia Country Study Guide
51. Cuba Country Study Guide
52. Cyprus Country Study Guide
53. Czech Republic Country Study Guide
54. Denmark Country Study Guide
55. Djibouti Country Study Guide
56. Dominica Country Study Guide
57. Dominican Republic Country Study Guide
58. Ecuador Country Study Guide
59. Egypt Country Study Guide
60. El Salvador Country Study Guide
61. Equatorial Guinea Country Study Guide
62. Eritrea Country Study Guide
63. Estonia Country Study Guide
64. Ethiopia Country Study Guide
65. Falkland Islands Country Study Guide
66. Faroes Country Study Guide
67. Fiji Country Study Guide
68. Finland Country Study Guide
69. France Country Study Guide
70. Gabon Country Study Guide
71. Gambia Country Study Guide

72.	Georgia Country Study Guide
73.	Germany Country Study Guide
74.	Ghana Country Study Guide
75.	Gibraltar Country Study Guide
76.	Greece Country Study Guide
77.	Greenland Country Study Guide
78.	Grenada Country Study Guide
79.	Guam Country Study Guide
80.	Guatemala Country Study Guide
81.	Guernsey Country Study Guide
82.	Guinea Country Study Guide
83.	Guinea-Bissau Country Study Guide
84.	Guyana Country Study Guide
85.	Haiti Country Study Guide
86.	Honduras Country Study Guide
87.	Hungary Country Study Guide
88.	Iceland Country Study Guide
89.	India Country Study Guide
90.	Indonesia Country Study Guide
91.	Iran Country Study Guide
92.	Iraq Country Study Guide
93.	Ireland Country Study Guide
94.	Israel Country Study Guide
95.	Italy Country Study Guide
96.	Jamaica Country Study Guide
97.	Japan Country Study Guide
98.	Jersey Country Study Guide
99.	Jordan Country Study Guide
100.	Kazakhstan Country Study Guide
101.	Kenya Country Study Guide
102.	Kiribati Country Study Guide
103.	Korea, North Country Study Guide
104.	Korea, South Country Study Guide
105.	Kuwait Country Study Guide
106.	Kyrgyzstan Country Study Guide
107.	Laos Country Study Guide
108.	Latvia Country Study Guide
109.	Lebanon Country Study Guide
110.	Lesotho Country Study Guide
111.	Liberia Country Study Guide

112. Libya Country Study Guide
113. Liechtenstein Country Study Guide
114. Lithuania Country Study Guide
115. Luxembourg Country Study Guide
116. Macau Country Study Guide
117. Macedonia, The Former Yugoslav Republic Country Study Guide
118. Madagascar Country Study Guide
119. Malawi Country Study Guide
120. Malaysia Country Study Guide
121. Maldives Country Study Guide
122. Mali Country Study Guide
123. Malta Country Study Guide
124. Man Country Study Guide
125. Marshall Islands Country Study Guide
126. Mauritania Country Study Guide
127. Mauritius Country Study Guide
128. Mayotte Country Study Guide
129. Mexico Country Study Guide
130. Micronesia Country Study Guide
131. Moldova Country Study Guide
132. Monaco Country Study Guide
133. Mongolia Country Study Guide
134. Monserrat Country Study Guide
135. Morocco Country Study Guide
136. Mozambique Country Study Guide
137. Myanmar Country Study Guide
138. Namibia Country Study Guide
139. Nauru Country Study Guide
140. Nepal Country Study Guide
141. Netherlands Country Study Guide
142. New Caledonia Country Study Guide
143. New Zealand Country Study Guide
144. Nicaragua Country Study Guide
145. Niger Country Study Guide
146. Nigeria Country Study Guide
147. Niue Country Study Guide
148. Northern Mariana Islands Country Study Guide
149. Norway Country Study Guide
150. Oman Country Study Guide
151. Pakistan Country Study Guide

152. Palau Country Study Guide
153. Palestine Country Study Guide
154. Panama Country Study Guide
155. Papua New Guinea Country Study Guide
156. Paraguay Country Study Guide
157. Peru Country Study Guide
158. Philippines Country Study Guide
159. Pitcairn Islands Country Study Guide
160. Poland Country Study Guide
161. Polynesia French Country Study Guide
162. Portugal Country Study Guide
163. Qatar Country Study Guide
164. Romania Country Study Guide
165. Russia Country Study Guide
166. Rwanda Country Study Guide
167. Saint Kitts and Nevis Country Study Guide
168. Saint Lucia Country Study Guide
169. Saint Vincent and The Grenadines Country Study Guide
170. Samoa (American) A Country Study Guide
171. Samoa (Western) Country Study Guide
172. San Marino Country Study Guide
173. Sao Tome and Principe Country Study Guide
174. Saudi Arabia Country Study Guide
175. Scotland Country Study Guide
176. Senegal Country Study Guide
177. Seychelles Country Study Guide
178. Sierra Leone Country Study Guide
179. Singapore Country Study Guide
180. Slovakia Country Study Guide
181. Slovenia Country Study Guide
182. Solomon Islands Country Study Guide
183. Somalia Country Study Guide
184. South Africa Country Study Guide
185. Spain Country Study Guide
186. Sri Lanka Country Study Guide
187. St. Helena Country Study Guide
188. St. Pierre & Miquelon Country Study Guide
189. Sudan Country Study Guide
190. Suriname Country Study Guide
191. Swaziland Country Study Guide

192. Sweden Country Study Guide
193. Switzerland Country Study Guide
194. Syria Country Study Guide
195. Taiwan Country Study Guide
196. Tajikistan Country Study Guide
197. Tanzania Country Study Guide
198. Thailand Country Study Guide
199. Togo Country Study Guide
200. Tonga Country Study Guide
201. Trinidad and Tobago Country Study Guide
202. Tunisia Country Study Guide
203. Turkey Country Study Guide
204. Turkmenistan Country Study Guide
205. Tuvalu Country Study Guide
206. Uganda Country Study Guide
207. Ukraine Country Study Guide
208. United Arab Emirates Country Study Guide
209. United Kingdom Country Study Guide
210. United States Country Study Guide
211. Uruguay Country Study Guide
212. Uzbekistan Country Study Guide
213. Vanuatu Country Study Guide
214. Vatican City Country Study Guide
215. Venezuela Country Study Guide
216. Vietnam Country Study Guide
217. Virgin Islands, British Country Study Guide
218. Wake Atoll Country Study Guide
219. Wallis & Futuna Country Study Guide
220. Western Sahara Country Study Guide
221. Yemen Country Study Guide
222. Yugoslavia Country Study Guide
223. Zambia Country Study Guide

Printed in the United States
19001LVS00001B/274

9 780739 758236